•Bartholomew•

WIGAN Street Finder ATLAS

Contents

Key to map pages	2-3
Map pages	4-67
Index to street names	68

Printed in Great Britain by The Edinburgh Press Limited

ISBN 0 7028 2928 5 HI 8008 CUNB

Bartholomew

An Imprint of HarperCollins*Publishers*

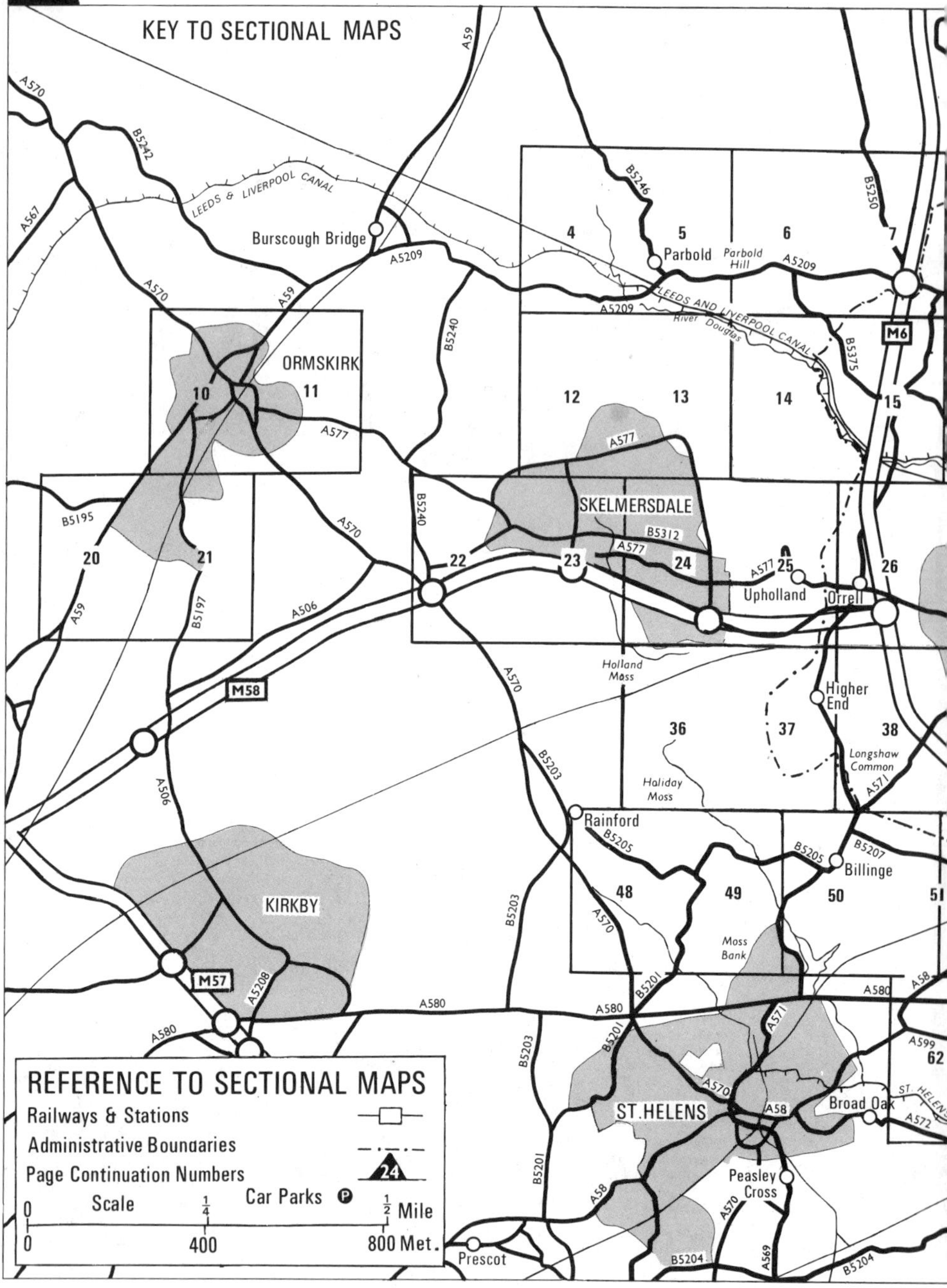
KEY TO SECTIONAL MAPS
A570
B5242
A567
LEEDS & LIVERPOOL CANAL
Burscough Bridge
A59
A5209
B5240
B5246
B5250
4
5
Parbold
Parbold Hill
6
7
A5209
LEEDS AND LIVERPOOL CANAL
River Douglas
B5375
M6
ORMSKIRK
10
11
A577
12
13
14
15
SKELMERSDALE
B5312
A577
B5195
20
21
A570
22
23
24
25
Upholland
26
Orrell
A59
B5197
A506
M58
Holland Moss
Higher End
36
37
38
Longshaw Common
A571
Haliday Moss
A506
B5203
Rainford
B5205
B5207
Billinge
48
49
50
51
KIRKBY
Moss Bank
M57
A5208
A580
B5201
A58
A599
62
ST. HELENS
Broad Oak
ST. HELENS
A572
Peasley Cross
B5204
A569
Prescot
REFERENCE TO SECTIONAL MAPS
Railways & Stations
Administrative Boundaries
Page Continuation Numbers
24
Car Parks
Scale
0
1/4
1/2 Mile
0
400
800 Met.

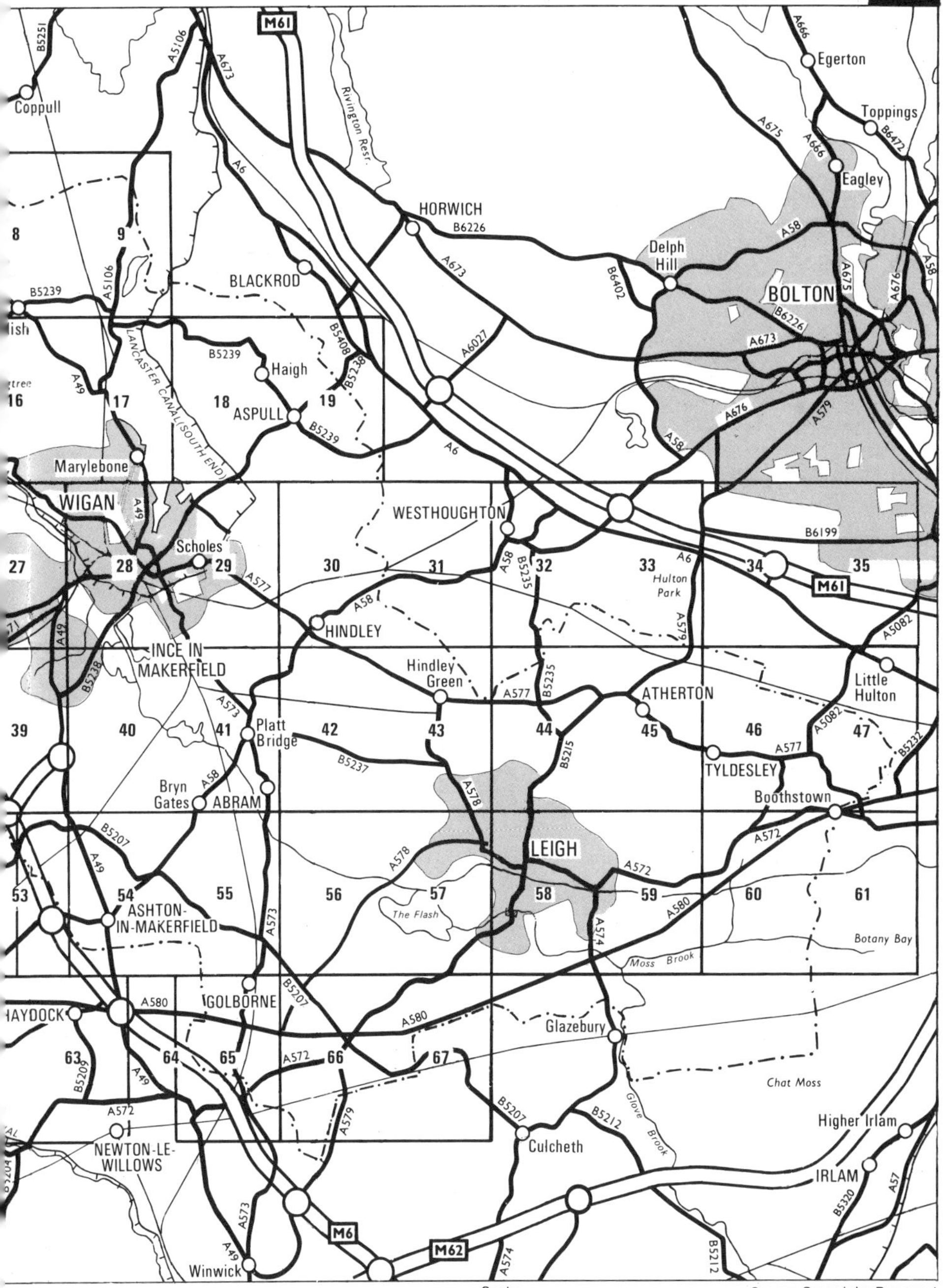

Scale

0 1 2 3 Miles

0 1 2 3 4 5 Kilometres

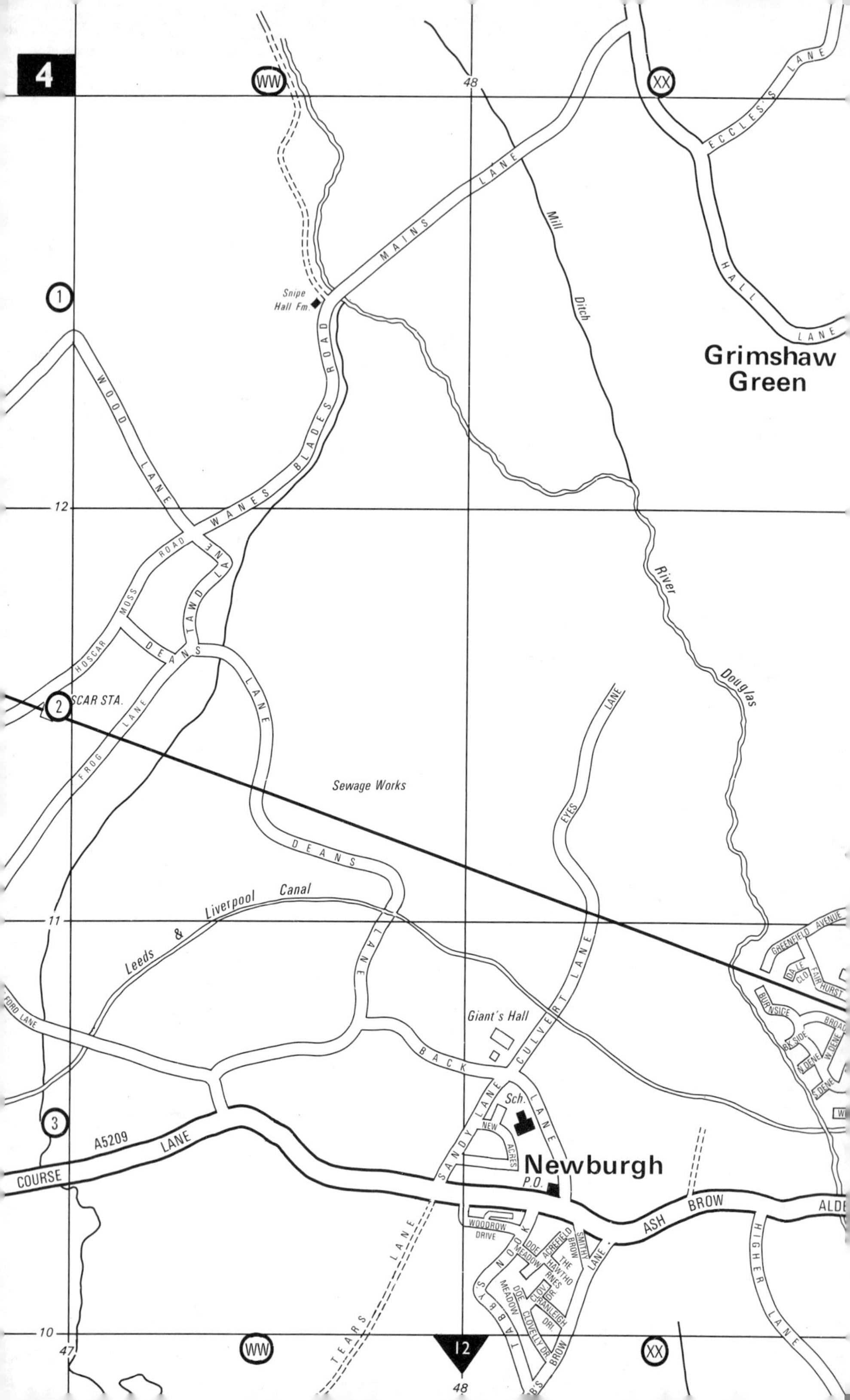
WW
XX
48
ECCLES'S LANE
MAINS LANE
Mill Ditch
HALL LANE
Grimshaw Green
1
Snipe Hall Fm.
BLADES ROAD
WOOD LANE
WANES
12
ROAD
MOSS
TAWD LANE
HOSCAR
DEANS
SCAR STA.
2
FROG LANE
LANE
River Douglas
LANE
Sewage Works
EYES
DEANS
Canal
Liverpool
&
Leeds
11
LANE
GREENFIELD AVENUE
FAIRHURST
BURNSIDE
BROAD
CULVERT LANE
FORD LANE
Giant's Hall
BACK
Sch.
LANE
SANDY LANE
NEW ACRES
3
A5209
LANE
COURSE
Newburgh
P.O.
ASH BROW
HIGHER LANE
WOODROW DRIVE
NOOK
DOE MEADOW
ACREFIELD
BROW
SMITHY LANE
THE HAWTHORNES
CRANLEIGH DR.
CLOVELLY DR.
BROW
TABBY'S
TEARS LANE
10
47
12
48

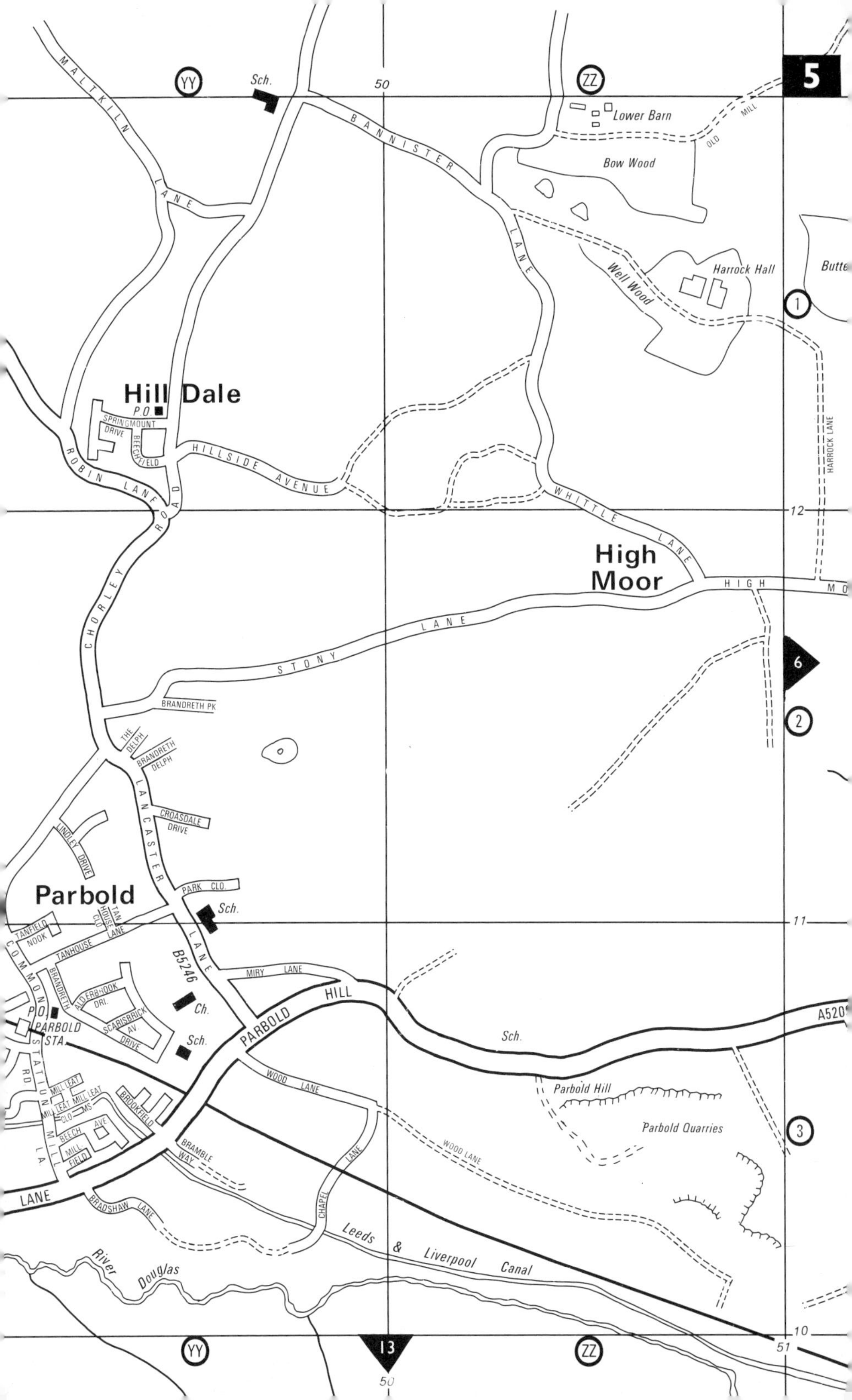
YY
ZZ
50
Sch.
MALTKILN LANE
BANNISTER LANE
Lower Barn
OLD MILL
Bow Wood
Well Wood
Harrock Hall
Butte
1
Hill Dale
P.O.
SPRINGMOUNT DRIVE
BEECHFIELD
HILLSIDE AVENUE
ROBIN LANE
ROAD
WHITTLE LANE
HARROCK LANE
12
High Moor
HIGH MO
STONY LANE
CHORLEY
6
2
BRANDRETH PK
THE DELPH
BRANDRETH DELPH
LANCASTER
CROASDALE DRIVE
LINDLEY DRIVE
PARK CLO.
Parbold
TAN HOUSE CLO.
11
TANFIELD NOOK
TANHOUSE LANE
COMMONS
B5246
MIRY LANE
PARBOLD HILL
A5209
BRANDRETH
ALDERBROOK DRI.
SCARISBRICK AV.
DRIVE
Ch.
P.O.
PARBOLD STA.
STATION RD.
MILL LEAT
MILL LEAT MEWS
MILL LEAT CLO.
BROOKFIELD
BEECH AVE
MILL FIELD
MILL LA.
WOOD LANE
CHAPEL LANE
BRAMBLE WAY
Parbold Hill
Parbold Quarries
3
LANE
BRADSHAW LANE
Leeds & Liverpool Canal
River Douglas
10
51
13

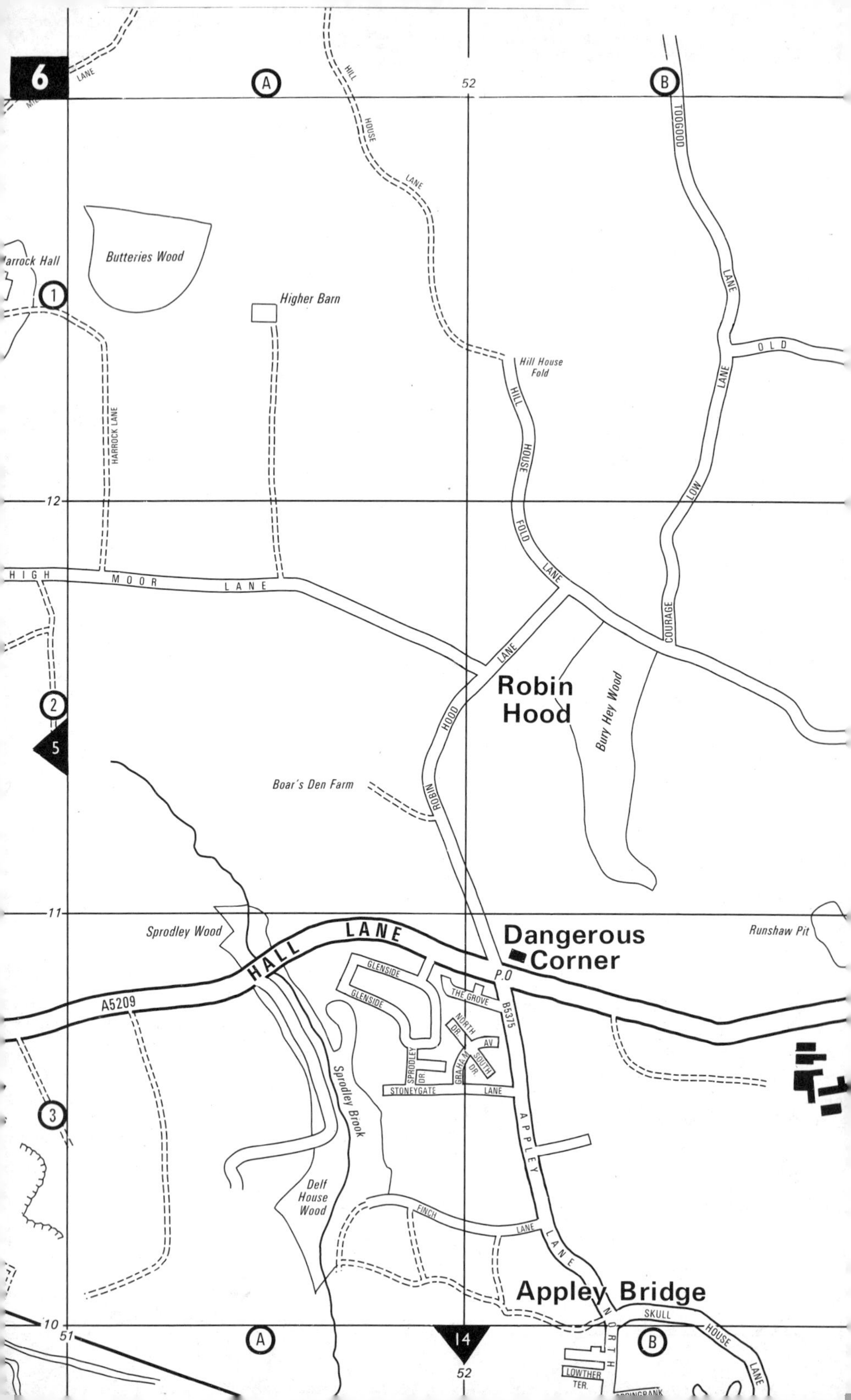
A
52
B
HILL HOUSE LANE
TOOGOOD LANE
Butteries Wood
Harrock Hall
1
Higher Barn
HARROCK LANE
Hill House Fold
HILL HOUSE FOLD LANE
OLD LANE
LOW COURAGE
12
HIGH MOOR LANE
LANE
Robin Hood
Bury Hey Wood
2
5
HOOD
ROBIN
Boar's Den Farm
11
Sprodley Wood
HALL LANE
Dangerous Corner
Runshaw Pit
P.O
GLENSIDE
GLENSIDE
THE GROVE
B5375
A5209
NORTH DR.
AV
SOUTH DR.
GRAHAM
SPRODLEY DR.
Sprodley Brook
STONEYGATE LANE
3
APPLEY LANE
Delf House Wood
FINCH LANE
Appley Bridge
NORTH
SKULL HOUSE LANE
10
51
A
14
52
B
LOWTHER TER.

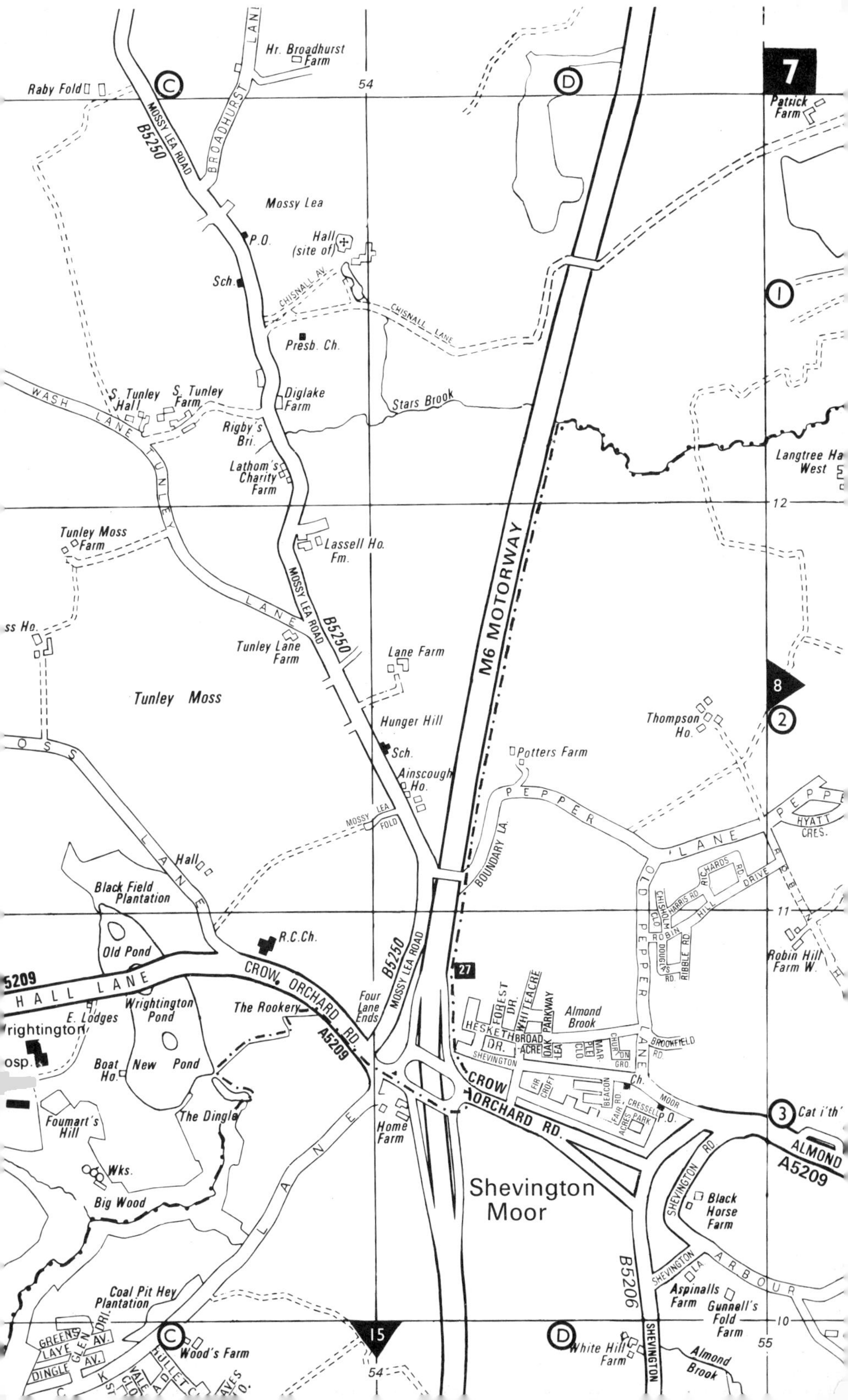
Raby Fold
Hr. Broadhurst Farm
BROADHURST LANE
MOSSY LEA ROAD
B5250
54
Patrick Farm
Mossy Lea
P.O.
Hall (site of)
Sch.
CHISNALL AV.
CHISNALL LANE
Presb. Ch.
WASH LANE
S. Tunley Hall
S. Tunley Farm
Diglake Farm
Stars Brook
Rigby's Bri.
Lathom's Charity Farm
Langtree Hall West
12
Tunley Moss Farm
Lassell Ho. Fm.
TUNLEY LANE
M6 MOTORWAY
ss Ho.
Tunley Lane Farm
Lane Farm
Tunley Moss
Hunger Hill
8
Thompson Ho.
Potters Farm
Sch.
Ainscough Ho.
PEPPER LANE
MOSSY LEA FOLD
BOUNDARY LA.
HYATT CRES.
RICHARDS RD
HARRIS RD
CHISHOLM CLO
ROBIN HILL DRIVE
MOSS LANE
Hall
Black Field Plantation
11
R.C.Ch.
DOUGLAS RD.
RIBBLE RD
OLD PEPPER LANE
Robin Hill Farm W.
Old Pond
B5209
HALL LANE
CROW ORCHARD RD.
Four Lane Ends
27
FOREST DR.
WHITEACRE
PARKWAY
Almond Brook
Wrightington Pond
The Rookery
E. Lodges
A5209
HESKETH DR.
BROAD ACRE
OAK LEA
MAR PLE CLO
CHURTON GRO.
BROOKFIELD RD.
Boat Ho.
New Pond
SHEVINGTON
FIR CROFT
BEACON
CRESSELL PARK
FAIR ACRES
Ch.
MOOR
P.O.
3
Cat i'th'
Foumart's Hill
The Dingle
Home Farm
CROW ORCHARD RD.
ALMOND
A5209
Wks.
Shevington Moor
SHEVINGTON RD.
Black Horse Farm
Big Wood
B5206
SHEVINGTON LA
ARBOUR
Coal Pit Hey Plantation
Aspinalls Farm
Gunnell's Fold Farm
10
GREENS
LAYE
GLEN AV.
DRI.
DINGLE AV.
Wood's Farm
15
White Hill Farm
SHEVINGTON
Almond Brook
55
54

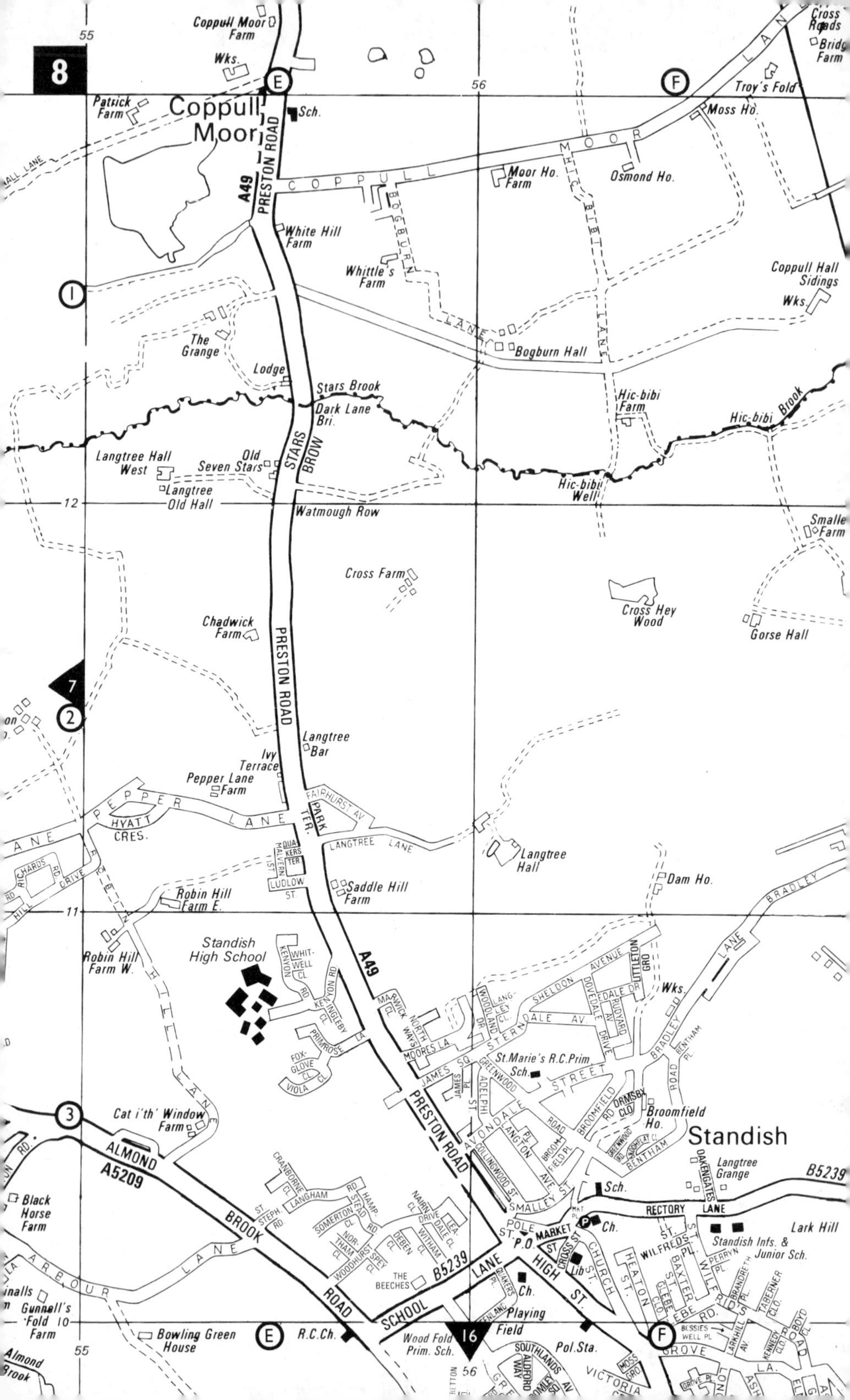
Coppull Moor Farm
Wks.
Patrick Farm
Coppull Moor
Sch.
PRESTON ROAD
A49
COPPULL MOOR LANE
Troy's Fold
Moss Ho.
Cross Roads
Moor Ho. Farm
Osmond Ho.
HIC BIBI LANE
BOGBURN LANE
White Hill Farm
Whittle's Farm
Coppull Hall Sidings
Wks.
The Grange
Lodge
Bogburn Hall
Stars Brook
Dark Lane Bri.
Hic-bibi Farm
Hic-bibi Brook
STARS BROW
Langtree Hall West
Old Seven Stars
Langtree Old Hall
Hic-bibi Well
Watmough Row
Cross Farm
Cross Hey Wood
Gorse Hall
Chadwick Farm
PRESTON ROAD
Langtree Bar
Ivy Terrace
Pepper Lane Farm
PEPPER LANE
HYATT CRES.
FAIRHURST AV.
PARK TER.
LANGTREE LANE
Langtree Hall
QUAKERS TER.
MALVERN ST.
LUDLOW ST.
Saddle Hill Farm
Dam Ho.
RICHARDS RD
Robin Hill Farm E.
BRADLEY LANE
Standish High School
WHIT-WELL CL.
KENYON RD
A49
Robin Hill Farm W.
HILL LANE
MARWICK CL.
NORTH WAYS
MOORES LA.
KINGLEBY CL.
PRIMROSE LA.
FOXGLOVE CL.
VIOLA CL.
WOODLAND DR.
LANGLEY CL.
SHELDON AVENUE
DOVEDALE DRIVE
EDALE DR.
RUDYARD AV.
LITTLETON GRO.
Wks.
STERNDALE AV.
JAMES SQ.
St. Marie's R.C. Prim. Sch.
STREET
GREENWOOD
ADELPHI ST.
JAMES PL.
BENTHAM PL.
BRADLEY ROAD
AVONDALE ROAD
BROOMFIELD RD
ORMSBY CLO.
Broomfield Ho.
Standish
LANGTON PL.
BROOMFIELD PL.
COLLINGWOOD ST.
AVE.
BENTHAM
OAKENGATES
Langtree Grange
B5239
Cat i'th' Window Farm
ALMOND BROOK
A5209
CRANBORNE CL.
LANGHAM
HAMPSTEAD RD
NAIRN CL.
DRIVE
LEADALE CL.
SMALLEY ST.
Sch.
RECTORY LANE
Lark Hill
Standish Infs. & Junior Sch.
ST. STEPH. RD
SOMERTON CL.
NORTHAM CL.
WOODHURST CL.
SPEY CL.
DEBEN CL.
WITHAM CL.
THE BEECHES
B5239
SCHOOL LANE
POLE ST.
P.O.
MARKET ST.
CROSS ST.
Lib.
CHURCH ST.
HIGH ST.
Ch.
HEATON ST.
WILFREDS PL.
BAXTER ST.
GLEBE CLO.
PERRYN PL.
BRANDRETH PL.
TABERNER CLO.
LARKHILL AV.
KENNEDY CLO.
BOYD CL.
Black Horse Farm
ARBOUR LANE
Gunnell's Fold Farm
Bowling Green House
R.C.Ch.
Wood Fold Prim. Sch.
Playing Field
Pol.Sta.
Ch.
QUAKERS PL.
SOUTHLANDS AV.
ALDFORD WAY
MOSS GRO.
VICTORIA
BLESSIES WELL PL.
GROVE
GROVE PL.
Almond Brook
55
56
12
11
10
E
F
1
2
3
7
16

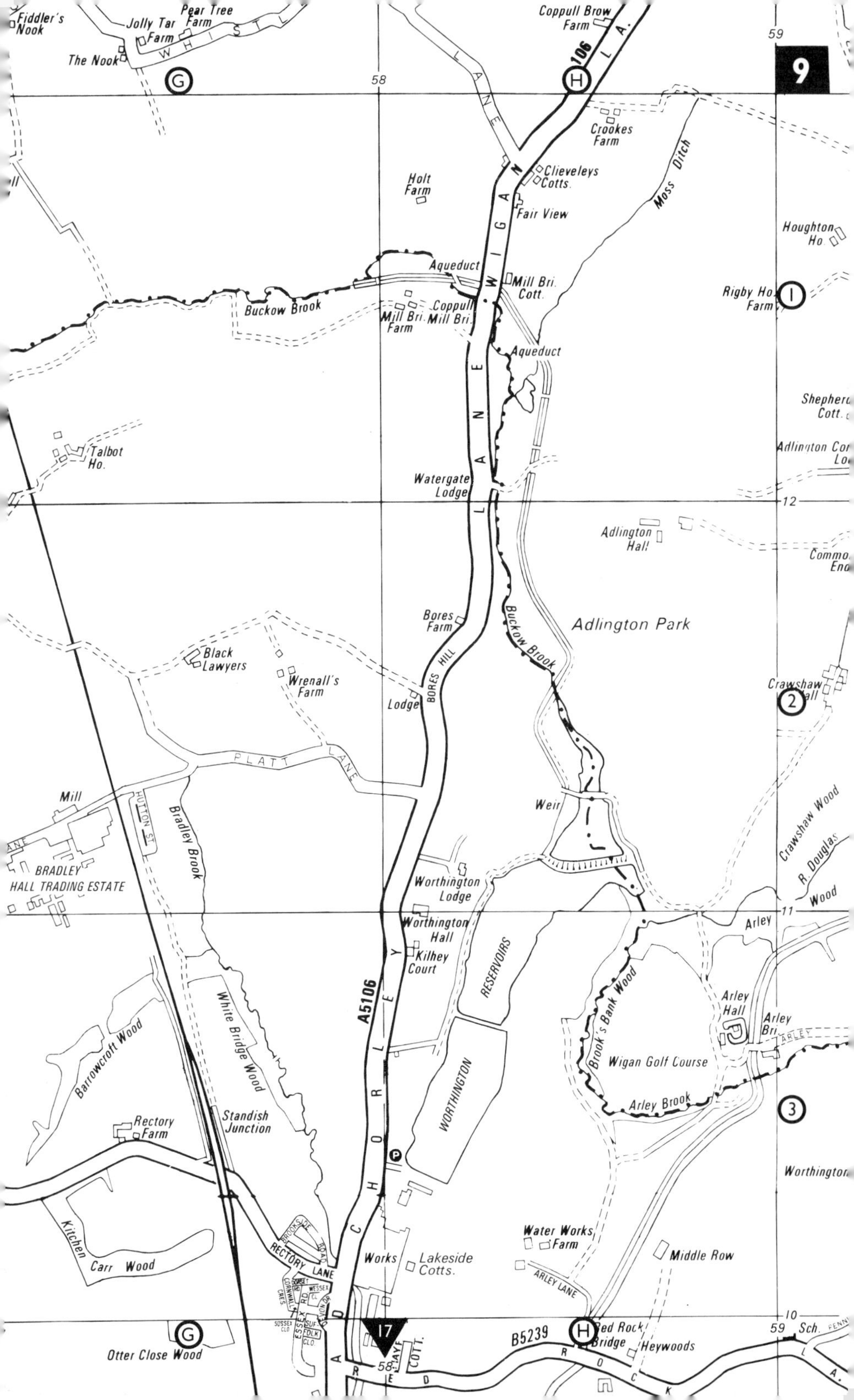

Fiddler's Nook
Pear Tree Farm
Jolly Tar Farm
The Nook
WHISTL
G
Coppull Brow Farm
106
LA.
H
58
59
LANE
Crookes Farm
Clieveleys Cotts.
Moss Ditch
Holt Farm
Fair View
Houghton Ho.
WIGAN
Aqueduct
Mill Bri. Cott.
Rigby Ho. Farm
1
Buckow Brook
Coppull Mill Bri.
Mill Bri. Farm
Aqueduct
LANE
Shepherd Cott.
Talbot Ho.
Adlington Co Lo
Watergate Lodge
12
Adlington Hall
Commo End
Bores Farm
Buckow Brook
Adlington Park
Black Lawyers
Wrenall's Farm
BORES HILL
Lodge
Crawshaw Hall
2
PLATT LANE
Mill
HUTTON ST
Bradley Brook
Weir
Crawshaw Wood
R. Douglas
BRADLEY
HALL TRADING ESTATE
Worthington Lodge
Wood
11
Worthington Hall
Arley
Kilhey Court
RESERVOIRS
Brook's Bank Wood
Arley Hall
Arley Bri.
ARLEY
A5106
White Bridge Wood
Barrowcroft Wood
WORTHINGTON
Wigan Golf Course
Arley Brook
3
CHORLEY
Rectory Farm
Standish Junction
P
Worthington
Water Works Farm
Kitchen
Carr Wood
BROOKSIDE ROAD
RECTORY LANE
Works
Lakeside Cotts.
Middle Row
ARLEY LANE
DORSET RD
WESSEX CL.
CORNWALL CRES.
ESSEX RD.
SUSSEX CLO
SUF-FOLK CLO.
DEVON DR.
10
G
17
H
Red Rock Bridge
Heywoods
B5239
59
Sch.
FENN
Otter Close Wood
58
LAYF COTT.
RED ROCK LA.

PP
QQ
41
4
5
6
09
08
07
40
21
ORMSKIRK
A570
A59
A577
MARSH LANE
NARROW MOSS LANE
BLACKACRE LANE
BLINDMAN'S LANE
ASMALL LANE
HESKIN LANE
RENFREY CLO.
RUTLAND CRES.
LUDLOW DRIVE
HASLAM DR.
MARIANS DRIVE
DOUGLAS DR.
COURT GRN.
COURTFIELD ROAD
HURLSTON DR.
SOUTHPORT ROAD
GRIMSHAW ROAD
Sch.
WHITTLE DRIVE
MAWDSLEY TER.
DAWSON RD.
TYRER RD.
CARROLL CRESCENT
PARKER CRESCENT
LEA CRESCENT
STURGESS CLO.
SCOTT DRIVE
SEPHTON DRIVE
YEW TREE ROAD
HAYFIELD ROAD
HIGHFIELD ROAD
COUNTY ROAD
GRO. PK.
LONSDALE AV.
CROFTSON AV.
BURSCOUGH STREET
OLD BOUNDARY WAY
SHELLEY DR.
WHITE-RAILS MS.
WORDSWORTH CLO.
TENNYSON DR.
WHITERAILS DR.
ASMALL CLO.
BROOKHOUSE RD.
COTTON DRIVE
HALSALL CT.
SANFIELD CLO.
HALSALL LANE
THE AVENUE
CHURCH HILL RD.
THE REEDS
LOVES COTTAGE
ELLERBROOK WY.
HILLCREST ROAD
FARRINGTON DRIVE
Hosp.
ASHCROFT AVENUE
CLUCAS GDN.
OWEN AV.
JUBILEE AV.
SCARISBRICK ST.
GREEN LA.
THE AVENUE
PENNINGTON AV.
GREEN LANE AV.
HANTS LA.
TUDOR CT.
HARDACRE STREET
STATION RD.
STA.
STATION APPROACH
BATH
Little Hall Farm
BRIGHOUSE CLO.
KINLOCH WAY
ROTHWELL CLO.
ROSECROFT CLO.
CHURCHFIELDS
Ch.
NEW COURT WAY
Lib.
Pol. Sta.
RAILWAY APP.
DERBY ST. WEST
THE STILES
CHURCH ST.
LEYLAND WAY
RAILWAY ROAD
STANLEY ST.
ABBOTS ROAD
DERBY
NORFIELD
Leisure Centre
VICARAGE WK.
PARK RD.
HUTTON WAY
Bus Sta.
P.O.
MOOR STREET
REDGATE
COTTAGE LA.
ASH CLO.
DR.
THE ORCHARD
COTTAGE GDNS.
BEECHWOOD
OAK AV.
GARNETT GREEN
COTTAGE CLO.
COTTAGE LANE
CEDAR CRES.
REDWOOD DR.
PARK AV.
DYERS CT.
Fire Sta.
AUGHTON STREET
BRIDGE AV.
GATE
QUEEN ST.
SOUTH TER.
MOOR
BRIDGE STREET
CHAPEL MEWS
CHAPEL ST.
KNOWSLEY RD.
MS.
WINDMILL AV.
MILL STREET
MILL GDNS.
RUFF LA.
WELDON DRIVE
ST. ANNES RD.
DYERS LANE
FURNESS AV.
RAVENSCROFT AV.
BROOK LANE
SMALL LA.
ST. HELENS
HOLBORN HILL
PRIORY GRD.
ROAD
PEET AVENUE
RYBURN ROAD
CALDER AVENUE
ELM PLACE
WAY
STATHAM
ALTY'S LANE
ST. BEDE'S CLO.
HILLSIDE CRES.
OLD MILL HILL
HILLTOP WK.
WIMBRECK
PRESCOT GRN.
PRESCOT
BLACKMOSS LANE
HOLBORN DR.
COLUMBINE
VANDER GARDENS
BEBLES ROAD
MILMAN CLO.
WOODFIELD RD.
Schs.
TARN BROW
SPINNEY CLO.
CLAREMONT DR.
HIGH MOSS
GORE DRIVE
BARNES RD.
REDSANDS
REDCLIFFE GDNS.
BUTTERFIELD GDNS.
PINE CREST
LONG
LYNWOOD AV.
LYNWOOD END
THE PADDOCK
VICTORIA ROAD
SHERWOOD AV.
STANDHOUSE LA.
ROSE PLACE
COVENT CLO.
LANE
HILL LA.

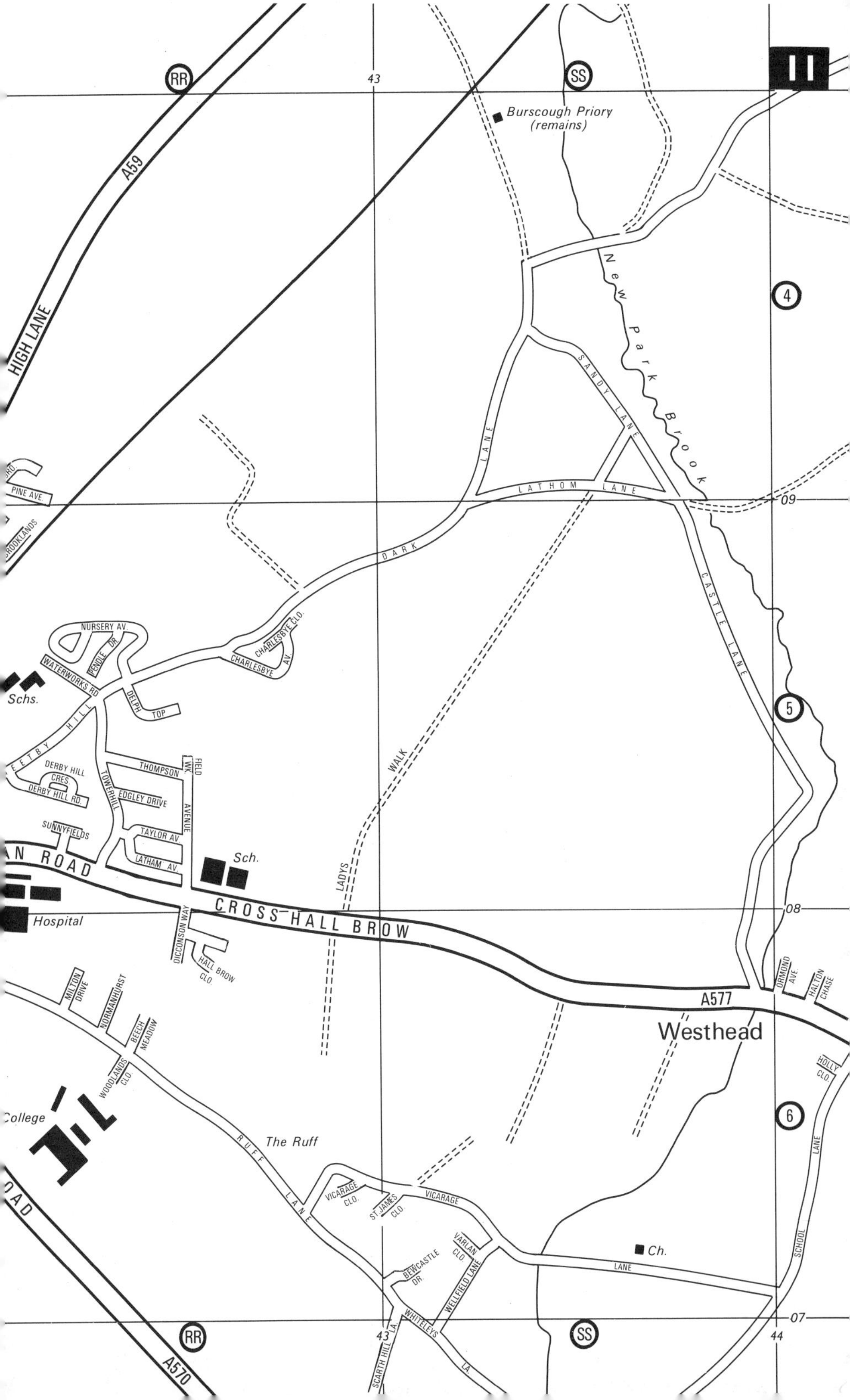

RR
SS
43
Burscough Priory (remains)
A59
HIGH LANE
4
New Park Brook
SANDY LANE
LANE
LATHOM LANE
09
PINE AVE.
BROOKLANDS
DARK
CASTLE LANE
NURSERY AV.
PENDLE DR.
WATERWORKS RD.
CHARLESBYE CLO.
CHARLESBYE AV.
Schs.
DELPH TOP
HILL
5
DERBY HILL CRES.
DERBY HILL RD.
TOWERHILL
THOMPSON
FIELD WK.
EDGLEY DRIVE
AVENUE
WALK
SUNNYFIELDS
TAYLOR AV
LATHAM AV.
ROAD
Sch.
LADYS
CROSS HALL BROW
Hospital
08
DICCONSON WAY
HALL BROW CLO.
ORMOND AVE
HALTON CHASE
A577
MILTON DRIVE
NORMANHURST
BEECH MEADOW
Westhead
WOODLANDS CLO.
HOLLY CLO.
College
6
The Ruff
RUFF LANE
LANE
VICARAGE CLO.
ST. JAMES CLO.
VICARAGE
ROAD
VARLAN CLO.
Ch.
BEWCASTLE DR.
LANE
SCHOOL
WELLFIELD LANE
WHITELEYS LA
07
RR
43
SS
44
A570
SCARTH HILL LA.

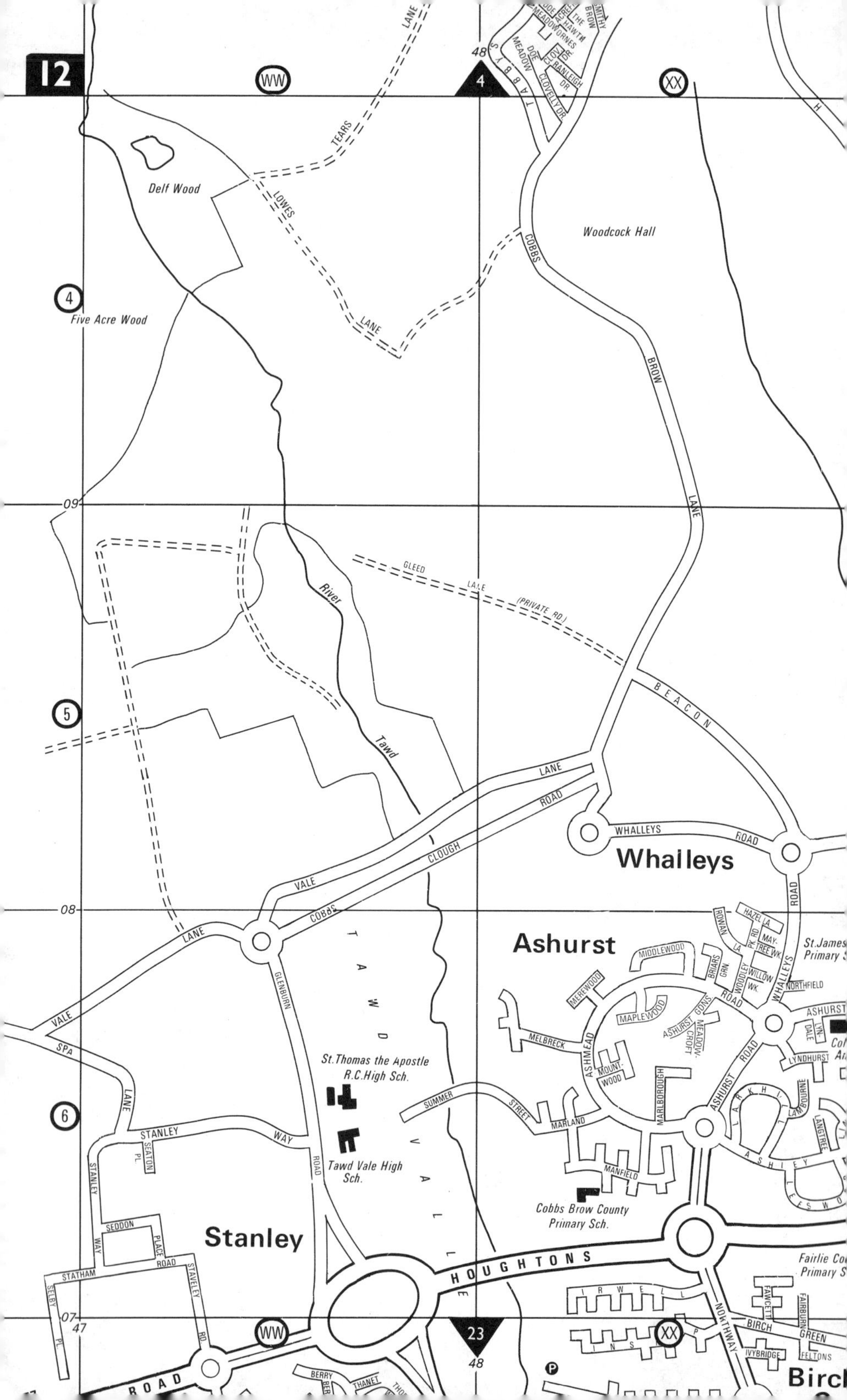
WW
4
XX
48
Delf Wood
Five Acre Wood
Woodcock Hall
TEARS LANE
LOWES LANE
COBBS BROW LANE
GLEED LANE (PRIVATE RD.)
River Tawd
BEACON LANE
VALE LANE
CLOUGH ROAD
COBBS
WHALLEYS ROAD
Whalleys
Ashurst
TAWD VALLE
St.Thomas the Apostle R.C.High Sch.
Tawd Vale High Sch.
GLENBURN ROAD
SPA LANE
STANLEY WAY
SEATON PL.
STANLEY WAY
SEDDON PLACE
STATHAM ROAD
STAVELEY RD.
SELBY PL.
Stanley
HOUGHTONS
ROAD
MIDDLEWOOD
MEREWOOD
MELBRECK
ASHMEAD
MAPLEWOOD
MOUNTWOOD
ASHURST GDNS
MEADOWCROFT
MARLBOROUGH
SUMMER STREET
MARLAND
MANFIELD
Cobbs Brow County Primary Sch.
ASHURST ROAD
BRIARS GRN
WOODLEY
ROWAN LA
HAZEL LA
PK RD
MAY-TREE WK
WILLOW WK
NORTHFIELD
LYNDHURST
LAMBOURNE
LANGTREE
ASHLEY
ST.James Primary
Fairlie Primary
IRWELL
NORTHWAY
BIRCH GREEN
FAWCETT
FAIRBURN
IVYBRIDGE
FELTONS
BERRY
THANET
09
08
07
47
5
6
23

River
Douglas
50
5
YY
ZZ
Prior's Wood Hill
4
LEES LANE
DUNGEON LA.
LANE
HILLOCK
09
14
5
LANE
Dalton
LANE
Ashurst's Beacon
HEYS
08
BEACON
KESTREL MS.
KESTREL PARK
KESTREL PARK
ELMERS GREEN LANE
LONG HEY
LUDLOW
LINDHOLME
KINGSBURY CT.
KING-FISHER PK.
ROAD
LONG
6
STANNANOUGHT
ROAD
FIR-WOOD DRIVE
PINEWOOD
OAKTREE CT
FOREST
BEECH-WOOD
SHERWOOD DR.
ELMERS GREEN LA.
LANE
CROW
Beacon Park
Golf Course
Playing
Fields
FAIRSTEAD
FALKLAND
FAIRLIE
FAIRHAVEN
FOXFOLD
FOSTERS GREEN RD
PARKLANDS
BIRCH GREEN ROAD
HEVERSHAM
HELMSDALE
HARTLAND
24
ZZ
YY
07
51
50
Playing

14
51
52
A
B
6
4
5
13
6
09
08
07
25
Pichill Wood
Hand Lane Bridge
Appley Locks
Lock Meadow Farm
Lock Cottages
Works
LOWTHER TER
SPRING BANK
ASHFIELD TER
NORTH
APPLEY LANE
SOUTH APPLEY LA.
HOUSE LANE
Works
Dawber Delf
Dawber Delf Farm
THE VALE
Appley Road Quarry
West Quarry
Appley Bridge
Central Quarry
BEECH TREE AV.
FINCH M
AV.
Works
Sch.
Hall
P.O.
STA.
MILL LANE
MILL BK.
CHISACRE
CARAWOOD
Finch House
THE BEACONS
GRO.
COXFIELD
TILBURY GRO
DR.
BROOMHOLME
CHISACRE
Appley Bridge
Calico Brook
Swing Bridge
LEEDS & LIVERPOOL
AYREFIELD GR
LEES LANE
Martin's Farm
Cross House Farm
Cassicar Wood
Atherton House
Halliwell Farm
Douglas Bank Farm
Aspinalls
Holland Lees
Swing Bridge
River Douglas
Bank Wood
Bank House
Ferndale
Coppice Bank Wood
STONE HALL LANE
Woodlands
Lees Wood
Lees Brook
Mellings
BANK BROW
Green Alley Wood
Woodcroft
Bank Top
Ayrefield House
AYREFIELD LANE
Whittle's Farm
Cliff's Farm
FARLEY LANE
Knights House
Knights Cottage
R.C. Sch
R C Sch.
Cemetery
Walthew Green
ST. GABRIELS CLO.
Roby Mill C.E. Sch
SCHOOL LANE
Mawdsley's Charity
Meth. Ch.
WHITTLE ROAD
Roby Mill
Knowles Farm
WIDE
LAFFOR
Johnson's
Chap.

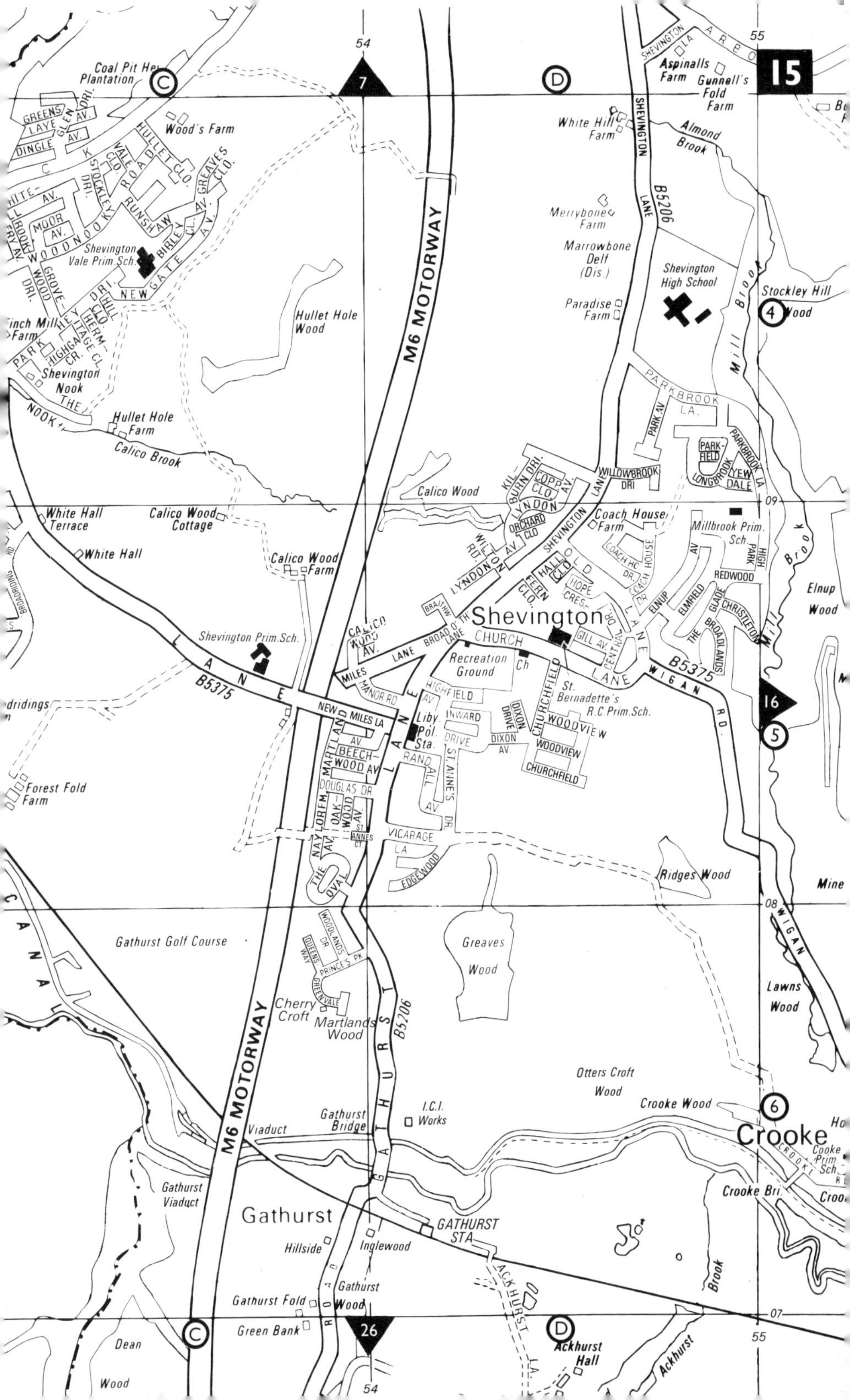
15
54
55
7
26
16
C
D
4
5
6
09
08
07
Coal Pit Hey Plantation
Wood's Farm
GREENS
LAYE
GLEN
DRI.
AV.
DINGLE
HULLET CLO.
VALE CLO.
ROAD
STOCKLEY DRI.
GREAVES CLO.
RUNSHAW
MOOR AV.
WOODNOOK
BIRLEY
Shevington Vale Prim.Sch.
NEW GATE AV.
GROVE
WOOD DRI.
HEY DRI.
HILL CLO.
HERMITAGE CL.
HIGHGATE CR.
PARK
Finch Mill Farm
Shevington Nook
THE NOOK
Hullet Hole Farm
Hullet Hole Wood
Calico Brook
M6 MOTORWAY
White Hill Farm
Aspinalls Farm
Gunnell's Fold Farm
SHEVINGTON LA
Almond Brook
SHEVINGTON LANE
B5206
Merrybone Farm
Marrowbone Delf (Dis.)
Paradise Farm
Shevington High School
Stockley Hill Wood
Mill Brook
PARKBROOK LA.
PARK AV
PARK-FIELD
PARKBROOK LA
LONGBROOK
YEW DALE
WILLOWBROOK DRI
KILBURN DRI.
COPPICE CLO.
LYNDON AV.
ORCHARD CLO
WILTON RD.
LYNDON AV.
Calico Wood
White Hall Terrace
Calico Wood Cottage
White Hall
Calico Wood Farm
BROADRIDING RD
Coach House Farm
COACH HO. DR.
COACH HOUSE DR
Millbrook Prim. Sch.
HIGH PARK
REDWOOD
ELNUP
ELMFIELD
THE GLADE
CHRISTLETON
THE BROADLANDS
Elnup Wood
Shevington
BRAITHWAITE
BROAD O' TH' LANE
CALICO WOOD AV.
MILES LANE
OLD LANE
FERN CLO.
HALL CLO
HOPE CRES.
CENTRAL DR.
GILL AV.
CHURCH LANE
B5375
WIGAN RD.
Shevington Prim.Sch.
LANE
B5375
Recreation Ground
Ch
St. Bernadette's R.C.Prim.Sch.
HIGHFIELD AV.
MANOR RD
NEW MILES LA
MARTLAND AV.
BEECHWOOD AV
DOUGLAS DR
LOREM AV.
NAYLOR
OAKWOOD AV.
ST. ANNES CT.
Liby. Pol. Sta.
INWARD DRIVE
DIXON DRIVE
DIXON AV.
CHURCHFIELD
WOODVIEW
RANDALL AV.
ST. ANNE'S DR.
VICARAGE LA
EDGEWOOD
THE OVAL
Forest Fold Farm
Broadridings
Ridges Wood
Mine
Gathurst Golf Course
CANAL
WOODLANDS DR.
QUEENS WAY
PRINCE'S PK
GREENVALE
Cherry Croft
Martlands Wood
Greaves Wood
GATHURST ROAD
B5206
WIGAN
Lawns Wood
Otters Croft Wood
Crooke Wood
Crooke
CROOKE
Crooke Prim. Sch.
Crooke Bri.
I.C.I. Works
Gathurst Bridge
Viaduct
Gathurst Viaduct
Gathurst
GATHURST STA
Hillside
Inglewood
ACKHURST LA.
Gathurst Wood
Gathurst Fold
Green Bank
Dean Wood
Ackhurst Hall
Ackhurst
Brook

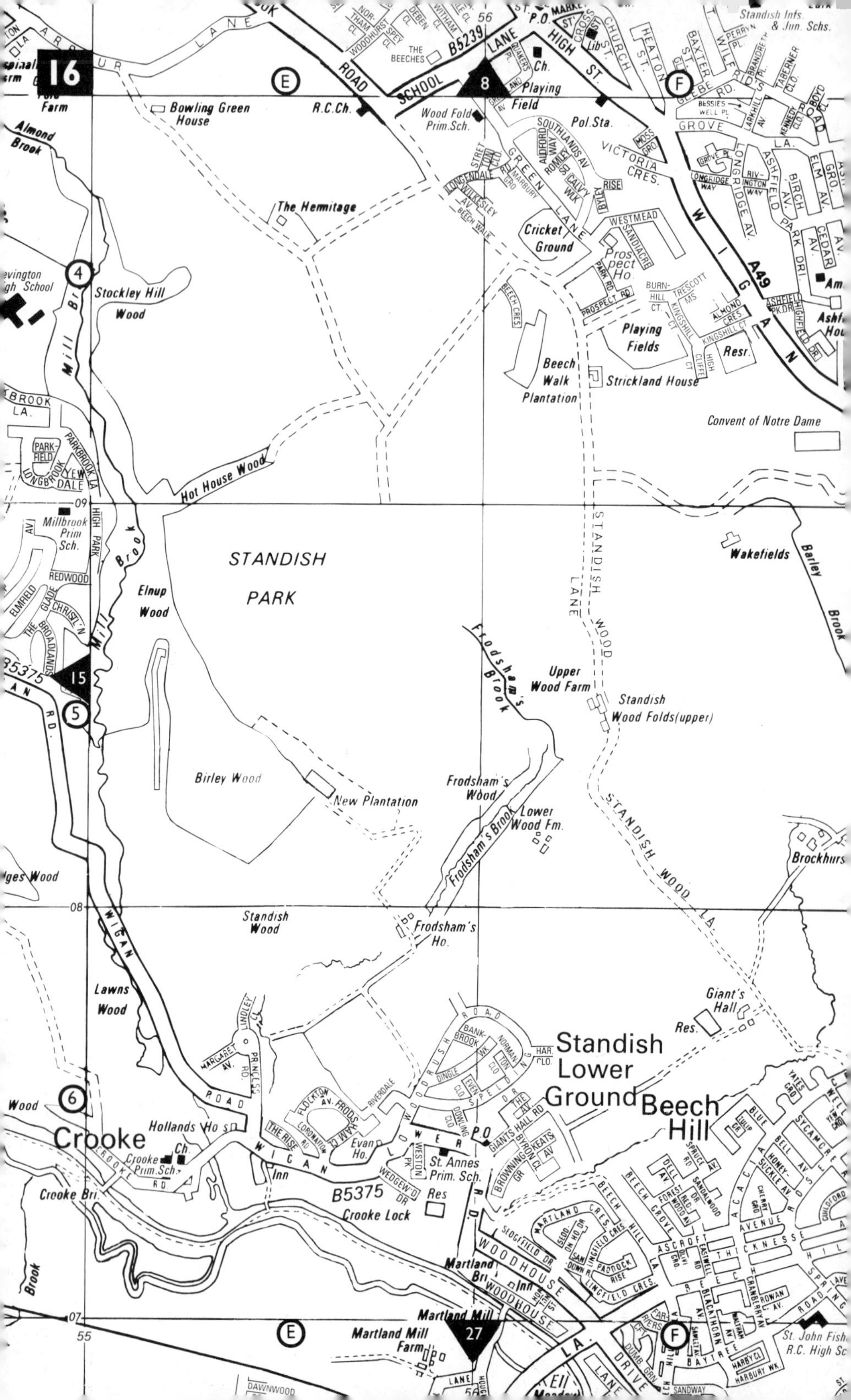

16
ARBOUR LANE
Farm
Almond Brook
Bowling Green House
The Hermitage
R.C.Ch.
SCHOOL LANE
ROAD
B5239
THE BEECHES
WOODHURST
NORTHAM CL.
DEBEN CL.
WITHAM CL.
SPEY CL.
P.O.
MARKET
CROSS ST.
HIGH ST.
Lib
CHURCH ST.
Ch.
QUAKERS PL.
HEATON ST.
BAXTER ST.
Standish Infs. & Jun. Schs.
8
Playing Field
Wood Fold Prim.Sch.
Pol.Sta.
GLEBE RD.
BESSIES WELL PL.
GROVE
LARKHILL AV.
KENNEDY CLO.
TABERNER CLO.
BOYD CL.
LA.
BRANDRETH PL.
PERRYN PL.
GREEN LANE
SOUTHLANDS AV
AUDFORD WAY
ROMLEY
CALV'Y WLK
LONGENDALE RD
WILKESLEY AV
MARBURY GRO
BEECH WALK
MOSS GRO.
VICTORIA CRES.
BYLEY RISE
GROVE PL
LONGRIDGE WAY
LONGRIDGE AV.
RIVINGTON WAY
ASHFIELD AV.
BIRCH AV.
ELM AV.
ASH GRO.
PARK DRI.
CEDAR AV.
AV.
WIGAN
A49
Cricket Ground
WESTMEAD
SANDIACRE
Prospect Ho.
PARK RD.
PROSPECT RD.
BURNHILL CT.
TRESCOTT MS.
KINGSHILL CT.
ALMOND CRES.
KINGSHILL CT
HIGH CLIFFE CT
ASHFIELD PK.DR.
HIGHFIELD DR.
Ashfield Ho
Am
Playing Fields
Resr.
BEECH CRES
Beech Walk Plantation
Strickland House
Convent of Notre Dame
Stockley Hill Wood
Mill Brook
Standish High School
BROOK LA.
PARKFIELD
PARKBROOK LA
LONGBROOK
YEW DALE
Hot House Wood
Millbrook Prim Sch.
HIGH PARK
AV
REDWOOD
ELMFIELD
THE GLADE
CHRISTLEA
THE BROADLANDS
B5375
15
WIGAN RD.
STANDISH PARK
Elnup Wood
STANDISH WOOD LANE
Wakefields
Barley Brook
Frodsham's Brook
Upper Wood Farm
Standish Wood Folds(upper)
Birley Wood
New Plantation
Frodsham's Wood
Lower Wood Fm.
Brockhurs
Standish Wood
Frodsham's Ho.
STANDISH WOOD LA.
Lawns Wood
Giant's Hall
Res.
Standish Lower Ground
Beech Hill
LINDLEY
MARGARET AV.
PRINCESS RD.
ROAD
BANKBROOK
ROAD
NORMANTON CLO
WOODRUSH
DINGLE CLO
EVENWK
SPELDING
HAR. CLO.
RIVERDALE
FLOCKTON AV.
CORONATION RD
FRODSHAM CL.
THE RISE
Evan Ho.
DOWLING CLO
LOWER RD.
P.O.
THE AV
GIANTS HALL RD
BYRON CL
KEATS AV
BROWNING GR
WESTON PK
St. Annes Prim. Sch.
WEDGEW'D DR
Res
Crooke Lock
Inn
Wood
Hollands Ho
Crooke
Ch.
Crooke Prim.Sch.
CROOKE RD.
Crooke Bri.
Brook
Martland Bri.
Martland Mill
Martland Mill Farm
27
WOODHOUSE LA.
STOCKFIELD DR
MARTLAND CRES
SANDOWN RD
LINGFIELD CRES.
PADDOCK RISE
BEECH HILL LA.
BEECH GROVE
FOREST RD.
DELL AV.
SPRUCE AV.
SANDALWOOD
ASCROFT
ACACIA AVENUE
THICKNESSE
TULIP
BLUE
YATES GRO
SYCAMORE
BELL AV.
HONEYSUCKLE AV.
CHERRY GRO
EASTWELL RD
OLIVE GRO.
BLACKTHORN AV.
CRANBERRY AV.
ROWAN AV.
WALTHAM AV.
HARBY CL
HARBURY WK
BAYTREE
SANDWAY
DRIVE
LANE
SPRING RD
St. John Fisher R.C. High Sc
DAWNWOOD
E
F
4
5
6
55
56
07
08
09

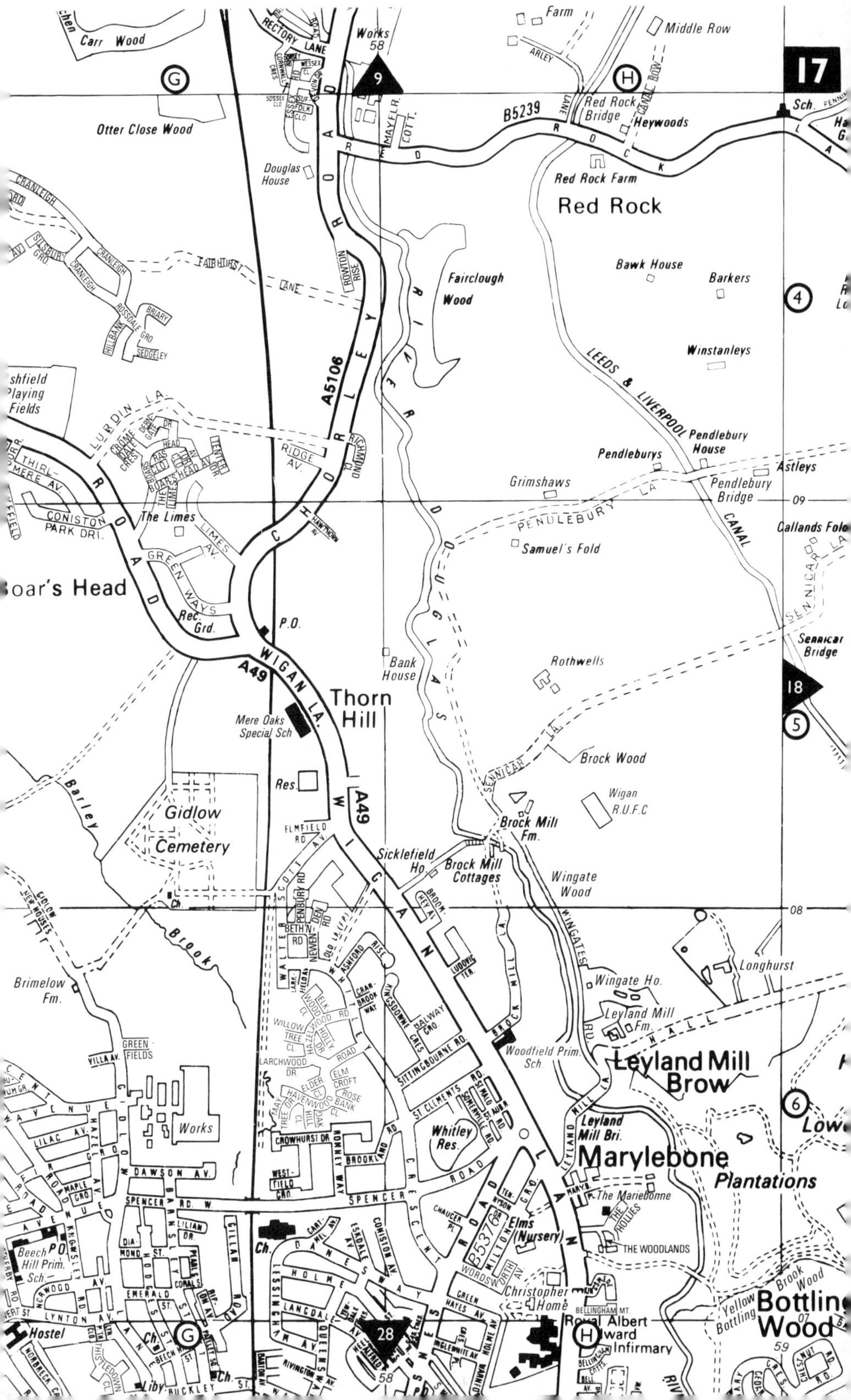
Carr Wood
Otter Close Wood
Rectory Lane
Works
58
9
Farm
Arley
Middle Row
Canal Row
Red Rock Bridge
Heywoods
B5239
Red Rock
Red Rock Farm
Sch.
Mayflr.
Cott.
Douglas House
Cranleigh
Silsbury Gro.
Fairhurst Lane
Rowton Rise
Rossdale Gro.
Briary
Hillbank
Sedgeley
Fairclough Wood
River Douglas
Bawk House
Barkers
Winstanleys
Leeds & Liverpool Canal
A5106
Chorley Road
Ashfield Playing Fields
Lurdin La.
Thirlmere Av.
Coniston Park Dri.
Ridge Av.
Richmond Cl.
Hawthorn Av.
Pendleburys
Pendlebury House
Pendlebury Bridge
Pendlebury La.
Astleys
Grimshaws
Samuel's Fold
Callands Fold
Sennicar La.
Sennicar Bridge
09
The Limes
Limes Av.
Green Ways
Boar's Head
Boar's Head Av.
Rec. Grd.
P.O.
Wigan La.
A49
Thorn Hill
Mere Oaks Special Sch
Bank House
Rothwells
18
4
5
Res.
Brock Wood
Wigan R.U.F.C
Barley Brook
Gidlow Cemetery
Brock Mill Fm.
Elmfield Rd.
Scott Av.
Sicklefield Ho.
Brock Mill Cottages
Wingate Wood
Wingates La.
08
Longhurst
Brook Hey Av.
Ludovic Ter.
Brock Mill La.
Wingate Ho.
Leyland Mill Fm.
Hall La.
Gidlow New Houses
Brimelow Fm.
Penbury Rd
Walter St.
Ashford Rise
Cranbrook Way
Kingsdowne Cres
Halway Gro.
Elkwood Cl.
Willow Tree Cl.
Hazelwood Dr.
Holly Rd
Larchwood Dr.
Elder Cl.
Elm Croft
Havenwood Rd
Rose Bank Cl.
Oak Hill Cl.
Maytree Dr.
Sittingbourne Rd.
St. Clements Rd.
Woodfield Prim. Sch.
Leyland Mill Brow
Leyland Mill La.
Leyland Mill Bri.
6
Green Fields
Villa Av.
Works
Crowhurst Dr
Romney Way
Brookland Rd
Whitley Res.
Westfield Gro.
Crescent Road
Marylebone
Plantations
Lilac Av.
Dawson Av.
Spencer Rd. W.
Spencer Rd.
Maple Gro.
Barnsley St.
Lilian Dr.
Gillan Road
Avenue
Beech Hill Prim. Sch.
P.O.
Diamond St.
Pearl St.
Corals
Emerald St.
Lynton Av.
Norwood Av.
Ch.
Danes Way
Holme
Eskdale Av.
Coniston Av.
Chaucer Pl.
Tennyson Gro.
Milton Dr.
B5376
Elms (Nursery)
The Marienbonne
The Hollies
The Woodlands
Wordsworth Av.
Christopher Home
Green Hayes Av.
Langdale
Lessingham Av.
Queensway
28
Royal Albert Edward Infirmary
Bellingham Mt.
Yellow Brook
Brook Wood
Bottling Wood
07
59
Chestnut Rd.
Hostel
Rivington Av.
Inglewhite Av.
Holme Av.
Buckley St.
Liby.
Norbreck
Thistledown
G
H

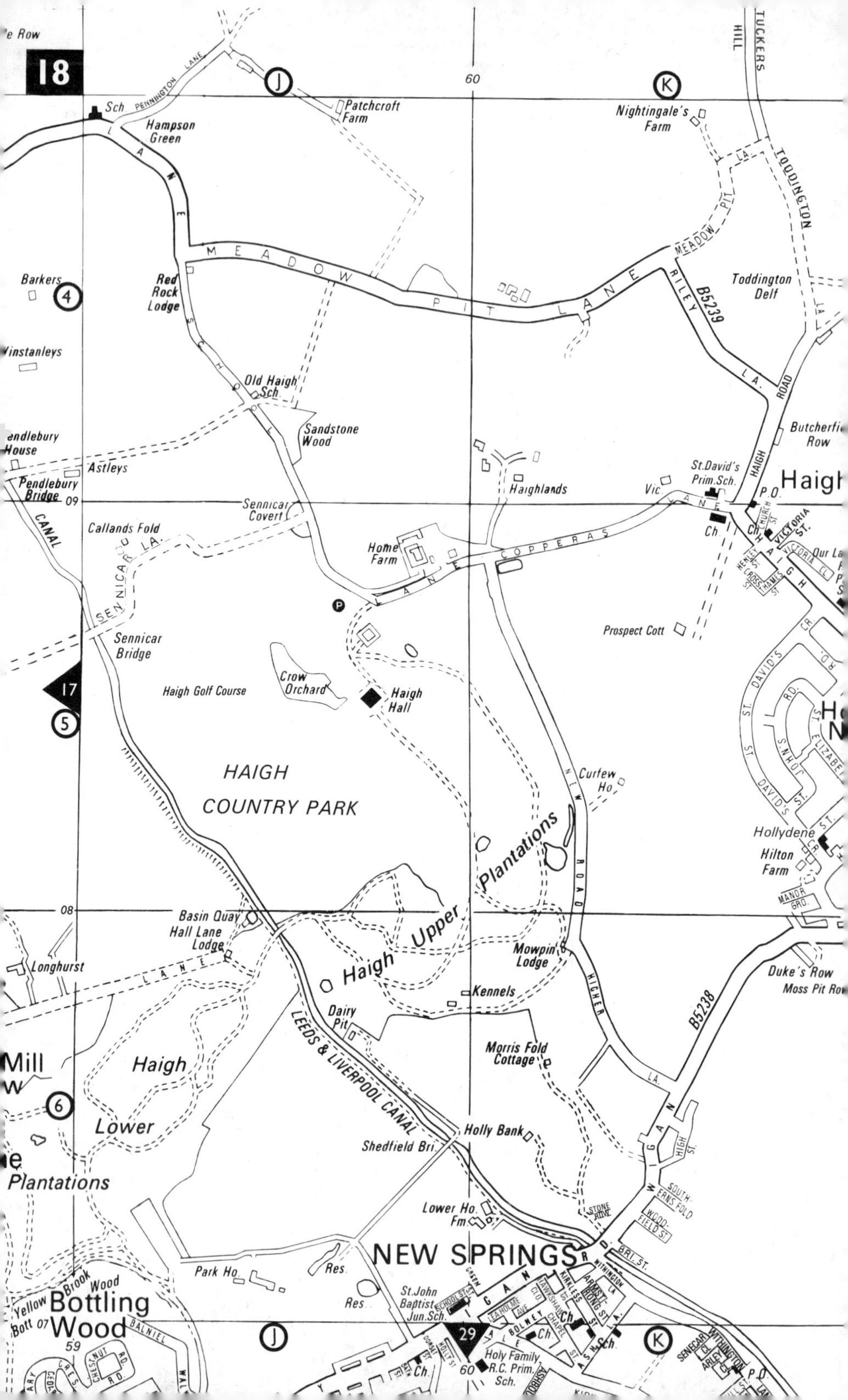
J
K
60
Patchcroft Farm
Nightingale's Farm
TUCKERS HILL
Sch
PENNINGTON LANE
Hampson Green
LANE
MEADOW PIT LANE
MEADOW PIT LA.
TODDINGTON LA.
Toddington Delf
RILEY LA.
B5239
HAIGH ROAD
Barkers
4
Red Rock Lodge
SCHOOL LA.
Winstanleys
Old Haigh Sch.
Sandstone Wood
Pendlebury House
Astleys
Pendlebury Bridge
09
CANAL
Sennicar Covert
Callands Fold
SENNICAR LA.
Haighlands
Vic.
St.David's Prim.Sch.
P.O.
Haigh
Ch.
CHURCH ST.
VICTORIA ST.
VICTORIA CL.
HEMLEY ST.
CROSS ST.
THAMES ST.
Our La
Home Farm
COPPERAS LANE
Sennicar Bridge
Prospect Cott
ST. DAVID'S CR.
17
5
Crow Orchard
Haigh Hall
Haigh Golf Course
ST. JOHN'S RD.
ST. ELIZABETH
ST. DAVID'S ST.
HAIGH COUNTRY PARK
NEW ROAD
Curfew Ho
Plantations
Hollydene
Hilton Farm
MANOR GRO.
08
Basin Quay
Hall Lane Lodge
Haigh Upper
Mowpin Lodge
Longhurst
LANE
Kennels
Duke's Row
Moss Pit Row
B5238
HIGHER LA.
Dairy Pit
LEEDS & LIVERPOOL CANAL
Morris Fold Cottage
Mill
6
Haigh
Lower
Plantations
Holly Bank
Shedfield Bri.
WIGAN
HIGH ST.
SOUTHERNS FOLD
WOODFIELD ST.
STONE ROW
Lower Ho. Fm.
NEW SPRINGS
BRI. ST.
WITHINGTON LA.
Park Ho.
Res.
Res
St.John Baptist Jun.Sch.
SCHOOL ST.
GREEN
KIRKLESS ST.
ARMSTRONG ST.
LEA HOLME AVE.
HAWKSHAW CLO.
BOLNEY
CHAPEL ST.
Ch.
Sch.
K
J
29
Brook Wood
Yellow Bott
Bottling Wood
07
59
BALNIEL
CHESNUT RD.
CRES.
WAL
HOLLY ST.
DORSET
Holy Family R.C. Prim. Sch.
60
SENECAR CL.
ARLEY CL.
WITHINGTON
P.O.

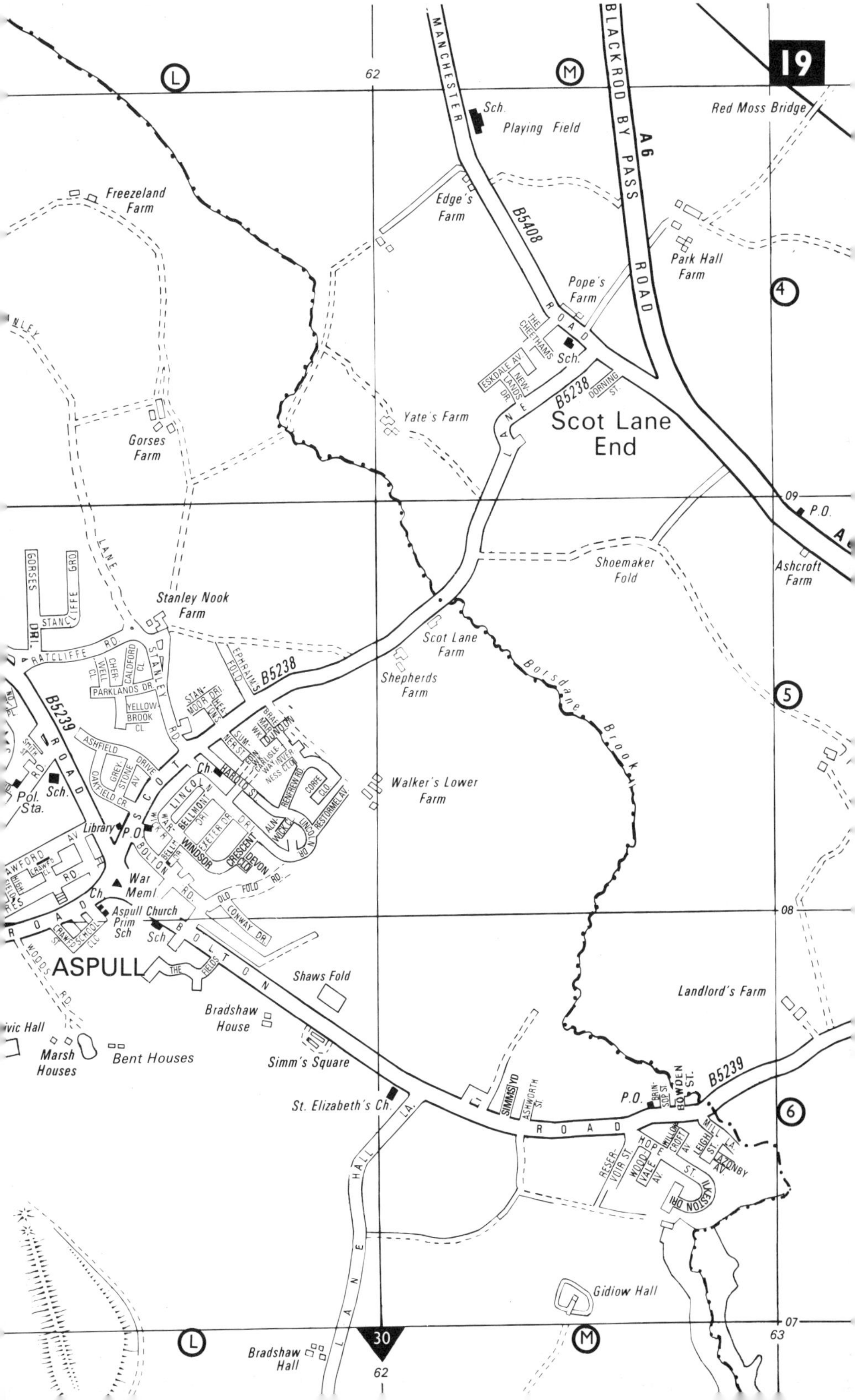
Red Moss Bridge
Sch.
Playing Field
MANCHESTER
BLACKROD BY PASS
A6
ROAD
B5408
Freezeland Farm
Edge's Farm
Park Hall Farm
Pope's Farm
THE CHEETHAMS
Sch.
ESKDALE AV.
NEW LANDS DR.
B5238
DORNING ST.
Yate's Farm
Scot Lane End
Gorses Farm
Shoemaker Fold
Ashcroft Farm
P.O.
Stanley Nook Farm
Scot Lane Farm
Shepherds Farm
Borsdane Brook
RATCLIFFE RD.
GORSES DRI.
STANCLIFFE GRO.
PARKLANDS DR.
YELLOW BROOK CL.
CALDFORD CL.
EPHRAIM'S FOLD
ASHFIELD DRIVE
OAKFIELD CR.
GREYSTONE AV.
B5239
Sch.
Pol. Sta.
Walker's Lower Farm
Library
P.O.
War Meml.
Aspull Church Prim Sch
Sch
ASPULL
BOLTON RD.
OLD FOLD RD.
CONWAY DR.
WINDSOR CRESCENT
DEVON CLO.
EXETER DR.
BELLMONT DRI.
LINCOLN DR.
HAROLD ST.
RENFREW RD.
CORFE CLO.
RESTORMEL AV.
DUNDON
Shaws Fold
Bradshaw House
Simm's Square
Civic Hall
Marsh Houses
Bent Houses
St. Elizabeth's Ch.
SIMMS YD
ASHWORTH ST.
P.O.
BOWDEN ST.
B5239
Landlord's Farm
RESERVOIR ST.
WOODVALE AV.
WILLOWCROFT AV.
LEIGH ST.
AZONBY AV.
ILKESTON DRI
HALL LANE
Gidlow Hall
Bradshaw Hall
62
63
08
09
07

30

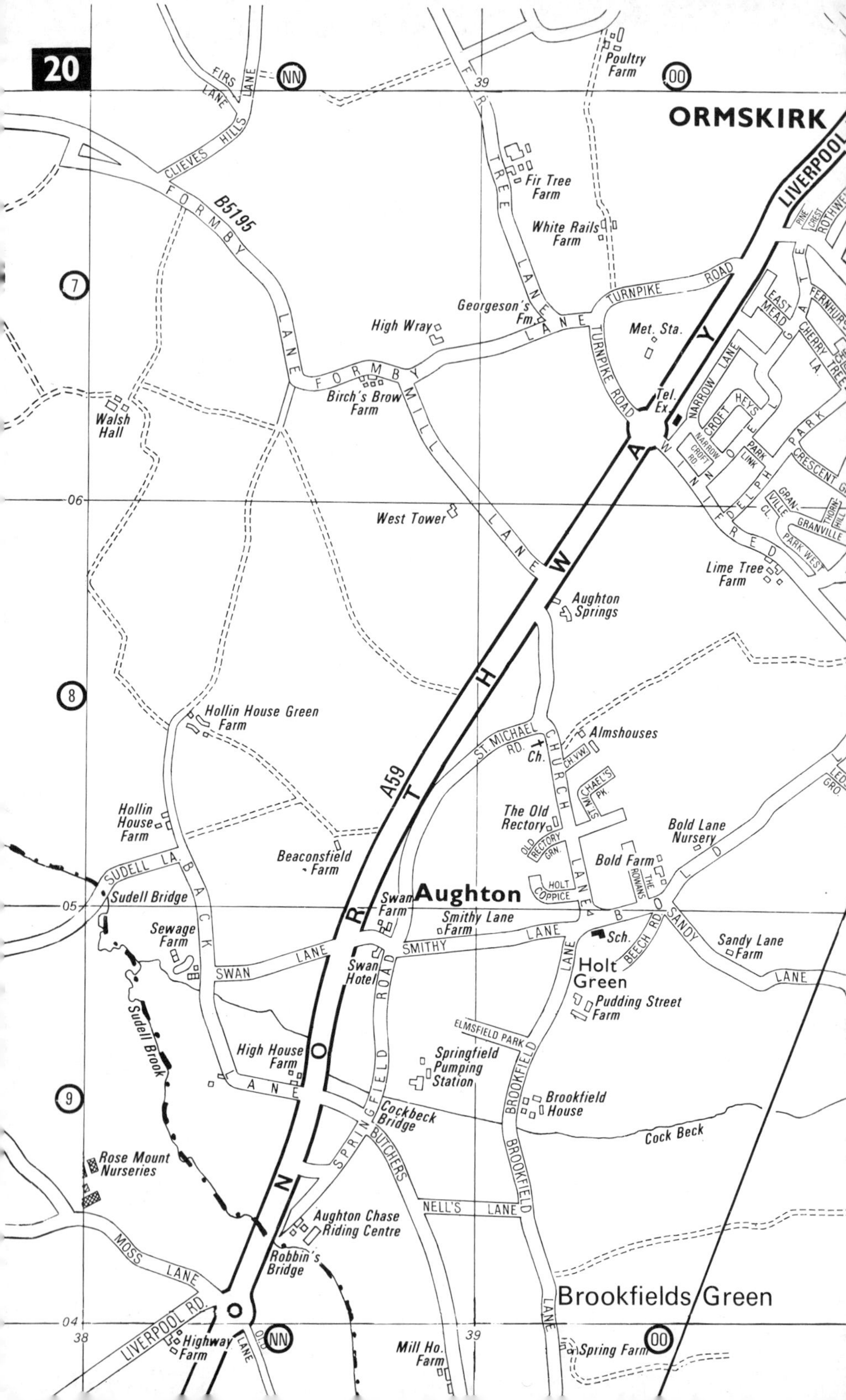
ORMSKIRK
FIRS LANE
CLIEVES HILLS LANE
NN
OO
39
Poultry Farm
FIR TREE LANE
LIVERPOOL
B5195
FORMBY LANE
Fir Tree Farm
White Rails Farm
7
TURNPIKE ROAD
Georgeson's Fm.
High Wray
Met. Sta.
EAST MEAD
FERNHURST
CHERRY TREE LA.
PINE CREST
ROTHWELL
FORMBY LANE
MILL LANE
Birch's Brow Farm
Walsh Hall
NARROW LANE
CROFT HEYS
Tel. Ex.
NARROW CROFT RD
PARK LINK
PARK CRESCENT
WINIFRED LANE
DELPH PARK
GRAN-VILLE CL.
GRANVILLE
THORN HILL
PARK WEST
06
West Tower
Lime Tree Farm
Aughton Springs
NORTHWAY
A59
8
Hollin House Green Farm
Almshouses
ST. MICHAEL RD.
CHURCH LANE
Ch.
CH. VW.
ST. MICHAEL'S PK.
LEDS GRO.
The Old Rectory
OLD RECTORY GRN.
Hollin House Farm
Bold Lane Nursery
BOLD LANE
Beaconsfield Farm
Bold Farm
SUDELL LA.
BACK LANE
Sudell Bridge
HOLT COPPICE
THE ROWANS
Swan Farm
Aughton
05
Smithy Lane Farm
SANDY LANE
Sewage Farm
SMITHY LANE
Sch.
BEECH RD.
Sandy Lane Farm
SWAN LANE
Swan Hotel
Holt Green
SPRINGFIELD ROAD
Pudding Street Farm
Sudell Brook
ELMSFIELD PARK
High House Farm
Springfield Pumping Station
BROOKFIELD
9
Brookfield House
Cockbeck Bridge
Cock Beck
Rose Mount Nurseries
BUTCHERS LANE
NELL'S LANE
BROOKFIELD LANE
Aughton Chase Riding Centre
MOSS LANE
Robbin's Bridge
Brookfields Green
LIVERPOOL RD.
04
38
OLD LANE
Highway Farm
Mill Ho. Farm
Spring Farm

Aughton Park
Town Green
Bowkers Green
AUGHTON PARK STA.
TOWN GREEN STA.
Sch.
Sch.
Moor Hall Farm
Lower End Farm
10
PP
QQ
PP
QQ
7
8
9
41
41
42
06
05
04
LONG LANE
PINE CREST
LYNWOOD AV
LYNWOOD END
SHERWOOD AV
VICTORIA ROAD
THE PADDOCK
TARN BROW
SPINNEY CLO.
BUTTERFIELD GDNS.
CLAREMONT DR.
REDSANDS
GORE DRIVE
BARNES RD.
REDCLIFFE
CONVENT CLO.
ROSE PLACE
GREYSTOKES
CROMWELL CLO.
CROMFIELD
ROSEHILL DRIVE
DRAKE CLO.
MALLARD CLO.
DELPH CLO.
MEADOW DR.
SWANPOOL LANE
TEAL CLO.
RYDER CLO.
RYDER CRES.
MOSS DELPH LANE
DELPH CLO.
DELPH LANE
QUARRY DRIVE
WESTHAVEN CRESCENT
GREENWOOD CLO.
DINGLE CLO.
HAVEN BROW
THE NOOK
NORRISHOUSE DRIVE
COLE CRES.
GRANVILLE PARK
ORCHARD VIEW
B5197
BEAUMONT CLO.
CARMEL CLO.
BLACKMOSS LANE
MOSS BANK
HALLMOOR CLO.
NEW LANE
SCARTH HILL LANE
ALTY'S LANE
CATHERINE'S LANE
CROPPERS LANE
PARR'S LANE
MALTKILN LANE
TOWN GREEN LANE
SAGAR FOLD
WHALLEY DRIVE
MOLYNEUX ROAD
THE SERPENTINE
PRESCOT ROAD
BLEASDALE CLOSE
SEFTON GARDENS
THE GROVE
MIDDLEWOOD ROAD
MIDDLEWOOD DR.
MIDDLEWOOD CLO.
SUNNYSIDE
MICKERING LANE
BOWKERS GREEN LANE

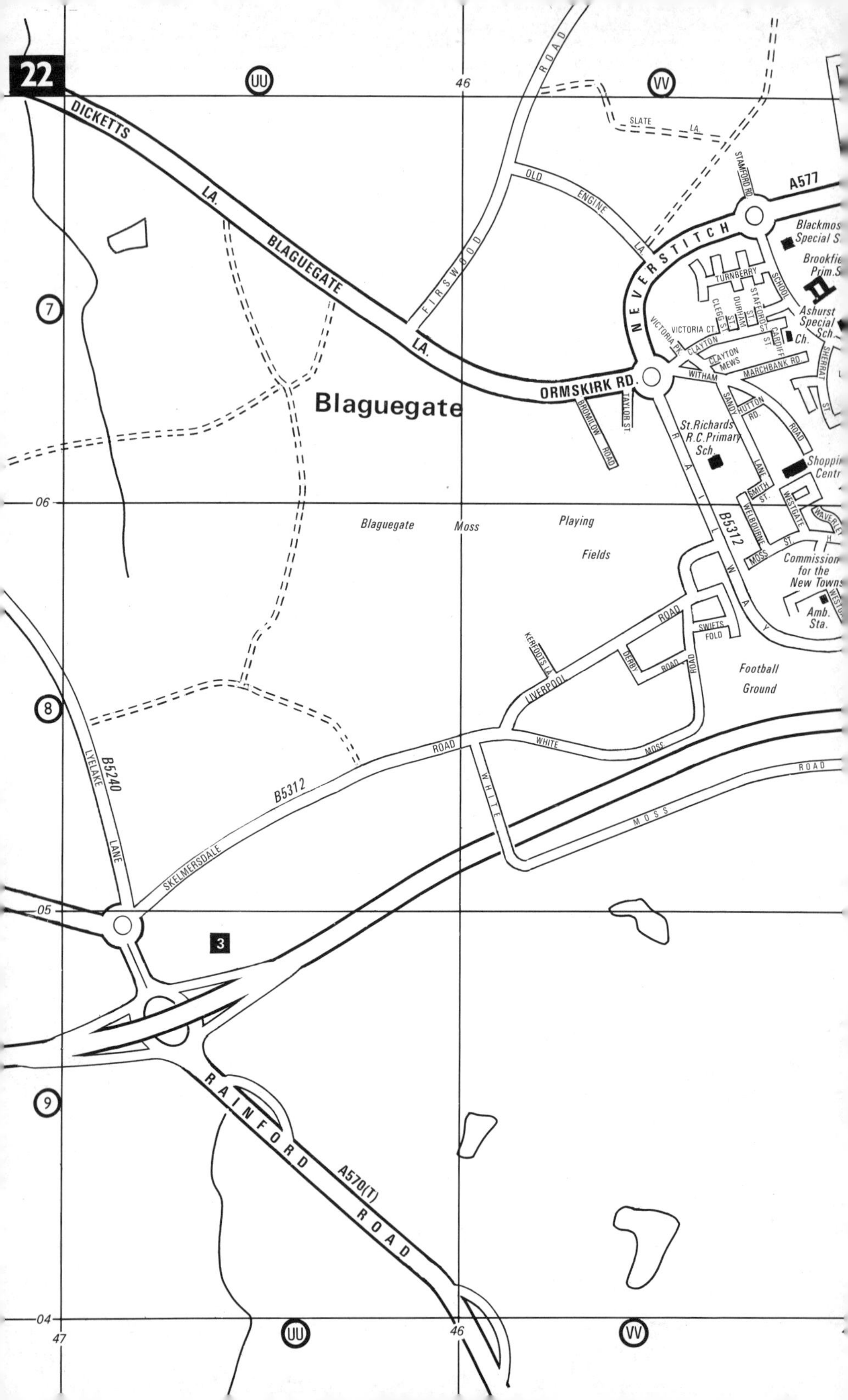
UU
46
VV
DICKETTS
LA.
BLAGUEGATE
LA.
ROAD
SLATE
LA.
OLD
ENGINE
LA.
FIRSWOOD
STAMFORD RD.
A577
NEVERSTITCH
Blackmoss
Special S.
Brookfield
Prim.S.
TURNBERRY
SCHOOL
CLEGG ST.
DURHAM ST.
STAFFORD ST.
Ashurst
Special
Sch.
VICTORIA CT.
VICTORIA PK.
CARDIFF ST.
Ch.
CLAYTON
CLAYTON MEWS
SHERRAT
WITHAM
MARCHBANK RD.
ST.
ORMSKIRK RD.
BROMILOW ROAD
TAYLOR ST.
SANDY
HUTTON RD.
Blaguegate
St.Richards
R.C.Primary
Sch.
ROAD
LANE
Shopping
Centre
SMITH ST.
WELBOURNE
WESTGATE
WAVERLEY
RAILWAY
B5312
06
Blaguegate
Moss
Playing
Fields
MOSS ST.
Commission
for the
New Towns
Amb.
Sta.
7
ROAD
SWIFTS FOLD
KERFOOTS LA.
DERBY
ROAD
ROAD
LIVERPOOL
Football
Ground
8
WHITE
MOSS
ROAD
WHITE
MOSS
ROAD
B5240
LYELAKE
LANE
B5312
SKELMERSDALE
05
3
9
RAINFORD
A570(T)
ROAD
04
47
46
UU
VV

Stanley
SEDDON
PLACE
ROAD
STAVELEY
RD.
WW
HOUGHTONS
48
12
IRWELL
XX
INSKIP
NORTHWAY
Fairlie County
Primary Sch.
23
FAIRLIE
HAVEN
FAWCETT
FAIRBURN
BIRCH
GREEN
ROAD
IVYBRIDGE
FELTONS
FELSTED
Birch
Green
INGLEWHITE
IVYDALE
INCHFIELD
FERNDALE
BIRCH
ROAD
KILN
THURCROFT
THEALBY CLO.
DR.
THURSTON
MILLBROOK
MILLROSE CLO.
BERRY
BERRY CLO.
THANET
THORNWOOD
TITCH CLO.
NEVERSTREET
Sch.
STREET
HORNBURY
SCHOOL
LANE
CLO.
THORNTON
MILL
LANE
ROMILEY
DEL AMERE
RD.
MERE CLO.
BRAMHALL
DR.
RD.
TIVERTON AV.
PARK
GLENBURN
A506
SKELMERSDALE
River
FINDON
7
FIRBECK
PALM CT.
THORPE
APPLETON RD.
TONGBARN
TILCROFT
SCHOOL
HOLLY CLO.
LAUREL DR.
WILLOW
POPLAR DR.
CHURCH ROAD
TARLSWOOD
TANFIELDS
INGRAM
Playing Fields
KILN
LARCH CLO.
PINE CLO.
DR.
LANE
TAN CASTER
LANCASTER
St. Edmunds
County Primary
Sch.
Skelmersdale
College
Old
Skelmersdale
Trinity
Primary Sch.
CHURCH
THE TAMNEYS
OXFORD RD.
CAMBRIDGE RD.
OLIVE GR.
ELM GR.
LILAC GR.
LIME CT.
Nye Bevan
Pool
Bus Sta.
P.S.
NORTHWAY
YEADON
THE CONCOURSE
SOUTHWAY
Tawd
WILLOW
HEY
WINDROWS
ROAD
WILCOVE
THE WINSTERS
ROSE
CEDAR GR.
CRES.
BEECH CLO.
Park County
Primary Sch.
MANOR GR.
CRES.
FERN CL.
HAWTHORN CRES.
ROAD
YEWDALE
06
Glenburn & Westbank
High Schools
BARNES
BIRCH ST.
ANN ST.
STREET
WIGAN RD.
WOLVERTON
WINSTANLEY RD.
WOODCROFT
WHITE STOCKS
WOODROW
WHITEHEY RD.
WHITE HEY
JUBILEE DR.
WALL CROFT ST.
WHEATACRE
ROAD
B5312
GRIMSHAW
Delphside County
Primary Sch.
ROAD
GLADDEN PL.
GARDINERS PL.
GILLIBRANDS
GREENHEY PL.
GLEBE
ROAD
GREETBY PL.
ROAD
GRIMROD
ORMSKIRK
8
SPENCERS
GREENWAY AV.
24
Gillibrands
GERRARD PL.
INDUSTRIAL
ESTATE
GRATTON PLACE
GLEBE
GARNETT PL.
WHITELEDGE ROAD
HILLCREST
AMBERGATE
GLENBURN ROAD
4
GORSEY PL.
ROAD
PL.
AMERSHAM
Ch.
DANIELS
LANE
SOUTH
GILLIBRANDS ROAD
ABBEYSTEAD
05
M58 MOTORWAY
Little Digmoor
Primary
Sch.
MOSS LANE VW.
MOSS
LANE
MIDGE NOOK
LANE
9
NIPE
04
WW
48
XX
49

24
Fairlie County Primary Sch.
Birch Green
Clough Fold County Primary Sch.
St.Johns R.C Primary Sch.
FINDON
FIRBECK
GREEN
ROAD
BIRCH GREEN ROAD
FELSTED
FERNDALE
BIRCH
FELTONS
FAIRBURN
FAIRLIE
FAIRSHEAD
FALKLAND
HEATHGATE
HEVERSHAM
HELMSDALE
HARTLAND
FOXFOLD
ELMERS GREEN LA
FOSTERS GREEN RD
PARKLANDS
HARSNIPS
HARTSHEAD
HAWKSCLOUGH
HALLCROFT
FLAMSTEAD
FLAXTON
FLIMBY
Playing Fields
Beacon Park
Golf Course
CROW
BEACON
Beacon Park Centre
LANE
PARK
A577
ROAD
ELMERS
GREEN
FELTONS MEWS
ELMERS WOOD RD
Elmers Green County Primary Sch.
EVINGTON
EVENWOOD
EVERSLEY
EASTLEIGH
NORTHWAY
Bus Sta.
THE CONCOURSE
SOUTHWAY
ESKBROOK
HOUGHTONS LA
FENNEY CT
DALE
ESKBANK
TANHOUSE ROAD
Delphside County Primary Sch.
ELSWICK
ELMSTEAD
FIMRIDGE
ENSTONE
ENNERDALE
EAVESDALE
EARLSWOOD
Tanhouse
Ch.
TAWD ROAD
Skelmersdale Hillside County Primary Sch.
EGERTON
St.Marks R.C. Primary Sch.
St.Richards R.C. High Sch.
Beacon Special Sch.
GRIMSHAW
B5312
WINDMILL RD.
NEWGATE RD.
Fire Station
ORMSKIRK ROAD
BLYTHEWOOD
BANKFIELD
AMBERGATE
AMERSHAM
DANILLS
Sports Centre
St.Mathews R.C. Primary Sch.
RR TREE CLO
LYNWOOD CLO
BLAYDON PARK
Holland Moor County Primary Sch.
COLINTON
CORNBROOK
Playing Fields
GARNETT LEES
BANKSBARN
BLAKEHALL
MARTINS
WHITSTONE DR
NEWLYN DR
NIXONS LANE
MEADOW CLO
MOOR DR
DIGMOOR ROAD
Digmoor
GILLIBRANDS ROAD
LANE
ABBEYSTEAD
ABBEYWOOD
ACREGATE
BEECHTREES
Bishop Martin Primary Sch.
BEARNCROFT
BIRKRIG
BIRLEYWOOD
BACK LA
CHERRYCROFT
CHARNOCK
BARNFIELD DR
BACK LA
BROW
CLAY
CASTLEHEY
CARFIELD
DARFIELD
DANBERS
CHEQUER
Little Digmoor Primary Sch.
ALDERLEY
BELFIELD
St.Lukes R.C. Primary Sch.
STANNANOUGHT ROAD
Playing Fields
WHITELEDGE RD.
PENNINE PL
BRIERFIELD
PENKETH PL
PIKELAW
PILLING PL
PIMBO
HEY PL
PIT
PADDOCK RD
INDUSTRIAL ESTATE
PEEL ROAD
PROSPECT PL
East Pimbo
West Pimbo
PAXTON PL
PRESTWOOD PL
PRIORSWOOD PL
ROAD
13
23
36
YY
ZZ
7
8
9
5
50
06
05
04
49

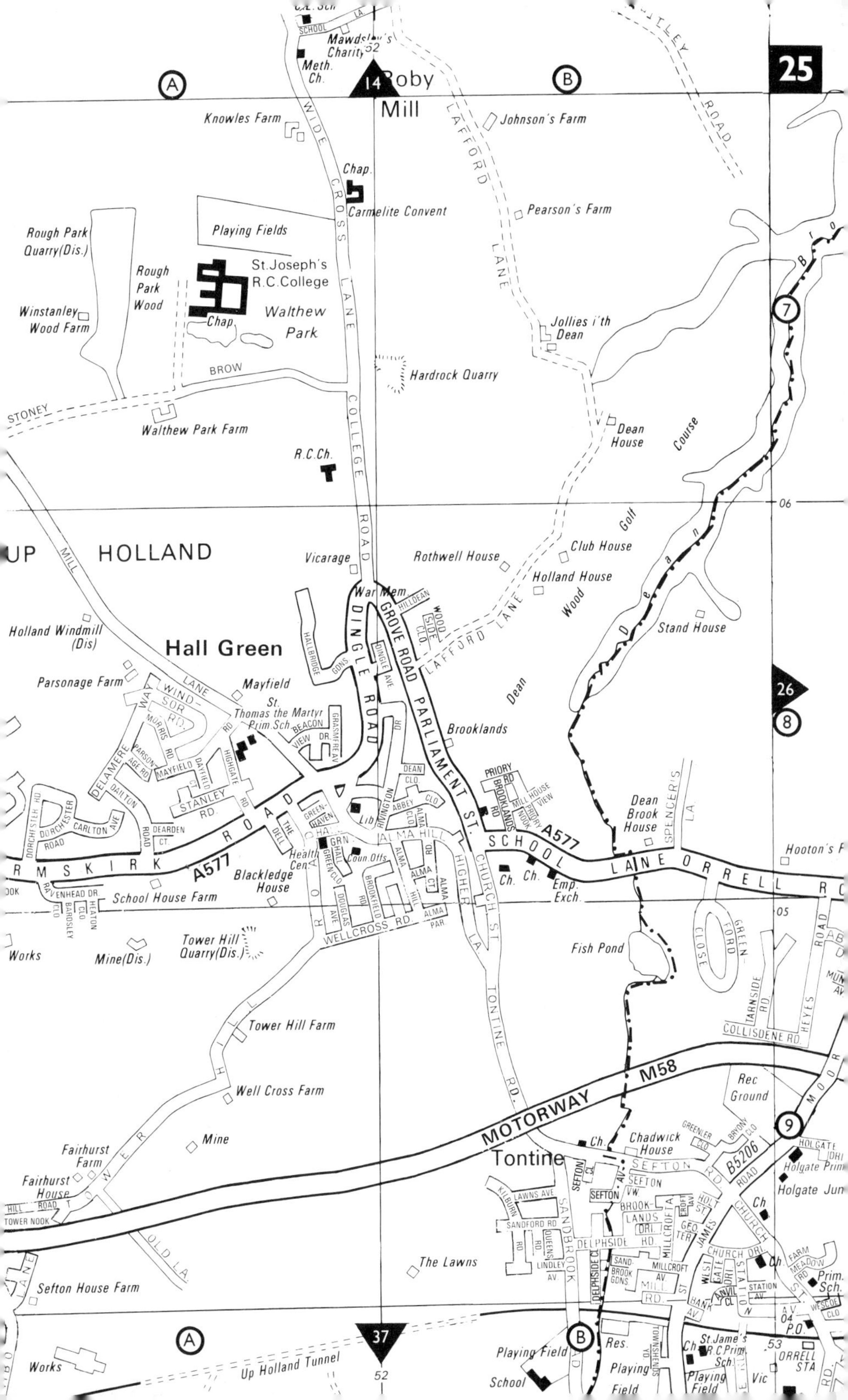
A
B
14
Roby Mill
Mawdsley's Charity
Meth. Ch.
SCHOOL LA.
52
Knowles Farm
Johnson's Farm
WIDE CROSS LANE
LAFFORD LANE
ROAD
Chap.
Carmelite Convent
Pearson's Farm
Playing Fields
Rough Park Quarry (Dis.)
Rough Park Wood
St. Joseph's R.C. College
Chap
Walthew Park
Winstanley Wood Farm
Jollies i'th Dean
BROW
STONEY
Hardrock Quarry
Walthew Park Farm
Dean House
Course
Golf
R.C.Ch.
COLLEGE ROAD
06
UP HOLLAND
MILL
Vicarage
Rothwell House
Club House
Holland House
Wood
Holland Windmill (Dis)
Hall Green
War Mem.
HILLDEAN
WOODSIDE CLO.
DINGLE ROAD
GROVE ROAD
PARLIAMENT ST.
LAFFORD LANE
Stand House
Dean
HALLBRIDGE GDNS
DINGLE AVE
Parsonage Farm
LANE
Mayfield
WINDSOR RD.
WAY
St. Thomas the Martyr Prim. Sch.
BEACON VIEW DR.
GRASMERE AV
DR
Brooklands
26
8
7
MORRIS RD
DELAMERE
PARSONAGE RD
MAYFIELD
DAYFIELD CT
HIGHGATE RD
STANLEY RD.
DEAN CLO.
PRIORY RD
BROOKLANDS RD
MILL HOUSE VIEW
PRIORY NOOK
Dean Brook House
SPENCER'S LA.
DORCHESTER RD
DORCHESTER ROAD
CARLTON AVE
DALTON
DEARDEN CT.
ROAD
THE DELL
GREENHAVEN
RIVINGTON
ABBEY CLO
ALMA CLO
Lib.
ALMA HILL
SCHOOL LANE
A577
ORRELL RD
Hooton's F
ORMSKIRK ROAD
A577
Health Cen.
GRN. HALL
GREEN CLO
Coun.Offs
ALMA RD.
HIGHER LA.
CHURCH ST.
Ch.
Emp. Exch.
Blackledge House
ALMA CT
ALMA HILL
RAVENHEAD DR.
School House Farm
BROOKFIELD RD
DOUGLAS AVE
BARDSLEY CLO
HEATON CLO
WELLCROSS RD.
ALMA PAR.
05
Fish Pond
GREEN FORD
CLOSE
ROAD
Works
Mine (Dis.)
Tower Hill Quarry (Dis.)
TONTINE RD.
TARNSIDE RD.
HEYES
COLLISDENE RD.
Tower Hill Farm
TOWER HILL
Well Cross Farm
M58
MOTORWAY
Rec Ground
MOOR
9
Mine
Chadwick House
GREENLEA CLO
BRYONY CLO
Fairhurst Farm
Fairhurst House
HILL ROAD
TOWER NOOK
Tontine
SEFTON CL.
SEFTON AV.
SEFTON RD.
SEFTON VW.
B5206
HOLGATE DRI
Holgate Prim
Holgate Jun
KILBURN RD
LAWNS AVE
SANDFORD RD.
QUEENS RD.
LINDLEY AV.
SANDBROOK
BROOKLANDS DRI.
MILLCROFT AV
CROFT AV
HOLT ST.
GEO. TER
JAMES
DELPHSIDE RD.
DELPHSIDE CL.
CHURCH ROAD
OLD LA.
The Lawns
SANDBROOK GDNS
MILLCROFT AV
MILL RD.
ST.
WESTGATE DRI
ANVIL CL
BANK AV.
STATION AV
CHURCH DRI
FARM MEADOW RD
Prim. Sch.
WESCOE CLO
Sefton House Farm
LANE
04
P.O.
B
37
Res.
Playing Field
TOWNSHEND RD
Playing Field
School
St. James's R.C. Prim. Sch.
53
ORRELL STA
Vic
Works
Up Holland Tunnel
52

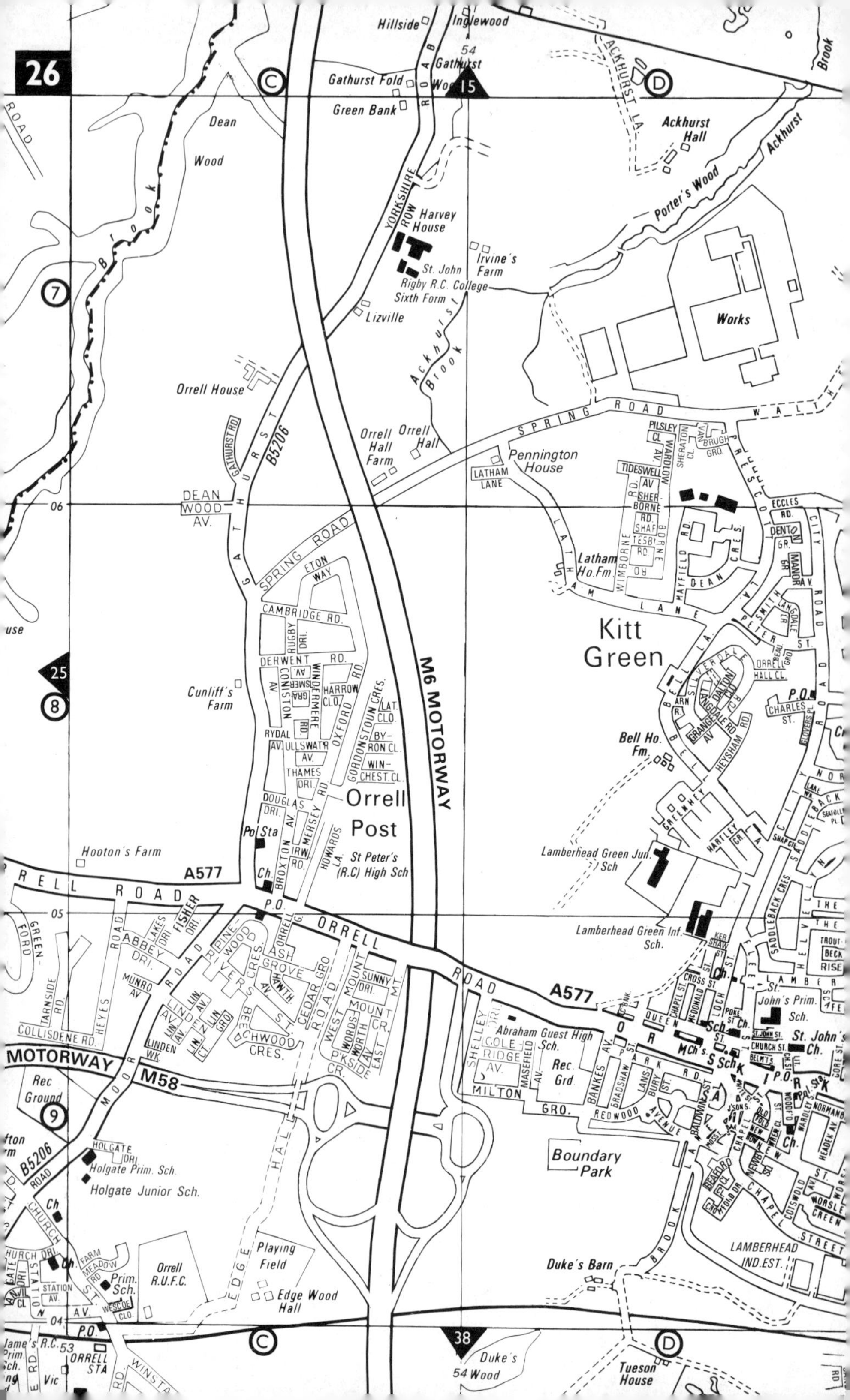
Hillside
St. Inglewood
54
Gathurst
Gathurst Fold
Wood
15
Green Bank
C
D
Ackhurst La.
Brook
Ackhurst Hall
Ackhurst
Porter's Wood
Dean
Wood
Brook
Road
Yorkshire Row
Harvey House
Irvine's Farm
St. John Rigby R.C. College Sixth Form
Lizville
Ackhurst Brook
Works
7
Orrell House
Gathurst Rd
B5206
Gathurst
Orrell Hall Farm
Orrell Hall
Spring Road
Walthew
Pennington House
Latham Lane
Pilsley Cl
Wardlow Av
Sheraton Cl
Vanbrugh Gro
Prescot
Tideswell Av
Sherborne Rd
Shaftesbury Rd
Wimborne Rd
Borne
Mayfield Rd
Dean Cres
Eccles Rd
Denton Gr
City Road
Manor Gr
Av
Dean Wood Av
06
Spring Road
Eton Way
Latham Ho. Fm.
Latham Lane
Cambridge Rd.
Rugby Dri.
Derwent Rd.
Windermere Rd
Grasmere Av
Coniston Av
Harrow Clo.
Oxford Rd
Gordonstoun Cres.
Lat. Clo.
Byron Cl.
Winchester Cl.
Rydal Av.
Ullswater Av.
Thames Dri.
Douglas Dri.
Kitt Green
Smith
Langdale
Peter St.
Bell La.
Silverdale
Dalton
Langdale
Grange Av
Heysham Rd
Beau Gro
Orrell Hall Cl.
P.O.
Charles St.
Glovers Pl
Bell Ho. Fm.
Bell La.
Greenhey
Hartley Gr.
Nor
Saddleback
Seafold Pl
Shap Gr.
Saddleback Cres
Helvellyn
City
25
8
Cunliff's Farm
Orrell Post
M6 Motorway
Pol Sta
Broxton Av.
Mersey Rd
Irwell Rd.
Howards La.
St Peter's (R.C) High Sch
Ch.
Hooton's Farm
A577
Orrell Road
Lamberhead Green Jun. Sch
Lamberhead Green Inf. Sch.
05
P.O.
Green Ford
Road
Lakes Dri
Fisher Dri.
Abbey Dri.
Munro Av
Tarnside Rd.
Heyes
Collisdene Rd.
Road
Pinewood
Ash Grove
Orrell Gro
Cedar Gro
Orrell
Sunny Dri.
Mount Mt.
Hawth.
Beechwood Cres.
Lin. Av.
Lind Av
Lin. Av.
Lin. Ct
Lin. Gro
Linden Wk
West Mount Road
Wordsworth Av
East Cr.
Pikside Cr.
Road
A577
Kershaw St.
Cross St
Chapel St.
McDonald
Loch
Ch.
Poke St
Sch.
Trout Beck Rise
Lamber
St. John's Prim. Sch.
St. John St.
Church St.
St. John's Ch.
Belmont
Shelley Dri.
Coleridge Av.
Masefield Av.
Abraham Guest High Sch.
Rec. Grd.
Bankes Av.
Queen St.
Park Rd.
Bradshaw
Lansbury St.
Milton Gro.
Redwood
Avenue
Baldwin St.
Motorway
M58
Rec Ground
9
Moor Road
Holgate Dri
Holgate Prim. Sch.
Holgate Junior Sch.
B5206
Road
Church
Ch
Edge Hall
Boundary Park
Brook La
Beaford
Cotswold Av
Worsley Green
Chapel
Street
Lamberhead Ind. Est.
Church Dri.
Farm Meadow Rd
Station Av.
Prim. Sch.
Wescoe Clo.
Orrell R.U.F.C.
Playing Field
Edge Wood Hall
Duke's Barn
04
P.O.
C
38
D
St. James's R.C. Prim. Sch.
53
Orrell Sta
Vic
Winstanley Rd.
Duke's Wood
54
Tueson House

Martland Mill Farm
Cuthbert Scotts
Meadow Lock
Works
Springfield Park F.C.
"Wigan Athletic" F.C.
St. John Fisher R.C. High Sch.
St. Andrew's Prim. Sch.
B5375
Stone Ho.
MARSH GREEN
Library
Marsh Green Prim. Sch.
Hope Special Sch
Pagefield Lock
RIVER DOUGLAS
LEEDS & LIVERPOOL CANAL
Robin Park
Robin Park Statium
Scot Lane Prim. Sch.
Logwood Ho.
St. Edward's R.C. Prim. Sch.
St. Thomas More High Sch
Pemberton Sch
Playing Fields
Playing Field
Newtown
Fire Sta.
St. Mark's Prim. Sch.
St. Cuthberts R.C. Jun. Infs. Sch.
Spring Bank
Pemberton Prim. Sch.
Rose Hill
Hostel
A577
A571
Alexandra Park
VICTORIA ROAD
ORMSKIRK ROAD
WARRINGTON ROAD INDUSTRIAL ESTATE
St. James R.C. Prim Sch.
St. Judes R.C. Jun. & Inf. Schs.
PEMBERTON
High-field Gdns
LAMBERHEAD GREEN INE. EST.
Highfield Prim. Sch.
PEMBERTON STA.
St. Paul's Vicarage
Playing Field
16
28
39
56
57

SWINLEY
WIGAN
Poolstock
Worsley Mesnes
Mesnes Park
Royal Albert Edward Infirmary
Christopher Home
The Woodlands
RIVER DOUGLAS
Bloody Mts. (Site of Battle)
Mab's Cross Prim. Sch.
Central Park R.F.C.
Tennis Grds.
Inland Rev.
Res.
Bull Hey
Cricket Grd.
Bow.Grn.
Delph Ho.
Wigan Deanery High Sch.
Wigan Coll.
Wigan Hall
Civic Bldgs
Play Field
Galleries Shopping Centre
Bus Sta.
G.P.O.
Mun Bldgs
Town Hall
Wigan Pool
Civic Centre
WALLGATE STA.
NTH. WESTERN STA.
Courts
Super Bowl
Wigan Pier
Trencherfield Mill
Bus Depot
Mills
Fire Sta.
Works
Pagefield Lock
Turn Bri.
LIVERPOOL CANAL
Park
Girobank
Westwood Hall
Home Fm.
Westwood Bri.
Lion Bri.
Swing Bri.
Lock
Crick.Grd.
Sewage Disposal Fm.
PEARSON'S FLASH
St. James R.C. Prim. Sch.
A49
B5238
A573
PARK RD.
POTTERY RD.
WALLGATE
NORTHWAY
STANDISHGATE
MILLGATE
WARRINGTON LANE
DARLINGTON ST.
POOLSTOCK LANE
CENTRAL PARK WAY
PARSON'S WALK
KING ST.
MARKET ST.
NEW MKT. ST.
MESNES RD.
KENYON RD.
CAROLINE ST.
QUEEN ST.
CHAPEL LANE
SCHOOL LA.
SPRINGFIELD ROAD
GIDLOW AV.
WESTWOOD
MESNES AVENUE
17
27
40
57
58

NEW SPRINGS
St. John Baptist Jun. Sch.
Park Ho.
Res.
Res.
Newsprings Inf. Sch.
Holy Family R.C. Prim. Sch.
KIRKLESS VILLAS
WITHINGTON HILL
Whelley Hospital
Plantation Gates
B5238
Lock
Lock Works
LEEDS & LIVERPOOL CANAL
Kirkless Hall
Platt Lane Play. Field
Clarington Brook
SCHOLES
Rec. Grd.
Rose Bridge High Sch
Peel Hall Bri.
Belle Green Prim. Sch.
Gidlow House
MANCHESTER ROAD
Rec. Grd.
INCE-IN-MAKERFIELD
Playing Fields
Ince-in-Makerfield Prim. Sch.
St. Williams R.C. Prim. Sch.
Works
A577
Walmesley Park
Brownlow
Common Nook
Hindley Junc.
INCE STA.
VIADUCT ROW
Council Off.
Works
Ince Forge
SEAMAN WAY
Moss Hall Farm
MAKERFIELD
A573
WARRINGTON
Ince Cemetery Chaps.
Works
Spring View
Amberswood Common
Ince Moss
18
30
41
60
61
06
05
04

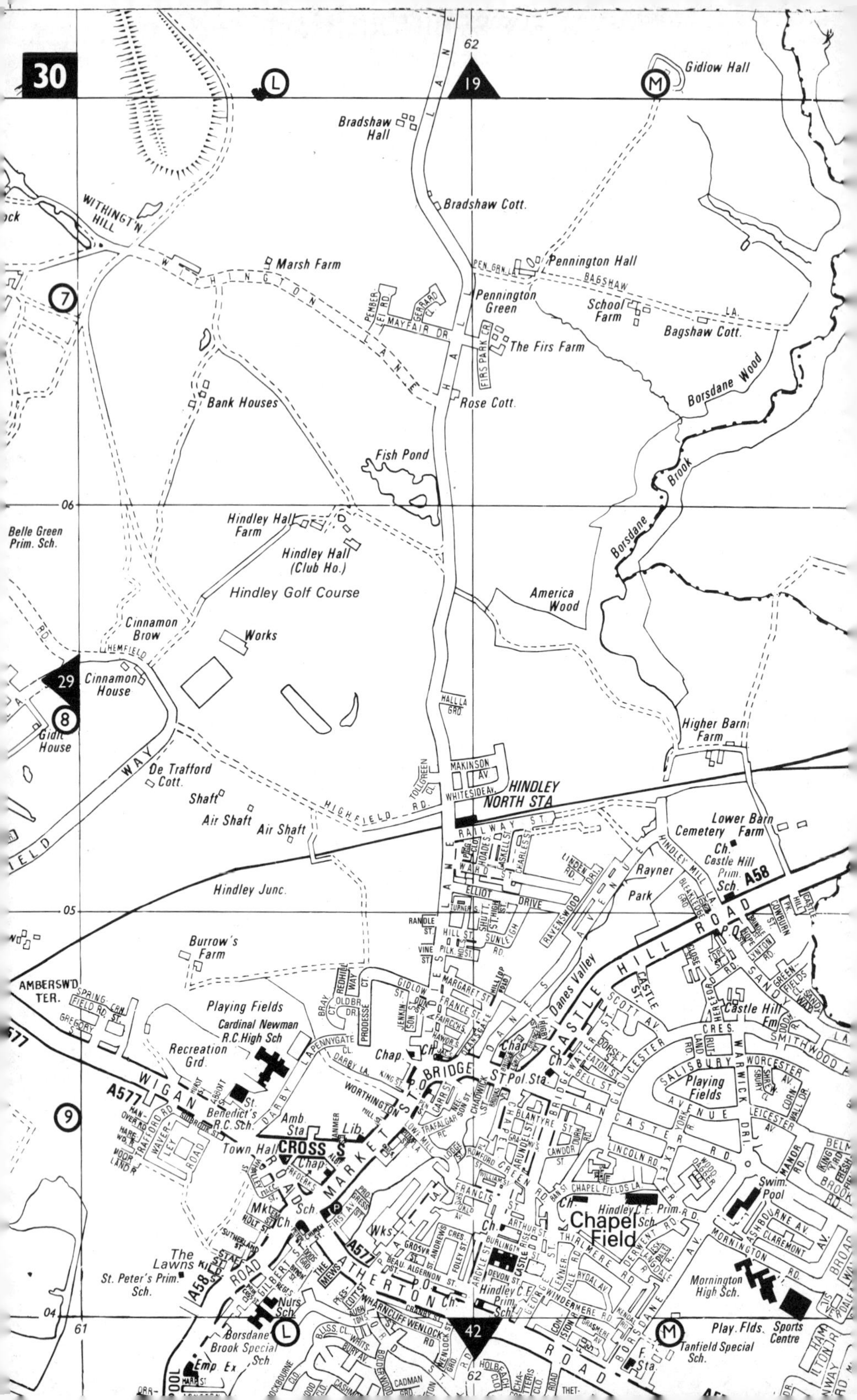

19
62
Gidlow Hall
Bradshaw Hall
Withingt'n Hill
Bradshaw Cott.
Marsh Farm
Withington Lane
Pennington Hall
Pen Grn La.
Bagshaw La.
Pennington Green
School Farm
Bagshaw Cott.
Pemberton Rd.
Gerrard Cl.
Mayfair Dr.
Firs Park Cr.
The Firs Farm
Hall Lane
Borsdane Wood
Bank Houses
Rose Cott.
Fish Pond
Borsdane Brook
06
Belle Green Prim. Sch.
Hindley Hall Farm
Hindley Hall (Club Ho.)
Hindley Golf Course
America Wood
Cinnamon Brow
Works
Hemfield
29
Cinnamon House
Gidlt House
Hall La Gro
Higher Barn Farm
De Trafford Cott.
Way
Makinson Av.
Tollgreen Cl.
Whiteside Av.
Hindley North Sta
Shaft
Air Shaft
Air Shaft
Highfield Rd.
Railway St.
Lower Barn Farm
Cemetery
Ch.
Castle Hill Prim. Sch.
A58
Linden Rd.
Hindley Mill La.
Rayner Park
Hindley Junc.
Elliot Drive
Ravenswood Dri.
Bleakledge Gro.
05
Randle St.
Hill St.
Sunleigh Rd.
Castle Hill Road
Cowburn St.
Vine St.
Pilk. St.
Lynton Rd.
Burrow's Farm
Danes Valley
Sandy Way
Ambersw'd Ter.
Spring Field Rd.
Gregory St.
Redhill Way
Gidlow St.
Margaret St.
France St.
Castle St.
Scott Av.
Hereford Rd.
Castle Hill Fm.
Playing Fields
Cardinal Newman R.C. High Sch
Bray Ct.
Old Br. Dr.
Prodesse Ct.
Jenkinson St.
Recreation Grd.
Lapennygate Cl.
Darby La.
King St.
Chap.
Ch.
Bridge St.
Pol. Sta.
Bridgewater St.
Dorset St.
Eaton St.
Bell St.
Gloucester
Cres.
Salisbury
Worcester Av.
Smithwood Av.
Playing Fields
Warwick Dri.
Avenue
Leicester Av.
Wigan Road
A577
St. Benedict's R.C. Sch.
Worthington St.
Chadwick St.
Lancaster Rd.
Blantyre St.
Hanover Rd.
Trafford Rd.
Waverley Road
Amb. Sta
Lib.
Trafalgar St.
Cawdor St.
Exeter Rd.
Moorland R.
Town Hall
Cross St.
Market St.
Lowe Mill La.
Romford St.
Lincoln Rd.
Wood Dale Rd.
Manor Rd.
Belmont
Swim. Pool
Chap.
Road
Francis St.
Chapel Green Rd.
Chapel Fields La.
Hindley C.E. Prim. Sch.
Chapel Field
Ashbourne Av.
Claremont
Brook
9
Mkt.
Sch.
Ch.
Wks.
Grosvr. St.
St. Andrews Cres.
Foley St.
Arthur St.
Thirlmere Rd.
Derwent Rd.
Mornington Rd.
Holt St.
Sutherland St.
The Lawns
St. Peter's Prim. Sch.
A58
Gilbert St.
The Mews
Atherton Rd.
A577
Beau.
Algernon St.
Argyle St.
Burlington St.
Castle Rise
Rydal Av.
Devon St.
Hindley C.E. Prim. Sch.
Windermere Rd.
Mornington High Sch.
Nurs. Sch.
Wharncliff
Wenlock Rd
Cranby St.
Grasmere Av.
Kendal
04
61
L
42
M
Play. Flds.
Sports Centre
Borsdane Brook Special Sch
Emp. Ex
Bliss Cl.
Whitsbury Av.
Cadman Gro.
Holbeach Cl.
62
Coniston
Road
Borsdane
F. Sta.
Tanfield Special Sch.
Hamilton
L
M
7
8

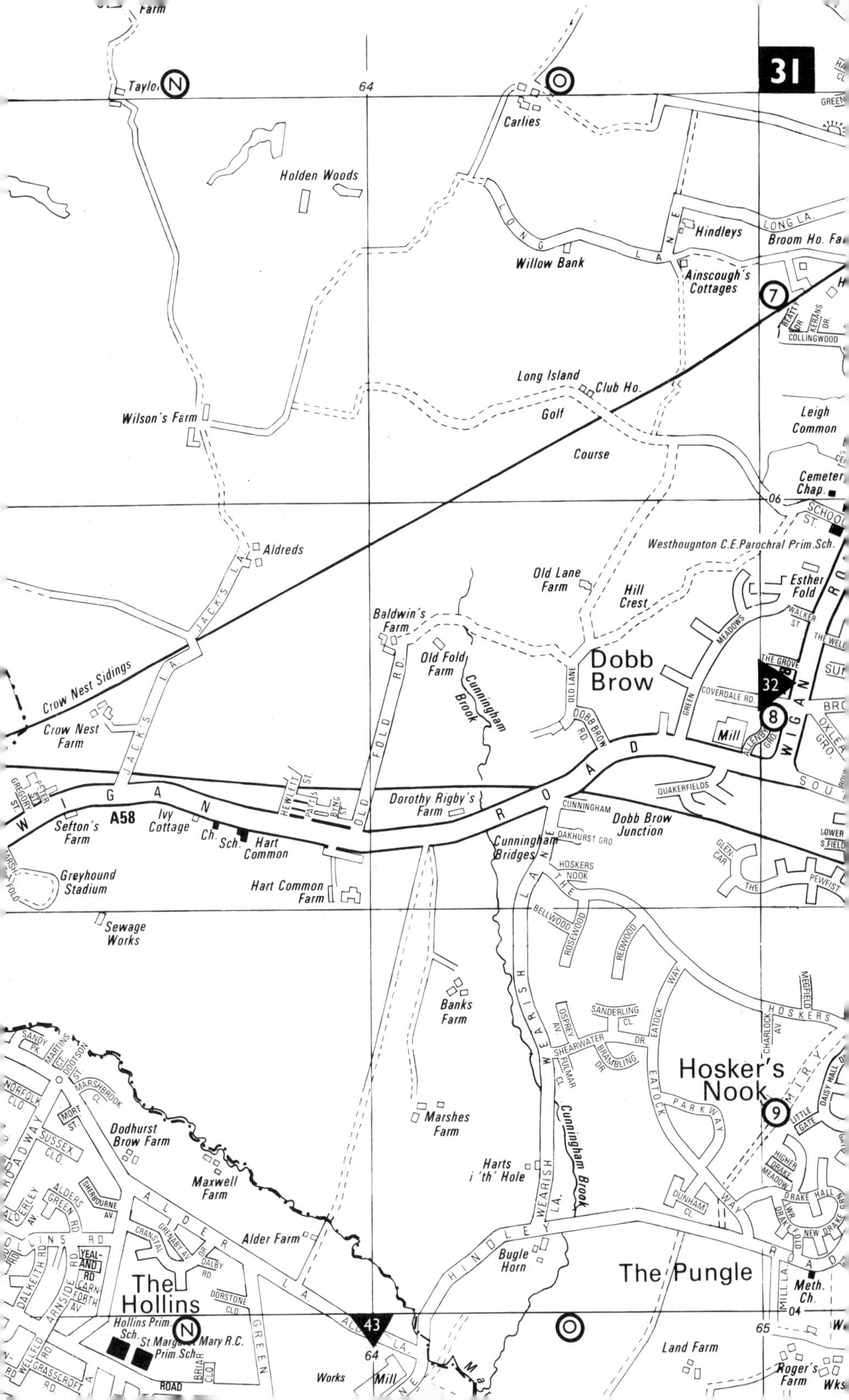
Farm
Taylor
64
Carlies
Holden Woods
Long Lane
Hindleys
Long La.
Broom Ho. Fa
Willow Bank
Ainscough's Cottages
7
Beatty Dr.
Kerans Dr.
Collingwood
Long Island
Club Ho.
Golf
Course
Leigh Common
Wilson's Farm
Cemetery Chap.
06
School St.
Westhoughton C.E. Parochral Prim. Sch.
Aldreds
Old Lane Farm
Hill Crest
Esther Fold
Jack's La.
Baldwin's Farm
Meadows
Walker St.
The Well
Old Fold Farm
Dobb Brow
The Grove
32
Crow Nest Sidings
Cunningham Brook
Old Lane
Coverdale Rd.
8
Crow Nest Farm
Old Fold Rd.
Dobb Brow Rd.
Green
Mill
Allenby Gro.
Wigan
Oxlea Gro.
Gregory St.
Peter St.
Hewlett St.
Patt's
Byng St.
Quakerfields
Wigan Road
A58
Sefton's Farm
Ivy Cottage
Ch.
Sch.
Hart Common
Dorothy Rigby's Farm
Cunningham
Dobb Brow Junction
Lower S.Field
Oakhurst Gro.
Cunningham Bridges
Hoskers Nook
Glen Car
Pewfist
Greyhound Stadium
Hart Common Farm
Marsh Fold
Bellwood
Rosewood
Redwood
Sewage Works
Way
Megfield
Hoskers
Banks Farm
Sanderling Cl.
Osprey Av.
Charlock Av.
Shearwater Dr.
Eatock
Bramblings Dr.
Fulmar Cl.
Hosker's Nook
Wearish La.
Cunningham Brook
Parkway
9
Miry
Little Gate
Daisy Hall Dr.
Sandy Pk.
Martins Ct.
Dootson St.
Marshbrook Cl.
Norfolk Clo.
Mort St.
Broadway
Sussex Clo.
Dodhurst Brow Farm
Marshes Farm
Harts i 'th' Hole
Higher Drake Meadow
Dunham Cl.
Maxwell Farm
Sherbourne Av.
Alders Green Rd.
Alderley Av.
Hollins Rd.
Alder Farm
Cranstal
Grenaby Av.
Dalby Rd.
Alder La.
Drake Hall
Lwr. Drake Fold
New Drake
Yeal-and Rd
Carnforth Av.
Dalkeith Rd.
Arnside Rd.
Hindley Rd.
Bugle Horn
The Pungle
Mill La.
Meth. Ch.
Road
The Hollins
Dorstone Clo.
Hollins Prim. Sch.
N
St. Margaret Mary R.C. Prim. Sch.
Green
43
04
65
Land Farm
Wellfield Rd.
Grasscroft Rd.
Briar Clo.
Road
Works
Mill
Roger's Farm
Wks

M61 MOTORWAY
A6
MANCHESTER ROAD
BOLTON ROAD
CHEW MOOR LANE
WIGAN ROAD
A58
CRICKETERS WAY
PARK ROAD
MILL ST.
MARKET STREET
CHURCH ST.
CENTRAL DRIVE
MOLYNEUX ROAD
LEIGH ROAD
LOWER LEIGH ROAD
B5235
HINDLEY ROAD
PLATT LANE
NORTH ROAD
GREEN COMMON LA.
SOUTHFIELD DRIVE
TOWNSFIELD RD.
WASHACRE
HOSKERS LANE
DAISY HALL DRIVE
OLD HALL LA.
JAMES ST.
LONG LA.
WELLINGTON ST
WESTHOUGHTON
Westhoughton Ind.Est.
Westhoughton High Sch. & Sports Centre
Westhoughton C.E.Parochral Prim.Sch.
Central Park
Roscoe Farm
Wade Lane Bridge
Hall Lee Bank Park
Lee Hall Farm
Fish Fold
Water's Nook
Bailey Fold Farm
Hooper Green
Green Common
Ashes Farm
Yew Tree Farm
Lower Whittles
Langley Hall Farm
Mountain Farm
Edges Farm
Daisy Hill Prim. Sch.
DAISY HILL STA.
Hall Lee Brook
Casson Fold
Old Sirs Fm.
Nicholas Fold
Fine Hoskars
Woodbine Ho.
Gillibrands
Roger's Farm
Hosker's Nook
Leigh Common
Cemetery Chap.
Broom Ho. Farm
Hindleys
Ainscough's Cottages
Esther Fold
Cricket Grd.
Foot Grd.
Pol. Sta.
Town Hall Info.Cen.
Lib.
R.C.Prim. Sch.
Play.Flds
Chequerbent C.E.Prim.Sch.
Motel
Snydale Gate Farm
Shafts (Dis.)
Monks Farm
Factory
Platts Farm
Recreation Ground
Beech House
Top o'th Slack
North Rd. Ind.Est.
Knight Farm
Works
Wks.
Meth. Ch.
STA.
P.O.
31
44
65
66
06
05
04

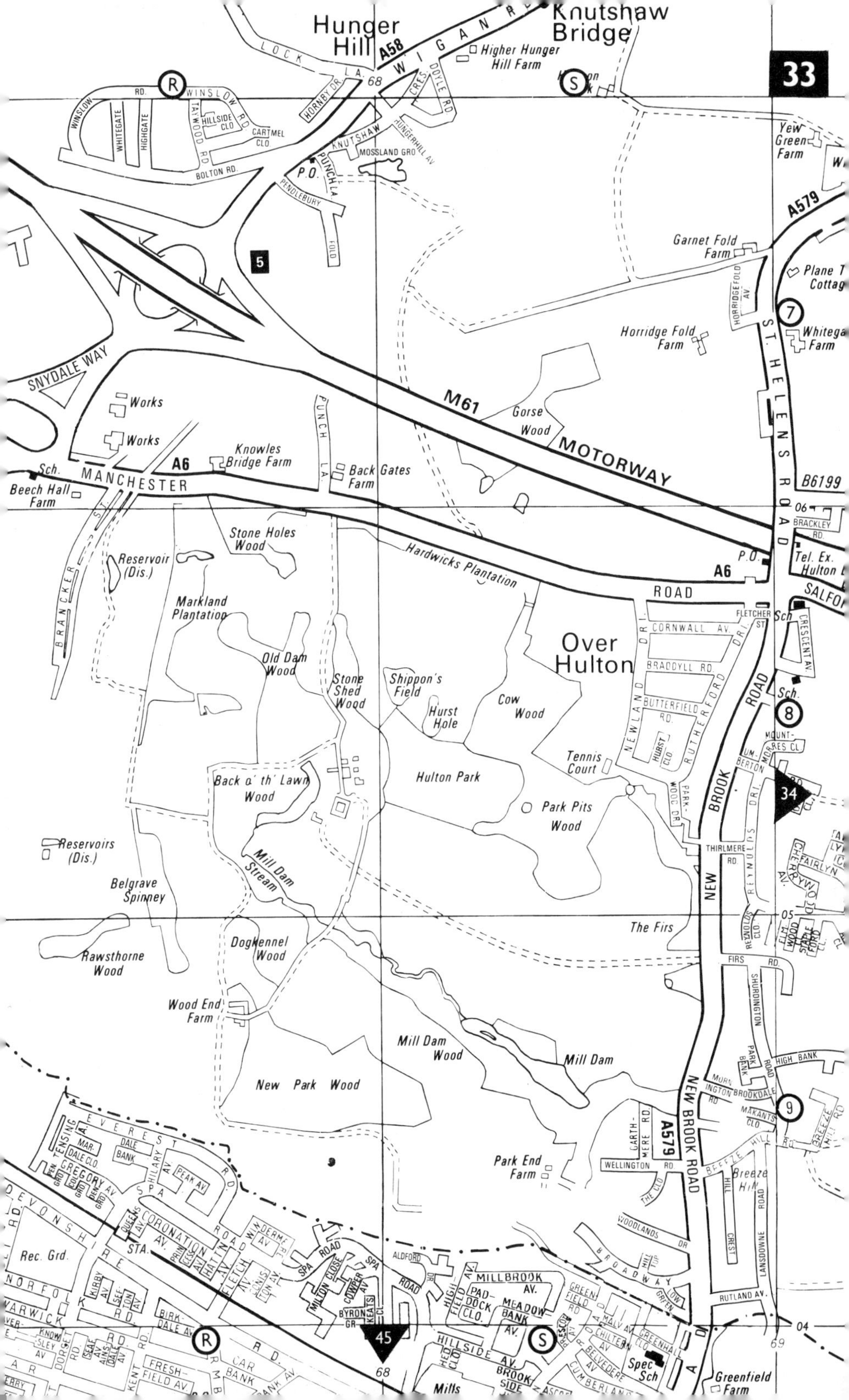
Hunger Hill
Knutshaw Bridge
A58
WIGAN RD.
Higher Hunger Hill Farm
LOCK LA.
68
HORNBY DR.
CRES.
DOYLE RD.
WINSLOW RD.
WINSLOW
WHITEGATE
HIGHGATE
TAYWOOD RD.
HILLSIDE CLO.
CARTMEL CLO.
BOLTON RD.
KNUTSHAW
HUNGERHILL AV.
MOSSLAND GRO.
P.O.
PUNCH LA.
PENDLEBURY FOLD
5
Yew Green Farm
A579
Garnet Fold Farm
Plane Tree Cottage
HORRIDGE FOLD AV.
7
Whitegate Farm
Horridge Fold Farm
ST. HELENS ROAD
SNYDALE WAY
Works
Works
PUNCH LA.
M61
Gorse Wood
MOTORWAY
A6
Knowles Bridge Farm
Back Gates Farm
Sch.
MANCHESTER
Beech Hall Farm
B6199
06
BRACKLEY RD.
Stone Holes Wood
Hardwicks Plantation
P.O.
A6
Tel. Ex.
Hulton
SALFORD
ROAD
Reservoir (Dis.)
BRANCKER ST.
Markland Plantation
Over Hulton
NEWLAND DRI.
CORNWALL AV.
BRADDYLL RD.
BUTTERFIELD RD.
HUBST CLO.
RUTHERFORD DRI.
FLETCHER ST.
Sch.
CRESCENT AV.
ROAD
Sch.
8
Old Dam Wood
Stone Shed Wood
Shippon's Field
Hurst Hole
Cow Wood
Tennis Court
MOUNTMORRES CL.
UMBERTON
34
Back a' th' Lawn Wood
Hulton Park
Park Pits Wood
PARKWOOD DR.
BROOK
REYNOLDS DRI.
Reservoirs (Dis.)
Mill Dam Stream
THIRLMERE RD.
NEW
CHERRYWOOD AV.
FAIRLYN CL.
Belgrave Spinney
05
The Firs
REYNOLDS CLO.
ELMWOOD
STAPLEFORD CL.
Rawsthorne Wood
Doghennel Wood
FIRS RD.
SHURDINGTON
Wood End Farm
Mill Dam Wood
Mill Dam
PARK BANK
ROAD
HIGH BANK
MORNINGTON RD.
BROOKDALE
New Park Wood
9
MAKANTS CLO.
BREEZE HILL RD.
NEW BROOK ROAD
A579
GARTHMERE RD.
EVEREST RD.
TENSING AV.
MARDALE CLO.
DALE BANK
HILARY AV.
PEAK AV.
GREGORY AV.
PEN GRO.
COL GRO.
DEN GRO.
SPA
Park End Farm
WELLINGTON RD.
THE CLO.
Breeze Hill
HILL CREST
LANSDOWNE ROAD
DEVONSHIRE RD.
QUEENS AV.
CORONATION AV.
WINDERMERE AV.
ROAD
WOODLANDS DR.
BROADWAY
HILL TOP
LOW GREEN
Rec. Grd.
STA.
PRINCESS AV.
HATTON AV.
FLETCHER AV.
CONISTON AV.
SPA ROAD
ALDFORD DR.
HIGHFIELD AV.
MILLBROOK AV.
PADDOCK CLO.
MEADOW BANK AV.
GREENFIELD RD.
NORFOLK
KIRBY AV.
SEFTON AV.
MILTON CLOSE
COWPER AV.
SPA ROAD
RUTLAND AV.
WARWICK
RD.
BIRKDALE AV.
KEATS CL.
BYRON GR.
45
PRESCOTT AV.
MALVERN AV.
CHILTERN AV.
GREENHALGH CLO.
04
69
KNOWSLEY AV.
DORSET RD.
SEAFORD RD.
AINSDALE AV.
KENT RD.
FRESHFIELD AV.
R
CAR BANK
BANK AV.
HILLSIDE AV.
HED CLO.
BROOKSIDE
BELVEDERE AV.
CUMBERLAND
Spec. Sch.
Greenfield Farm
68
Mills
S

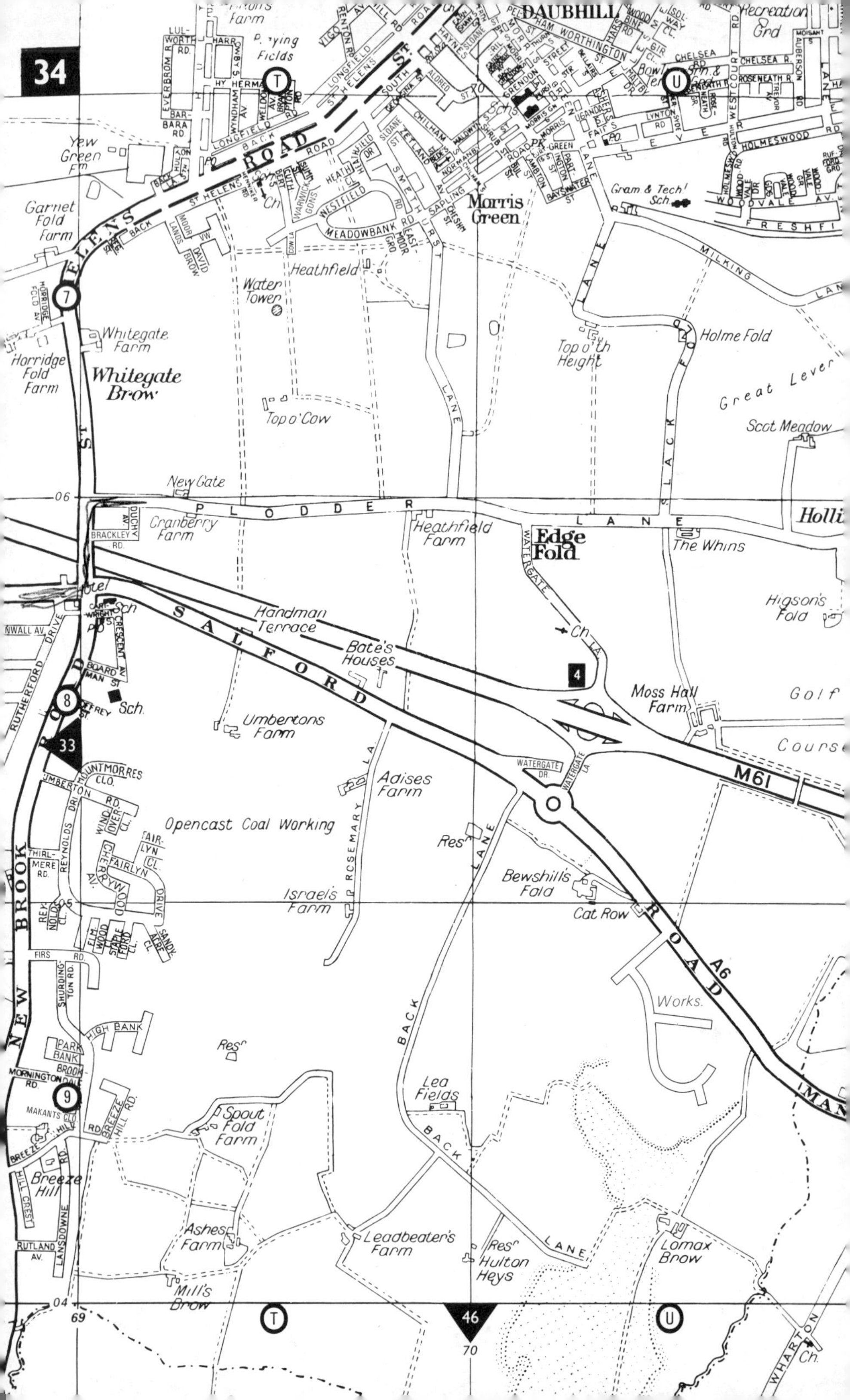
DAUBHILL
Recreation Grd
Playing Fields
Yew Green Fm
Garnet Fold Farm
ST HELENS ROAD
BACK ST HELENS
LEVER
Morris Green
MEADOWBANK RD.
WESTFIELD
Heathfield
Water Tower
Gram & Tech! Sch.
MILKING LANE
Holme Fold
Top o'th Height
Great Lever
Scot Meadow
Whitegate Farm
Horridge Fold Farm
Whitegate Brow
Top o'Cow
SLACK
New Gate
06
PLODDER LANE
Heathfield Farm
Edge Fold
The Whins
Holli
Cranberry Farm
BRACKLEY RD.
DUCHY AV.
WATERGATE
Hotel
Sch
P.O.
CRESCENT
Handman Terrace
Bate's Houses
SALFORD ROAD
Ch.
4
Higson's Fold
Moss Hall Farm
Golf Course
M61
BOARDMAN ST.
RUTHERFORD DRIVE
8
Sch.
33
Umbertons Farm
MOUNTMORRES CLO.
UMBERTON RD.
WATERGATE DR.
WATERGATE LA.
Adises Farm
Opencast Coal Working
ROSEMARY LA.
Res
LANE
REYNOLDS DRI.
FAIRLYN DRIVE
CHERRYWOOD AV.
Israels Farm
Bewshills Fold
Cat Row
05
THIRLMERE RD.
NEW BROOK ROAD
FIRS RD.
SHURDINGTON RD.
SANDY ACRE CL.
A6
Works.
BACK LANE
HIGH BANK
PARK BANK
BROOKDALE
Res
MORNINGTON RD.
9
MAKANTS CLO.
BREEZE HILL RD.
Lea Fields
Spout Fold Farm
Breeze Hill
HILL CREST
LANSDOWNE RD
RUTLAND AV.
Ashes Farm
Leadbeater's Farm
Res
Hulton Heys
Lomax Brow
Mill's Brow
04
69
T
46
70
U
WHARTON
Ch.
MAN

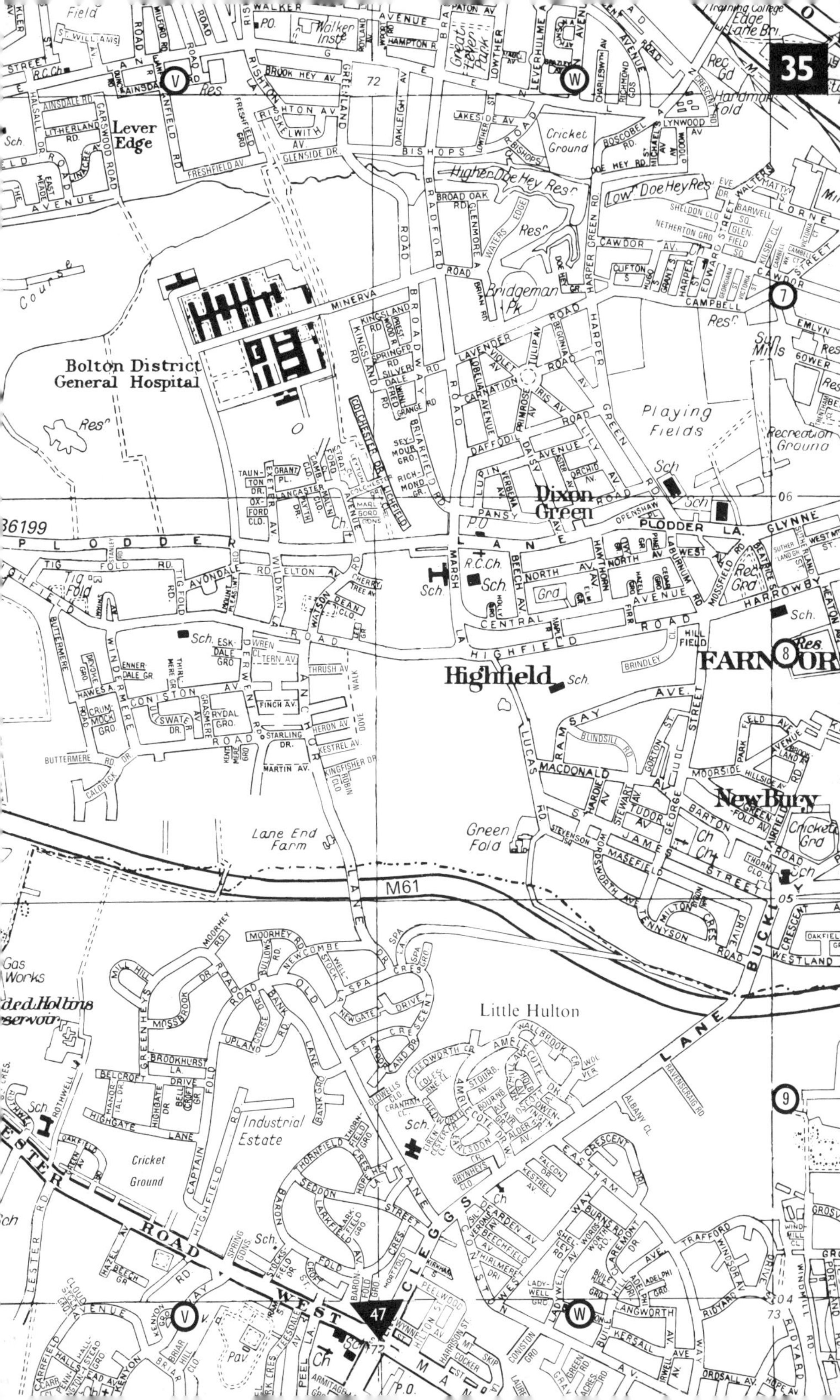

Lever Edge
Bolton District General Hospital
Dixon Green
Highfield
FARNWORTH
New Bury
Little Hulton
Great Lever Park
Cricket Ground
Higher Doe Hey Res.
Low Doe Hey Res.
Bridgeman Pk
Playing Fields
Recreation Ground
Sun Mills
Tig Fold
Lane End Farm
Green Fold
Industrial Estate
Gas Works
Walker Inst.
Training College
Hardman Fold
Rec Gd
B6199
PLODDER LANE
HIGHFIELD ROAD
MINERVA
BISHOPS ROAD
BRADFORD ROAD
BROADWAY
HARPER GREEN RD.
HARROWBY
GLYNNE
CAMPBELL
CAWDOR
LUCAS RD.
MACDONALD AV.
GEORGE STREET
JAMES STREET
TENNYSON ROAD
BUCKLEY LANE
WESTLAND
M61
CLEGGS LANE
CAPTAIN FOLD
HIGHFIELD RD
WEST ROAD
MANCHESTER ROAD
ANCHOR LANE
WINDERMERE RD
CONISTON AV.
MOORHEY RD
OLD BANK LANE
SPA CRESCENT
EASTHAM WAY
SEDDON STREET
LESTER RD
47
V
W
7
8
9
06
05
04
72
73

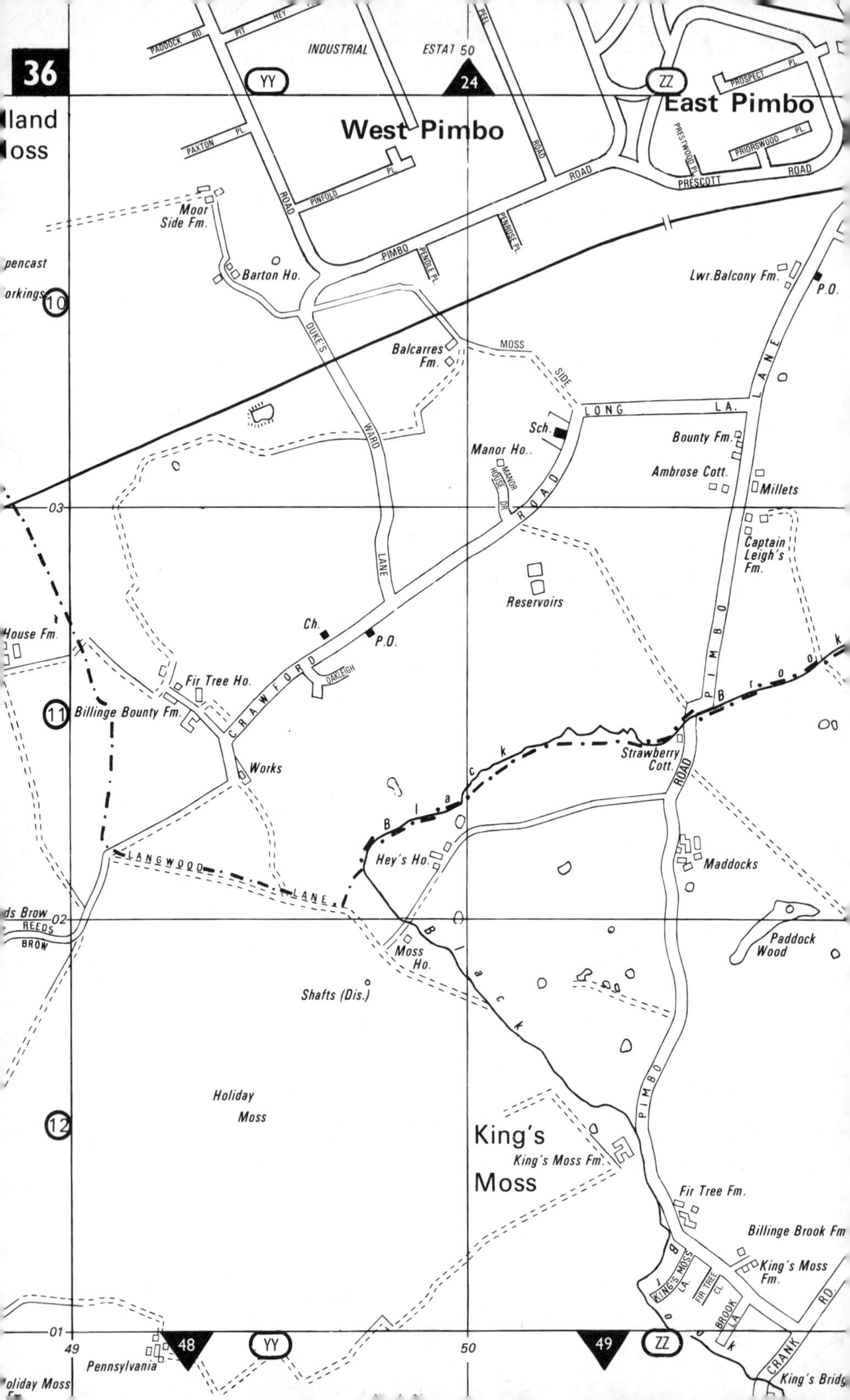

PADDOCK RD.
PIT HEY
INDUSTRIAL ESTATE
PEEL
24
YY
ZZ
PROSPECT PL.
East Pimbo
West Pimbo
PAXTON PL.
PINFOLD PL.
ROAD
PRESTWOOD PL.
PRIORSWOOD PL.
PRESCOTT ROAD
Moor Side Fm.
PENROSE PL.
PIMBO
PENDLE PL.
Barton Ho.
Lwr. Balcony Fm.
P.O.
DUKE'S
Balcarres Fm.
MOSS SIDE
LONG LA.
LANE
WARD
Sch.
Manor Ho.
MANOR HOUSE DR.
Bounty Fm.
Ambrose Cott.
Millets
Captain Leigh's Fm.
Reservoirs
LANE
PIMBO
Ch.
P.O.
House Fm.
CRAWFORD ROAD
OAKLEIGH
Fir Tree Ho.
Billinge Bounty Fm.
Brook
Works
Strawberry Cott.
ROAD
Black
LANGWOOD LANE
Hey's Ho.
Maddocks
REEDS BROW
Moss Ho.
Paddock Wood
Shafts (Dis.)
Black
Holiday Moss
King's Moss
King's Moss Fm.
PIMBO
Fir Tree Fm.
Billinge Brook Fm
King's Moss Fm.
KING'S MOSS LA.
FIR TREE CL.
BROOK LA.
CRANK RD.
Pennsylvania
Holiday Moss
King's Bridg
48
49
YY
ZZ
03
02
01
10
11
12
49
50

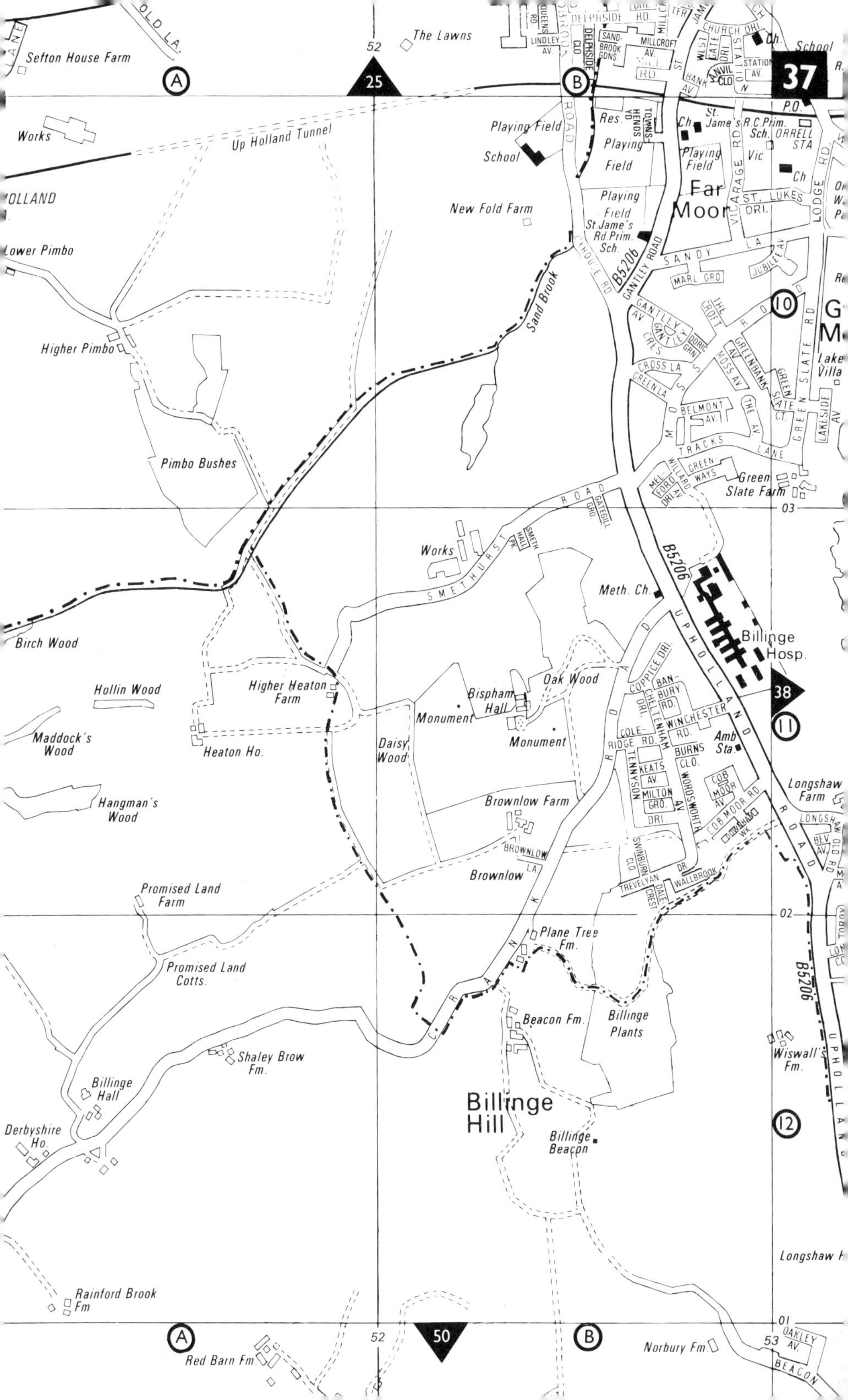
37
25
50
38
A
B
52
03
02
01
53
10
11
12
Sefton House Farm
OLD LA.
The Lawns
Works
Up Holland Tunnel
OLLAND
Lower Pimbo
Higher Pimbo
Pimbo Bushes
Sand Brook
New Fold Farm
Playing Field
School
Res.
Playing Field
Playing Field
St. James's Rd Prim. Sch.
B5206
GANTLEY ROAD
DELPHSIDE RD.
DELPHSIDE CLO.
SANDBROOK GDNS
MILLCROFT AV.
MILL RD.
LINDLEY AV.
QUEENS RD.
CHURCH DRI.
WESTGATE DRI.
ANVIL CLO.
STATION AV.
BANK AV.
Ch.
School
P.O.
St. James's R.C. Prim. Sch.
ORRELL STA.
Ch.
Vic
Playing Field
Far Moor
VICARAGE RD.
ST. LUKES DRI.
LODGE RD.
SANDY LA.
JUBILEE AV.
MARL GRO.
THE CROFT
GANTLEY AV.
GANTLEY CRES.
DORIC GRN.
CROSS LA.
GREEN LA.
MOSS AV.
GREENBANK AV.
GREEN SLATE CT.
SLATE RD.
GREEN SLATE
Lake Villa
LAKESIDE AV.
BELMONT AV.
THE AV.
TRACKS LANE
MELFORD DRI.
WILLARD AV.
GREENWAYS
Green Slate Farm
SMETHURST ROAD
GATEGILL GRO.
SMETHALL PK.
Works
Meth. Ch.
Billinge Hosp.
UPHOLLAND ROAD
Birch Wood
Hollin Wood
Maddock's Wood
Higher Heaton Farm
Heaton Ho.
Bispham Hall
Oak Wood
Monument
Monument
Daisy Wood
Hangman's Wood
Brownlow Farm
BROWNLOW LA.
Brownlow
COPPICE DRI.
BANBURY RD.
CHELTENHAM DRI.
WINCHESTER RD.
COLERIDGE RD.
BURNS CLO.
Amb Sta.
TENNYSON
KEATS AV.
MILTON GRO.
WORDSWORTH AV.
DRI.
COB MOOR AV.
COB MOOR RD.
Longshaw Farm
LONGSHAW
BEV. AV.
OLD RD.
SWINBURN CLO.
TREVELYAN DR.
DALECREST
WALLBROOK
Promised Land Farm
Promised Land Cotts
Plane Tree Fm.
CRANK ROAD
Beacon Fm.
Billinge Plants
Shaley Brow Fm.
Billinge Hall
Derbyshire Ho.
Billinge Hill
Billinge Beacon
Wiswall's Fm.
B5206
Longshaw
Rainford Brook Fm
Red Barn Fm.
Norbury Fm.
OAKLEY AV.
BEACON

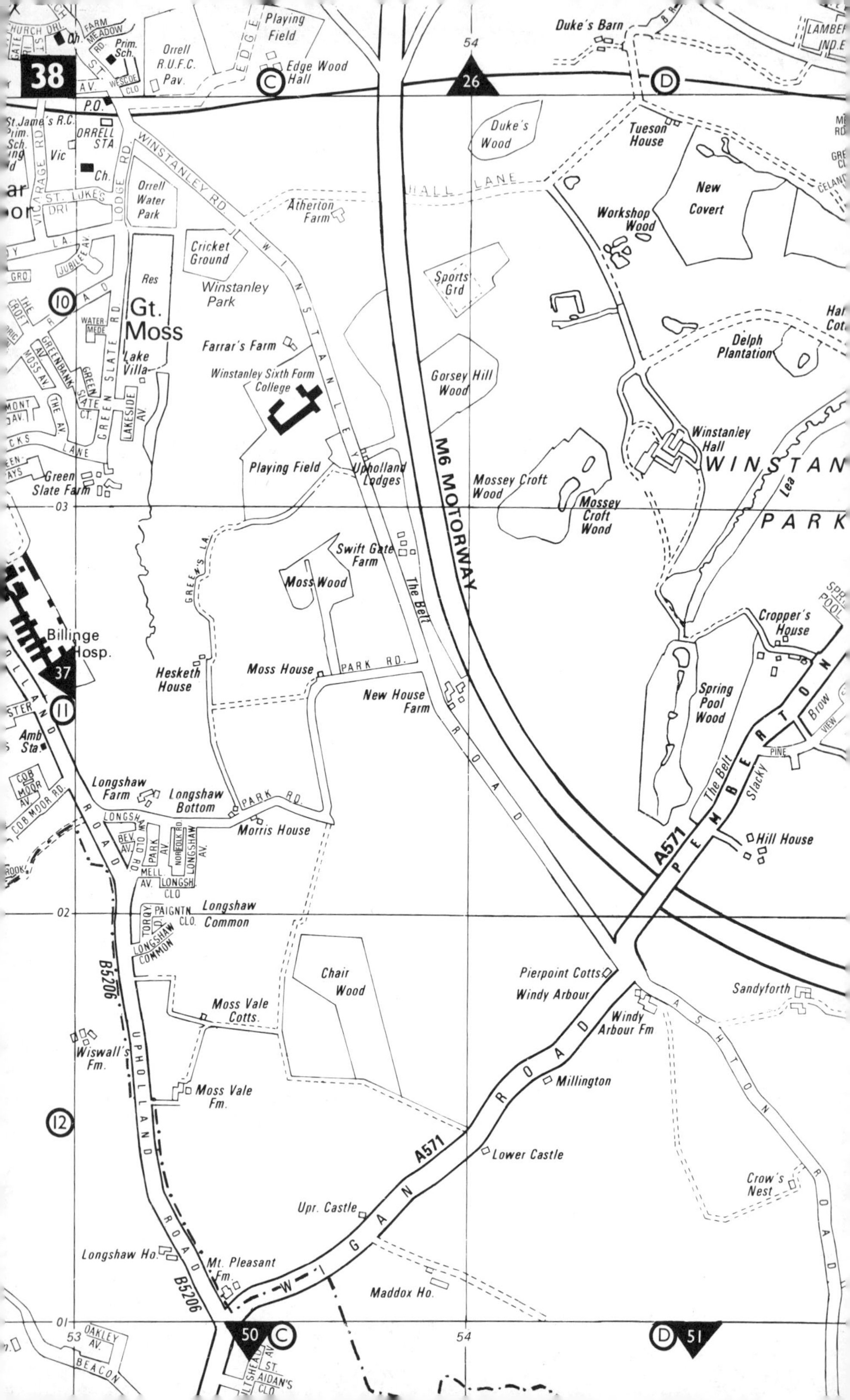
38
Church Dri.
Farm Meadow
Ch.
Prim. Sch.
Orrell R.U.F.C. Pav.
Playing Field
Edge
Edge Wood Hall
C
26
54
Duke's Barn
D
Lamber Ind. E
Wescoe Clo
Av.
P.O.
St. James's R.C. Prim. Sch.
Orrell Sta
Vic
Ch.
Winstanley Rd.
Duke's Wood
Tueson House
Vicarage Rd.
St. Luke's Dri.
Lodge Rd.
Orrell Water Park
Hall Lane
Atherton Farm
New Covert
Workshop Wood
Jubilee Av.
La.
Cricket Ground
Res
Winstanley Park
Winstanley
Sports Grd
Gro.
The Croft
10
Water Mede
Gt. Moss
Slate Rd.
Delph Plantation
Farrar's Farm
Greenbank Av.
Moss Av.
Green Slate Ct.
Lake Villa
Lakeside Av.
Winstanley Sixth Form College
Gorsey Hill Wood
The Av.
Green Slate Rd.
Winstanley Hall
Winstan
Lane
Playing Field
Upholland Lodges
M6 Motorway
Mossey Croft Wood
Green Slate Farm
03
Mossey Croft Wood
Park
Green's La.
Swift Gate Farm
Moss Wood
The Belt
Billinge Hosp.
37
Park Rd.
Moss House
Hesketh House
New House Farm
Cropper's House
11
Amb Sta.
Spring Pool Wood
Road
Cob Moor Av.
Cob Moor Rd.
Longshaw Farm
Longshaw Bottom
Park Rd.
Pemberton
Brow
View
Pine
The Belt
Slacky
Longshaw Old Rd.
Morris House
Bev. Av.
Park Av.
Norfolk Rd.
Longshaw Av.
A571
Hill House
Mell. Av.
Longsh. Clo
Road
02
Longshaw Common
Torqy Paigntn. Clo.
Longshaw Common
Chair Wood
Pierpoint Cotts
Windy Arbour
Sandyforth
B5206
Moss Vale Cotts.
Windy Arbour Fm
Ashton
Wiswall's Fm.
Upholland Road
Millington
Moss Vale Fm.
12
Road
A571
Lower Castle
Crow's Nest
Upr. Castle
Road
Wigan
Longshaw Ho.
Mt. Pleasant Fm.
Maddox Ho.
B5206
01
53
50
C
54
D
51
Oakley Av.
Beacon
St. Aidan's Clo

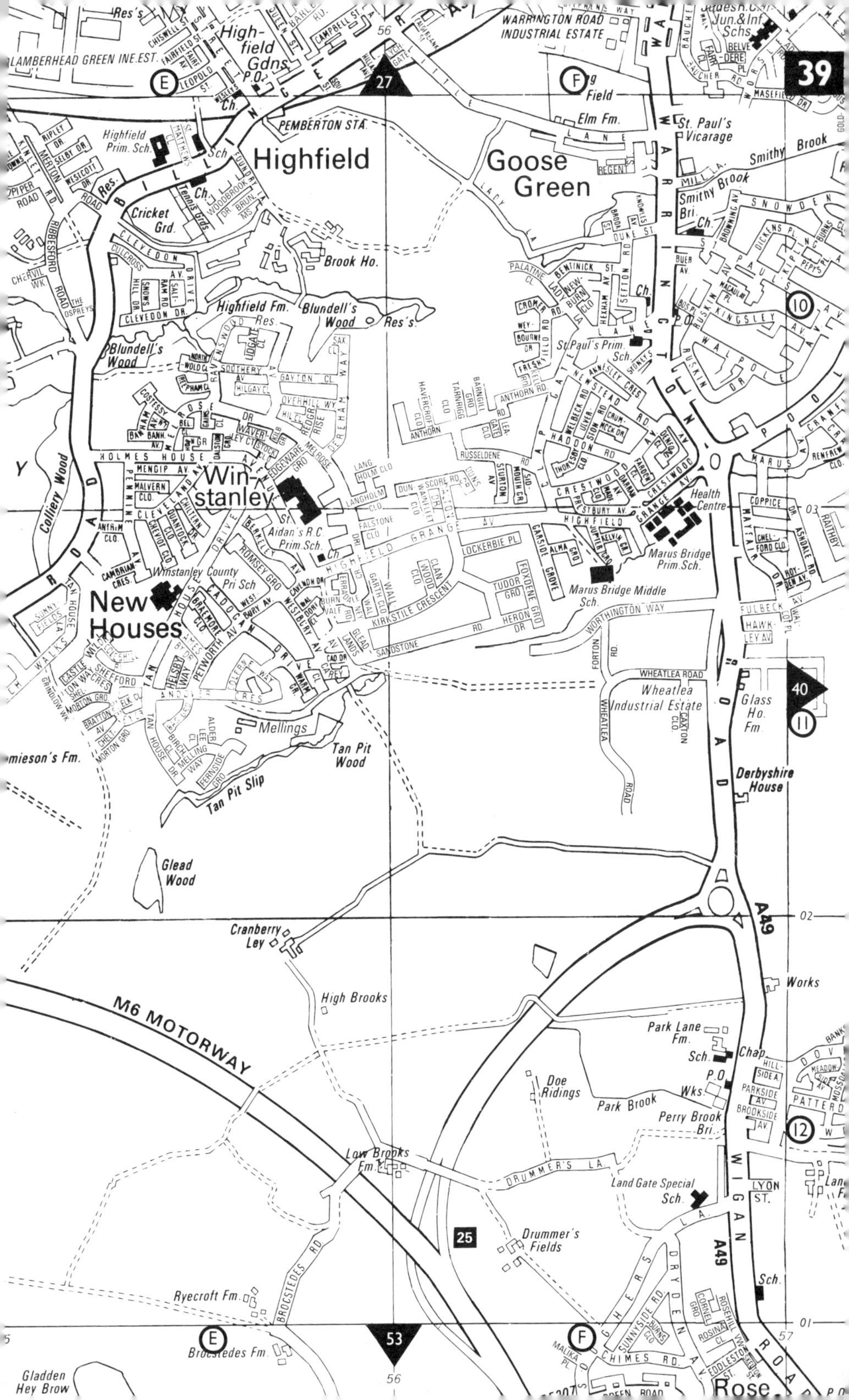
LAMBERHEAD GREEN INE. EST.
Highfield Gdns
Highfield
Goose Green
WARRINGTON ROAD INDUSTRIAL ESTATE
Fg Field
Elm Fm.
St. Paul's Vicarage
Smithy Brook
Smithy Brook Bri.
PEMBERTON STA.
Highfield Prim. Sch.
Cricket Grd.
Tennis Grds
Brook Ho.
Highfield Fm.
Blundell's Wood
Res's.
St. Paul's Prim. Sch.
Win-stanley
St. Aidan's R.C. Prim. Sch.
Health Centre
Marus Bridge Prim. Sch.
Marus Bridge Middle Sch.
Winstanley County Pri Sch
New Houses
Colliery Wood
WORTHINGTON WAY
WHEATLEA ROAD
Wheatlea Industrial Estate
Glass Ho. Fm.
Derbyshire House
Mellings
Tan Pit Wood
Tan Pit Slip
Glead Wood
Cranberry Ley
High Brooks
M6 MOTORWAY
A49
Works
Park Lane Fm.
Sch.
Chap.
P.O.
Wks.
Doe Ridings
Park Brook
Perry Brook Bri.
Low Brooks Fm.
DRUMMER'S LA.
Land Gate Special Sch.
Drummer's Fields
Ryecroft Fm.
Brocstedes Fm.
BROCSTEDES RD.
Gladden Hey Brow
WIGAN ROAD
CHIMES RD.
Rose
27
40
53
25
10
11
12
E
F
56
57
03
02
01

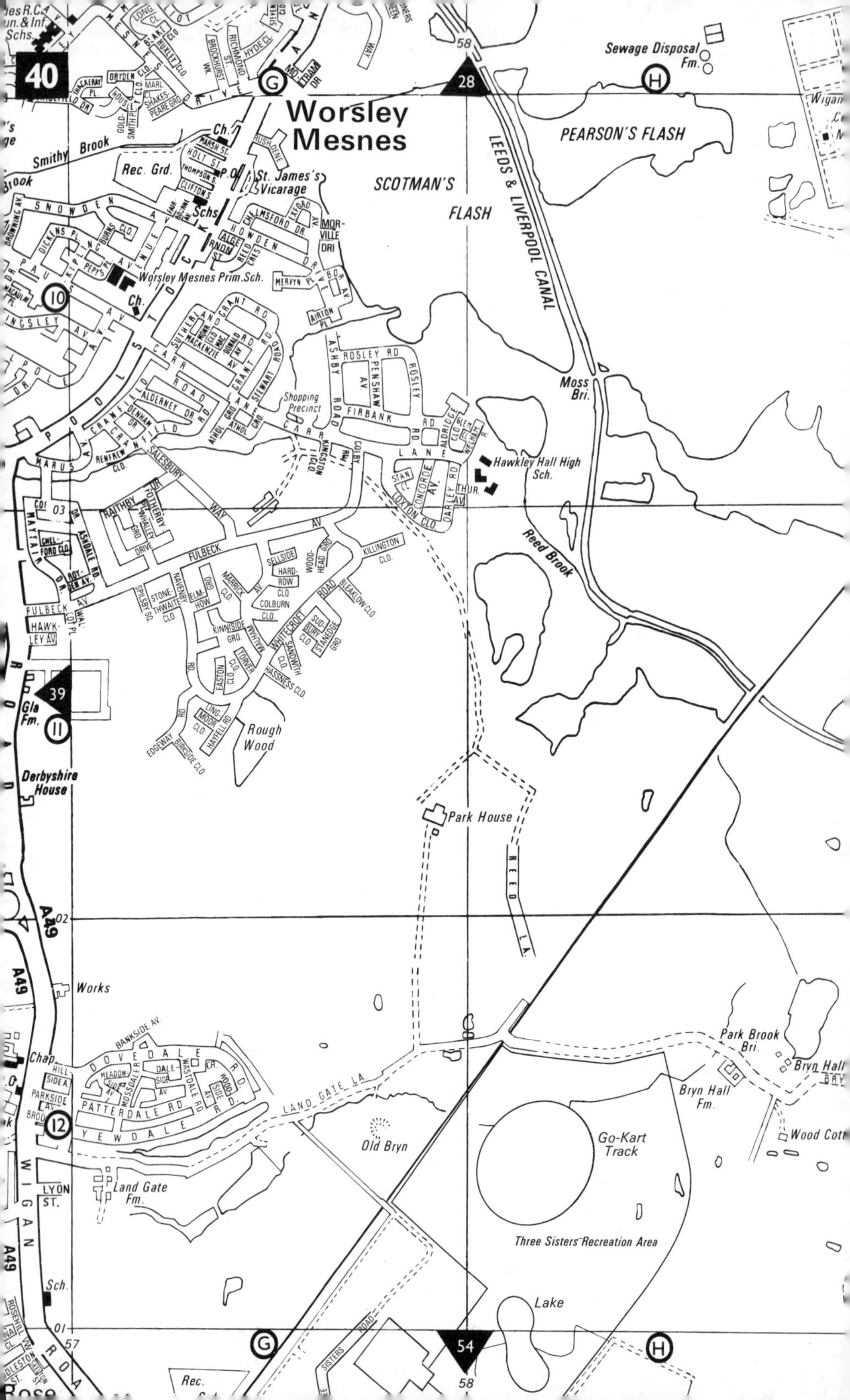
Worsley Mesnes
SCOTMAN'S FLASH
PEARSON'S FLASH
Sewage Disposal Fm.
LEEDS & LIVERPOOL CANAL
Moss Bri.
Smithy Brook
Rec. Grd.
Ch.
P.O.
St. James's Vicarage
Schs
Worsley Mesnes Prim.Sch.
SNOWDEN AV.
KIPLING AVENUE
DICKENS PL.
BURNS CLO.
PEPYS PL.
POOLSTOCK
CARR LANE
CRANFIELD RD.
ALDERNEY DR.
DENHAM DR.
RENFREW CLO.
MARUS AV.
SUTHERLAND RD.
GRANT RD.
MACKENZIE AV.
STEWART ROAD
ATHOL GRO.
CHELMSFORD DR.
HOWDEN DRIVE
EXFORD AV.
MORVILLE DRI
MERVYN PL.
AIRTON PL.
ASHBY ROAD
ROSLEY RD.
PENSHAW AV.
FIRBANK RD.
ALDRIDGE CLO.
WELHAM
Shopping Precinct
KINGSTON CLO.
COLBY
STAN CL.
CONCORDE AV.
LOXTON CLO.
DARLEY RD.
THUR. AV.
Hawkley Hall High Sch.
Reed Brook
SALESBURY WAY
RAITHBY
FOTHERBY DR.
WHALLEY GRO.
DRIVE
ASHDALE RD.
MAYFAIR DR.
ROYDEN AV.
FULBECK AV.
HAWKLEY AV.
SPILSBY SQ.
STONETHWAITE CLO.
NAVENBY
ELMHOW GRO.
MARRICK CLO.
SELLSIDE
HARDROW CLO.
WOODHEAD GRO.
COLBURN CLO.
KILLINGTON CLO.
BLEAKLOW CLO.
KINNISIDE GRO.
MALHAM
WHITECROFT ROAD
SUDBURY CLO.
STANEDGE GRO.
SANDSMITH
HASSNESS CLO.
EASTON CLO.
TORVER
LINGMOOR CLO.
HAYFELL RD.
EDGEWAY RD.
BIRKSIDE CLO.
Rough Wood
Gla Fm.
Derbyshire House
Park House
REED LA.
A49
Works
WIGAN ROAD
BANKSIDE AV.
DOVEDALE RD.
DALESIDE AV.
MEADOW SIDE AV.
MOSSDALE RD.
WASTDALE RD.
WOODSIDE RD.
PATTERDALE RD.
YEWDALE
HILL SIDE A.
PARKSIDE AV.
Chap.
LAND GATE LA.
Land Gate Fm.
LYON ST.
Sch.
Old Bryn
Park Brook Bri.
Bryn Hall
Bryn Hall Fm.
Wood Cott
Go-Kart Track
Three Sisters Recreation Area
Lake
SISTERS ROAD
Rec.
28
39
54
G
H
10
11
12
58
57
03
02
01

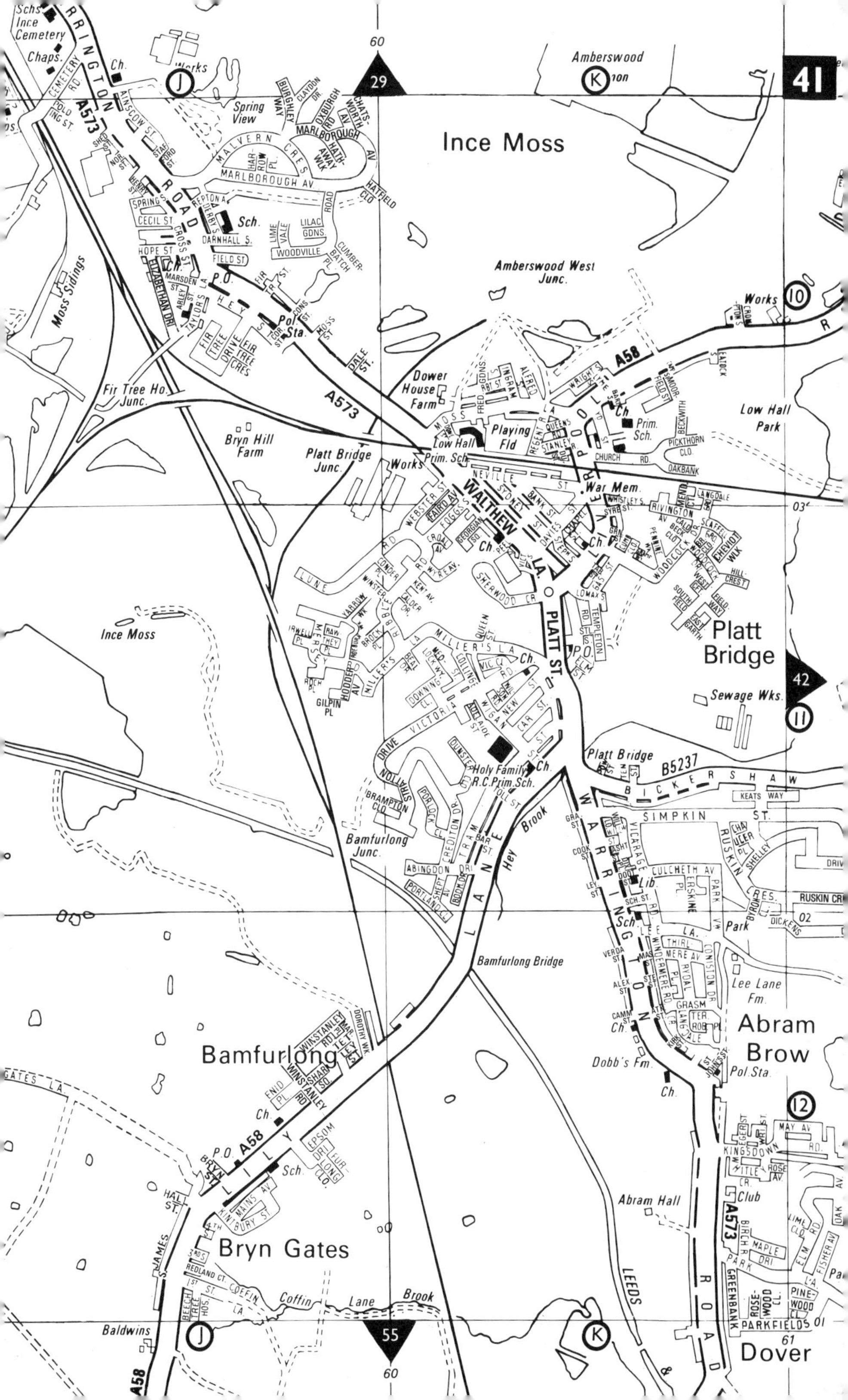
Ince Moss
Amberswood West Junc.
Amberswood
Spring View
Works
Dower House Farm
Playing Fld
Low Hall Prim. Sch.
Platt Bridge Junc.
Fir Tree Ho. Junc.
Bryn Hill Farm
Moss Sidings
Low Hall Park
WALTHEW LA.
PLATT ST.
War Mem.
Platt Bridge
Sewage Wks.
B5237
BICKERSHAW
A58
A573
Ince Moss
Holy Family R.C.Prim.Sch.
Bamfurlong Junc.
Bamfurlong Bridge
Hey Brook
WARRINGTON ROAD
Lee Lane Fm.
Abram Brow
Pol.Sta.
Dobb's Fm.
Abram Hall
Bamfurlong
Bryn Gates
Coffin Lane Brook
Baldwins
LEEDS
Dover
Club
29
42
55
60
61
02
03
01

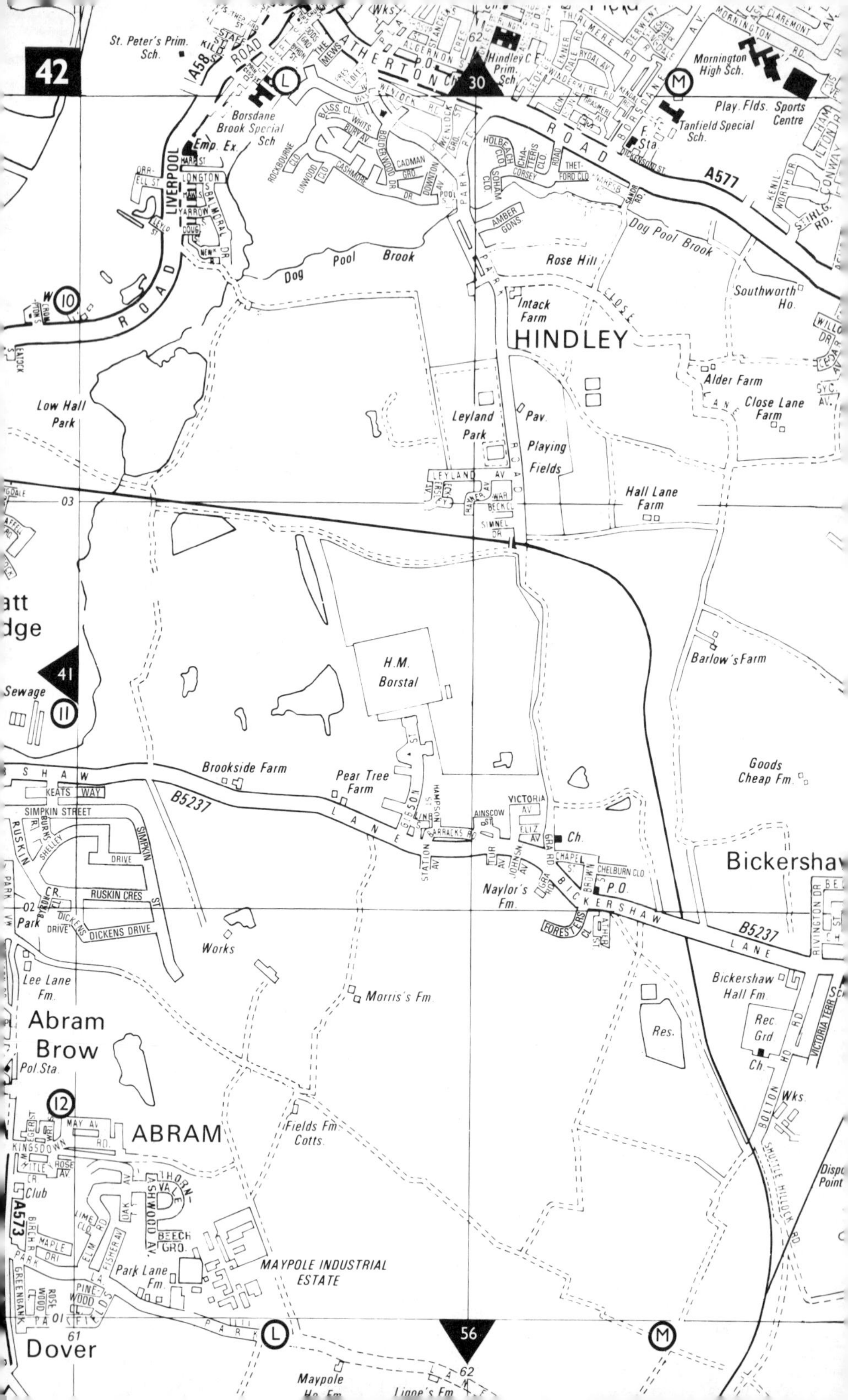

St. Peter's Prim. Sch.
A58
ROAD
ATHERTON
THE MEWS
ALGERNON
Hindley C.E. Prim. Sch.
30
THIRLMERE RD.
DERWENT
RYDAL AV.
WINDERMERE RD.
BORSDANE AV.
MORNINGTON RD.
CLAREMONT
Mornington High Sch.
Play. Flds.
Sports Centre
Tanfield Special Sch.
F. Sta.
DICKENSON ST.
A577
Borsdane Brook Special Sch.
Emp. Ex.
LIVERPOOL
LONGTON
YARROW
BALMORAL DR.
BLISS CL.
WHITSBURY AV.
ROCKBOURNE CLO.
LINWOOD CLO.
CASHMORE DR.
BOLDERWOOD DR.
CADMAN GRO.
DOWNTON AV.
WENLOCK RD.
PARK RD.
HOLBEACH CLO.
CHATTERIS CLO.
SOHAM CLO.
CORSEY
THETFORD CLO.
AMBER GDNS.
SANDR RD.
KENILWORTH DR.
CONWAY
HAMILTON
STIRLG. RD.
Dog Pool Brook
Rose Hill
CLOSE
Southworth Ho.
Intack Farm
HINDLEY
10
ROAD
Low Hall Park
Alder Farm
LANE
Close Lane Farm
Leyland Park
Pav.
Playing Fields
LEYLAND AV.
RAMSEY AV.
WAR
BECK CL.
SIMNEL DR.
Hall Lane Farm
03
att
dge
41
Sewage
11
H.M. Borstal
Barlow's Farm
SHAW
KEATS WAY
SIMPKIN STREET
RUSKIN
BURNS
SHELLEY
DRIVE
SIMPKIN ST.
RUSKIN CRES
DICKENS DRIVE
B5237
Brookside Farm
Pear Tree Farm
LANE
GIBSON
HAMPSON ST.
BARRACKS RD.
AINSCOW ST.
VICTORIA AV.
ELIZ AV.
Ch.
CHAPEL ST.
CHELBURN CLO.
BROWN ST.
P.O.
STATION AV.
JOHNSON AV.
Goods Cheap Fm.
Bickershaw
Naylor's Fm.
BICKERSHAW
FORESTERS CL.
B5237
LANE
RIVINGTON DR.
02
Park
Works
Lee Lane Fm.
Morris's Fm.
Bickershaw Hall Fm.
Rec. Grd.
Ch.
Res.
VICTORIA TERR.
Abram Brow
Pol. Sta.
12
MAY AV.
KINGSDOWN RD.
ABRAM
Fields Fm. Cotts.
BOLTON HO. RD.
Wks.
SHUTTLE HILLOCK RD.
Disp. Point
ROSE AV.
Club
ASHWOOD AV.
THORNVALE
A573
OAK
BEECH GRO.
MAPLE DRI.
ELM RD.
FISHER AV.
MAYPOLE INDUSTRIAL ESTATE
Park Lane Fm.
GREENBANK
ROSEWOOD CL.
PINEWOOD
PARK
61
Dover
56
62
Maypole Ho. Fm.
Ligoe's Fm.

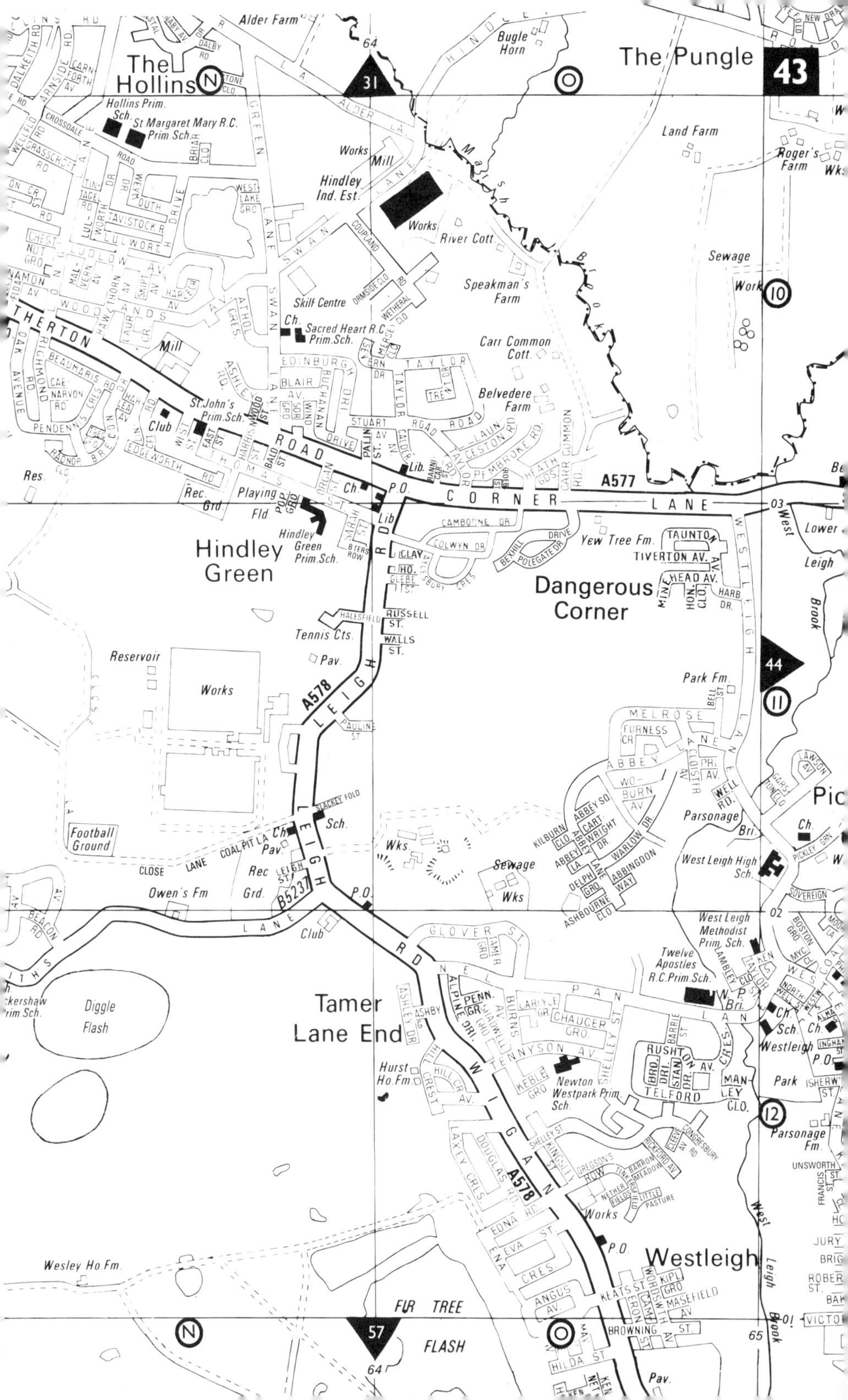
The Hollins
The Pungle
31
Alder Farm
Bugle Horn
Hollins Prim. Sch.
St Margaret Mary R.C. Prim.Sch.
Land Farm
Roger's Farm
Works
Mill
Hindley Ind. Est.
River Cott.
Sewage Works
10
Speakman's Farm
Skill Centre
Sacred Heart R.C. Prim.Sch.
Ch.
Carr Common Cott.
Belvedere Farm
Mill
St.John's Prim.Sch.
Club
Lib.
P.O.
A577
CORNER LANE
ROAD
Res.
Rec. Grd.
Playing Fld.
Hindley Green Prim.Sch.
Hindley Green
Yew Tree Fm.
Dangerous Corner
Lower Leigh
Brook
Tennis Cts.
Pav.
Reservoir
Works
A578
LEIGH RD
44
11
Park Fm.
Football Ground
Sch.
Wks.
Sewage Wks
Parsonage
West Leigh High Sch.
Owen's Fm
Rec Grd.
B5237
Club
West Leigh Methodist Prim. Sch.
Twelve Apostles R.C.Prim.Sch.
Diggle Flash
Tamer Lane End
Hurst Ho.Fm.
Newton Westpark Prim. Sch.
Westleigh
Park
12
Parsonage Fm.
WIGAN RD
Works
P.O.
Wesley Ho.Fm.
Westleigh
FIR TREE FLASH
57
64
65
West Leigh Brook
Pav.

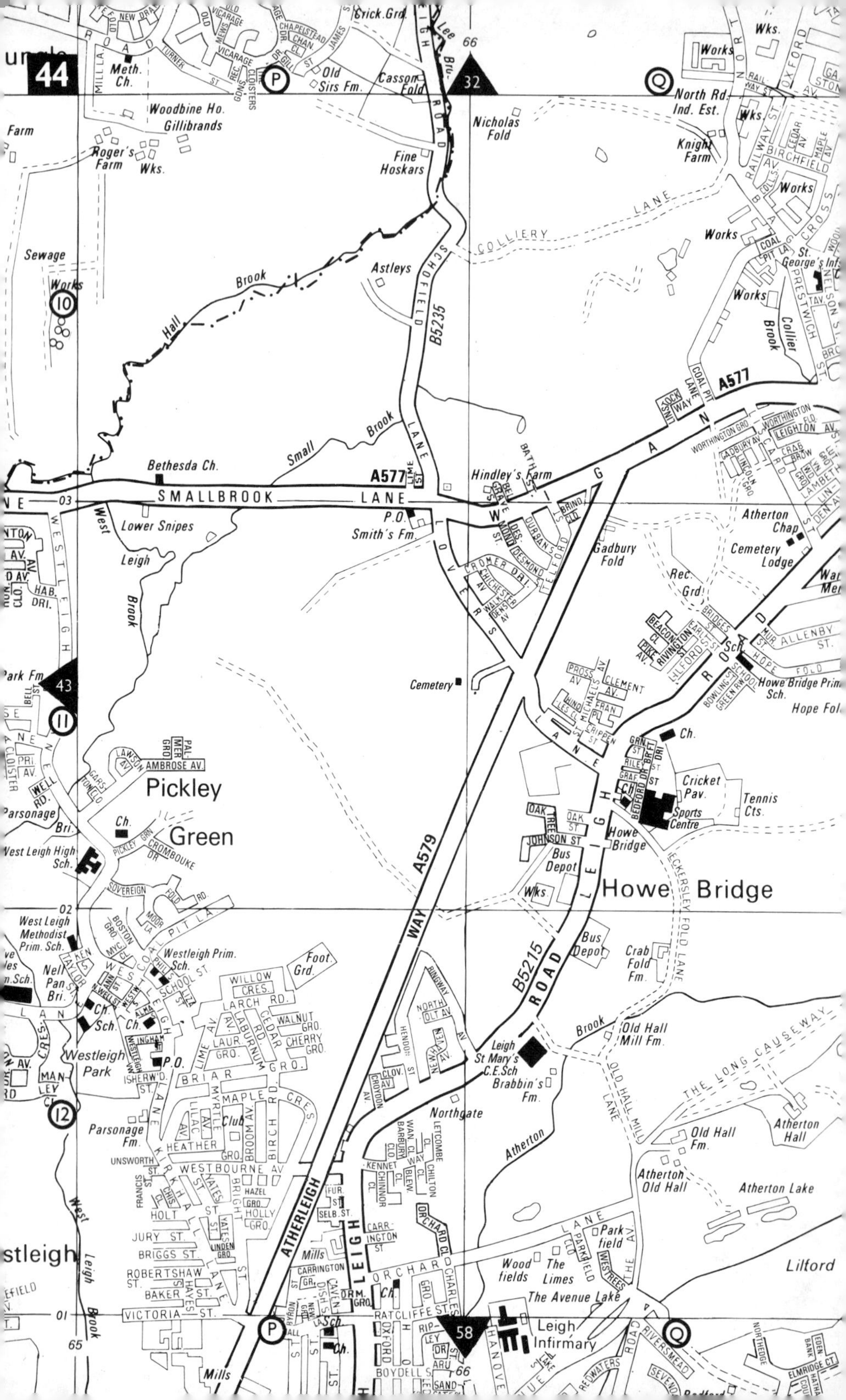
44
Meth. Ch.
Woodbine Ho.
Gillibrands
Farm
Roger's Farm
Wks.
Old Sirs Fm.
Casson Fold
Crick.Grd.
32
North Rd. Ind. Est.
Works
Wks.
Nicholas Fold
Fine Hoskars
Knight Farm
OXFORD
RAILWAY ST.
CEDAR AV.
MAPLE AV.
BIRCHFIELD AV.
COLLIERY LANE
Sewage Works
10
Hall Brook
Astleys
SCHOFIELD LANE
B5235
St. George's Infs.
PRESTWICH
Collier Brook
COAL PIT LANE
A577
LINSTOCK WAY
WORTHINGTON GRO.
LEIGHTON AV.
GADBURY AV.
LAMBETH
Bethesda Ch.
Small Brook
A577
Hindley's Farm
SMALLBROOK LANE
Lower Snipes
West Leigh Brook
P.O.
Smith's Fm.
LOVERS LANE
WIGAN ROAD
DURBAN ST.
DESMOND
TELFORD
CROMER DRI.
CHICHESTER AV.
WALKSTER
Gadbury Fold
Atherton Chap.
Cemetery Lodge
Rec. Grd.
BEACON CL.
PIKE AV.
RIVINGTON
HILFORD ST.
ALLENBY ST.
HOPE FOLD
Howe Bridge Prim. Sch.
Hope Fold
Cemetery
Park Fm.
43
11
WESTLEIGH
Pickley Green
AMBROSE AV.
LAWSON AV.
PROSS AV.
CLEMENT AV.
ST. MICHAEL'S AV.
Ch.
Cricket Pav.
Tennis Cts.
Sports Centre
BEDFORD DR.
Parsonage Bri.
West Leigh High Sch.
PICKLEY GRN.
CROMBOUKE DR.
A579
ATHERLEIGH WAY
OAK TREE
OAK ST.
JOHNSON ST
Howe Bridge
Bus Depot
Wks.
Howe Bridge
ECKERSLEY FOLD LANE
SOVEREIGN FOLD RD.
COAL PIT LA.
West Leigh Methodist Prim. Sch.
Westleigh Prim. Sch.
SCHOOL ST.
Foot. Grd.
WILLOW CRES.
LARCH RD.
CEDAR RD.
WALNUT GRO.
CHERRY GRO.
LABURNUM
B5215
LEIGH ROAD
Bus Depot
Crab Fold Fm.
Brook
Old Hall Mill Fm.
THE LONG CAUSEWAY
Westleigh Park
P.O.
BRIAR GRO.
MAPLE CRES.
Club
BIRCH RD.
BROOM AV.
HEATHER GRO.
RINGWAY
NORTH OLT AV.
HENDON
CROYDON AV.
CLOV. AV.
Leigh St Mary's C.E.Sch
Brabbin's Fm.
Northgate
OLD HALL MILL LANE
Atherton Hall
Old Hall Fm.
12
Parsonage Fm.
WESTBOURNE AV
KIRKHALL LANE
HAZEL GRO.
HOLLY GRO.
HOLT ST.
JURY ST.
BRIGGS ST.
ROBERTSHAW ST.
BAKER ST.
VICTORIA ST.
West Leigh Brook
stleigh
Atherton
Atherton Old Hall
Atherton Lake
KENNET CL.
CHINNOR CL.
LETCOMBE
CHILTON
ORCHARD CL.
CARRINGTON ST
LEIGH
Mills
ORCHARD
Wood fields
The Limes
Park field
The Avenue Lake
Lilford
RATCLIFFE ST.
58
Leigh Infirmary
RIVERSMEAD
REDWATERS
NORTHEDGE
ELMRIDGE CT.
OXFORD
BOYDELL ST.
Mills
65
66
03
02
01

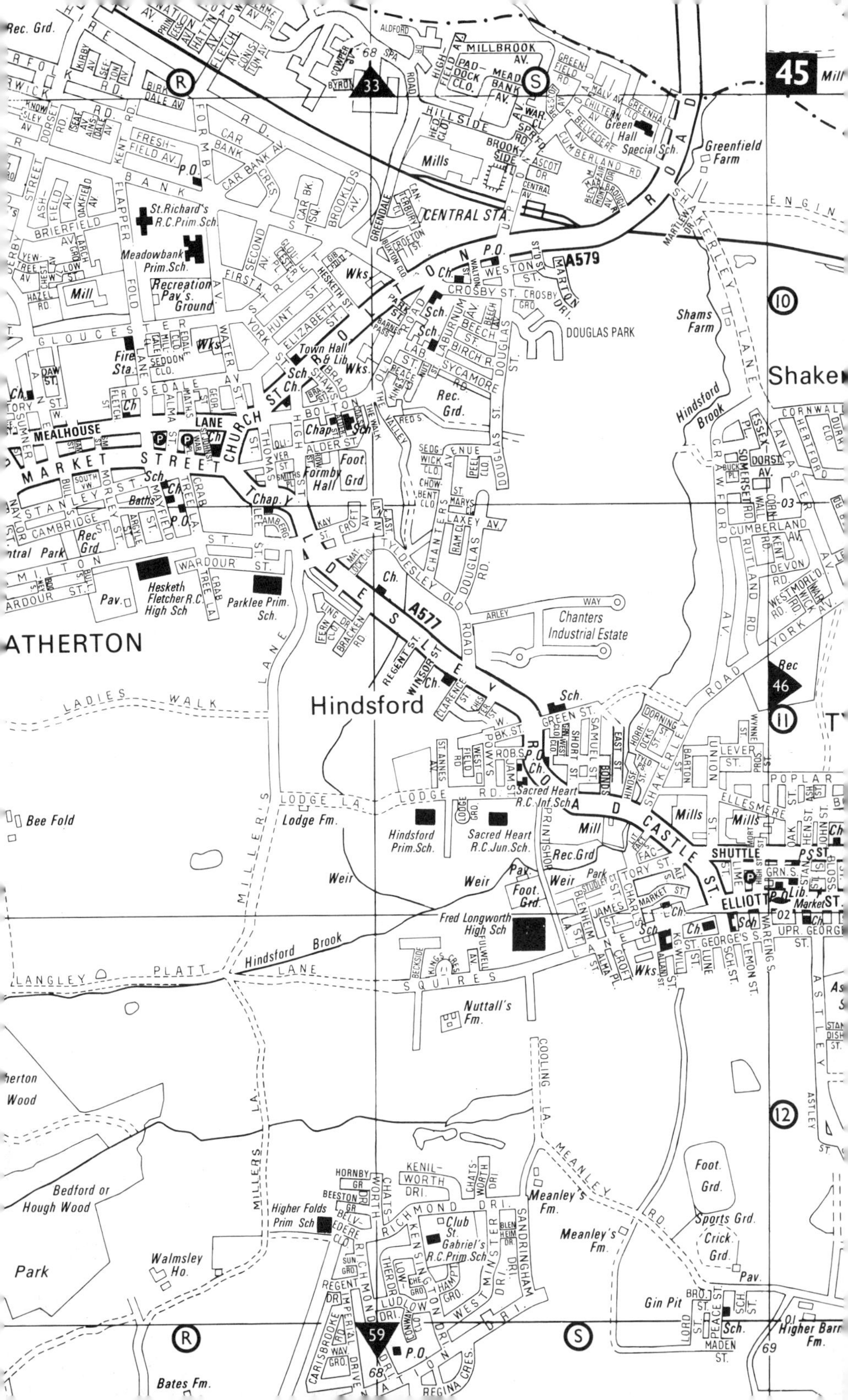
45
33
59
46
10
11
12
ATHERTON
Hindsford
Shaker
Rec. Grd.
Millbrook Av.
Padock Clo.
Mead Bank Av.
Hillside
Green Hall Special Sch.
Greenfield Farm
Cumberland Rd.
Central Sta.
Mills
A579
A577
St. Richard's R.C. Prim. Sch.
Meadowbank Prim. Sch.
Recreation Pav's. Ground
Mill
Flapper Fold
Gloucester St.
Fire Sta.
Town Hall & Lib.
Mealhouse Lane
Market Street
Church St.
Formby Hall
Foot. Grd.
Douglas Park
Shams Farm
Hindsford Brook
Shakerley Lane
Chanters Industrial Estate
Hesketh Fletcher R.C. High Sch
Parklee Prim. Sch.
Ladies Walk
Lodge La.
Lodge Fm.
Bee Fold
Hindsford Prim. Sch.
Sacred Heart R.C. Jun. Sch.
Sacred Heart R.C. Inf. Sch
Castle St.
Shuttle St.
Elliott St.
Market St.
Weir
Fred Longworth High Sch
Langley Platt Lane
Squires Lane
Nuttall's Fm.
Millers La.
Cooling La.
Meanley Rd.
Meanley's Fm.
Bedford or Hough Wood
Park
Walmsley Ho.
Higher Folds Prim Sch
Club
St. Gabriel's R.C. Prim. Sch
Richmond Dri.
Sandringham Dri.
Westminster Dri.
Foot. Grd.
Sports Grd.
Crick. Grd.
Pav.
Gin Pit
Higher Barr Fm.
Bates Fm.
Regina Cres.
Astley St.
Upr. George St.
St. George's St.
York Av.
Tyldesley Old Road
68
69
02
03

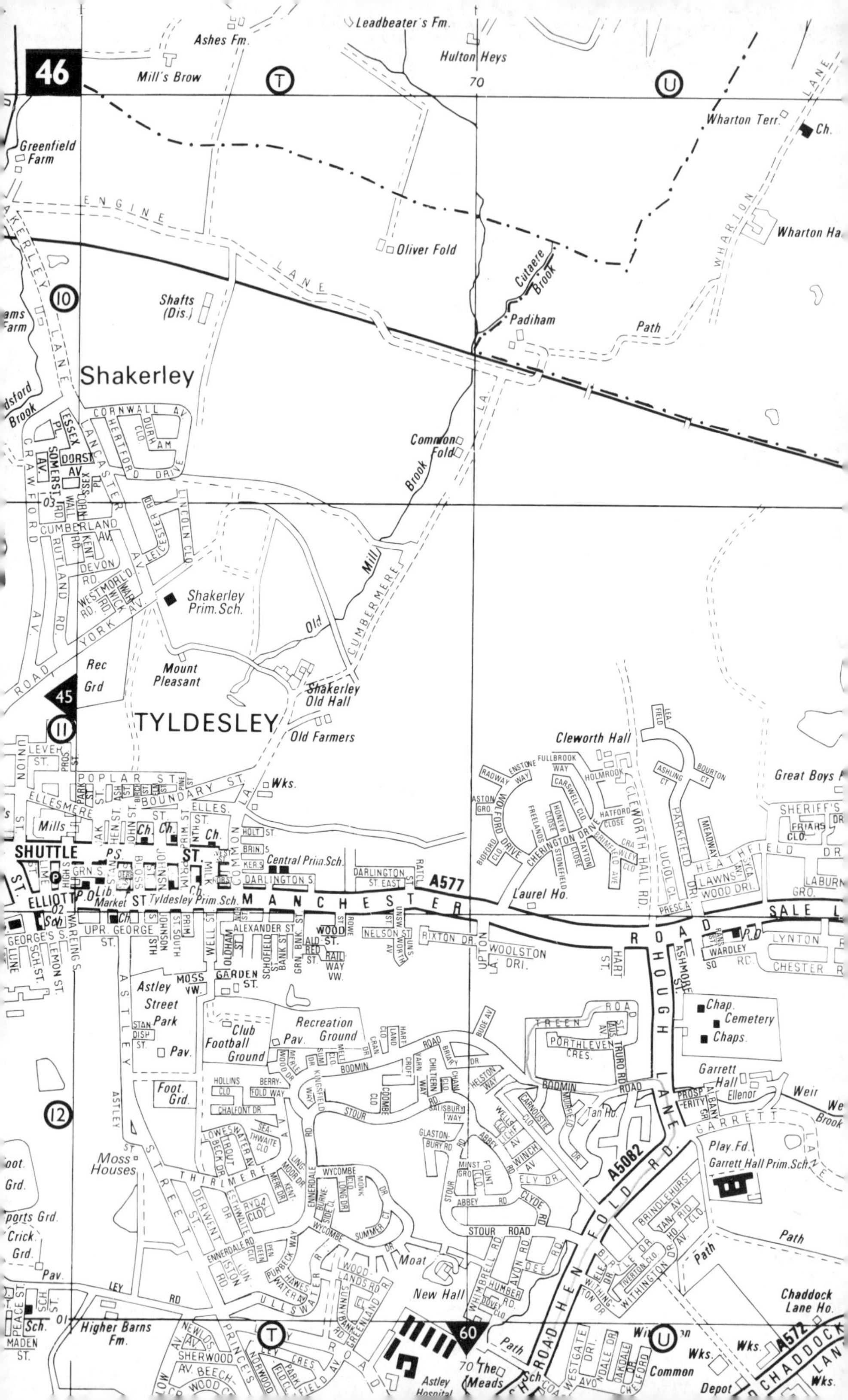

46
Leadbeater's Fm.
Ashes Fm.
Hulton Heys
Mill's Brow
T
70
U
Wharton Terr.
Ch.
Greenfield Farm
ENGINE LANE
Oliver Fold
Wharton Hall
WHARTON LANE
Cutacre Brook
SHAKERLEY LANE
10
Shafts (Dis.)
Padiham
Path
Shakerley
Brook
CORNWALL AV.
ESSEX PL.
LANCASTER AV.
HERTFORD DRIVE
DURHAM CLO.
CRAWFORD AV.
SOMERST. AV.
DORST AV
ESSEX PL.
Common Fold
Brook
03
WALL RD.
CORN. RD.
LEICESTER RD.
LINCOLN CLO.
CUMBERLAND AV.
RUTLAND RD.
KENT RD.
DEVON RD.
WESTMORL'D. RD.
WAR. WICK RD.
YORK AV.
Mill
CUMBERMERE LA.
Shakerley Prim. Sch.
Old
ROAD
Rec Grd
Mount Pleasant
45
Shakerley Old Hall
11
TYLDESLEY
Old Farmers
UNION ST.
LEVER ST.
PROS. ST.
POPLAR ST.
PARK ST.
ASH ST.
BIRCH ST.
PINE ST.
BOUNDARY ST.
ELLESMERE ST.
ELLES. ST.
COMMON LA.
Wks.
Mills
Ch.
Ch.
Ch.
HOLT ST.
BRIN. S.
KER. S.
Central Prim. Sch.
SHUTTLE ST.
P.S.
ST.
GRN. S.
Lib.
P.O.
Market ST
Tyldesley Prim. Sch.
DARLINGTON S.
DARLINGTON ST. EAST
RATCL.
A577
MANCHESTER ROAD
Cleworth Hall
LEA FIELD
BOURTON CT
ASHLING CT
Great Boys
RADWAY WAY
ENSTONE WAY
FULLBROOK WAY
HOLMROOK
ASTON GRO.
WOLFORD DRIVE
CARSWELL CLO.
HONEYB. CLOSE
FREELANDS
HATFORD CLOSE
CLEWORTH HALL RD.
PARKFIELD DRI.
MEADWAY
SHERIFF'S
FRIARS CLO.
BIDEFORD CLO.
CHERINGTON DRIVE
STONEFIELD
LAYTON CLOSE
BRIMFIELD AVE
CRAWLEY CLO.
LUCIOL CL.
HEATHFIELD DR
LAWNS AV.
WOOD DRI.
LABURN. GRO.
Laurel Ho.
PRESCA.
ELLIOTT ST.
02
Sch.
Ch.
UPR. GEORGE ST.
GEORGE'S S.
JOHNSON ST.
ST. SOUTH
WELL ST.
ALEXANDER ST.
WOOD ST.
NELSON ST.
RIXTON DR.
UPTON LA.
WOOLSTON DRI.
HART ST.
SALE LANE
LYNTON
WARDLEY SQ
CHESTER RD.
ASHMORE ST.
LUNE
SCH. ST.
LEMON ST.
WAREING S.
ASTLEY ST.
OLDHAM ST.
SCHOFIELD ST.
BANK ST.
ALD. RED ST.
RAIL WAY VW.
UNSWORTH AV.
Astley Street Park
MOSS VW.
GARDEN ST.
HOUGH LANE
TREEN ROAD
Chap.
Cemetery
Chaps.
BUDE AV.
STANDISH ST.
Pav.
Club Football Ground
Recreation Ground
Pav.
HARTLAND
PORTHLEVEN CRES.
TRURO RD
BODMIN ROAD
BRIARY DR.
CHILTERN WAY
HELSTON WAY
Foot. Grd.
HOLLINS CLO.
BERRYFOLD WAY
KINGSFIELD
COOMBE CLO.
CHALFONT DR.
STOUR ROAD
SALISBURY WAY
CARNOUSTIE CLO.
MUIRFIELD DR
Tan Ho.
Garrett Hall
Ellenor
PROSPERITY
ALBANY GR.
GARRETT LANE
Weir
Brook
12
LOWESWATER AV.
TROUT BECK DR.
SEATHWAITE CLO.
GLASTONBURY RD.
WELLS AV.
LICHF.
ABBEY
WINCH AV.
ELY DR.
Play. Fd.
Garrett Hall Prim. Sch.
A5082
FOLD RD.
Moss Houses
THIRLMERE AV.
MERE DR.
KENT.
LING MOOR DR.
ENNERDALE RD.
WYCOMBE DR.
MINST GRO.
FOUNT CLO.
ABBEY RD.
CLYDE RD.
DERWENT ST.
ESTHWAITE DR.
RYDAL CLO.
BURNE. SIDE CL.
LONG DR.
MONK. DR.
SUMMER CT.
STOUR ROAD
BRINDLEHURST
TAN. AV.
Path
Foot. Grd.
Sports Grd.
Crick. Grd.
Pav.
ENNERDALE RD.
PURBECK WAY
WYCOMBE
Moat
WHIMBRELL RD.
AVON RD.
DEE
HUMBER RD.
DOVEY CLO.
BIRTLE DR.
TIVERTON CLO.
WITHINGTON DR.
Path
Path
LEY RD
HAWES WATER AV.
ULLSWATER
WOODLANDS RD.
SUNNYBANK
GREENLAND R.
New Hall
Chaddock Lane Ho.
PEACE ST.
SCH. ST.
01
Sch.
MADEN ST.
Higher Barns Fm.
NEWLDS. AV.
SHERWOOD AV.
BEECH WOOD
PRINCE'S
NORWOOD
60
70
The Meads
Astley Hospital
HENFOLD ROAD
Sch.
WESTGATE DRI.
OAKDALE DR
CHELFORD
Common
Wks.
Wks.
Depot
A572
CHADDOCK LANE
Wks.

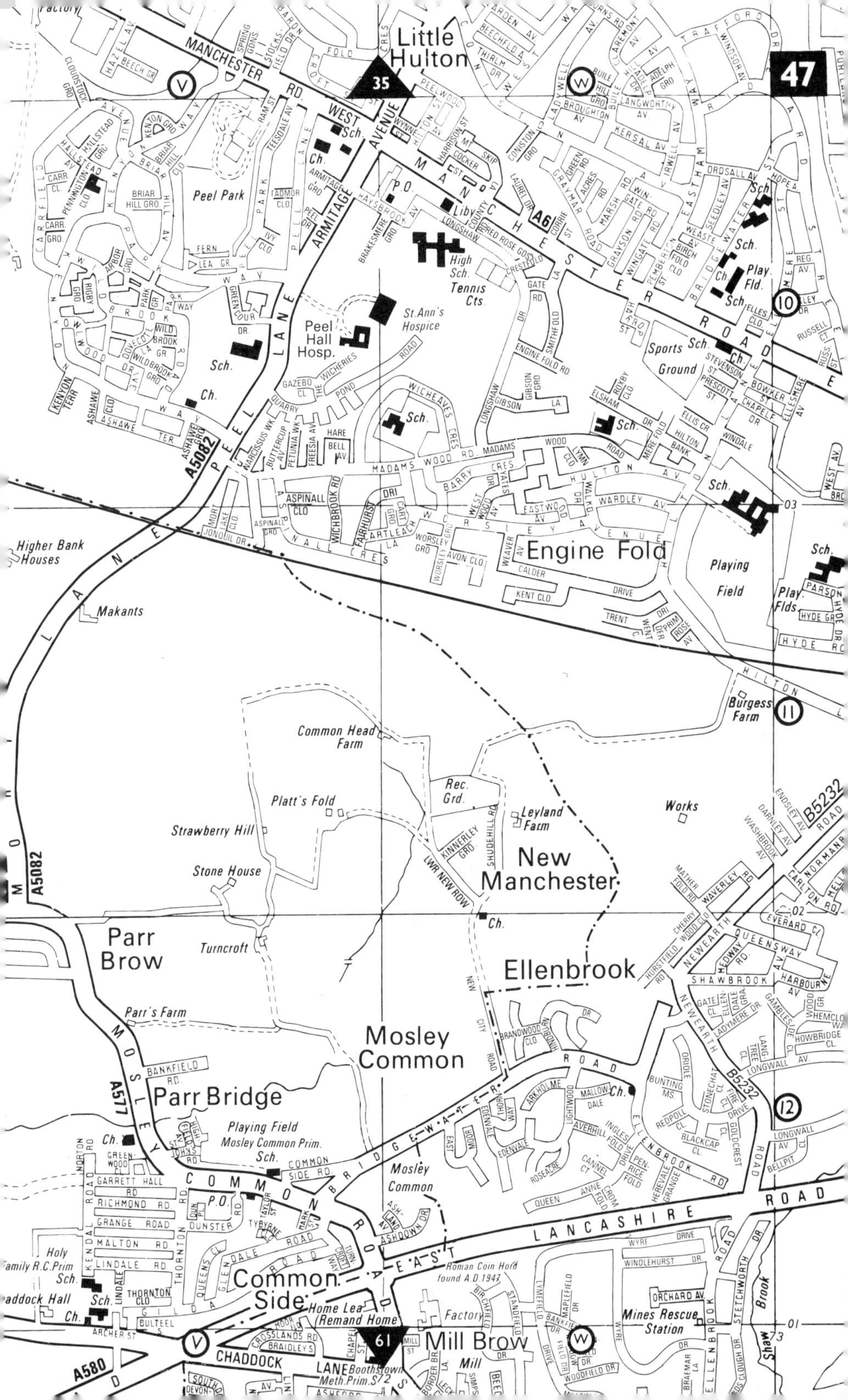
Little Hulton
35
MANCHESTER RD.
WEST
AVENUE
ARMITAGE AV
Peel Park
PEEL LANE
A5082
A6
MANCHESTER ROAD
High Sch.
Tennis Cts.
St. Ann's Hospice
Peel Hall Hosp.
Sch.
Ch.
P.O.
Liby
Sports Ground
Playing Field
Play. Flds.
Play. Fld.
MADAMS WOOD RD.
HULTON AV.
WORSLEY AVENUE
WARDLEY AV.
Engine Fold
KENT CLO.
HILTON LA.
Higher Bank Houses
Makants
Burgess Farm
Common Head Farm
Platt's Fold
Strawberry Hill
Stone House
Rec. Grd.
Leyland Farm
Works
B5232
New Manchester
LWR NEW ROW
NEW CITY ROAD
Parr Brow
Turncroft
Ellenbrook
Parr's Farm
Mosley Common
BANKFIELD RD.
Parr Bridge
A577
MOSLEY COMMON ROAD
Playing Field
Mosley Common Prim. Sch.
BRIDGEWATER ROAD
ELLENBROOK RD
NEWEARTH RD
LONGWALL AV.
EAST LANCASHIRE ROAD
Roman Coin Hord found A.D. 1947
Holy Family R.C.Prim Sch.
Common Side
Home Lea (Remand Home)
Factory
Mines Rescue Station
CHADDOCK LANE
A580
61
Mill Brow
Mill
Boothstown Meth. Prim. S
Shaw Brook
10
11
12
V
W

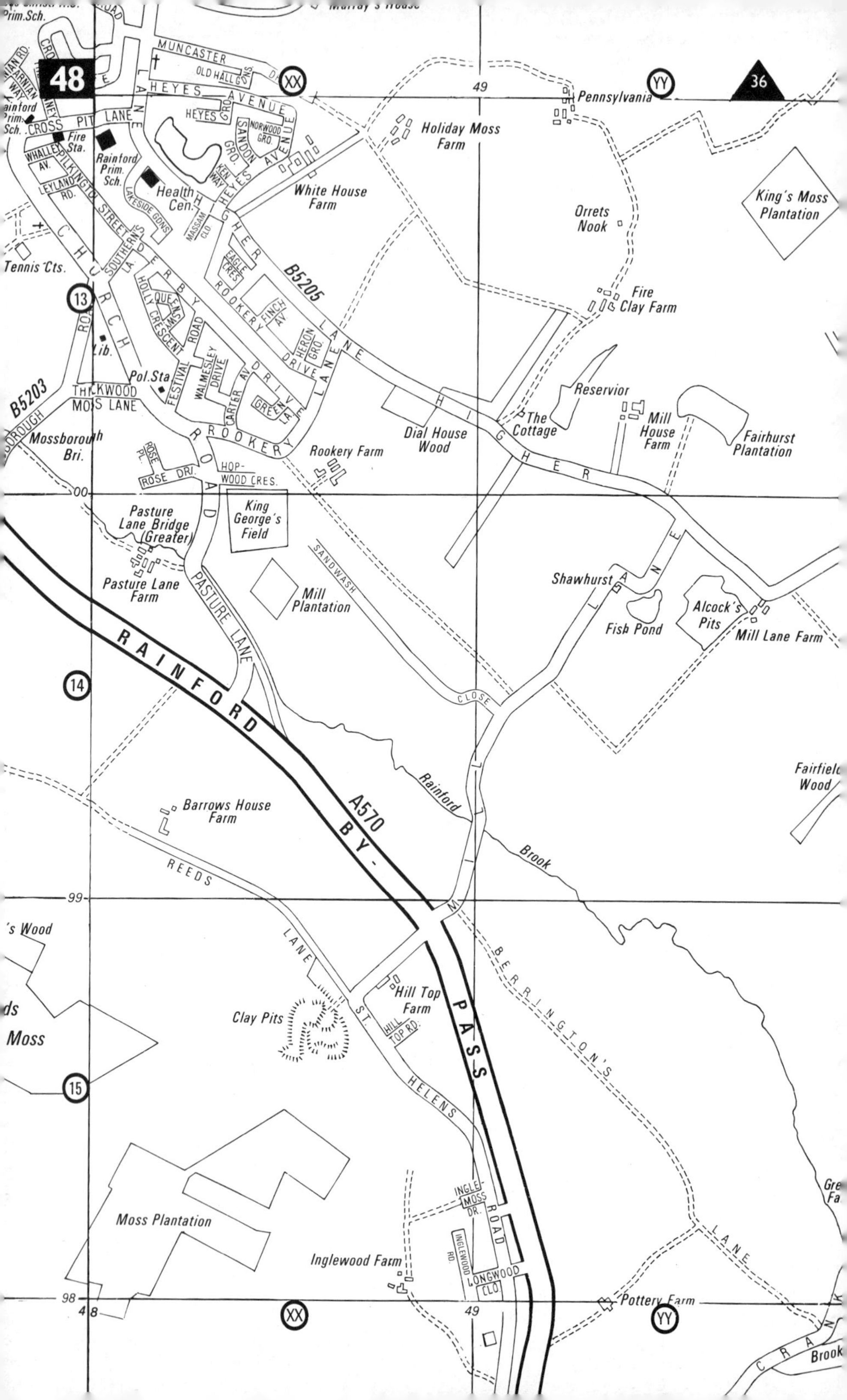

48
36
XX
YY
49
Prim.Sch.
MUNCASTER
OLD HALL GDNS.
HEYES AVENUE
HEYES GRO.
NORWOOD GRO.
SANDON GRO.
KEN WAY
Pennsylvania
Holiday Moss Farm
CROSS PIT LANE
Fire Sta.
Rainford Prim. Sch.
WHALLEY AV.
LEYLAND RD.
PILKINGTON STREET
Health Cen.
LAKESIDE GDNS
MASSAM CLO.
White House Farm
King's Moss Plantation
Orrets Nook
Tennis Cts.
CHURCH
SOUTHERN'S LA.
DERBY
HOLLY CRESCENT
QUEEN'S
EAGLE CRES.
ROOKERY
FINCH AV.
B5205
HIGHER LANE
Fire Clay Farm
13
Lib.
FESTIVAL ROAD
WALMESLEY DRIVE
CARTER AV
DRIVE
HERON GRO.
LANE
Pol.Sta
B5203
THICKWOOD MOSS LANE
GREEN LA.
Reservior
The Cottage
Mill House Farm
Fairhurst Plantation
Dial House Wood
Mossborough Bri.
ROSE PL.
ROSE DRI.
ROOKERY ROAD
HOP-WOOD CRES.
Rookery Farm
00
King George's Field
Pasture Lane Bridge (Greater)
Pasture Lane Farm
PASTURE LANE
SANDWASH CLOSE
Mill Plantation
Shawhurst
Fish Pond
Alcock's Pits
Mill Lane Farm
RAINFORD BY-PASS
A570
14
Rainford Brook
MILL LANE
Fairfield Wood
Barrows House Farm
REEDS LANE
99
's Wood
ds Moss
Hill Top Farm
HILL TOP RD.
Clay Pits
ST. HELENS
BERRINGTON'S LANE
15
Moss Plantation
INGLE-MOSS DR.
ROAD
INGLEWOOD RD.
Inglewood Farm
LONGWOOD CLO.
98
48
Pottery Farm
CRANK
Brook

49
36
37
50
ZZ
A
13
14
15
51
00
99
98
Kings Moss
KING'S MOSS LA.
FIR TREE CL.
BROOK LA.
Rainford Brook Farm
Red Barn Farm
Haughwood Farm
RED BARN RD.
King's Bri.
Black Brook
Little Moss Farm
GORE'S LANE
Gore's Farm
BACK LANE
RED CAT LANE
Chadwick Wood
Guild Hall
Gore's Bri.
B5205
RAINFORD LANE
Rose Farm
Alderley Farm
ALDER LANE
Rainford Delf Farm
CRANK HILL
HIGHFIELD DR.
Crank Hill Prim. Sch.
Crank
Fir Wood
HEYSOME CLO.
Heysome Ho.
Rainford Old Delf
CRANK ROAD
B5201
Crank Farm
Crank Hall Farm
GUN SITE LANE
Windle Gorse Coverts
Cray Wood
Shoots Delf Wood
Brooklands
BIRCHLEY
A571
Moss Bank Bri
High Wood
Crank House Hall
FAIRFIELD GDNS.
Fairfield Hospital
MARTINDALE RD.
Rainford Hall
BIRCHLEY VW.
BROAD OAK ROAD
Nursery
Shoots's Delph Farm
Lion House Wood
Nursery Wood
CHERRY TREE LA.
CHERRY TREE COTTAGES
TROUTBECK GRO.
MILLBECK GRO.
Caleb
The Nursery
MANOR HOUSE CLO.
DALSTON DR.
CROSSDALE WAY
ROSTHWAITE GR.
MOSEDALE AV.
LINGMELL
GREENB AV.
Fenny Bank Rough
Fenny Bank Farm
BANK
Rec. Grd.
CRAG GRO.
GHYLL GRO.
BAMPTON AV.
DALEHEAD PL.
LOUGHRIGG AV.
AVENUE
DUNMAIL
CALDBECK
Carr Jun.
Winstanley Wood
Poverty Plantation
CLUBS
P.O.
MOSS
Clinkham Wood
gnals Bri.
SANDY LA.
HILLBRAE AV.
DEV. OKE AV.
LORTON AV.
FELL GR.
KINGSWAY
SILVER
ENNERDALE
MARDALE AV.
AVENUE
WINDERMERE AV.
BOWNESS AV.
YEWDALE
WASDALE
AV.
Moss Bank
Windle Park Wood
WOODSIDE AV.
ood

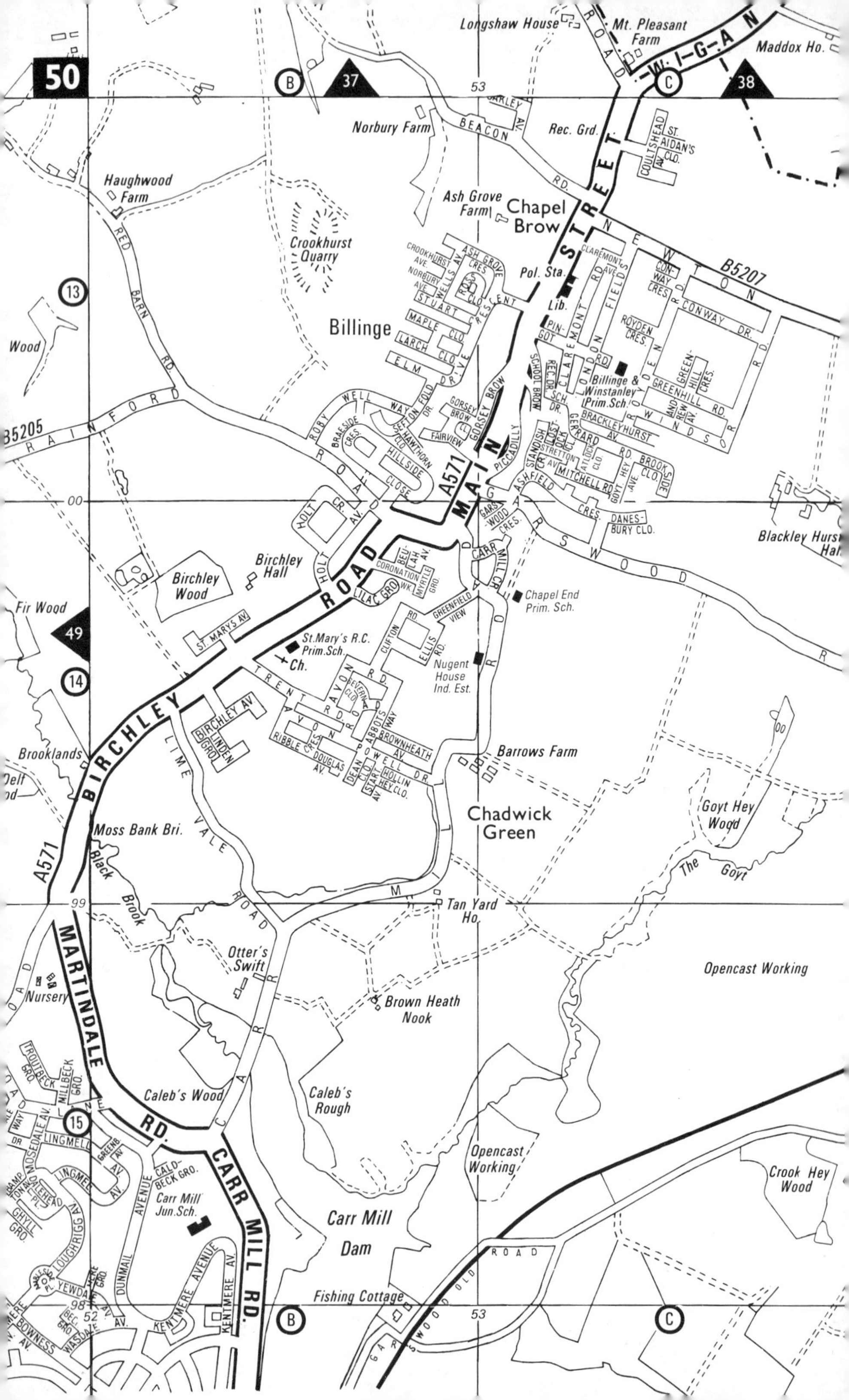
37
38
49
B
C
13
14
15
53
00
99
98
52
Longshaw House
Mt. Pleasant Farm
Maddox Ho.
WIGAN
ROAD
Norbury Farm
BEACON RD.
BARLEY AV.
Rec. Grd.
COULTSHEAD AV.
ST. AIDAN'S CLO.
Haughwood Farm
Ash Grove Farm
Chapel Brow
STREET
MAIN
NEWTON
B5207
Crookhurst Quarry
CROOKHURST AVE.
NORBURY AVE.
WELLS AV.
ASH GROVE CRES.
ROSS CLO.
CRESCENT
STUART
Pol. Sta.
Lib.
CLAREMONT AVE.
CLAREMONT RD
FIELDS
LONDON RD
CONWAY CRES.
CONWAY DR.
ROYDEN CRES.
ROYDEN RD
PINGOT
SCHOOL BROW
REC. DR.
SCH. DR.
Billinge & Winstanley Prim. Sch.
GREENHILL CRES.
GREENHILL RD.
ANDREW AV.
WINDSOR RD
BRACKLEYHURST AV.
GERRARD RD.
Billinge
MAPLE CLO.
LARCH CLO.
ELM DRIVE
Wood
RED BARN RD.
RAINFORD ROAD
B5205
ROBY WELL WAY
BRAESIDE CRES.
SEFTON FOLD DR.
HAWTHORN CLO.
HILLSIDE CLOSE
GORSEY BROW
GORSEY BROW CL.
FAIRVIEW
PICCADILLY
A571
STANDISH CL.
LOSTOCK CL.
STRETTON AV.
ATLOCK CLO.
GOYT HEY AVE.
MITCHELL RD.
BROOK CLO.
BROOKSIDE
ASHFIELD CRES.
DANESBURY CLO.
GARSWOOD RD
GARSWOOD CRES.
Blackley Hurst Hall
HOLT CR.
HOLT AV.
HOLT
ROAD
BEULAH AV.
CORONATION WK.
MYRTLE GRO.
LILAC GRO
CARR MILL CR.
CARR MILL ROAD
Chapel End Prim. Sch.
Birchley Hall
Birchley Wood
Fir Wood
ST. MARYS AV.
St. Mary's R.C. Prim. Sch.
Ch.
GREENFIELD VIEW
CLIFTON RD
ELLIS RD.
Nugent House Ind. Est.
TRENT RD.
AVON RD.
SEVERN CLO.
ABBOTS WAY
BROWNHEATH AV.
AVON
RIBBLE CRES.
DOUGLAS AV.
DEAN CLO.
POWELL DR.
HOLLIN CLO.
STARTHEY AV.
BIRCHLEY
BIRCHLEY AV.
LINDEN GRO.
LIME VALE ROAD
Brooklands
Delf
Barrows Farm
Chadwick Green
Goyt Hey Wood
The Goyt
Moss Bank Bri.
Black Brook
Tan Yard Ho.
MILL
Otter's Swift
Nursery
MARTINDALE RD.
CARR MILL RD.
Brown Heath Nook
Opencast Working
TROUTBECK GRO.
MILLBECK GRO.
LINGMELL
MOSEDALE AV.
DALEHEAD PL.
LOUGHRIGG AV.
GHYLL GRO.
YEWDALE
BOWNESS AV.
WASDALE AV.
GREENBANK AV.
CALDBECK GRO.
AVENUE
DUNMAIL AV.
Carr Mill Jun. Sch.
KENTMERE AVENUE
KENTMERE AV.
Caleb's Wood
Caleb's Rough
Carr Mill Dam
Fishing Cottage
GARSWOOD OLD ROAD
Crook Hey Wood

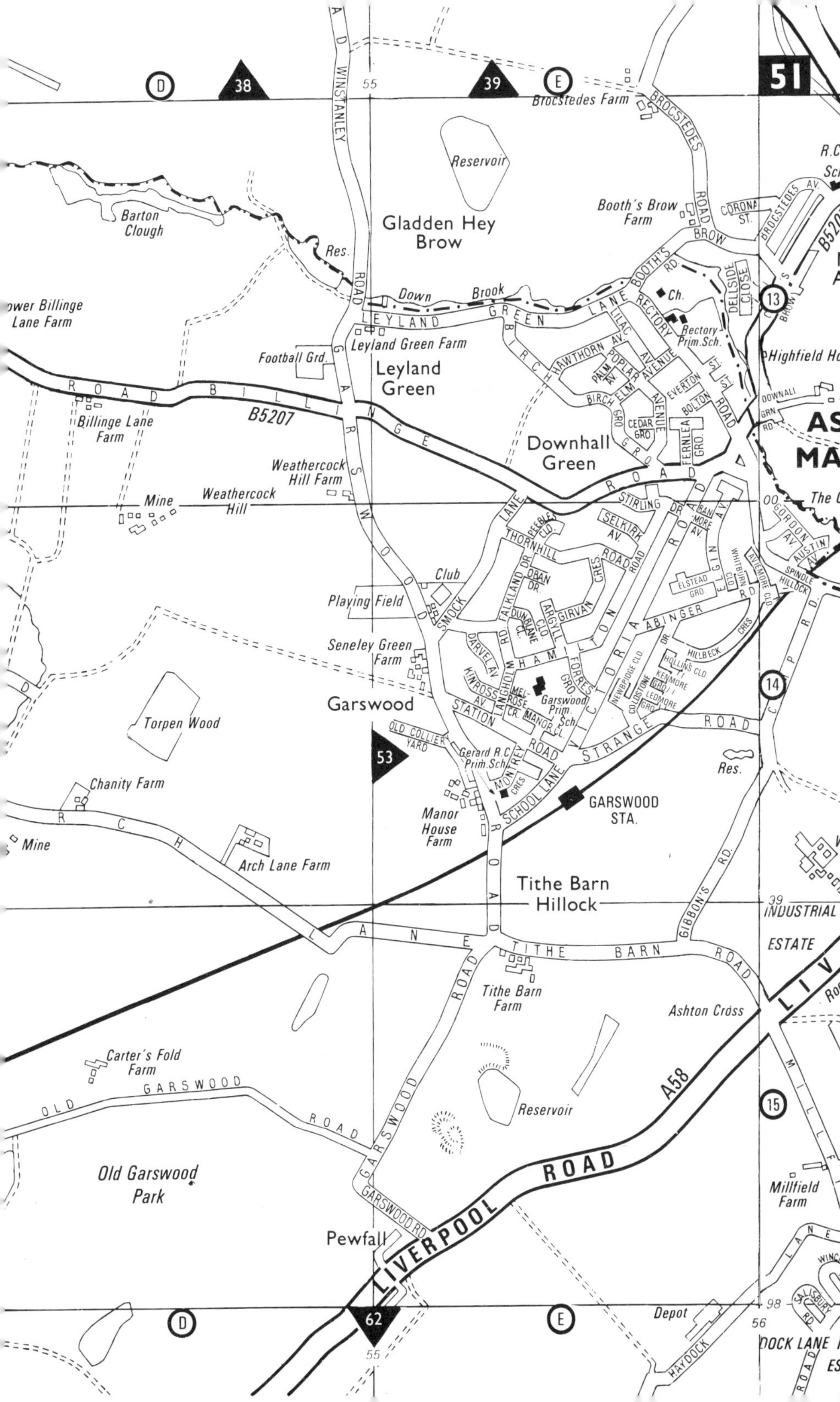
D
38
39
E
55
Brocstedes Farm
BROCSTEDES ROAD
WINSTANLEY ROAD
Reservoir
Barton Clough
Res.
Gladden Hey Brow
Booth's Brow Farm
BROW
CORONA ST.
BROCSTEDES AV.
R.C Sch
B5207
Down Brook
LEYLAND GREEN LANE
BOOTH'S RD.
Ch.
RECTORY
Rectory Prim.Sch.
DELLSIDE CLOSE
13
Lower Billinge Lane Farm
Leyland Green Farm
Football Grd.
Leyland Green
HAWTHORN AV.
LILAC AV.
PALM AV.
POPLAR AV.
ELM AVENUE
AVENUE
EVERTON ST.
BOLTON ST.
ROAD
Highfield Ho
BIRCH GRO.
BIRCH
CEDAR GRO.
FERNLEA GRO.
DOWNALL GRN RD.
AS
MA
ROAD BILLINGE ROAD
B5207
Billinge Lane Farm
GARSWOOD
Downhall Green
ROAD
Weathercock Hill Farm
Mine
Weathercock Hill
LANE
STIRLING DR.
ROAD
PEEBLES CLO.
SELKIRK AV.
BAN MORE AV.
ELGIN AV.
GORDON AV.
AUSTIN AV.
The C
THORNHILL ROAD
WHITBURN CLO
AVIEMORE CLO
SPINDLE HILLOCK
Club
OBAN DR.
CRES.
ELSTEAD GRO.
RD.
Playing Field
SMOCK
FALKLAND DR.
DUNBLANE CL.
ARGYLL CLO.
GIRVAN
HAMILTON
ABINGER
VICTORIA
CRES
Seneley Green Farm
DARVEL AV.
HILLBECK
HOLLINS CLO.
KINROSS AV.
LANGHOLM RD.
MELROSE CR.
FORRES GRO.
NEWBRIDGE CLO.
COLDSTONE GRO.
KENMORE GRO.
LEDMORE GRO.
Garswood
Garswood Prim. Sch.
14
Torpen Wood
STATION ROAD
MANOR CL.
STRANGE ROAD
OLD COLLIERY YARD
53
Gerard R.C. Prim.Sch.
MONTREY CRES.
SCHOOL LANE
GARSWOOD STA.
Res.
Chanity Farm
ARCH LANE
Mine
Manor House Farm
Arch Lane Farm
ROAD
Tithe Barn Hillock
GIBBON'S RD.
39
INDUSTRIAL ESTATE
TITHE BARN ROAD
ROAD
Tithe Barn Farm
Ashton Cross
LIV
Roc
Carter's Fold Farm
GARSWOOD
OLD GARSWOOD ROAD
A58
Reservoir
15
MILLFIELD
Old Garswood Park
ROAD
LIVERPOOL
Millfield Farm
GARSWOOD RD
Pewfall
LANE
WINCE
98
SALISBURY RD.
D
62
E
Depot
56
HAYDOCK
DOCK LANE I
ES
55
ROAD

OTHER STREETFINDER MAPS & ATLASES IN THE BARTHOLOMEW & NICHOLSON RANGE

Streetfinder Maps

	ISBN	Price
Aberdeen Colour	0 7028 2156 X	£1.99
Barnet	0 7028 2519 0	£1.99
Belfast	0 7028 2224 8	£2.99
Blackburn	0 7028 2364 3	£1.99
Blackpool	0 7028 2223 X	£1.99
Bromley	0 7028 2265 5	£1.99
Burnley	0 7028 2227 2	£1.99
Cardiff Colour	0 7028 2365 1	£2.99
Cheltenham	0 7028 2645 6	£1.99
Croydon and Sutton	0 7028 2264 7	£1.99
Dartford	0 7028 2518 2	£1.99
Docklands	0 7028 2517 4	£1.99
Dublin Colour	0 7028 2281 7	£3.25
Dublin Illustrated Map	0 7028 2296 5	£2.99
Dundee	0 7028 2162 4	£2.25
Ealing, Wembley and Harrow	0 7028 2266 3	£1.99
Edinburgh Colour	0 7028 2684 7	£2.99
Edinburgh Illustrated Map	0 7028 2377 5	£2.99
Enfield	0 7028 2514 X	£1.99
Epsom & Ewell	0 7028 2451 8	£1.99
Official Glasgow Colour	0 7028 2708 8	£2.99
Glasgow	0 7028 2280 9	£1.99
Gloucester	0 7028 2143 8	£1.99
Gravesend	0 7028 2607 3	£1.99
Guildford	0 7029 2456 9	£1.99
Halifax & Brighouse	0 7028 2679 0	£2.25
Harlow	0 7028 2446 1	£1.99
Harrogate & Knaresborough	0 7028 2226 4	£1.99
Heathrow to Hammersmith	0 7028 2592 1	£1.99
Hemel Hempstead	0 7028 2601 4	£1.99
Hertford & Ware	0 7028 2604 9	£1.99
Huddersfield	0 7028 2458 5	£1.99
Ilford	0 7028 2442 9	£1.99
Inverness Colour	0 7028 2600 6	£2.25
Kingston	0 7028 2267 1	£1.99
Leatherhead & Dorking	0 7028 2450 X	£1.99
Leeds Colour	0 7028 2282 5	£2.50
London Illustrated Map	0 7028 2160 8	£3.50
Perth	0 7028 2682 0	£2.25
Preston Colour	0 7028 2225 6	£2.50
Reigate & Redhill	0 7028 2452 6	£1.99
Romford & Hornchurch	0 7028 2454 2	£1.99
St. Albans	0 7028 2447 X	£1.99
Sevenoaks	0 7028 2608 1	£1.99
Slough & Windsor	0 7028 2457 7	£1.99
Wakefield	0 7028 2445 3	£2.25
Watford	0 7028 2441 0	£1.99
Welwyn & Hatfield	0 7028 2602 2	£1.99
Weybridge & Esher	0 7028 2615 4	£1.99
Woking	0 7028 2455 0	£1.99
York Colour	0 7028 2167 5	£1.99

Streetfinder Atlases & Guides

Aberdeen	0 7028 1681 7	£2.50
Belfast	0 7028 2435 6	£2.99
Blackburn, Accrington & Darwen	0 7028 2704 5	£2.99
Dublin Colour Atlas & Guide	0 7028 2283 3	£2.99
Edinburgh Colour	0 7028 1857 7	£2.99
Edinburgh	0 7028 2705 3	£2.75
Glasgow	0 7028 2787 8	£2.99
Glasgow Colour	0 7028 2788 6	£3.99
Leeds Colour	0 7028 2418 6	£3.25
Luton and Dunstable	0 7028 2367 8	£1.99
Merseyside	0 7028 2681 2	£3.99
York Colour	0 7028 2166 7	£2.50

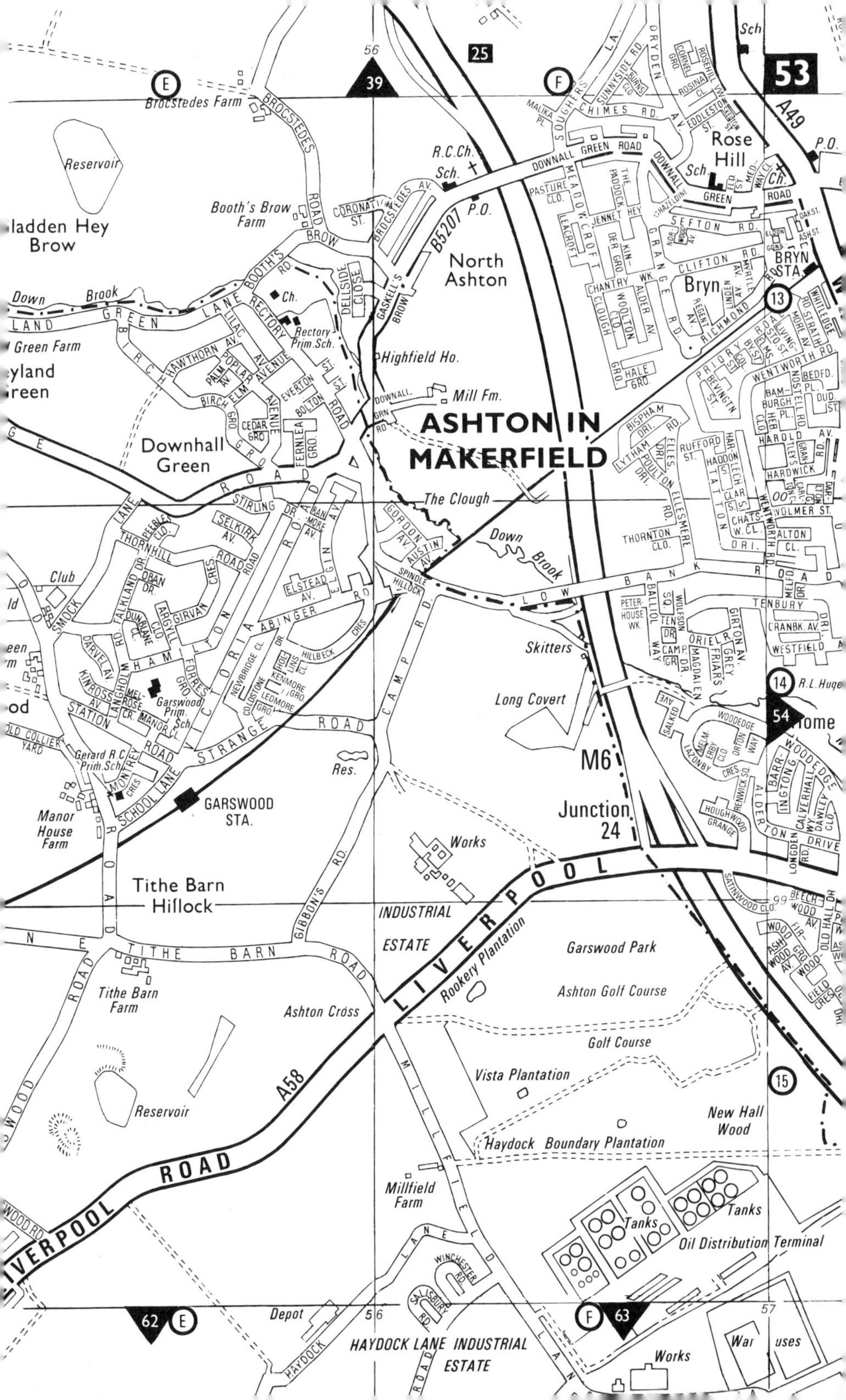

Brocstedes Farm
Reservoir
Booth's Brow Farm
Gladden Hey Brow
Down Brook
Downhall Green
ASHTON IN MAKERFIELD
North Ashton
R.C.Ch.
Sch.
P.O.
B5207
Highfield Ho.
Mill Fm.
The Clough
Rectory Prim.Sch.
Ch.
Rose Hill
Bryn
BRYN STA.
A49
DOWNALL GREEN ROAD
CHIMES RD.
SOUGHERS
SEFTON RD.
CLIFTON RD.
RICHMOND RD.
GRANGE RD.
WENTWORTH RD.
LOW BANK ROAD
TENBURY DRI.
WESTFIELD
Skitters
Long Covert
M6
Junction 24
Club
SMOCK
Garswood Prim. Sch.
GARSWOOD STA.
STATION ROAD
SCHOOL LANE
STRANGE ROAD
VICTORIA ROAD
HAMILTON
ABINGER RD.
CAMP RD.
Res.
Works
Gerard R.C. Prim.Sch.
Manor House Farm
Tithe Barn Hillock
TITHE BARN ROAD
GIBBON'S RD.
Tithe Barn Farm
INDUSTRIAL ESTATE
Ashton Cross
LIVERPOOL ROAD
A58
Rookery Plantation
Garswood Park
Ashton Golf Course
Golf Course
Vista Plantation
Haydock Boundary Plantation
New Hall Wood
Reservoir
MILLFIELD LANE
Millfield Farm
Tanks
Oil Distribution Terminal
WINCHESTER RD.
SALISBURY RD.
Depot
HAYDOCK LANE INDUSTRIAL ESTATE
HAYDOCK
Works
War uses
56
57
25
39
62
63
54
13
14
15
E
F

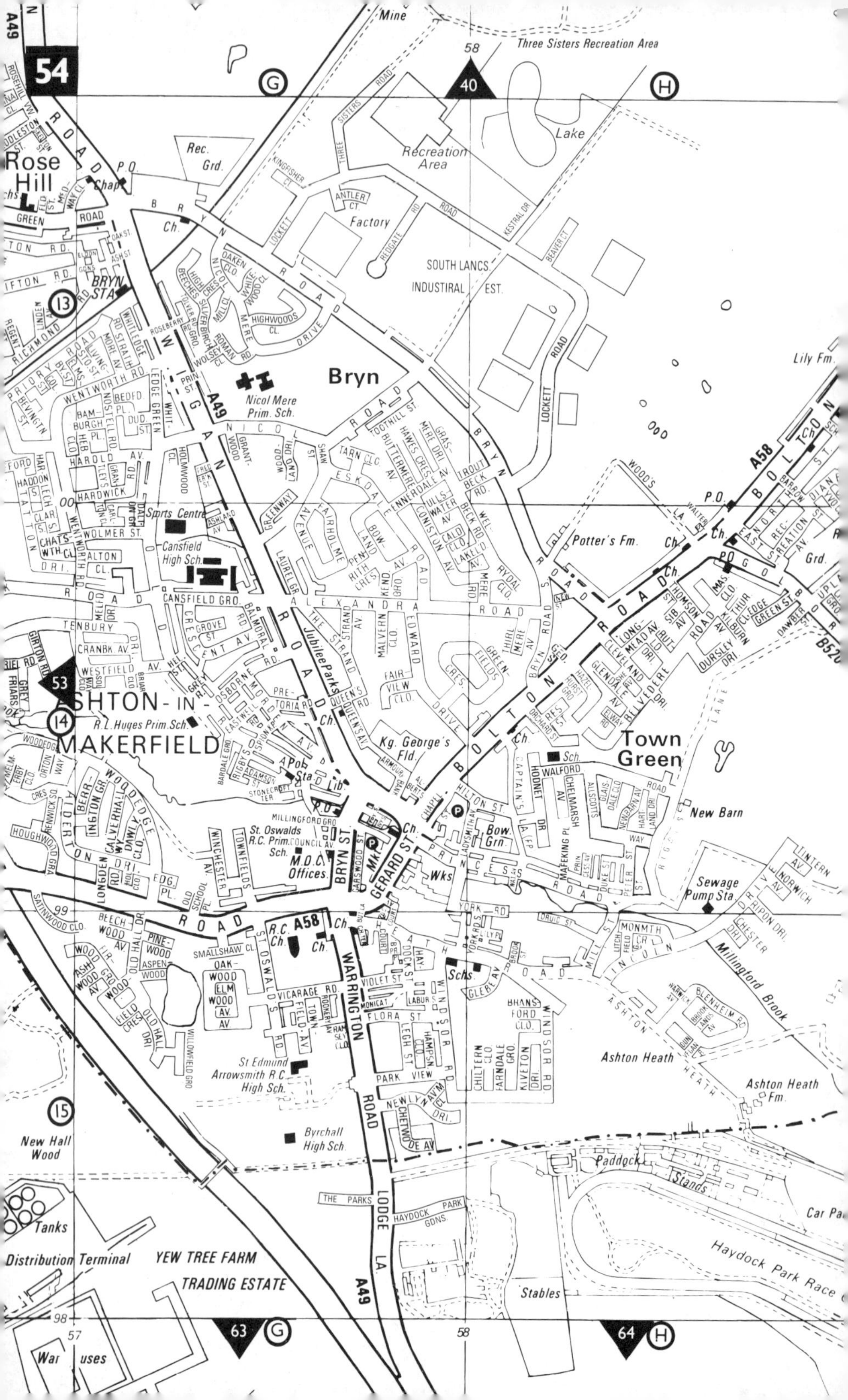

Three Sisters Recreation Area
Mine
Lake
Recreation Area
Factory
SOUTH LANCS. INDUSTRIAL EST.
Rose Hill
Rec. Grd.
BRYN STA
Bryn
Nicol Mere Prim. Sch.
Sports Centre
Cansfield High Sch.
Lily Fm.
Potter's Fm.
Town Green
New Barn
Sewage Pump Sta.
ASHTON-IN-MAKERFIELD
R.L. Huges Prim. Sch.
Jubilee Park
Kg. George's Fld.
St. Oswalds R.C. Prim. Sch.
M.D.C. Offices
Wks
Bow. Grn.
Millingford Brook
Ashton Heath
Ashton Heath Fm.
St Edmund Arrowsmith R.C. High Sch.
Byrchall High Sch.
New Hall Wood
Tanks
Distribution Terminal
YEW TREE FARM TRADING ESTATE
Paddock
Stands
Car Pa
Haydock Park Race C
Stables
War uses
BRYN ROAD
WIGAN ROAD
BOLTON ROAD
WARRINGTON ROAD
LODGE LA.
ALEXANDRA ROAD
GERARD ST.
BRYN ST.
LOCKETT ROAD
A49
A58
B520
40
53
63
64
13
14
15
57
58
98
99

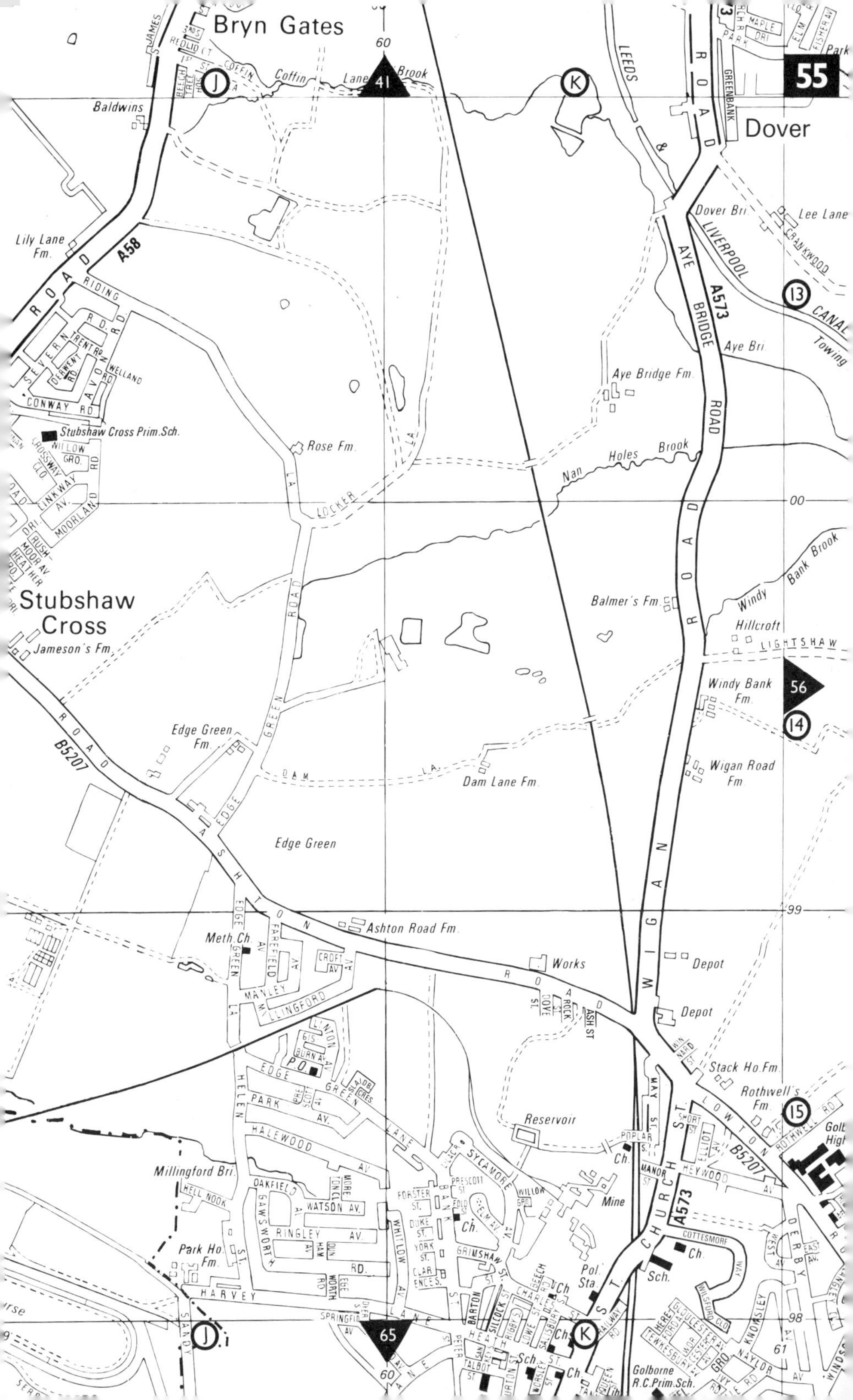

55
Bryn Gates
Dover
Baldwins
Coffin Lane Brook
41
LEEDS & LIVERPOOL CANAL
ROAD
Park
MAPLE DRI
ELM AV
FISHER AV
GREENBANK
Dover Bri.
Lee Lane
CRANKWOOD
13
Towing
Lily Lane Fm.
A58
ROAD
RIDING
SEVERN
TRENT RD.
DERWENT RD.
AVON RD.
WELLAND
CONWAY RD.
Stubshaw Cross Prim. Sch.
WILLOW GRO.
CROSSWAY CLO.
LINKWAY AV.
MOORLAND RD
RUSHMOOR AV.
HEATHER
Stubshaw Cross
Jameson's Fm.
Rose Fm.
LOCKER LA
AYE BRIDGE ROAD
A573
Aye Bri.
Aye Bridge Fm.
Nan Holes Brook
00
Windy Bank Brook
Balmer's Fm.
Hillcroft
LIGHTSHAW
Windy Bank Fm.
56
14
Wigan Road Fm.
GREEN ROAD
Edge Green Fm.
DAM LA.
Dam Lane Fm.
B5207
ROAD
ASHTON ROAD
Edge Green
99
Meth. Ch.
EDGE GREEN LA
FAIRFIELD AV
Ashton Road Fm.
CROFT AV
MANLEY AV
MILLINGFORD
Works
Depot
DOVE ST.
ROCK
ASH ST
WIGAN ROAD
WINNARD ST.
Stack Ho. Fm.
L'NTON AV
BURN AV
P.O.
EDGE GREEN LANE
HELEN
PARK AV.
PRESCOTT
Reservoir
Rothwell's Fm.
15
LOWTON ROTHWELL RD
Golb High
HALEWOOD AV
SYCAMORE
POPLAR ST.
Ch.
MAY ST.
SHORT ST
ELLIOT AV
Millingford Bri.
HELL NOOK
OAKFIELD
GAWSWORTH
WATSON AV.
RINGLEY AV.
FORSTER ST.
BANK ST.
DUKE ST.
YORK ST.
CLARENCES ST.
GRIMSHAW ST.
ELM AV.
WILLOW GRO
Mine
MANOR ST
HEYWOOD AV
B5207
CHURCH ST.
A573
Park Ho. Fm.
HARVEY ST.
RD.
WHITLOW AV
BARTON
SILCOCK ST.
RIGBY'S
LOWE ST
CHARLES ST
SALISBURY ST.
Pol. Sta.
Sch.
COTTESMORE WAY
WILSFORD CLO
WEST AV
EAST AV.
DERBY RD
98
SANDY
J
K
SPRINGFIELD AV
65
LANE
PETER
HEATH
TALBOT ST.
BURTON ST.
WORSLEY ST.
QUEEN
RAILWAY RD
Golborne R.C. Prim. Sch.
HEREFORD
GLOUCESTER AV
TEWKESBURY
KNOWSLEY
NAYLOR AV
IVY RD
61
WINDSOR
60

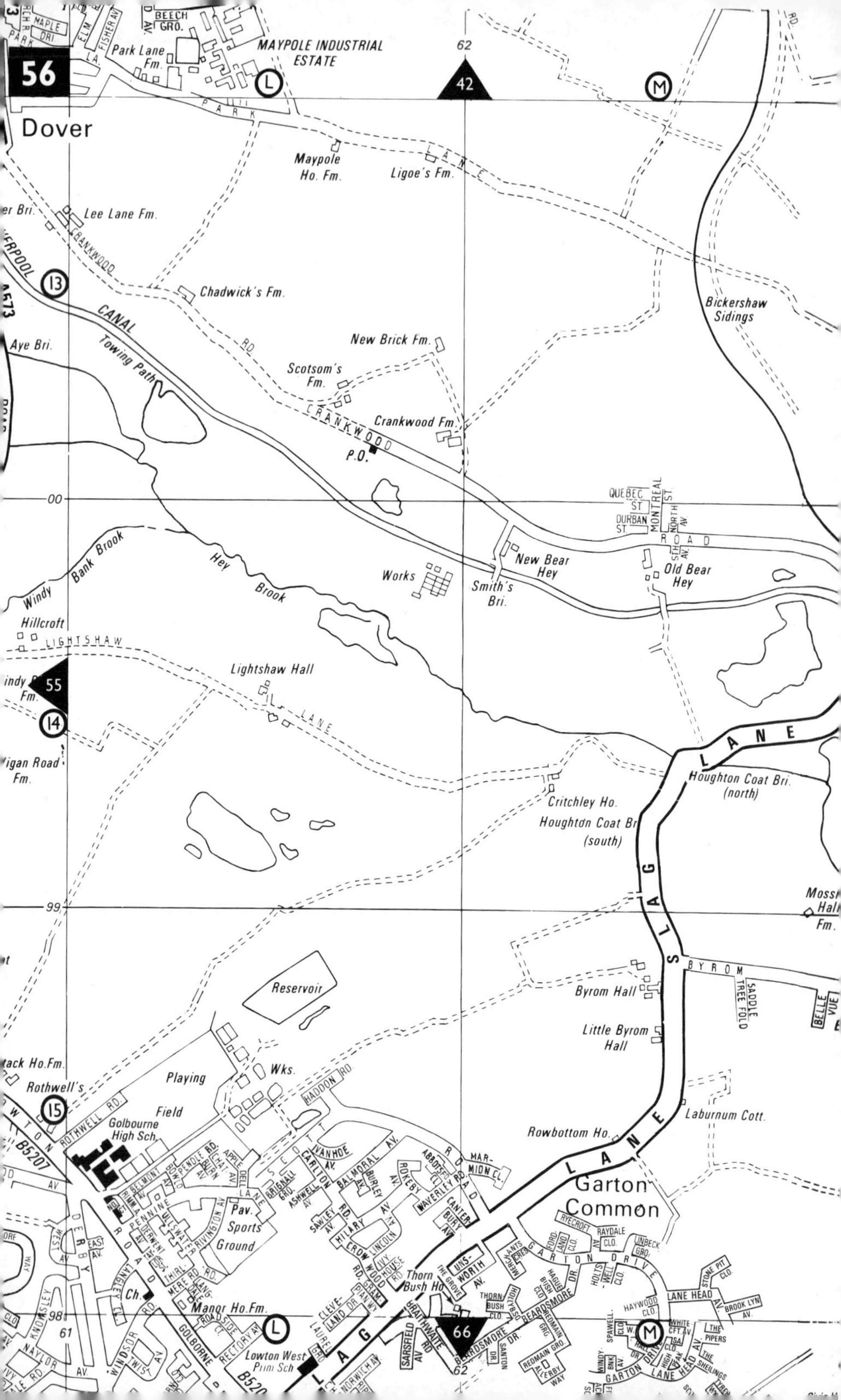
Dover
MAYPOLE INDUSTRIAL ESTATE
Park Lane Fm.
BEECH GRO.
MAPLE DRI.
ELM
FISHER AV.
62
42
PARK
LANE
Maypole Ho. Fm.
Ligoe's Fm.
Lee Lane Fm.
CRANKWOOD
13
A573
CANAL
Towing Path
Chadwick's Fm.
Aye Bri.
RD.
New Brick Fm.
Scotsom's Fm.
CRANKWOOD
Crankwood Fm.
P.O.
Bickershaw Sidings
00
QUEBEC ST.
DURBAN ST.
MONTREAL ST.
NORTH AV.
STH. AV.
ROAD
New Bear Hey
Old Bear Hey
Works
Smith's Bri.
Windy Bank Brook
Hey Brook
Hillcroft
LIGHTSHAW
Lightshaw Hall
LANE
55
14
Wigan Road Fm.
LANE
Houghton Coat Bri. (north)
Critchley Ho.
Houghton Coat Bri. (south)
SLAG
99
Moss Hall Fm.
BYROM
SADDLE TREE FOLD
BELLE VUE
Byrom Hall
Little Byrom Hall
Reservoir
Wks.
Playing Field
Rothwell's
15
ROTHWELL RD.
Golbourne High Sch.
B5207
HADDON RD.
SCOTT
IVANHOE AV.
CARLTON
BALMORAL AV.
ROAD
MARMION CL.
Laburnum Cott.
Rowbottom Ho.
LANE
Garton Common
BELMONT
PENNINE
ULLSWATER
RIVINGTON AV.
PENDLE RD.
APPLE DEL LANE
BRIGNALL GRO.
ASHWELL AV.
BURLEY AV.
ROKEBY
ABBOTSFORD CL.
WAVERLEY RD.
CANTERBURY AV.
Pav.
Sports Ground
DERBY
ROAD
EAST AV.
WEST AV.
SAWLEY AV.
HILARY
CROW WOOD RD.
LINCOLN AV.
IVY HOUSE RD.
Thorn Bush Ho.
THE GROVE
UNSWORTH AV.
THORN BUSH CLO.
HOLTBY GRO.
RYECROFT
RAYDALE CLO.
LINBECK GRO.
GARTON DRIVE
FORDLAND CLO.
BEARDSMORE DR.
HOLTSWELL CLO.
STONE PIT CLO.
LANE HEAD AV.
BROOK LYN AV.
HAYWOOD CLO.
Ch.
THIRLMERE RD.
Manor Ho.Fm.
ROADSIDE CT.
RECTORY AV.
GOLBORNE
KNOWSLEY
NAYLOR
WINDSOR
98
61
Lowton West Prim Sch.
B520
SLAG
CLEVELAND DR.
SARSFIELD AV.
BRAITHWAITE RD.
66
SANTON
REDMAIN GRO.
ALVERBY WAY
WHITE CFT. AV.
THE PIPERS
THE SHEILINGS
GARTON
LANE HEAD AV.
Rack Ho.Fm.

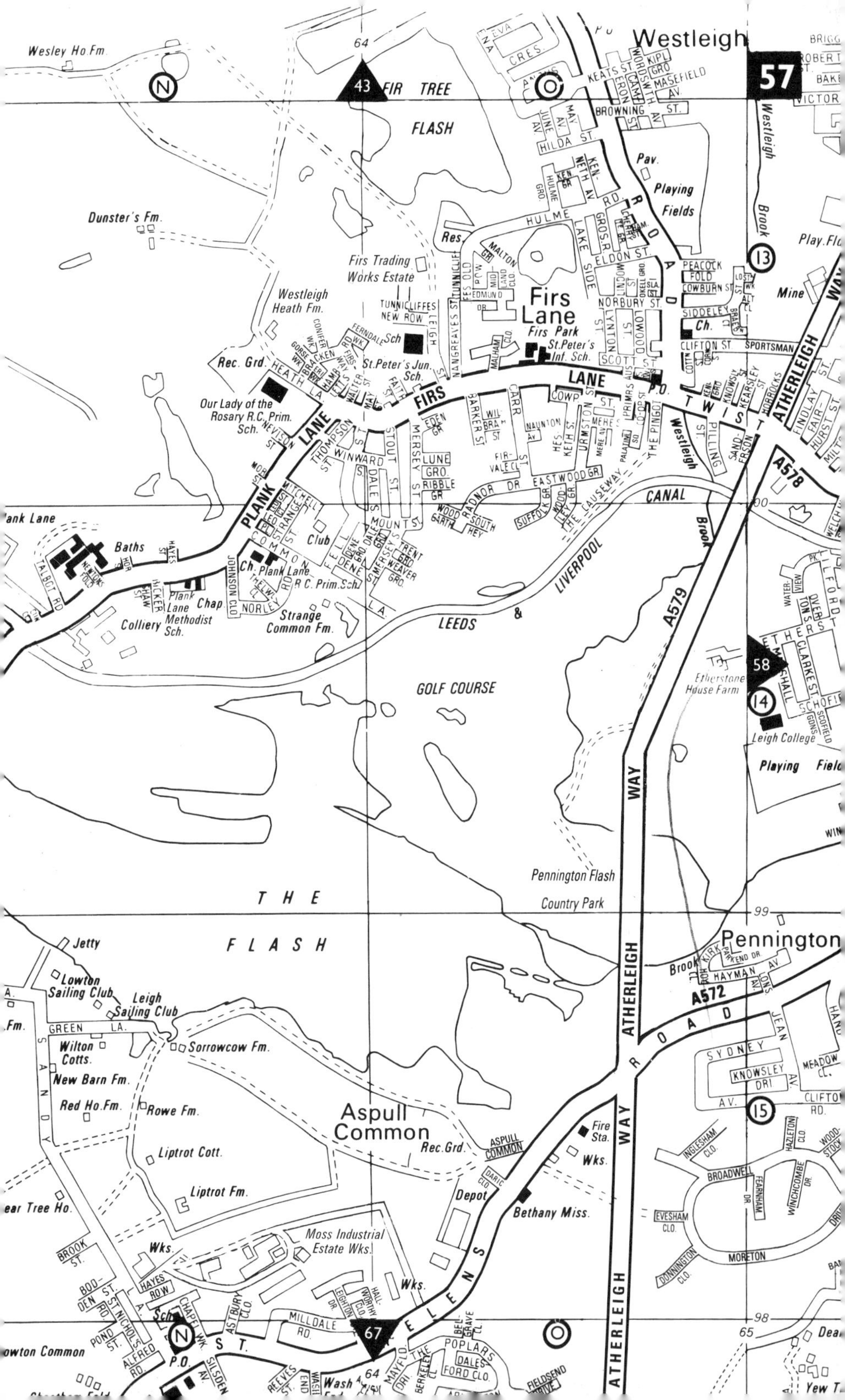

57
Westleigh
Wesley Ho.Fm.
64
43
FIR TREE
FLASH
EVA
CRES.
KEATS ST.
WORDSWORTH AV.
KIPL
GRO
MASEFIELD AV.
BROWNING ST.
JUNE AV.
MAY AV.
HILDA ST.
KEN-NETH AV.
HULME GRO.
HULME RD.
Pav.
Playing Fields
Westleigh Brook
Play.Fld
13
Dunster's Fm.
Res.
MALTON GR.
LAKE SIDE
GROS.R.
ELDON ST.
ROAD
Firs Trading Works Estate
PEACOCK FOLD
COWBURN ST.
Mine
Westleigh Heath Fm.
TUNNICLIFFES NEW ROW
NANGREAVES ST.
EDMUND DR.
Firs Lane
Firs Park
NORBURY ST.
LYNTON ST.
LOWOOD ST.
SIDDELEY ST.
Ch.
Sch
LEIGH ST.
St.Peter's Inf. Sch.
St.Peter's Jun. Sch.
MALHAM CLO.
SCOTT ST.
CLIFTON ST.
SPORTSMAN
ATHERLEIGH WAY
Rec. Grd.
HEATH LA.
FIRS LANE
P.O.
TWIST
KNOWSLEY
KEARSLEY ST.
HORROCKS
FINDLAY
FAIRHURST ST.
Our Lady of the Rosary R.C. Prim. Sch.
NEVISON ST.
PLANK LANE
THOMPSON ST.
WINWARD ST.
STOUT ST.
MERSEY ST.
BARKER ST.
WILBRAHAM ST.
CARR ST.
EDEN GR.
LUNE GRO.
RIBBLE GR.
NAUNTON AV.
HESKETH ST.
URMSTON ST.
COWP ST.
PRIMRS
THE PINGOT
Westleigh
PILLING ST.
SANDERSON
A578
FIR-VALE CL.
RADNOR DR
EASTWOOD GR.
SUFFOLK GR.
WOODLEY GR.
THE CAUSEWAY
CANAL
WOOD GARTH
SOUTH HEY
MOUNTS
DALE ST.
Brook
Plank Lane
Baths
HAYES ST.
TALBOT RD
MITCHELL
STRANGE ST.
COMMON
Club
FELL
DENE
TRENT GRO
WEAVER GRO.
LIVERPOOL
A579
Ch.
Plank Lane R.C. Prim.Sch.
JOHNSON CLO
THELWL RD
NORLEY
Plank Lane Methodist Sch.
Chap
Colliery
Strange Common Fm.
LEEDS
&
LA.
58
Etherstone House Farm
14
CLARKE ST.
SCHOFIELD
Leigh College
Playing Fields
GOLF COURSE
WAY
Pennington Flash
Country Park
THE
FLASH
99
Pennington
Jetty
Lowton Sailing Club
Leigh Sailing Club
Brook
PARKEND DR.
HAYMAN AV.
A572
ROAD
ATHERLEIGH WAY
GREEN LA.
SANDY
Wilton Cotts.
Sorrowcow Fm.
New Barn Fm.
SYDNEY
KNOWSLEY DRI.
MEADOW CL.
CLIFTON RD.
Red Ho.Fm.
Rowe Fm.
Aspull Common
Fire Sta.
15
Liptrot Cott.
Rec.Grd.
ASPULL COMMON
Wks.
INGLESHAM CLO.
HAZLETON CLO.
WOODSTOCK
Liptrot Fm.
DARIC CLO.
Depot
BROADWELL
FEARNHAM DR.
WINCHCOMBE DR.
Pear Tree Ho.
Bethany Miss.
EVESHAM CLO.
Moss Industrial Estate Wks.
BROOK ST.
Wks.
MORETON
DONINGTON CLO.
HAYES ROW
Wks.
BODDEN ST.
ST NICHOL'S RD.
CHAPEL WK.
ASTBURY CLO.
LEIGHTON DR.
HALLWORTHY CLO.
ST. HELENS
MILLDALE RD.
67
BELGRAVE CL.
98
65
POND ST.
ALFRED RD.
Sch
P.O.
ST.
Lowton Common
SILSDEN AV.
REEVES
Wash
64
MAYFLO DRI.
THE BERKELEY CL.
POPLARS
DALESFORD CLO.
FIELDSEND DRIVE
Yew T

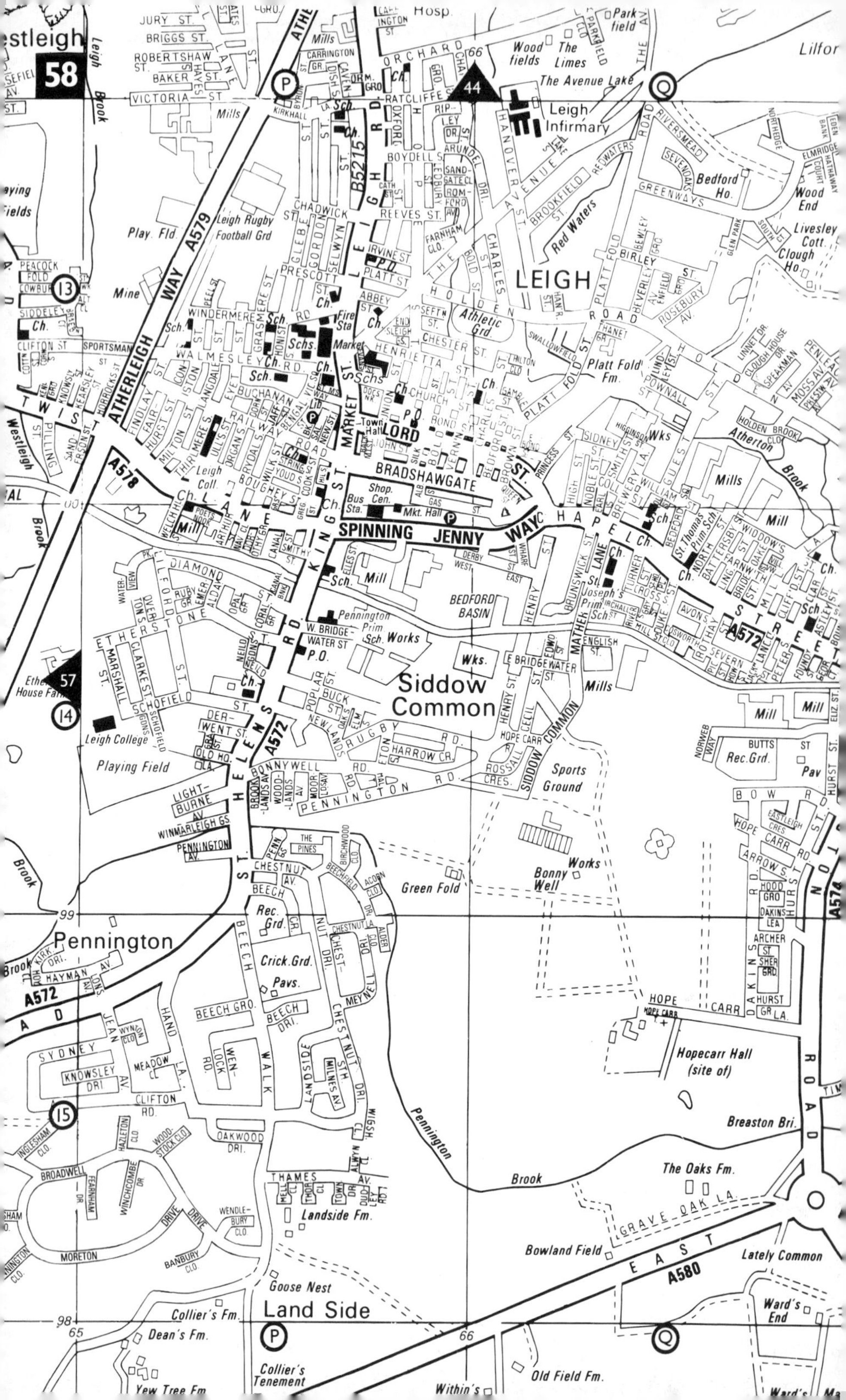
58
Westleigh
44
57
LEIGH
Leigh Infirmary
The Avenue Lake
Wood fields
The Limes
Park field
Lilford
Bedford Ho.
Wood End
Livesley Cott.
Clough Ho.
Red Waters
Athletic Grd.
Platt Fold Fm.
Atherton Brook
Mills
Mill
Leigh Rugby Football Grd
Play. Fld.
Mine
A579
ATHERLEIGH WAY
A578
A572
A574
A580
B5215
LEIGH RD
Leigh Coll.
Town Hall
BRADSHAWGATE
SPINNING JENNY WAY
CHAPEL STREET
Shop. Cen.
Bus Sta.
Mkt. Hall
BEDFORD BASIN
Siddow Common
Wks.
Pennington Prim. Sch.
Works
St. Joseph's Prim. Sch.
St. Thomas Prim. Sch.
Leigh College
Playing Field
Sports Ground
Bonny Well
Green Fold
Rec. Grd.
Crick. Grd.
Pavs.
Pennington
Pennington Brook
Hopecarr Hall (site of)
Breaston Bri.
The Oaks Fm.
GRAVE OAK LA.
Landside Fm.
Bowland Field
EAST LANCASHIRE ROAD
Lately Common
Ward's End
Goose Nest
Land Side
Collier's Fm.
Dean's Fm.
Collier's Tenement
Yew Tree Fm.
Old Field Fm.
Within's
ST. HELENS RD.
KING ST.
MARKET ST.
LORD ST.
HOLDEN ROAD
PENNINGTON RD.
RUGBY RD.
BUTTS ST
Rec.Grd.
Pav
HOPE CARR
BEECH WALK
CHESTNUT DRI.
LANDSIDE
MORETON
BROADWELL DR
99
98
65
66
13
14
15

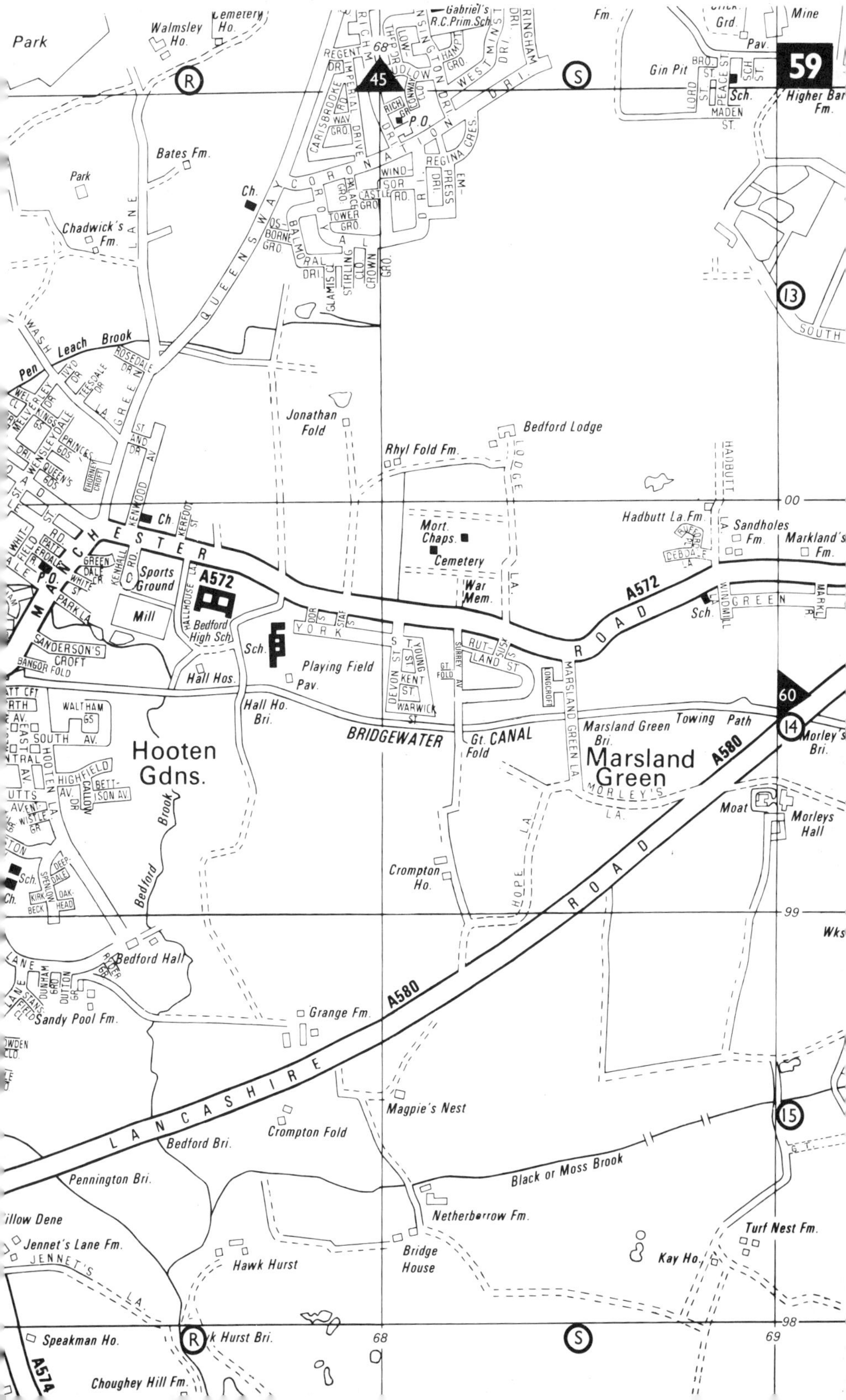

Park
Walmsley Ho.
Cemetery Ho.
Gabriel's R.C.Prim.Sch.
Fm.
Crick. Grd.
Mine
Pav.
Gin Pit
Sch.
Higher Bar Fm.
MADEN ST.
PEACE ST.
LORD ST.
68
45
REGENT DR.
IMPERIAL DRIVE
CARISBROOKE RD.
WAV GRO.
LUDLOW
CONWAY
P.O.
RINGHAM
WEST MINST DRI.
REGINA CRES.
EMPRESS DRI.
CORONATION DRI.
WINDSOR RD.
CASTLE GRO.
TOWER GRO.
BALMORAL DRI.
OSBORNE GRO.
GLAMIS CL.
STIRLING CLO.
CROWN GRO.
Bates Fm.
Ch.
Chadwick's Fm.
QUEENSWAY
LANE
13
SOUTH
Leach Brook
Pen
WASH
ROSEDALE DR.
TEESDALE DR.
GREEN LA.
KINGS GS.
WENSLEYDALE DRI.
PRINCES GDS.
QUEEN'S GDS.
THORNEY CROFT
KENWOOD AV.
KERFOOT ST.
Ch.
Jonathan Fold
Bedford Lodge
Rhyl Fold Fm.
LODGE LA.
HADBUTT LA.
00
Hadbutt La. Fm.
Sandholes Fm.
Markland's Fm.
DEBDALE LA.
Mort. Chaps.
Cemetery
War Mem.
MANCHESTER ROAD
A572
A572
Sch.
WINDMILL LA.
GREEN
P.O.
PARK LA.
Sports Ground
Mill
HALLHOUSE LA.
Bedford High Sch.
Sch.
YORK ST.
Playing Field
Pav.
YOUNG ST.
KENT ST.
DEVON ST.
WARWICK ST.
SURREY AV.
RUTLAND ST.
SUSSEX
GT. FOLD
LONGCROFT
SANDERSON'S CROFT
BANGOR FOLD
Hall Hos.
Hall Ho. Bri.
WALTHAM GS.
SOUTH AV.
HOOTEN LA.
HIGHFIELD AV.
CALLOW DR.
BETTISON AV.
Hooten Gdns.
BRIDGEWATER
Gt. Fold
CANAL
MARSLAND GREEN LA.
Marsland Green Bri.
Towing Path
Marsland Green
60
14
Morley's Bri.
A580
MORLEY'S LA.
Moat
Morleys Hall
Bedford Brook
Crompton Ho.
HOPE LA.
ROAD
99
Wks
Sch.
Ch.
DEEPDALE
KIRKBECK
OAKHEAD
Bedford Hall
DUNHAM GRO.
DUTTON GR.
Sandy Pool Fm.
Grange Fm.
A580
LANCASHIRE
Magpie's Nest
Crompton Fold
15
Bedford Bri.
Pennington Bri.
Black or Moss Brook
Willow Dene
Netherbarrow Fm.
Turf Nest Fm.
Jennet's Lane Fm.
JENNET'S LA.
Hawk Hurst
Bridge House
Kay Ho.
98
Speakman Ho.
Hawk Hurst Bri.
68
69
A574
Choughey Hill Fm.

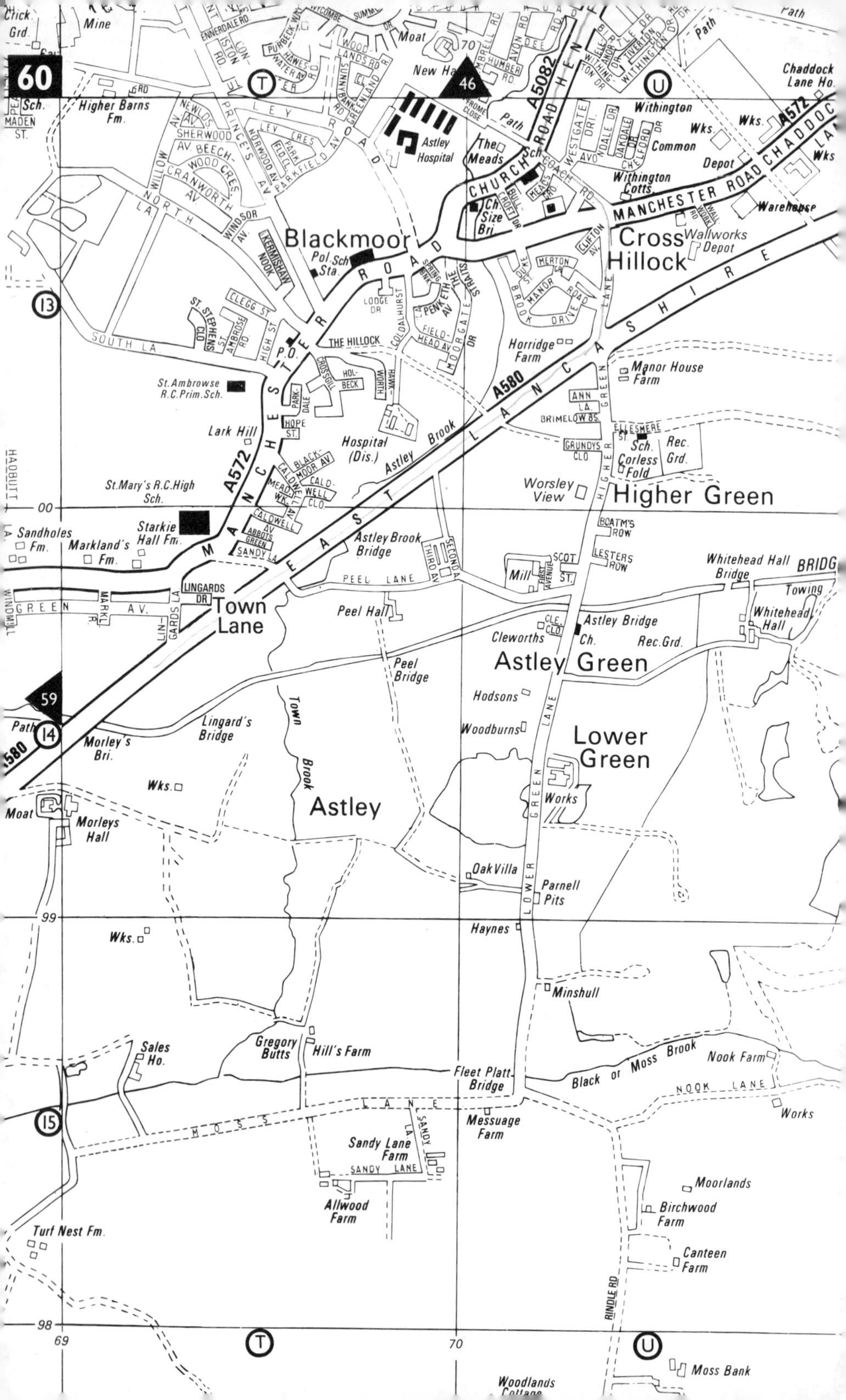

60
46
59
13
14
15
T
U
Mine
Moat
New Hall
Higher Barns Fm.
Sch.
MADEN ST.
ENNERDALE RD.
PURBECK WAY
HAWES WATER AV.
WOODLANDS RD.
SUNNYBANK RD.
GREENLAND RD.
AVON RD.
DEE RD.
HUMBER RD.
FROME CLOSE
Path
A5082
CHURCH ROAD
WESTGATE DRI.
AVONDALE DR.
OAKDALE DR.
CHELFORD DR.
Withington
Withington Common
Withington Cotts.
Chaddock Lane Ho.
Wks.
Depot
A572
CHADDOCK LA.
MANCHESTER ROAD
Warehouse
Wallworks Depot
Cross Hillock
SHERWOOD AV.
BEECH WOOD CRES.
CRANWORTH AV.
WILLOW AV.
NEWLANDS AV.
PRINCES AV.
NORWOOD AV.
LEY CRES
PARK FIELD CL.
PARKFIELD AV.
NORTH LA.
WINDSOR AV.
KERMISHAW NOOK
Astley Hospital
The Meads
Sch.
Ch.
Size Bri.
BULLCROFT DR.
MEADS GRO.
COACH RD.
Blackmoor
Pol. Sta.
Sch.
ROAD
SPRING BANK
PENKETH AV.
THE STRAITS
MERTON GR.
DUKE ST.
MANOR ROAD
BROOK DRIVE
CLIFTON AV.
LANE
CLEGG ST.
ST. STEPHENS CLO.
ST. AMBROSE RD.
HIGH ST.
SOUTH LA.
P.O.
THE HILLOCK
LODGE DR.
COLDALHURST
FIELDHEAD AV.
MOORGATE DR.
Horridge Farm
Manor House Farm
A580
EAST LANCASHIRE
CROSSGILL
HOLBECK
HAWKWORTH
PARKDALE
HOPE ST.
St. Ambrowse R.C. Prim. Sch.
Lark Hill
Hospital (Dis.)
Astley Brook
BLACKMOOR AV.
CALDWELL AV.
CALDWELL CLO.
MEADOW WK.
CALDWELL AV.
ABBOTS GREEN
SANDY LA.
A572
MANCHESTER
ANN LA.
BRIMELOW BS.
GREEN
ELLESMERE ST.
GRUNDYS CLO.
Sch.
Corless Fold
Rec. Grd.
Worsley View
HIGHER
Higher Green
HADBUTT LA.
St. Mary's R.C. High Sch.
00
Sandholes Fm.
Markland's Fm.
Starkie Hall Fm.
Astley Brook Bridge
THIRD AV
SECOND AV
BOATM'S ROW
LESTERS ROW
Mill
FIRST AVENUE
SCOT ST.
Whitehead Hall Bridge
BRIDG
Towing
Whitehead Hall
WINDMILL
GREEN AV.
MARKLAND R.
LINGARDS LA
LINGARDS DR.
Town Lane
PEEL LANE
Peel Hall
CLE. CLO.
Cleworths
Astley Bridge
Ch.
Rec. Grd.
Astley Green
Peel Bridge
Town Brook
Hodsons
Woodburns
LANE
Lower Green
Path
A580
Lingard's Bridge
Morley's Bri.
Wks.
Astley
Works
Moat
Morleys Hall
LOWER GREEN
Oak Villa
Parnell Pits
99
Wks.
Haynes
Minshull
Sales Ho.
Gregory Butts
Hill's Farm
Fleet Platt Bridge
Black or Moss Brook
Nook Farm
NOOK LANE
Works
MOSS LANE
SANDY LA
Messuage Farm
Sandy Lane Farm
SANDY LANE
Allwood Farm
Moorlands
Birchwood Farm
Turf Nest Fm.
Canteen Farm
RINDLE RD
98
69
70
Moss Bank
Woodlands Cottage

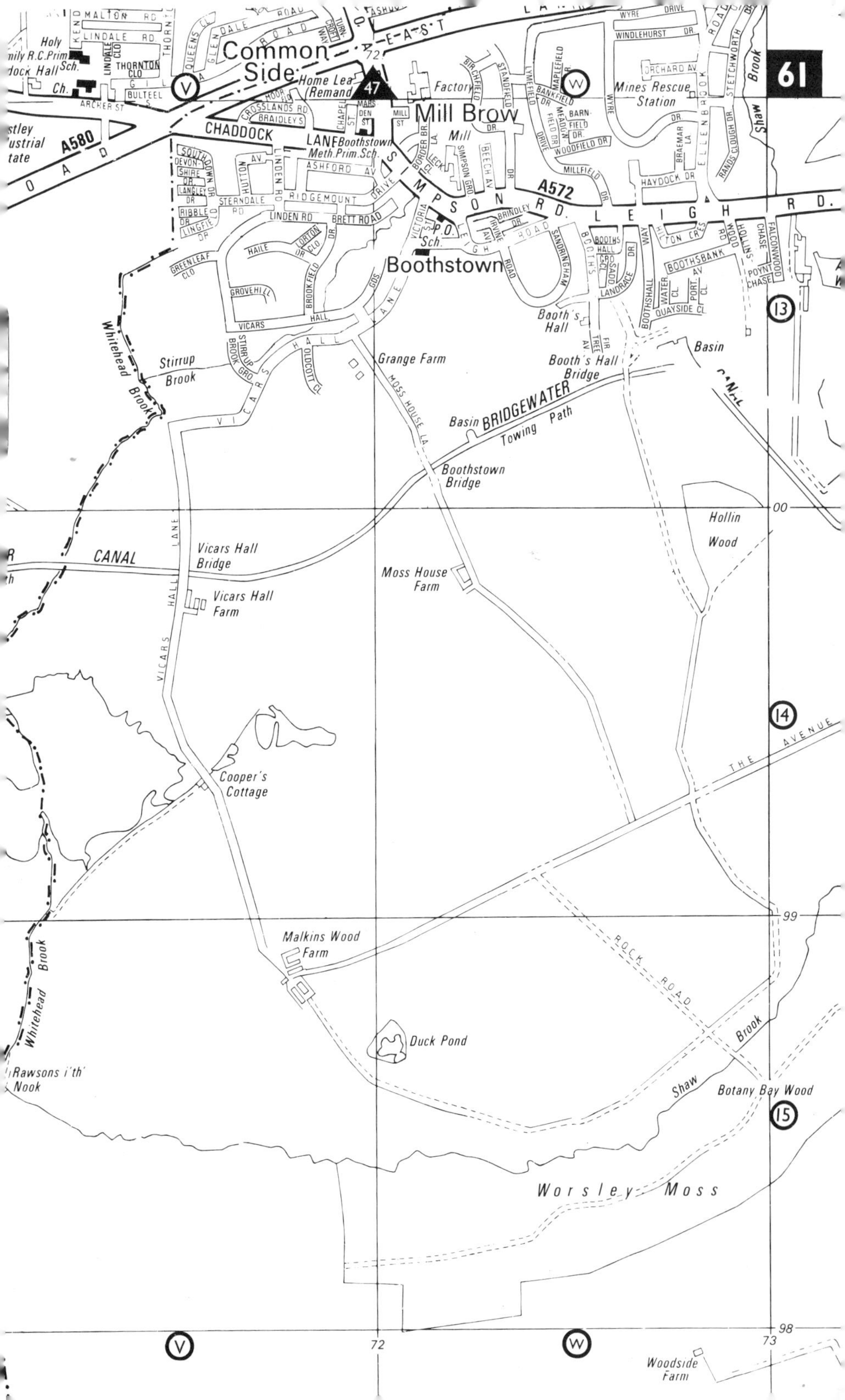
Common Side
Mill Brow
Boothstown
Holy Family R.C.Prim Sch.
Haydock Hall
Ch.
Home Lea (Remand
47
Factory
Mines Rescue Station
Mill
Boothstown Meth.Prim.Sch.
P.O.
Sch.
Booth's Hall
Basin
Booth's Hall Bridge
BRIDGEWATER
Towing Path
Boothstown Bridge
Stirrup Brook
Whitehead Brook
Grange Farm
MOSS HOUSE LA.
Hollin Wood
CANAL
Vicars Hall Bridge
Moss House Farm
Vicars Hall Farm
VICARS HALL LANE
Cooper's Cottage
THE AVENUE
Malkins Wood Farm
ROCK ROAD
Duck Pond
Shaw Brook
Botany Bay Wood
Rawsons i'th' Nook
Worsley Moss
Woodside Farm
A580
A572
CHADDOCK LANE
SIMPSON RD.
LEIGH RD.
MALTON RD
LINDALE RD.
THORNTON CLO
BULTEEL S.
ARCHER ST
CROSSLANDS RD
BRAIDLEY S.
WYRE DRIVE
WINDLEHURST DR.
ORCHARD AV.
STETCHWORTH
HAYDOCK DR
MILLFIELD DR
WOODFIELD DR
ASHFORD AV
RIDGEMOUNT DRIVE
STERNDALE RD
LINDEN RD
BRETT ROAD
HAILE
GROVEHILL
VICARS HALL GDS.
GREENLEAF CLO
OLDCOTT CL
SANDRINGHAM
BOOTHSBANK
QUAYSIDE CL
LANDRACE DR.
BRINDLEY DR.
V
W
13
14
15
72
73
00
99
98

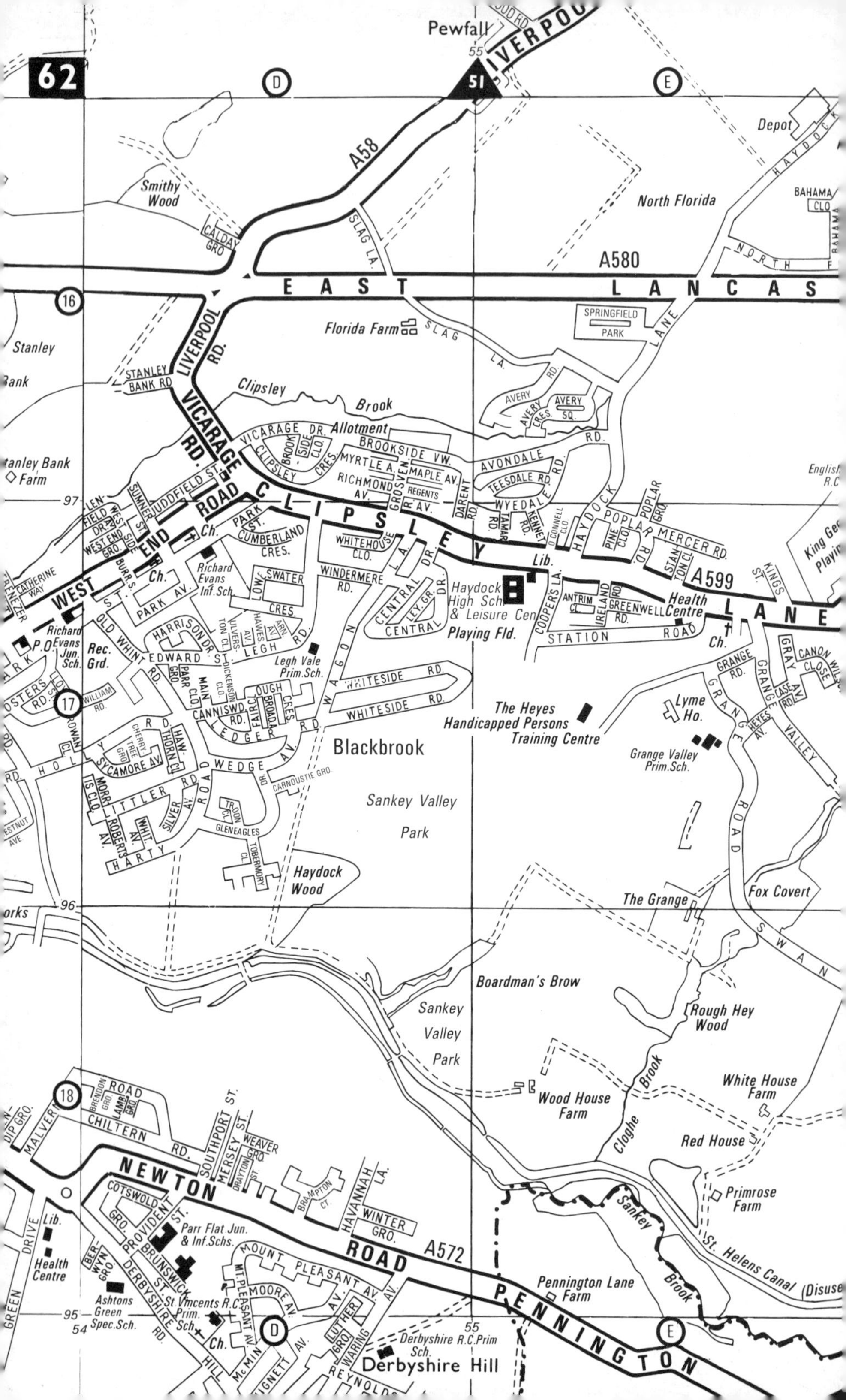
Pewfall
LIVERPOOL
51
D
E
A58
Smithy Wood
CALDAY GRO
SLAG LA.
Depot
HAYDOCK
North Florida
BAHAMA CLO
NORTH
A580
EAST LANCAS
16
Stanley Bank
LIVERPOOL RD.
Florida Farm
SLAG LA.
SPRINGFIELD PARK
LANE
STANLEY BANK RD
Clipsley Brook
AVERY RD.
AVERY CRES.
AVERY SQ.
VICARAGE RD.
Allotment
VICARAGE DR.
BROOKSIDE CLO.
BROOKSIDE VW.
CLIPSLEY CRES.
MYRTLE A.
MAPLE AV.
RICHMOND AV.
REGENTS AV.
GROSVENOR AV.
AVONDALE RD.
TEESDALE RD.
Stanley Bank Farm
English R.C
JUDDFIELD ST.
SUMNER ST.
LENFIELD DR.
WEST END GRO.
WESTSIDE
WEST END ROAD
CLIPSLEY LANE
PARK ST.
CUMBERLAND CRES.
WHITEHOUSE CLO.
DARENT RD.
TAMAR RD.
WYEDALE RD.
KENNET RD.
O'CONNELL CLO.
HAYDOCK
POPLAR RD.
POPLAR GRO.
PINE CLO.
MERCER RD.
STANTON CL.
KINGS ST.
King George Playing
Ch.
Richard Evans Inf.Sch.
BURR ST.
CATHERINE WAY
LOWESWATER CRES.
WINDERMERE RD.
CENTRAL DR.
LEY GR.
CENTRAL DR.
Haydock High Sch. & Leisure Cen.
Lib.
COOPER'S LA.
ANTRIM CL.
IRELAND RD.
GREENWELL RD.
A599
Health Centre
PARK AV.
WEST
Richard Evans Jun. Sch.
P.O.
Rec. Grd.
OLD WHINT RD.
HARRISON DR.
ULVERSTON CL.
HAWES AV.
ARN AV.
LEGH RD.
Playing Fld.
STATION ROAD
Ch.
GRAY AV.
CANON WILSON CLOSE
GRANGE RD.
Legh Vale Prim.Sch.
EDWARD ST.
PARR GRO
PARR CLO.
DICKENSON CLO.
MAIN
WAGON LA.
WHITESIDE RD.
ROUGH CRES.
BROADOAK
FAIRCL
CANNISWD RD.
LEDGER RD.
WHITESIDE RD.
LASE RD.
HEYES AV.
GRANGE VALLEY
Lyme Ho.
The Heyes Handicapped Persons Training Centre
GRANGE ROAD
Grange Valley Prim.Sch.
FOSTERS RD.
17
WILLIAM RD.
ROWAN CL.
HOLLY RD.
HAWTHORN CL.
CHERRY TREE GRO
SYCAMORE AV.
WEDGE AV.
Blackbrook
CARNOUSTIE GRO.
MORRIS CLO.
LITTLER RD.
ROAD
TROON CL
DR.
Sankey Valley Park
ROBERTS AV.
WHIT. AV.
SILVER AV.
GLENEAGLES
CHESTNUT AVE.
HARTY
TOBERMORY CL.
Haydock Wood
The Grange
Fox Covert
Works
SWAN
Boardman's Brow
Rough Hey Wood
Sankey Valley Park
Cloghe Brook
White House Farm
Wood House Farm
Red House
18
BRENDON GRO
ROAD
LAMB GRO
CHILTERN RD.
MALVERN
SOUTHPORT ST.
MERSEY ST.
WEAVER GRO
DRAYTON ST.
NEWTON ROAD
A572
BRAMPTON CT.
HAVANNAH LA.
WINTER GRO.
COTSWOLD GRO.
PROVIDENT ST.
Parr Flat Jun. & Inf.Schs.
BRUNSWICK ST.
Lib.
Health Centre
GREEN DRIVE
BERWYN GRO
DERBYSHIRE RD.
Ashtons Green Spec.Sch.
MOUNT PLEASANT AV.
MT.PLEASANT AV.
MOORE AV.
LUTHER GRO
St.Vincents R.C. Prim. Sch.
Ch.
McMIN
WARING AV.
Sankey Brook
Primrose Farm
St. Helens Canal (Disused)
Pennington Lane Farm
PENNINGTON
Derbyshire R.C.Prim Sch.
Derbyshire Hill
HILL
REYNOLDS

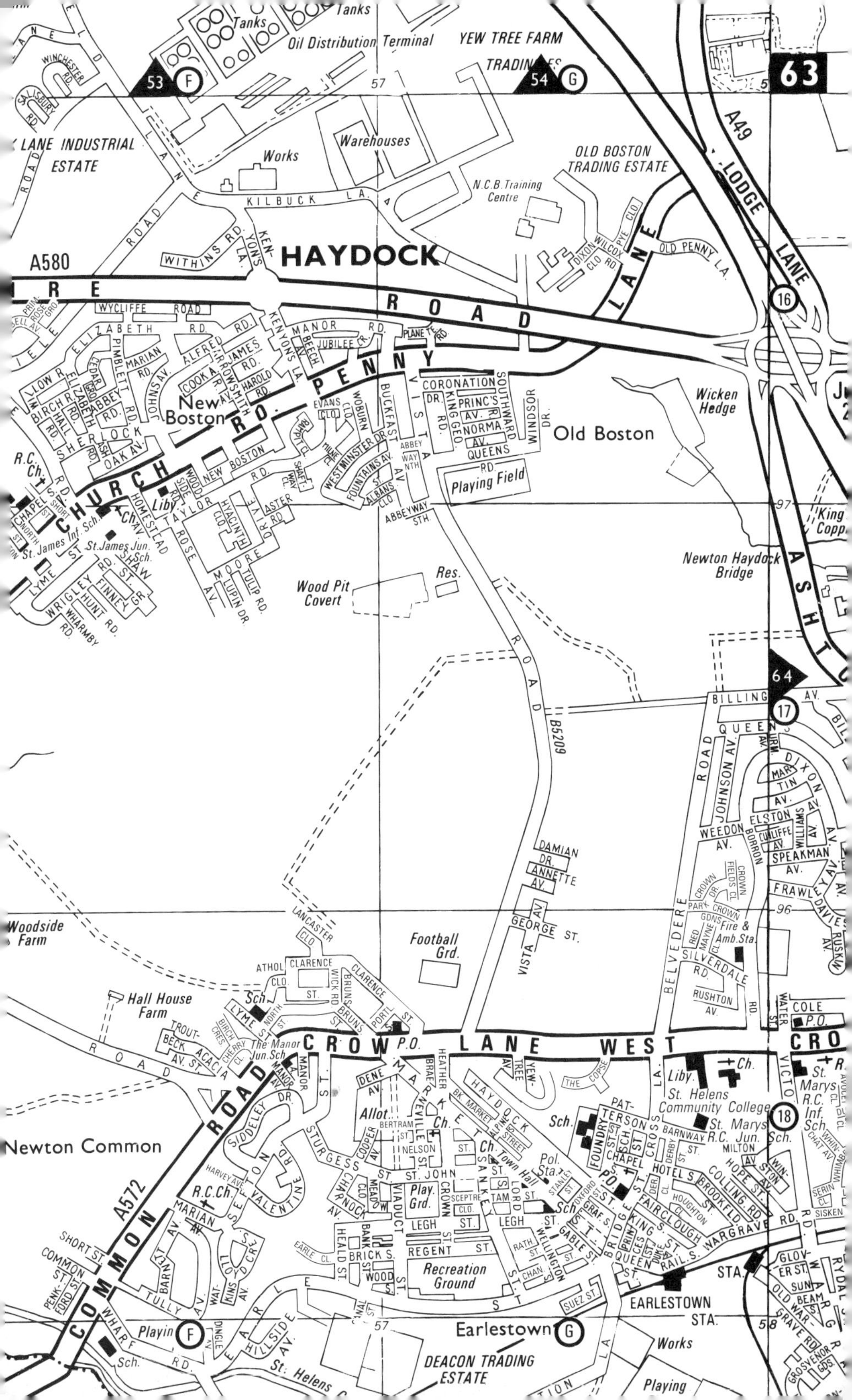
Tanks
Oil Distribution Terminal
YEW TREE FARM TRADING ES
53 F
54 G
57
WINCHESTER RD.
SALISBURY RD.
LANE INDUSTRIAL ESTATE
Warehouses
Works
KILBUCK LA.
OLD BOSTON TRADING ESTATE
N.C.B. Training Centre
A49
LODGE LANE
A580
HAYDOCK
WITHINS RD.
KENYON'S LA.
DIXON CLO.
WILCOX RD.
PYE CLO.
OLD PENNY LA.
LANE
16
ROAD
WYCLIFFE ROAD
ELIZABETH RD.
MANOR RD.
JUBILEE CR.
PLANETREE RD.
PENNY
CORONATION
SOUTHWARD
WINDSOR DR.
PRINC'S AV.
KING GEO. RD.
NORMA AV.
QUEENS RD.
Wicken Hedge
Old Boston
New Boston
PIMBLETT RD.
MARIAN RD.
JOHNS AV.
ALFRED RD.
JAMES RD.
HAROLD RD.
ARROWSMITH AV.
COOK AV.
BIRCH RD.
ELIZABETH RD.
ABBEY RD.
HALL RD.
SHERLOCK AV.
OAK AV.
CHURCH RD.
EVANS CLO.
WOBURN CLO.
BUCKFAST AV.
VISTA
WESTMINSTER DR.
FOUNTAINS AV.
ST. ALBANS CLO.
ABBEYWAY NTH.
ABBEYWAY STH.
Playing Field
NEW BOSTON
R.C. Ch.
Liby
HOMESTEAD AV.
TAYLOR
HYACINTH CLO.
DRIVE
ASTER RD.
ROSE AV.
MOORE AV.
LUPIN DR.
TULIP RD.
St. James Inf. Sch.
St. James Jun. Sch.
LYME ST.
SHAW ST.
FINNEY GR.
WRIGLEY RD.
HUNT RD.
WHARMBY RD.
97
Kings Copp
Newton Haydock Bridge
ASHTON
Wood Pit Covert
Res.
ROAD
B5209
64
17
BILLING AV.
QUEENS AV.
ROAD
JOHNSON AV.
DIXON
MARTIN AV.
WEEDON AV.
ELSTON AV.
CUNLIFFE AV.
WILLIAMS AV.
SPEAKMAN AV.
BORRON
CROWN FIELDS CL.
FRAWLEY AV.
DAVIES AV.
RUSKIN AV.
96
DAMIAN DR.
ANNETTE AV.
GEORGE ST.
VISTA AV.
BELVEDERE
Fire & Amb. Sta.
SILVERDALE RD.
RUSHTON AV.
COLE
P.O.
Woodside Farm
LANCASTER CLO.
Football Grd.
ATHOL CLO.
CLARENCE ST.
WICK RD.
BRUNS
CLARENCE
PORTL ST.
Hall House Farm
Sch.
TROUTBECK AV.
ACACIA
The Manor Jun. Sch.
CROW LANE WEST
CRO
P.O.
MANOR
DENE AV.
MARKET
HEATHER
BRAE
YEW TREE
THE COPSE
HAYDOCK STREET
ALPINE
BK. MARKET
Liby
Ch.
St. Helens Community College
St. Marys R.C. Jun. Sch.
St. Marys R.C. Inf. Sch.
18
Newton Common
ROAD
SIDDELEY DR.
STURGESS
Allot.
BERTRAM ST.
NEVILLE ST.
NELSON ST.
Ch.
Town Hall
Pol. Sta.
Sch.
FOUNDRY
PATTERSON
CHAPEL
CROSS
BARNWAY
MILTON
HOPE ST.
COLLING RD.
BROOKFLD.
HOTEL S.
FAIRCLOUGH
WARGRAVE RD.
A572
R.C. Ch.
HARVEY AVE.
SEFTON RD.
VALENTINE
MARIAN
CHARNOCK
COOPER AV.
ST. JOHN
CROWN
SANKEY
LORD
Play. Grd.
VIADUCT
LEGH ST.
REGENT ST.
BANK
BRICK S.
WOOD S.
Recreation Ground
HEALD ST.
EARLE CL.
SCEPTRE CLO.
WELLINGTON S.
CHAN. S.
GABLE ST.
BRIDGE ST.
KING S.
QUEEN ST.
RAIL S.
STA.
EARLESTOWN STA.
SHORT ST.
COMMON ST.
PENKFORD ST.
COMMON
BARN ST.
LLOYD CRES.
WATKINS AV.
TULLY AV.
EARLE
HILLSIDE AV.
SUEZ ST.
Earlestown G
Playin F
WHARF RD.
Sch.
DINGLE AV.
57
58
Works
DEACON TRADING ESTATE
St. Helens
Playing
GLOVER ST.
SUNBEAM S.
OLD WARGRAVE RD.
GROSVENOR GDS.
RYDAL
VICTORIA

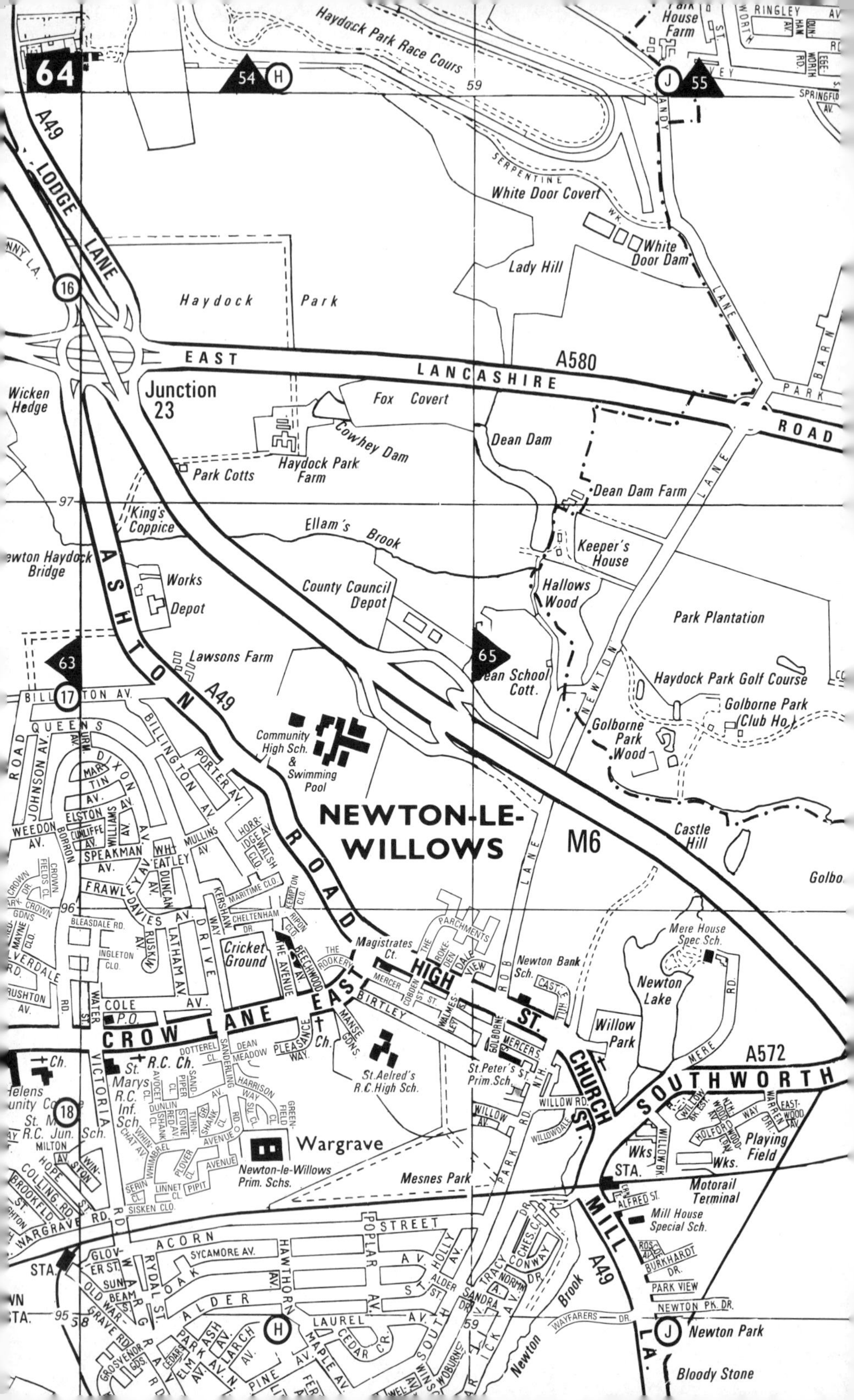
64
54
H
Haydock Park Race Cours
59
Park House Farm
RINGLEY AV.
J
55
SPRINGFLD AV.
A49
LODGE LANE
SERPENTINE WK.
White Door Covert
White Door Dam
Lady Hill
16
Haydock Park
EAST LANCASHIRE ROAD
A580
PARK
LANE
Wicken Hedge
Junction 23
Fox Covert
Cowhey Dam
Haydock Park Farm
Park Cotts
Dean Dam
Dean Dam Farm
97
King's Coppice
Ellam's Brook
Keeper's House
Newton Haydock Bridge
Works
Depot
County Council Depot
Hallows Wood
Park Plantation
63
Lawsons Farm
65
Dean School Cott.
Haydock Park Golf Course
Golborne Park (Club Ho.)
17
BILLINGTON AV.
QUEENS ROAD
ASHTON ROAD
A49
Community High Sch. & Swimming Pool
NEWTON
Golborne Park Wood
JOHNSON AV.
DIXON AV.
MARTIN AV.
BILLINGTON AV.
PORTER AV.
NEWTON-LE-WILLOWS
M6
Castle Hill
ELSTON AV.
CUNLIFFE AV.
WILLIAMS AV.
WEEDON AV.
BORRON RD.
SPEAKMAN AV.
WHEATLEY AV.
MULLINS AV.
HORRIDGE AV.
WALSH CLO.
ROB LANE
Golbo
CROWN FIELDS CL.
FRAWLEY AV.
DUNCAN AV.
KERSHAW WAY
MARITIME CLO.
KEMPTON CLO.
96
BLEASDALE RD.
DAVIES AV.
CHELTENHAM DR.
RIPON CLO.
THE PARCHMENTS
Mere House Spec. Sch.
INGLETON CLO.
RUSKIN AV.
LATHAM AV.
DRIVE
Cricket Ground
THE AVENUE
BEECHWOOD AV.
THE ROOKERY
Magistrates Ct.
ROKEDEN
DALE VIEW
Newton Bank Sch.
CASTLE HILL
Newton Lake
DERWENTDALE RD.
RUSHTON AV.
WATER ST.
COLE AV.
EAST
MERCER
COBDEN ST.
HIGH ST.
WALMESLEY
Willow Park
P.O.
CROW LANE
BIRTLEY
MANSE GDNS.
Ch.
GOLBORNE
MERCERS
ST.
CHURCH ST.
MERE
A572
SOUTHWORTH
Ch.
VICTORIA
R.C. Ch.
St. Marys R.C. Inf. Sch.
DOTTEREL CL.
SANDERLING CL.
DEAN MEADOW
PLEASANCE WAY
St. Aelred's R.C. High Sch.
St. Peter's Prim. Sch.
NTH.
St. Helens Community Co
18
St. M R.C. Jun. Sch.
HARRISON WAY
GREENFIELD
WILLOW RD.
WILLOW AV.
WILLOWDALE
PARK RD.
WILLOW BK.
HOLFORD WAY
WARREN DR.
EASTWOOD AV.
Playing Field
MILTON AV.
WINSTON
HOPE
COLLING RD.
BROOKFLD.
WARGRAVE RD.
Wargrave
Newton-le-Willows Prim. Schs.
Mesnes Park
Wks.
STA.
Motorail Terminal
Wks.
AVENUE
PLOVER CL.
PIPIT
LINNET CL.
SERIN CL.
SISKEN CLO.
ALFRED ST.
Mill House Special Sch.
MILL
POPLAR STREET
ACORN
SYCAMORE AV.
HAWTHORN AV.
HOLLY AV.
CHES. CL.
CONWAY
STA.
GLOVER ST.
SUN
BEAM ST.
RYDAL ST.
OAK
ALDER
ALDER ST.
TRACY
NORMAN DR.
Brook
A49
BURKHARDT DR.
PARK VIEW
NEWTON PK. DR.
95
58
OLD WARGRAVE RD.
LAUREL AV.
SANDRA DR.
59
WAYFARERS DR.
J
Newton Park
H
GROSVENOR GDS.
PARK AV.
ASH AV.
LARCH AV.
ELM AV.
CEDARS
CEDAR CR.
MAPLE AV.
PINE
SOUTH
WOBURN
Newton
LA.
Bloody Stone

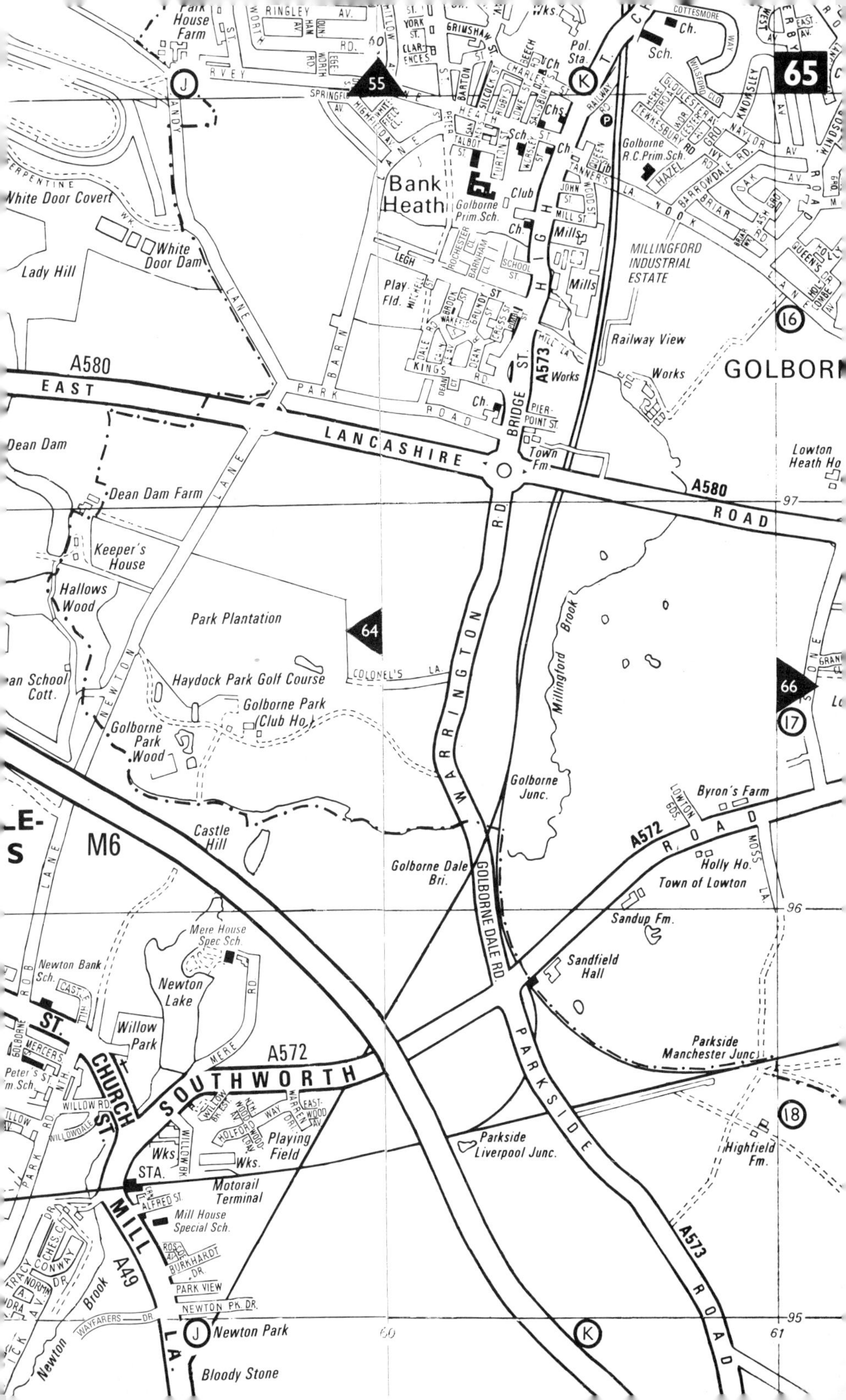
55
64
66
Park House Farm
RINGLEY AV.
YORK ST.
GRIMSHAW ST.
CLARENCES
BARTON ST.
SILCOCK ST.
CHARLES ST.
BEECH
Pol. Sta.
Ch.
Sch.
COTTESMORE WAY
WILSFORD CLO.
GLOUCESTER AV.
TEWKESBURY RD.
KNOWSLEY AV.
NAYLOR AV.
WINDSOR RD.
Golborne R.C.Prim.Sch.
HAZEL RD.
BARROWDALE RD.
BRIAR
ASH GRO.
OAK AV.
NOOK LA.
QUEEN'S DR.
HOLCOMBE AV.
SPRINGFIELD AV.
HIGHFIELD AV.
Bank Heath
TALBOT ST.
TURTON ST.
WORSLEY ST.
SALISBURY ST.
LOWE ST.
RIGBY'S ST.
Chs.
Club
Golborne Prim.Sch.
JOHN ST.
MILL ST.
TANNER'S LA.
Mills
MILLINGFORD INDUSTRIAL ESTATE
SERPENTINE WK.
White Door Covert
White Door Dam
Lady Hill
LEGH ST.
ROCHESTER CL.
BARNHAM CL.
SCHOOL ST.
HIGH ST.
Play. Fld.
MITCHELL ST.
BROOK ST.
GRUNDY ST.
CROSS ST.
KINGS RD.
DEANE AV.
Railway View
Works
GOLBORNE
A580
EAST LANCASHIRE ROAD
PARK ROAD
BARN LANE
Ch.
BRIDGE ST.
A573
PIERPOINT ST.
Town Fm.
Lowton Heath Ho.
Dean Dam
Dean Dam Farm
Keeper's House
Hallows Wood
Park Plantation
COLONEL'S LA.
Haydock Park Golf Course
Golborne Park (Club Ho.)
Golborne Park Wood
NEWTON LANE
WARRINGTON RD.
Millingford Brook
Golborne Junc.
Byron's Farm
LOWTON GDS.
A572
ROAD
Holly Ho.
Town of Lowton
MOSS LA.
Castle Hill
M6
Golborne Dale Bri.
GOLBORNE DALE RD.
Sandup Fm.
Sandfield Hall
Mere House Spec.Sch.
Newton Bank Sch.
Newton Lake
Willow Park
MERE RD.
CHURCH ST.
ST.
A572
SOUTHWORTH
Parkside Manchester Junc.
PARKSIDE
Parkside Liverpool Junc.
Highfield Fm.
Playing Field
Wks.
STA.
Motorail Terminal
ALFRED ST.
Mill House Special Sch.
MILL
A49
BURKHARDT DR.
PARK VIEW
NEWTON PK. DR.
WAYFARERS DR.
Newton Brook
Newton Park
LA.
Bloody Stone
A573 ROAD
16
17
18
97
96
95
60
61

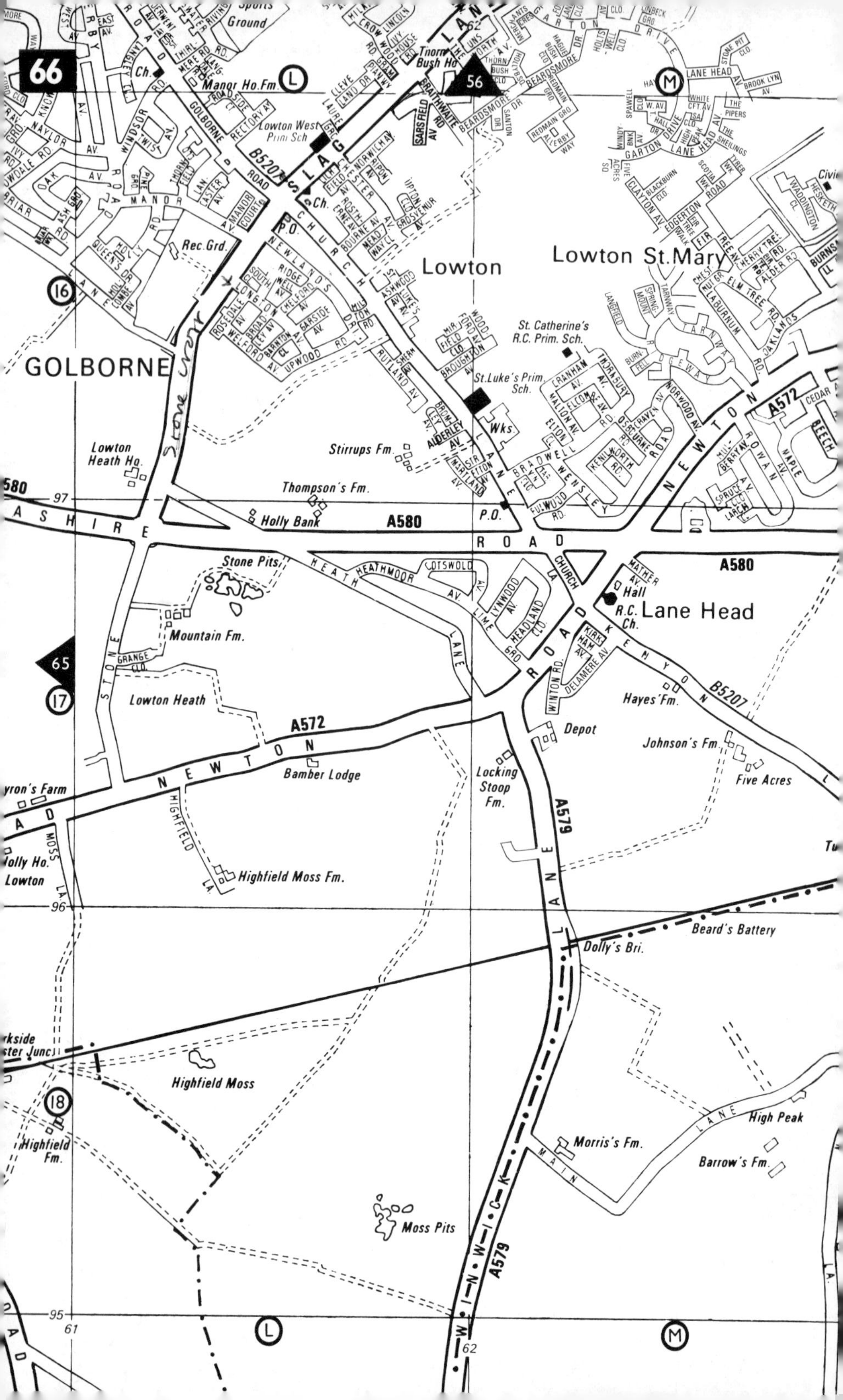
GOLBORNE
Lowton
Lowton St.Mary
Lane Head
Lowton Heath
Manor Ho.Fm.
Lowton West Prim Sch
Thorn Bush Ho
Rec.Grd.
St. Catherine's R.C. Prim. Sch.
St.Luke's Prim. Sch.
Wks.
Stirrups Fm.
Thompson's Fm.
Holly Bank
P.O.
Lowton Heath Ho.
Stone Pits
Mountain Fm.
Hall
R.C. Ch.
Hayes' Fm.
Depot
Johnson's Fm.
Five Acres
Bamber Lodge
Locking Stoop Fm.
Highfield Moss Fm.
Beard's Battery
Dolly's Bri.
Highfield Moss
Highfield Fm.
Morris's Fm.
High Peak
Barrow's Fm.
Moss Pits
Holly Ho. Lowton
A580
A572
A579
B5207
SLAG LANE
CHURCH LANE
NEWTON ROAD
KENYON ROAD
STONE CROSS LANE
HEATH LANE
HEATHMOOR AV.
WINWICK LANE
MAIN LANE
MOSS LA.
HIGHFIELD LA.
LANE HEAD AV.
GARTON DRIVE
BEARDSMORE DR.
NEWLANDS DR.
MANOR ROAD
GOLBORNE ROAD
WINDSOR ROAD
56
65
16
17
18
L
M
97
96
95
61
62

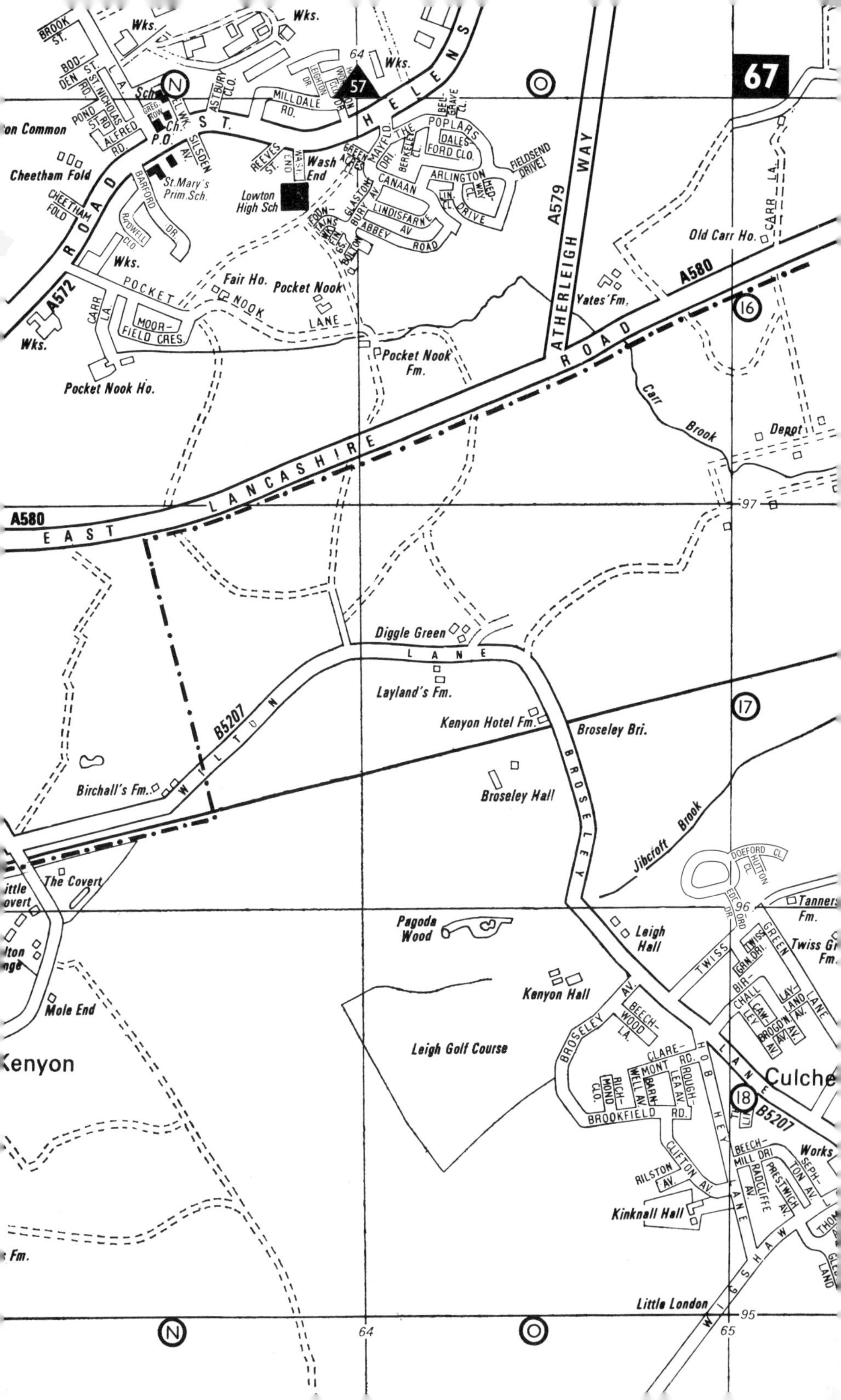

Wks.
BROOK ST.
BOD-DEN ST.
ST. NICHOLAS RD.
POND ST.
ALFRED RD.
Sch.
GREG. ROW
EL. WK. AV.
Ch.
P.O.
ASTBURY CLO.
MILLDALE RD.
LEIGHTON DR.
WOODLANDS CLO.
57
64
Wks.
ST. HELENS ROAD
SILSDEN AV.
REEVES ST.
WASH END
Wash End
Lowton High Sch
on Common
Cheetham Fold
CHEETHAM FOLD
BARFORD AV.
St. Mary's Prim. Sch.
RADWELL CLO.
BARFORD DR.
Wks.
A572
Wks.
CARR LA.
POCKET NOOK LANE
MOOR-FIELD CRES.
Fair Ho.
Pocket Nook
Pocket Nook Ho.
Pocket Nook Fm.
GREEN ACRES
MAYFLO. DRI.
THE BERKELEY CL.
BEL-GRAVE CL.
POPLARS
DALES FORD CLO.
CANAAN
GLASTONBURY AV.
FOUN-TAINS WELLS
BOLTON CL.
LINDISFARNE AV
ABBEY ROAD
ARLINGTON CL.
MED-WAY CL.
LIN. CL.
DRIVE
FIELDSEND DRIVE
A579
ATHERLEIGH WAY
Old Carr Ho.
CARR LA.
A580
Yates' Fm.
16
Carr Brook
Depot
EAST LANCASHIRE ROAD
A580
97
Diggle Green
LANE
Layland's Fm.
Kenyon Hotel Fm.
Broseley Bri.
17
B5207
WILTON
Birchall's Fm.
Broseley Hall
BROSELEY
Jibcroft Brook
DOEFORD CL.
HUTTON CL.
EDEFORD DR.
Tanners Fm.
96
The Covert
ittle overt
lton nge
Pagoda Wood
Leigh Hall
TWISS GRN. DRI.
TWISS GREEN LANE
Twiss Gr Fm.
Mole End
Kenyon Hall
BROSELEY AV.
BEECH-WOOD LA.
BIR-CHALL AV.
CAW-LEY AV.
BROGD'N AV.
LAY-LAND AV.
Kenyon
Leigh Golf Course
CLARE-MONT RD.
HOB HEY LANE
Culche
RICH-MOND CLO.
WELL AV.
BARN
ROUGH-LEA AV.
18
B5207
BROOKFIELD RD.
CLIFTON AV.
BEECH-MILL DRI.
SEPH-TON AV.
Works
RILSTON AV.
RADCLIFFE AV.
PRESTWICH AV.
Kinknall Hall
WIGSHAW LANE
THOM
GLEB LAND
Fm.
Little London
95
64
65

INDEX TO STREETS

General Abbreviations

App.	Approach	E.	East	Lwr.	Lower	Sq.	Square
Arc.	Arcade	Est.	Estate	Mkt.	Market	St.	Street
Av.	Avenue	Fld.	Field	Ms.	Mews	Ter.	Terrace
Bk.	Bank	Flds.	Fields	Mt.	Mount	Twr.	Tower
Bldgs.	Buildings	Fm.	Farm	N.	North	Vill.	Villa
Bri.	Bridge	Gdn.	Garden	Par.	Parade	Vw.	View
Cft.	Croft	Gdns.	Gardens	Pas.	Passage	W.	West
Ch.	Church	Gra.	Grange	Pk.	Park	Wd.	Wood
Clo.	Close	Grn.	Green	Pl.	Place	Wk.	Walk
Cotts.	Cottages	Gro.	Grove	Rd.	Road	Yd.	Yard
Cres.	Crescent	Ho.	House	Ri.	Rise		
Ct.	Court	La.	Lane	S.	South		
Dr.	Drive	Lo.	Lodge	Sch.	School		

District Abbreviations

App.Br.	Appley Bridge	Hay.	Haydock	Rainh.	Rainhill
Asht.	Ashton-in-Makerfield	Hind.	Hindley	Shev.	Shevington
Asp.	Aspull	Ince	Ince-in-Makerfield	Skel.	Skelmersdale
Ath.	Atherton	K.Moss	King's Moss	St.H.	St. Helens
Aug.	Aughton	Lath.	Lathom	Stand.	Standish
Bam.	Bamfurlong	Litt.H.	Little Hulton	Stand.L.G.	Standish Lower Ground
Bick.	Bickershaw	Low.	Lowton	Swin.	Swinley
Bill.	Billinge	Mos.Com.	Mosley Common	Tyld.	Tyldesley
Bisp.	Bispham	New.	Newtown	Up. Holl.	Up Holland
Black.	Blackrod	Newt.	Newton-le-Willows	Westho.	Westhoughton
Bolt.	Bolton	Orm.	Ormskirk	Wgn.	Wigan
Booth.	Boothstown	Orr.	Orrell	Win.	Winstanley
Cop.	Coppull	Parb.	Parbold	Wors.	Worsley
Cul.	Culcheth	Pemb.	Pemberton	Wors.M.	Worlsey Mesnes
Farn.	Farnworth	Platt. Br.	Platt Bridge	Wri.	Wrightington
G.Grn.	Goose Green	R.Mill	Roby Mill		
Gol.	Golborne	Rainf.	Rainford		

NOTES

This index contains some street names in standard text which are followed by another street named in italics. In these cases the street in standard text does not actually appear on the map due to insufficient space but can be located close to the street named in italics.

'A' Ct., Asht. 54 G15
Abberley Way, Wgn. 39 E10
Abbey Clo., Up Holl. 25 B8
Abbey Dr., Orr. 26 C9
Abbey La., Leigh 43 O11
Abbey Rd., Hay. 63 F16
Abbey Rd., Leigh 67 O16
Abbey Rd., Tyld. 46 T12
Abbey Sq., Leigh 43 O11
Abbey St., Leigh 58 P13
Abbey Way N., Hay. 63 G16
Abbeydale, App.Br. 14 B4
Abbeyfields, Wgn. 27 F7
Dumbarton Grn.
Abbeystead, Skel. 24 YY8
Abbeyway S., Hay. 63 G17
Abbeywood, Skel. 24 YY8
Abbingdon Way, Leigh 43 O11
Abbot Cft., Westho. 32 P9
Abbots Rd., Orm. 10 QQ5
Abbots Way, Bill. 50 B14
Abbotsfold Rd., Booth. 47 W12
Stetchworth Dr.
Abbotsford Clo., Low. 56 L15
Abbott St., Hind. 30 L9
Abbotts Grn., Astley 60 T14
Abingdon Dr., Platt Br. 41 K11
Abinger Rd., Asht. 53 E14
Abley Way, Wgn. 39 E10
Acacia Cres., Wgn. 16 F6
Acacia St., Newt. 63 F18
Ackhurst La., Orr. 15 D6
Acorn Clo., Leigh 58 P14
Acorn St., Newt. 64 H18
Acrefield, Parb. 4 XX3
Acregate, Skel. 24 YY9
Acresfield, Tyld. 46 U12
Withington Dr.
Acresfield Rd., Litt.H. 47 W10
Acton St., Wgn. 28 H7
Acton Ter., Wgn. 28 H7
Actons Wk., Wgn. 28 H8
Adams Dr., Wgn. 27 F9
Adamson St., Asht. 54 G14
Addison St., Wgn. 28 G8
Adelaide St., Platt Br. 41 K11
Adelphi Dr., Litt.H. 35 W9
Adelphi Gro., Litt.H. 35 W9
Adelphi St., Stand. 8 F3
Ainscow St., Bick. 42 M11
Ainscow St., Ince 29 J9
Ainsdale Av., Ath. 45 R10
Ainsdale Rd., Farn. 35 V7
Airton Pl., Wors.M. 40 G10
Albany Clo., Litt.H. 35 W9
Albany Gro., Tyld. 46 U12
Albert St., Asht. 54 G14
Albert St., Hind. 30 L9
Albert St., Ince 29 J8
Albert St., Wgn. 27 F9
Albion Dr., Asp. 29 K7
Albion St., Ince 29 K7
Withington La.
Albion St., Leigh 58 P13
Albion St., Westho. 32 P6
Albury Way, Wgn. 29 J7
Aldcliffe, Gol. 66 M16
Tarnway
Alder Av., Asht. 53 F13
Alder Av., Bill. 50 B13
Maple Clo.
Alder Av., Wgn. 27 E9
Alder Clo., Leigh 58 P15
Alder La., Hind. 31 N9
Alder La., Parb. 4 XX3
Alder La., Rainf. 49 ZZ14
Alder Lee Clo., Win. 39 E11
Alder Rd., Low. 66 M16
Alder St., Ath. 45 R10
Alder St., Newt. 64 H18
Alderbrook Dr., Parb. 5 YY3
Alderfold St., Ath. 45 R10
Alderley, Skel. 24 YY9
Alderley Av., Hind. 31 N9
Alderley Av., Low. 66 L16
Alderley Clo., Bill. 50 C13
Ashfield Cres.
Alderley La., Leigh 59 R14
Alderminster Av., Litt.H. 35 W9
Alderney Dr., Wors.M. 40 G10
Alders Grn. Rd., Hind. 31 N9
Aldersyde St., Farn. 34 U7
Alderton Dr., Asht. 53 F14
Aldford Dr., Ath. 33 S9
Aldford Way, Stand. 16 F4
Aldred St., Farn. 34 T6
Aldred St., Hind. 42 L10
Lord St.
Aldred St., Tyld. 46 T12
Aldridge Clo., Wgn. 40 G10
Alexander St., Tyld. 46 T12
Alexandra Cres., New. 27 F9
Alexandra Rd., Asht. 54 G14
Alexandra St., Abram 41 K12
Alexandra St., Wgn. 27 F8
Alexandria Dr., Westho. 32 Q8
Alfred Rd., Gol. 67 N16
Alfred Rd., Hay. 63 F16
Alfred St., Ince 28 H9
Alfred St., Newt. 64 H18
Alfred St., Platt Br. 41 K10
Alfred St., Tyld. 45 S11
Alfred St., Wgn. 28 G7
Algernon St., Hind. 30 L9
Algernon St., Wgn. 40 G10
Alicks Fold, Westho. 32 P7
Lord St.
Alker St., Wgn. 27 F9
All Saints Gro., Hind. 30 M9
Allan St., Tyld. 45 S12
Allenby Gro., Westho. 31 O8
Allenby St., Ath. 44 Q11
Allerby Way, Gol. 66 M16
Allerton Clo., Westho. 32 Q7
Upper Lees Dr.
Allesley Clo., Westho. 32 Q7

Alliance St., Wgn. 28 H8
Orchard St.
Allscotts Way, Asht. 54 H14
Alma Clo., Up Holl. 25 B8
Alma Ct., Up Holl. 25 B8
Alma Gro., Wgn. 39 F11
Alma Hill, Up Holl. 25 B8
Alma Par., Up Holl. 25 B9
Alma Rd., Up Holl. 25 B8
Alma Rd., Westho. 32 P8
Alma St., Ath. 45 R10
Alma St., Leigh 44 P12
Alma St., Newt. 63 G18
Suez St.
Alma St., Tyld. 45 S12
Almond Brook Rd., Stand. 8 E3
Almond Cres., Stand. 16 F4
Almond Gro., Wgn. 27 F9
Alnwick Clo., Asp. 19 L5
Alpine Dr., Leigh 43 O12
Alpine St., Newt. 63 G18
Alston Rd., Wgn. 29 J7
Alt Clo., Leigh 57 O13
Alton Clo., Asht. 54 G14
Altys La., Orm. 10 QQ6
Alvanley Clo., Wgn. 26 D7
Alwyn Clo., Leigh 58 P15
Alwyn St., Wgn. 28 H7
Alwyn Ter., Wgn. 28 H7
Amar St., Ince 29 J8
Amber Gdns., Hind. 42 M10
Amber Gro., Westho. 32 P7
Ambergate, Ath. 45 R11
Ambergate, Skel. 23 XX8
Amberley Clo., Wgn. 29 J7
Amberswood Clo., Ince 29 K8
Amberswood Ter., Hind. 29 K9
Amblecote Dr. E., Litt.H. 35 W9
Amblecote Dr. W., Litt.H. 35 W9
Ambleside, Ince 29 K8
Ambleside, Wgn. 27 E8
Ambleside Pl., St.H. 49 A15
Ambrose Av., Leigh 44 P11
Amersham, Skel. 24 YY8
Amesbury Dr., Wgn. 39 E11
Amethyst Clo., Wgn. 29 K7
Anchor La., Farn. 35 V8
Anderton St., Ince 29 J8
Anderton Way, Asp. 29 K7
Andover Cres., Wgn. 39 E11
Andrew Av., Bill. 50 C13
Andrews Ter., Westho. 32 P7
Anfield Rd., Farn. 35 V7
Angus Av., Leigh 43 O12
Ann La., Tyld. 60 U13
Ann St., Leigh 44 P12
Ann St., Skel. 23 WW8
Annan Gro., Asht. 55 J13
Annesley Cres., Wgn. 39 F10
Annette Av., Newt. 63 G17
Ansdell Rd., Wgn. 27 E9
Anson Pl., Wgn. 27 E8
Anson St., Wgn. 27 F8
Albert St.
Anthorn Rd., Win. 39 F10
Antler Ct., Asht. 54 G13
Antrim Clo., Hay. 62 E17
Antrim Clo., Wgn. 39 E11
Anvil Clo., Orr. 25 B9
Appledell Av., Gol. 56 L15
Applethwaite, Ince 29 K8
Appleton Rd., Skel. 23 WW7
Appleton St., Wgn. 28 G8
Appley Clo., Wri. 6 B3
The Gro.
Appley La. N., App.Br. 6 B3
Appley La. S., App.Br. 14 B5
Arbor Gro., Litt.H. 47 V10
Arbory Clo., Leigh 59 R13
Arbour La., Stand. 7 D3
Arcade St., Wgn. 28 H8
Arch La., Asht. 51 D14
Archer St., Leigh 58 Q15
Archer St., Tyld. 61 V13
Argyle St., Ath. 45 R11
Argyle St., Hind. 30 L9
Argyll Clo., Asht. 53 E14
Argyll St., Wgn. 27 F9
Arkholme, Tyld. 47 W12
Arley Clo., Asp. 29 J7
Arley La., Haigh 9 H3
Arley St., Ince 41 J10
Arley Way, Ath. 45 R11
Arlington Dr., Leigh 67 O16
Armitage Av., Litt.H. 47 V10
Armitage Gro., Litt.H. 47 V10
Armoury Bk., Asht. 54 G14
Armstrong St., Asp. 18 K6
Arnside Av., Hay. 62 D17
Arnside Av., Ince 29 K8
Arnside Rd., Hind. 31 N9
Arnside Rd., Orr. 26 D8
Arrow St., Leigh 58 Q14
Arrowsmith Rd., Hay. 63 F16
Arthur St., Hind. 30 M9
Arthur St., Leigh 58 P14
Arundale, Westho. 32 P7
Arundel Dr., Leigh 58 P13
Arundel St., Hind. 30 M9
Arundel St., New. 27 F9
Ascot Dr., Ath. 45 S10
Ascroft Av., Wgn. 16 F6
Ascroft St., Wgn. 29 J8
Ash Brow, Parb. 4 XX3
Ash Clo., App.Br. 14 B4
Ash Clo., Orm. 10 PP5
Ash Gro., Gol. 65 K16
Ash Gro., Orr. 26 C9
Ash Gro., Skel. 22 VV7
Ash Gro., Stand. 16 F4
Ash Gro., Westho. 32 P8
Ash Gro. Cres., Bill. 50 B13
Ash La., Asp. 29 K7
Ash Rd., Hay. 63 F16
Ash St., Asht. 54 G13
Ash St., Gol. 55 K15
Ash St., Tyld. 46 T11
Ash St., Wgn. 39 F11
Ashawe Clo., Litt.H. 47 V10
Ashawe Clo., Tyld. 47 V10
Ashawe Gro., Litt.H. 47 V10
Ashawe Gro., Tyld. 47 V10
Ashawe Ter., Litt.H. 47 V10
Ashbourne Av., Asp. 29 J7
Ashbourne Av., Hind. 30 M9
Ashbourne Clo., Leigh 43 O11
Ashbourne Gdns., Hind. 30 M9
Claremont Av.
Ashby Gro., Leigh 43 O12
Ashby Rd., Wgn. 40 G10
Ashcroft Av., Orm. 10 QQ5
Ashdale Rd., Hind. 30 M9
Ashdale Rd., Wgn. 40 G11
Ashdown Dr., Tyld. 47 V12
Asher St., Farn. 34 U7
Ashfield Av., Ath. 45 R10
Ashfield Av., Hind. 42 M10
Ashfield Cres., Bill. 50 C13
Ashfield Dr., Asp. 19 L5
Ashfield Pk. Dr., Stand. 16 F4
Ashfield Ter., App.Br. 14 B4
Ashford Av., Tyld. 61 V13
Ashford Ri., Wgn. 17 G6
Ashland Av., Asht. 54 G14
Ashland Av., Tyld. 47 W12
Ashland Av., Wgn. 28 H7
Ashley Dr., Leigh 43 O12
Ashley Rd., Hind. 43 N10
Ashley Rd., Skel. 12 XX6
Ashling Ct., Tyld. 46 U11
Ashmore St., Tyld. 46 U12
Ashton Heath, Asht. 54 H15
Ashton Rd., Asht. 38 D12
Ashton Rd., Newt. 64 H17
Ashton St., Abram 41 K11
Ashurst Fold, Orr. 26 D9
Baldwin St.
Ashurst Gdns., Skel. 12 XX6
Ashurst Rd., Skel. 12 XX6
Ashurst Rd., Stand. 7 D3
Beacon Rd.
Ashwall St., Skel. 23 WW8
Ashwell Av., Gol. 56 L15
Ashwood, Skel. 13 YY6
Forest Dr.
Ashwood Av., Abram 42 L12
Ashwood Av., Asht. 54 G15
Ashwood Av., Gol. 66 L16
Ashworth St., Asp. 19 M6
Asmall Clo., Orm. 10 PP5
Asmall La., Orm. 10 PP5
Aspen Clo., Westho. 32 P7
Aspen Way, Skel. 23 WW7
Laurel Dr.
Aspenwood, Asht. 54 G13
Aspinall Clo., Litt.H. 47 V10
Aspinall Cres., Litt.H. 47 V11
Aspinall Gro., Litt.H. 47 V11
Aspinall St., Platt Br. 41 K10
Platt St.
Aspull Common, Leigh 57 O15
Astbury Clo., Gol. 67 N16
Aster Av., Farn. 35 W7
Aster Rd., Hay. 63 F17
Astley St., Leigh 58 Q14
Astley St., Tyld. 46 T12
Aston Gro., Tyld. 46 U11
Atherleigh Gro., Leigh 44 P12
Leigh Rd.
Atherleigh Way, Leigh 57 O15
Atherton Rd., Hind. 30 L9
Atherton St., Bick. 42 M12
Atherton St., Wgn. 27 F9
Warrington Rd.
Athol Clo., Newt. 63 F18
Athol Cres., Hind. 43 N10
Athol Gro., Wgn. 40 G10
Aticks Fold, Westho. 32 P7
Lord St.
Atkinson St., Abram 41 K12
Aughton Clo., Bill. 50 C14
Ashfield Cres.
Aughton St., Hind. 30 L9
Aughton St., Orm. 10 QQ6
Austin Av., Asht. 53 F14
Austin St., Leigh 57 O13
Avenue, The, Bill. 37 B10
Avenue, The, Booth. 61 W14
Avenue, The, Leigh 58 P13
Avenue, The, Newt. 64 H18
Avenue, The (Halsall La.), Orm. 10 PP5
Avenue, The (Southport Rd.), Orm. 10 QQ5
Avenue, The, Stand.L.G. 16 F6
Avenue, The, Westho. 32 P7
Avenue, The, Wgn. 28 H7
Averham Clo., Asht. 54 G15
Averhill, Tyld. 47 W12
Avery Cres., Hay. 62 E16
Avery Rd., Hay. 62 E16
Avery Sq., Hay. 62 E16
Aviemore Clo., Asht. 53 E14
Avocet Clo., Newt. 64 H18
Avon Clo., Litt.H. 47 W11
Avon Rd., Asht. 55 J13
Avon Rd., Bill. 50 B14
Avon Rd., Tyld. 46 U12
Avon Rd., Wgn. 27 E8
Avon St., Leigh 58 Q14
Avondale Dr., Tyld. 60 U13
Avondale Rd., Farn. 35 V8
Avondale Rd., Hay. 62 E16
Avondale Rd., Wgn. 28 H7
Avondale St., Stand. 8 E3
Aye Bri. Rd., Abram 55 K13
Aylesbury Cres., Hind. 43 O11
Ayrefield Gro., App.Br. 14 B5
Ayrefield La., R.Mill 14 B6
Ayrton Gro., Litt.H. 35 W9

B

Back Brow, Up Holl. 25 B8
Higher La.
Back Hulton La. S., Farn. 34 T7
Back La., App.Br. 14 B4
Back La., Aug. 20 NN8
Back La., Farn. 34 T9
Back La., Parb. 4 WW3
Back La., Rainf. 49 ZZ13
Back La., Skel. 24 YY9
Back La. (Holland Moor), Skel. 24 ZZ8
Back Mkt. St., Leigh 58 P13
Back Mkt. St., Newt. 63 G18
Back St. Helens Rd. N., Farn. 34 T7

Back St. Helens Rd. S., Farn.	34	T7
Back Salford, Leigh	58	P13
Back Shakerley Rd., Tyld.	45	S11
Hindsford St.		
Back Short St., Tyld.	45	S11
Short St.		
Baclaw Clo., Wgn.	29	J7
Bag La., Ath.	44	Q10
Bagshaw La., Asp.	30	M7
Bahama Clo., Hay.	62	E16
Bahama Rd., Hay.	62	E16
Bailey Fold, Westho.	32	Q8
Baker St., Leigh	44	P12
Baker St., Wgn.	28	G9
Balcarres Av., Wgn.	28	H7
Balcarres Rd., Asp.	18	K5
Baldwin St., Hind.	43	N10
Baldwin St., Ince	28	H9
Baldwin St., Orr.	26	D9
Baldwin St., Wgn.	28	H8
Balfern Clo., Westho.	32	P7
Winward St.		
Balfern Fold, Westho.	32	P7
Church St.		
Ball St., Wgn.	27	F7
Balliol Way, Asht.	53	F14
Balmoral Av., Gol.	56	L15
Balmoral Dr., Hind.	42	L10
Balmoral Dr., Leigh	59	R13
Balmoral Rd., Asht.	54	G14
Balmoral Rd., Wgn.	27	F9
Balniel Wk., Wgn.	29	J7
Bamburgh Pl., Asht.	54	G13
Bamford Dr., Wgn.	29	J7
Bampton Av., St.H.	49	A15
Banbury Clo., Leigh	58	P15
Banbury Rd., Bill.	37	B11
Bangor Fold, Leigh	59	R14
Banham Av., Wgn.	39	E10
Bank Av., Orr.	25	B9
Bank Brow, R.Mill	14	B6
Bank Gro., Litt.H.	35	V9
Bank La., Litt.H.	35	V9
Bank St., Gol.	55	K15
Bank St., Newt.	63	F18
Bank St., Platt Br.	41	K10
Bank St., Tyld.	46	T12
Bank St., Wgn.	27	F9
Bankbrook, Stand.L.G.	16	E6
Bankes Av., Orr.	26	D9
Bankfield, Skel.	24	YY8
Bankfield, Westho.	32	Q8
Bankfield Dr., Booth.	47	W12
Bankfield Rd., Tyld.	47	V12
Banksbarn, Skel.	24	YY8
Bankside, Westho.	32	P8
Bankside Av., Asht.	40	G12
Bankwood, App.Br.	15	C5
Banner St., Hind.	30	M9
Banner St., Ince	29	J9
Bannister La., Bisp.	5	YY1
Bar St., Platt Br.	41	K11
Barbara Rd., Farn.	34	T7
Barbury Clo., Leigh	44	P12
Bardale Gro., Asht.	54	G14
Bardsley Clo., Up Holl.	25	A8
Barford Dr., Low.	67	N16
Barker St., Leigh	57	O13
Barlborough Rd., Pemb.	27	E9
Barley Brook St., Wgn.	28	G7
Barn Hill, Westho.	32	P7
Barn Hill Ter., Westho.	32	P7
Tithe Barn St.		
Barn La., Gol.	64	H16
Barnes Pas., Ath.	45	S10
Barnes Rd., Orm.	10	QQ6
Barnes Rd., Skel.	23	WW7
Barnett Av., Newt.	63	F18
Barnfield Dr., Booth.	61	W13
Barnfield Dr., Skel.	24	ZZ8
Barnfield Dr., Westho.	32	Q7
Barngill Gro., Win.	39	F10
Barnham Clo., Gol.	65	K16
Barnsley St., Wgn.	17	G6
Barnton Clo., Low.	66	L16
Barnway St., Newt.	63	G18
Barnwell Av., Cul.	67	O18
Baron Fold Cres., Litt.H.	35	V9
Baronfold Gro., Litt.H.	35	V9
Barons Ter., Ince	29	K9
Barrack Sq., Wgn.	28	H8
Library St.		
Barracks Rd., Bick.	42	L11
Barrie St., Leigh	43	O12
Barron Meadow, Leigh	43	O12
Barrow St., Asht.	54	H13
Barrowdale Rd., Gol.	65	K16
Barry Cres., Litt.H.	47	W10
Barton Av., Wgn.	28	G7
Barton Clough, Bill.	50	C13
Mitchell Rd.		
Barton Rd., Farn.	35	W8
Barton St., Gol.	65	K16
Barton St., Platt Br.	41	K10
Barton St., Tyld.	45	S11
Basset Gro., Wgn.	39	E11
Bath Springs, Orm.	10	QQ5
Bath St., Ath.	44	Q10
Bath St., Wgn.	29	J7
Battersby St., Ince	29	K8
Battersby St., Leigh	58	Q14
Baucher Rd., Wgn.	27	F9
Baxter St., Stand.	8	F3
Baxters Row, Hind.	43	N11
Bayswater St., Farn.	34	U7
Baytree Rd., Wgn.	27	F7
Beacon Clo., Ath.	44	Q11
Beacon La., Skel.	12	XX5
Beacon La., Up Holl.	25	A8
Beacon Rd., Bick.	43	N12
Beacon Rd., Bill.	50	B13
Beacon Rd., Stand.	7	D3
Beacon Vw. Dr., Up Holl.	25	A8
Beacons, The, App.Br.	14	B4
Beaconsfield St., Wgn.	29	J7
Beaford Clo., Pemb.	26	D9
Beal Dr., Platt Br.	41	K11
Beardsmore Dr., Gol.	66	L16
Bearncroft, Skel.	24	YY9
Beatrice St., Farn.	35	W8
Beatty Dr., Westho.	32	P7
Beaufort St., Hind.	30	L9
Beaufort St., Wgn.	27	F9
Beaumaris Clo., Leigh	57	O13
Edmund Dr.		
Beaumaris Rd., Hind.	43	N10
Beaumont Clo., Aug.	21	PP7
Beaumont Gro., Orr.	26	D8
Beaver Ct., Asht.	54	H13
Beavers La., Skel.	24	YY9
Bebles Rd., Orm.	10	PP6
Beckside, Tyld.	45	S12
Beckwith, Platt Br.	41	K10
Bedford Dr., Ath.	44	Q11
Bedford Gdns., Hind.	30	M9
Bedford Pl., Asht.	54	G13
Bedford Sq., Leigh	58	Q14
Bedford St., Leigh	58	Q13
Bedford St., Pemb.	27	E9
Bedford St., Wgn.	29	J7
Bee Fold La., Ath.	45	R11
Beech Av., Ath.	45	S10
Beech Av., Booth.	61	W13
Beech Av., Farn.	35	W8
Beech Av., Gol.	66	M16
Beech Av., Hay.	63	F16
Beech Av., Parb.	5	YY3
Beech Clo., Skel.	23	WW7
Beech Cres., Leigh	58	P14
Beech Cres., Stand.	16	F4
Beech Dr., Leigh	58	P15
Beech Gro., Abram	42	L12
Beech Gro., Leigh	58	P15
Beech Gro., Litt.H.	35	V9
Beech Gro., Wgn.	16	F6
Beech Hall St., Wgn.	28	G7
Beech Hill Av., Wgn.	16	F6
Beech Hill La., Wgn.	16	F6
Beech Meadow, Orm.	11	RR6
Beech Rd., Aug.	20	OO9
Beech Rd., Gol.	55	K15
Beech St., Ath.	45	S10
Beech Tree Av., App.Br.	14	B4
Beech Tree Hos., Bam.	41	J12
Beech Wk., Leigh	58	P15
Beech Wk., Stand.	16	E4
Beech Wk., Win.	39	E11
Beechfield, Wri.	5	YY1
Beechfield Av., Hind.	43	N10
Beechfield Av., Litt.H.	35	W9
Beechfield Dr., Leigh	58	P14
Beechtrees, Skel.	24	YY8
Beechwood, Skel.	13	YY6
Beechwood Av., Asht.	54	G15
Beechwood Av., Newt.	64	H18
Beechwood Av., Shev.	15	C5
Beechwood Cres., Orr.	26	C9
Beechwood Cres., Tyld.	60	T13
Beechwood Dr., Orm.	10	PP6
Beechwood La., Cul.	67	O18
Beehive Grn., Westho.	32	Q7
Beeston Gro., Leigh	45	R12
Begonia Av., Farn.	35	W7
Belcroft Dr., Litt.H.	35	V9
Belcroft Gro., Litt.H.	35	V9
Belfield, Skel.	24	YY9
Belgrave Clo., Leigh	67	O16
Belgrave Clo., Wgn.	39	E10
Belgrave St., Ath.	44	Q10
Bell La., Orr.	26	D8
Bell St., Hind.	30	M9
Bell St., Leigh	43	O11
Belldean, Ince	29	K8
Belle Grn. La., Ince	29	K8
Belle Vue, Gol.	56	M15
Belle Vue St., Wgn.	27	E9
Bellingham Av., Wgn.	28	H7
Bellingham Cotts., Wgn.	28	H7
Bellingham Dr., Wgn.	28	H7
Bellingham Mt., Wgn.	17	H6
Bellpit Clo., Booth.	47	W12
Bellwood, Westho.	31	O8
Belmont Av., Ath.	45	S10
Belmont Av., Bick.	42	M11
Belmont Av., Bill.	37	B10
Belmont Av., Gol.	56	L15
Belmont Dr., Asp.	19	L5
Belmont Rd., Hind.	30	M9
Belmont St., Wgn.	26	D9
Belvedere Av., Ath.	45	S10
Belvedere Clo., Leigh	45	R12
Belvedere Pl., Wgn.	27	F9
Belvedere Rd., Asht.	54	H14
Belvedere Rd., Newt.	63	G18
Belvoir Ct., Wgn.	29	J8
Belvoir St., Wgn.	28	H8
Bengairn Clo., Wgn.	29	J7
Bengal St., Leigh	58	P13
Bentham Pl., Stand.	8	F3
Bentham Rd., Stand.	8	F3
Bentinck St., Wgn.	39	F10
Beresford St., Wgn.	28	G7
Berkeley Av., Wgn.	39	E11
Berkeley Clo., Leigh	67	O16
Berrington Gro., Asht.	54	G14
Berrington's La., St.H.	48	YY15
Berry Clo., Skel.	23	WW7
Berry St., Skel.	23	WW7
Berryfold Way, Tyld.	46	T12
Bertram St., Newt.	63	G18
Berwick Pl., Wgn.	29	J7
Berwyn Gro., St.H.	62	D18
Bessies Well Pl., Stand.	16	F4
Bethersden Rd., Wgn.	17	G6
Bettison Av., Leigh	59	R14
Beulah Av., Bill.	50	B14
Beverley Av., Bill.	38	C11
Beverley Av., Leigh	58	Q13
Beverley Rd., Wgn.	26	D8
Bevington St., Asht.	53	F13
Bewcastle Dr., Orm.	11	SS6
Bewley Gro., Leigh	58	Q13
Bexhill Dr., Hind.	43	O11
Bexley St., Hind.	43	N10
Atherton Rd.		
Bickershaw La., Abram	41	K11
Bickershaw La., Bick.	42	M11
Bickershaw St., Leigh	57	N14
Bidford Clo., Tyld.	46	U11
Bigmoor Rd., Skel.	24	YY8
Billinge Rd., Asht.	53	E13
Billinge Rd., Wgn.	39	E10
Billington Av., Newt.	63	G17
Birch Av., Stand.	16	F4
Birch Av., Westho.	32	P8
Birch Cres., Newt.	63	F18
Birch Grn. Rd., Skel.	23	XX7
Birch Gro., Asht.	53	E13
Birch Rd., Abram	41	K12

Birch Rd., Ath. 45 S10
Birch Rd., Hay. 63 F16
Birch Rd., Leigh 44 P12
Birch St., Hind. 30 L9
Platt La.
Birch St., Skel. 23 WW8
Birch St., Tyld. 46 T11
Birch St., Wgn. 28 G7
Birch Tree Rd., Low. 66 M16
Birchall St., Leigh 58 Q14
Birchfield Av., Ath. 44 Q10
Birchfield Dr., Booth. 47 W12
Birchfold Clo., Litt.H. 47 W10
Birchley Av., Bill. 50 B14
Birchley Rd., Bill. 50 B14
Birchley Vw., St.H. 49 A15
Birchwood Clo., Leigh 58 P14
Birchwood Clo., Win. 39 E11
Bird St., Ince 29 J8
Birkdale Av., Ath. 33 R9
Birkett Bk., Wgn. 29 J8
Birkett Bk. Ter., Wgn. 29 J8
Birkett St., Wgn. 29 J8
Birkrig, Skel. 24 YY9
Birkside Clo., Wors.M. 40 G11
Birley Clo., App.Br. 15 C4
Birley St., Leigh 58 Q13
Birleywood, Skel. 24 YY9
Birtle Dr., Tyld. 46 U12
Birtley St., Newt. 64 H18
Bishop Reeves Rd., Hay. 63 F16
Elizabeth Rd.
Bishopgate, Wgn. 28 H8
Bishops Clo., Farn. 35 W7
Bishops Rd., Farn. 35 W7
Bispham Dr., Asht. 53 F13
Blackacre La., Orm. 10 QQ4
Blackburn Clo., Low. 66 M16
Blackcap Clo., Booth. 47 W12
Blackmoor Av., Tyld. 60 T13
Blackmoss La., Orm. 10 PP6
Blackrod Bypass Rd., Black. 19 M4
Blackthorn Av., Wgn. 16 F6
Blaguegate La., Skel. 22 UU7
Blair Av., Hind. 43 N10
Blake Av., Ath. 33 R9
Milton Clo.
Blake Clo., Wgn. 28 G9
Blakehall, Skel. 24 YY8
Blantyre St., Hind. 30 M9
Blaydon Clo., Asp. 19 L5
Lincoln Dr.
Blaydon Pk., Skel. 24 YY8
Bleakledge Gro., Hind. 30 M8
Bleaklow Clo., Wgn. 40 G11
Bleasdale Clo., Orm. 21 PP8
Bleasdale Rd., Hind. 31 N9
Bleasdale Rd., Newt. 63 G18
Blenheim Dr., Leigh 45 S12
Blenheim Rd., Asht. 54 H15
Blenheim Rd., Wgn. 27 E8
Blenheim St., Tyld. 45 S11
Blewbury Clo., Leigh 44 P12
Bligh Rd., Westho. 32 P7
Blindman's La., Orm. 10 PP4
Blindsill Rd., Farn. 35 W8
Blissford Clo., Hind. 30 L9
Bloomfield Dr., Booth. 47 W12
Standfield Dr.
Blossom St., Tyld. 46 T11
Blue Bell Av., Wgn. 16 F6
Bluebell Av., Hay. 63 F16
Blythewood, Skel. 24 YY8
Boardman St., Westho. 34 T8
Boars Head Av., Stand. 17 G4
Boatmans Row, Tyld. 60 U14
Bodden St., Gol. 57 N15
Bodmin Dr., Platt Br. 41 K11
Bodmin Rd., Tyld. 46 T12
Bogburn La., Cop. 8 E1
Bold La., Aug. 20 OO9
Bold St., Leigh 58 P13
Bold St., Wgn. 27 F9
Bolderwood Dr., Hind. 42 L10
Bolney St., Asp. 29 K7
Bolton Clo., Leigh 67 N16
Bolton Ho. Rd., Bick. 42 M12
Bolton Old Rd., Ath. 45 R10
Bolton Rd., Asht. 54 H14
Bolton Rd., Asp. 19 L6
Bolton Rd., Ath. 45 R10
Bolton Rd., Bolt. 33 R7
Bolton Rd., Westho. 32 P7
Bolton St., Asht. 53 E13
Bolton St., Ince 29 J8
Bombay Rd., Wgn. 27 E8
Bond St., Leigh 58 P13
Bond St., Tyld. 45 S11
Bonnywell Rd., Leigh 58 P14
Booth St., Newt. 63 G18
Wellington St.
Booths Brow Rd., Asht. 53 E13
Booths Hall Gro., Booth. 61 W13
Booths Hall Rd., Booth. 61 W13
Boothsbank Av., Booth. 61 W13
Boothshall Way, Booth. 61 W13
Bor Av., Wgn. 40 G10
Borden Clo., Wgn. 29 J7
Border Brook La., Booth. 61 W13
Bordesley Av., Litt.H. 35 W9
Bournbrook Av.
Bores Hill, Stand. 9 H2
Borrow Rd., Newt. 63 G17
Borrowdale, Wgn. 26 D8
Borsdane Av., Hind. 42 M10
Boscobel Rd., Farn. 35 W7
Boston Gro., Leigh 44 P12
Boswell Pl., Wgn. 39 F10
Botany Clo., Asp. 29 K7
Boughey St., Leigh 58 P13
Boundary La., Wri. 7 D2
Boundary St., Leigh 58 Q14
Boundary St., Tyld. 46 T11
Boundary St., Wgn. 28 H8
Bournbrook Av., Litt.H. 35 W9
Bourne Av., Gol. 66 L16
Bourton Ct., Tyld. 46 U11
Bow Rd., Leigh 58 Q14
Bowden Clo., Leigh 59 R15
Bowden St., Asp. 19 M6
Bowker St., Litt.H. 47 W10
Bowkers Grn., Aug. 21 PP9
Bowkers Grn. La., Aug. 21 PP9
Bowland Av., Asht. 54 G14
Bowland Av., Gol. 56 L15
Bowling Grn. Row, Ath. 44 Q11
Bowlings, The, Wgn. 28 G7
Bowness Pl., Ince 29 K8
Boyd Clo., Stand. 16 F4
Boydell St., Leigh 58 P13
Brabazon Pl., Wgn. 27 E8
Bracken Lea, Westho. 32 P9
Leigh Rd.
Bracken Rd., Ath. 45 R11
Bracken Rd., Leigh 57 N13
Brackley Rd., Farn. 34 T8
Brackleyhurst Av., Bill. 50 C13
Braddyll Rd., Westho. 33 S8
Bradford Rd., Farn. 35 W7
Bradford St., Wgn. 28 H8
Bradley La., Stand. 8 F3
Bradshaw La., Parb. 5 YY3
Bradshaw St., Ath. 45 R10
Bradshaw St., Orr. 26 D9
Bradshaw St., Wgn. 28 H7
Bradshawgate, Leigh 58 P13
Bradshawgate, Wgn. 28 H8
Bradwell Rd., Gol. 66 M16
Braeburn Ct., Leigh 57 O13
Braemar La., Booth. 61 W13
Braemar Wk., Asp. 19 L5
Braemore Clo., Wgn. 39 E11
Braeside Cres., Bill. 50 B13
Braidhaven, App.Br. 15 C4
Braidley St., Tyld. 61 V13
Braithwaite, Shev. 15 D5
Braithwaite Rd., Gol. 56 L15
Brakesmere Gro., Litt.H. 47 V10
Bramble Gro., Wgn. 27 F8
Bramble Way, Parb. 5 YY3
Brambling Dr., Westho. 31 O9
Bramhall Rd., Skel. 23 WW7
Brampton Clo., Platt Br. 41 K11
Brampton Ct., St.H. 62 D18
Brampton Rd., Farn. 34 T7
Brampton St., Ath. 45 R10
Branch St., Ince 29 K8
Brancker St., Westho. 33 R8
Brandreth Delph, Parb. 5 YY2
Brandreth Dr., Parb. 5 YY3
Brandreth Pk., Parb. 5 YY2
Brandreth Pl., Stand. 8 F3
Brandwood Clo., Tyld. 47 W12
Bransford Clo., Asht. 54 H15
Branthwaite, Ince 29 K7
Bratton Av., Wgn. 39 E11
Brayton Ct., Hind. 30 L9
Breaktemper, Westho. 32 P7
Cemetery St.
Breaston Av., Leigh 58 Q14
Brecon Clo., Platt Br. 41 K11
Brecon Dr., Hind. 43 N10
Breeze Hill Rd., Westho. 33 S9
Brendon Gro., St.H. 62 D18
Brentwood, Pemb. 27 E9
Brethertons Row, Wgn. 28 H8
Arcade St.
Brett Rd., Booth. 61 V13
Brewery Clo., Wgn. 28 G9
Brewery La., Leigh 58 Q14
Brian Rd., Farn. 35 W7
Briar Clo., Asht. 54 G14
Briar Clo., Hind. 43 N10
Briar Gro., Leigh 44 P12
Briar Hill Av., Litt.H. 47 V10
Briar Rd., Gol. 65 K16
Briar Rd., Wgn. 27 E8
Briar Wk., Gol. 65 K16
Briarcroft Dr., Ath. 44 Q11
Briarfield Rd., Farn. 35 W7
Briars Grn., Skel. 12 XX6
Briary, Stand. 17 G4
Briary Dr., Tyld. 46 T12
Brick St., Newt. 63 F18
Brideoake St., Leigh 58 Q14
Bridge Av., Orm. 10 QQ6
Bridge St., Asp. 18 K6
Bridge St., Gol. 65 K16
Bridge St., Hind. 30 L9
Bridge St., Newt. 63 G18
Bridge St., Orm. 10 QQ6
Bridge St., Wgn. 28 H8
Bridgehall Dr., Up Holl. 25 A8
Rivington Dr.
Bridgeman Ter., Wgn. 28 H7
Bridges St., Ath. 44 Q11
Bridgewater Rd., Tyld. 47 V12
Bridgewater St., Hind. 30 M9
Bridgewater St., Ince 29 J8
Bridgewater St., Leigh 58 P14
Bridgewater St., Litt.H. 47 W10
Bridgewater St., New. 27 F9
Bridgewater St., Wgn. 28 G8
Brierfield, Skel. 24 YY9
Brierfield Av., Ath. 45 R10
Briggs St., Leigh 44 P12
Brighouse Clo., Orm. 10 PP5
Bright St., Leigh 44 P12
Brignall Gro., Gol. 56 L15
Brimelow Bldgs., Tyld. 60 U13
Brimfield Av., Tyld. 46 U11
Brindle St., Hind. 30 M9
Brindle St., Tyld. 46 T11
Brindlehurst Av., Tyld. 46 U12
Brindley Clo., Ath. 44 Q11
Brindley Clo., Farn. 35 W8
Brindley Dr., Booth. 61 W13
Brindley St., Wgn. 27 E9
Brinsop St., Asp. 19 M6
Britannia Rd., Wgn. 27 E8
Broad La., St.H. 49 A15
Broad o' th' La., Shev. 15 D5
Broad Oak Av., Hay. 62 D17
Broad Oak Rd., Farn. 35 W7
Broad Wk., Westho. 32 P8
Broadacre, Shev. 7 D3
Broadheath Clo., Westho. 32 Q7
Broadhurst La., Wri. 7 C1
Broadlands, Shev. 15 D5
Broadley Av., Gol. 66 L16
Broadmead, Parb. 4 XX3
Broadriding Rd., App.Br. 15 C5
Broadriding Rd., Shev. 15 C5
Broadway, Bolt. 33 S9
Broadway, Farn. 35 W7
Broadway, Hind. 30 M9
Broadwell Dr., Leigh 57 O15
Brock Mill La., Wgn. 17 H6

Brock Pl., Platt Br.	41	J11
Brock St., Ince	29	J8
John St.		
Brocken Leg, Westho.	32	P9
Leigh Rd.		
Brockhurst Wk., Wgn.	28	G9
Brocstedes Av., Asht.	53	F13
Brocstedes Rd., Asht.	39	E12
Bromilow Rd., Skel.	22	VV7
Bromley Av., Gol.	66	L16
Bromley Clo., Wgn.	29	K7
Bromley Dr., Leigh	43	O12
Brook Dr., Tyld.	60	U13
Brook La., K.Moss	36	ZZ12
Brook La., Orm.	10	QQ6
Brook La., Pemb.	26	D9
Brook Lynn Av., Gol.	56	M15
Brook Meadow, Westho.	32	Q7
Brook Side, Parb.	4	XX3
Brook St., Asht.	54	H15
Brook St., Ath.	44	Q10
Brook St., Gol.	65	K16
Brook St., G.Grn.	39	F10
Brook St., Ince	29	K8
Brook St., Low.	57	N15
Brook St., Wgn.	28	G9
Pool St.		
Brookdale, Bolt.	33	S9
Brookdale Rd., Hind.	30	M9
Brookfield, Parb.	5	YY3
Brookfield Dr., Tyld.	61	V13
Brookfield La., Aug.	20	OO9
Brookfield Rd., Cul.	67	O18
Brookfield Rd., Stand.	7	D3
Brookfield Rd., Up Holl.	25	A8
Brookfield St., Leigh	58	Q13
Brookfield St., Newt.	63	G18
Brookhouse Rd., Orm.	10	PP5
Brookhouse St., Wgn.	28	H8
Brookhouse Ter., Wgn.	28	H8
Brookhurst La., Litt.H.	35	V9
Brookland Av., Hind.	30	L9
Brookland Rd., Wgn.	17	G6
Brooklands, Orm.	11	RR5
Brooklands Av., Asht.	54	H14
Brooklands Av., Ath.	45	R10
Brooklands Av., Leigh	58	P14
Brooklands Dr., Orr.	25	B9
Brooklands Rd., Up Holl.	25	B8
Brookside, Wgn.	28	G9
Mesnes Dr.		
Brookside Av., Asht.	39	F12
Brookside Clo., Ath.	45	S10
Brookside Clo., Bill.	50	C13
Brookside Clo., Hay.	62	D16
Brookside Pl., Hind.	30	M9
Brookside Rd., Stand.	9	G3
Brookside Vw., Hay.	62	D16
Brookvale, Wgn.	28	G7
Broom Av., Leigh	44	P12
Broom Rd., Wgn.	27	E9
Broom Way, Westho.	32	Q7
Broomfield Pl., Stand.	8	F3
Broomfield Rd., Stand.	8	F3
Broomfield Ter., Ince	29	J8
Broomflat Clo., Stand.	8	F3
Broomhey Av., Wgn.	17	H5
Broomhey Ter., Ince	29	J8
Broomholme, App.Br.	14	B4
Broseley Av., Cul.	67	O18
Broseley La., Cul.	67	O17
Broughton Av., Gol.	66	L16
Broughton Av., Litt.H.	47	W10
Brown St., Bick.	42	M11
Brown St., Ince	29	K8
Brown St., Leigh	57	O13
Brown St., Tyld.	45	S12
Brown St., Wgn.	28	G8
Browning Av., Ath.	33	R9
Spa Rd.		
Browning Av., Wgn.	39	F10
Browning Gro., Stand.L.G.	16	F6
Browning St., Leigh	57	O13
Browning Wk., Ath.	33	R9
Spa Rd.		
Brownlow Av., Ince	29	K8
Brownlow La., Bill.	37	B11
Brownmere, Wgn.	27	F7
Broxton Av., Orr.	26	C8
Brundell Ms., Win.	39	E10
Brunswick Rd., Newt.	63	F18
Brunswick St., Leigh	58	Q14
Brunswick St., Newt.	63	F18
Brunswick St., St.H.	62	D18
Bryham St., Wgn.	28	H8
Bryn Gates La., Bam.	40	H12
Bryn Rd., Asht.	54	G13
Bryn Rd. S., Asht.	54	H14
Bryn St., Asht.	54	G14
Bryn St., Bam.	41	J12
Bryn St., Ince	29	J9
Brynheys Clo., Litt.H.	35	W9
Bryony Clo., Orr.	25	B9
Buchanan Dr., Hind.	43	N10
Buchanan Rd., Wgn.	27	F8
Buchanan St., Leigh	58	P13
Buck St., Leigh	58	P14
Buckfast Av., Hay.	63	G16
Buckingham Clo., Wgn.	27	F9
Buckingham Pl., Tyld.	45	S10
Buckley La., Farn.	35	W9
Buckley St., Wgn.	28	G7
Buckley St. W., Wgn.	28	G7
Buckthorn Clo., Westho.	32	P7
Bude Av., Tyld.	46	U12
Buer Av., Wgn.	39	F10
Buile Hill Av., Litt.H.	47	W10
Buile Hill Gro., Litt.H.	35	W9
Bullcroft Dr., Tyld.	60	U13
Bullough St., Ath.	45	R10
Bullows Rd., Litt.H.	35	V9
Bulteel St., Farn.	34	U7
Bulteel St., Tyld.	47	V12
Bulteel St., Wgn.	27	E9
Bunting Ms., Booth.	47	W12
Burgess St., Ince	29	J9
Burghley Way, Ince	41	J10
Burkhardt Dr., Newt.	64	H18
Burland St., Wgn.	27	F8
Burley Av., Gol.	56	L15
Burley Cres., Wgn.	39	E11
Burlington St., Hind.	30	M9
Burlton Gro., Wgn.	29	K7
Burneside Clo., Tyld.	46	T12
Burnfell, Gol.	66	M16
Burnham Gro., Wgn.	29	J7
Burnhill Ct., Stand.	16	F4
Burns Av., Ath.	33	R9
Spa Rd.		
Burns Av., Leigh	43	O12
Burns Clo., Asht.	53	F13
Burns Clo., Bill.	37	B11
Burns Clo., Wgn.	40	G10
Burns Rd., Litt.H.	35	W9
Burnsall Av., Low.	66	M16
Burnside, Parb.	4	XX3
Burnvale, Win.	39	E11
Burr St., Hay.	62	D17
Burrows Yd., Wgn.	28	H8
Millgate		
Burscough Rd., Orm.	10	QQ5
Burscough St., Orm.	10	QQ5
Butchers La., Asht.	54	G15
Butchers La., Aug.	20	NN9
Butler St., Wgn.	28	H8
Buttercup Av., Litt.H.	47	V10
Butterfield Gdns., Orm.	10	PP6
Butterfield Rd., Westho.	33	S8
Buttermere Av., Asht.	54	G13
Buttermere Rd., Farn.	35	V8
Buttermere Rd., Wgn.	27	E8
Butts Av., Leigh	59	R14
Butts St., Leigh	58	Q14
Buxton Clo., Ath.	45	S10
Byley Ri., Stand.	16	F4
Byng St., Westho.	31	N8
Byrom La., Gol.	56	M15
Byrom St., Wgn.	28	G9
Byron Clo., Orr.	26	C8
Byron Clo., Platt Br.	41	K11
Byron Clo., Stand.L.G.	16	F6
Byron Gro., Ath.	33	R9
Byron Gro., Leigh	44	P12
Byron St.		
Byron St., Hind.	30	L9
Byron St., Leigh	44	P12
Byron Wk., Farn.	35	W9
Bywater St., Wgn.	28	G8

C

Cadman Gro., Hind.	42	L10
Cadogan Dr., Wgn.	39	E11
Caernarvon Rd., Hind.	43	N10
Caldbeck Clo., Asht.	54	G14
Caldbeck Clo., Platt Br.	41	K11
Caldbeck Dr., Farn.	35	V8
Caldbeck Gro., St.H.	50	B15
Calder Av., Hind.	43	O10
Calder Av., Orm.	10	QQ6
Calder Dr., Litt.H.	47	W11
Calder Dr., Platt Br.	41	K11
Calder Pl., Wgn.	27	E8
Calderbank, Orr.	26	D9
Calderbank St., Wgn.	27	F9
Caldford Dr., Asp.	19	L5
Caldwell Av., Tyld.	60	T13
Caldwell Clo., Tyld.	60	T13
Caldwell St., Westho.	32	P9
Cale La., Asp.	29	K7
Calico Wd. Av., Shev.	15	C5
Callow Dr., Leigh	59	R14
Calton Gro., Hind.	42	M10
Calveley Wk., Stand.	16	F4
Calverhall Way, Asht.	54	G14
Calverhey, Westho.	33	R7
Calverley Clo., Westho.	32	Q7
Camberwell Cres., Wgn.	29	J7
Camborne Dr., Hind.	43	O11
Cambrian Cres., Wgn.	39	E11
Cambridge Clo., Farn.	35	V7
Cambridge Rd., Orr.	26	C8
Cambridge Rd., Skel.	23	WW7
Cambridge St., Ath.	45	R11
Camelot Clo., Newt.	63	F18
Swan Rd.		
Cameron Pl., Wgn.	27	F8
Cameron St., Leigh	43	O12
Camm St., Abram	41	K12
Camp Rd., Asht.	53	F14
Campbell St., Farn.	35	W7
Campbell St., Wgn.	27	E9
Campion Gro., Asht.	53	F14
Canaan, Low.	67	O16
Canal Bk., Leigh	58	P14
Canal Bk., Wgn.	28	H8
Canal Row, Haigh	17	H4
Canal St., Asp.	29	K7
Canal St., Ince	29	J9
Canal St., Leigh	58	P14
Canal St., Newt.	63	F18
Canal St., Wgn.	27	F7
Canal Ter., Ince	29	J8
Canberra Rd., Wgn.	27	E8
Cannel Ct., Booth.	47	W12
Canniswood Rd., Hay.	62	D17
Canon Wilson Clo., Hay.	62	E17
Cansfield Gro., Asht.	54	G14
Canterbury Av., Gol.	56	L15
Canterbury Clo., Ath.	45	S10
Capilano Pk., Orm.	21	PP8
Capp St., Platt Br.	41	K10
Captain Fold Rd., Litt.H.	35	V9
Captain Lees Gdns., Westho.	32	Q8
Captain Lees Rd., Westho.	32	Q8
Captains La., Asht.	54	H14
Car Bk. Av., Ath.	45	R10
Car Bk. Cres., Ath.	45	R10
Car Bk. Sq., Ath.	45	R10
Car Bk. St., Ath.	45	R10
Carawood Gro., App.Br.	14	B4
Cardiff St., Skel.	22	VV7
Careless La., Ince	29	J8
Carey Clo., Wgn.	39	E11
Carfield, Skel.	24	ZZ9
Carisbrooke Rd., Leigh	59	R13
Carlisle St., Hind.	30	M9
Castle Hill Rd.		
Carlisle St., Wgn.	27	E9
Carlisle Way, Asp.	19	L5
Carlton Av., Wgn.	28	G9
Carlton Clo., Asht.	54	G14
Carlton Gro., Hind.	42	M10

Carlton Rd., Gol.	56	L15
Carlyle Gro., Leigh	43	O12
Carmel Clo., Aug.	21	PP7
Carnation Rd., Farn.	35	W7
Carnforth Av., Hind.	31	N9
Carnoustie Clo., Tyld.	46	U12
Caroline St., Ince	29	J8
Caroline St., Wgn.	28	H8
Carr Common Rd., Hind.	43	O10
Carr La., Gol.	67	N16
Carr La., Leigh	67	P16
Carr La., Wgn.	40	G10
Carr Mill Cres., Bill.	50	C14
Carr Mill Rd., Bill.	50	B15
Carr Mill Rd., St.H.	50	B15
Carr St., Hind.	30	L9
Carr St., Leigh	57	O13
Carr St., Platt Br.	41	K11
Carrfield Av., Litt.H.	47	V10
Carrfield Clo., Litt.H.	47	V10
Carrfield Gro., Litt.H.	47	V10
Carrington Gro., Leigh	44	P12
Carrington St., Leigh	44	P12
Carroll Cres., Orm.	10	QQ4
Carswell Clo., Tyld.	46	U11
Carter Av., Rainf.	48	XX13
Carter St., Ince	29	J9
Cartleach Gro., Litt.H.	47	W11
Cartleach La., Litt.H.	47	V11
Cartmel Av., Wgn.	17	G6
Cartmel Clo., Bolt.	33	R7
Cartwright Gro., Leigh	43	O11
Cartwright St., Westho.	34	T8
Case Rd., Hay.	62	E17
Cashmore Dr., Hind.	42	L10
Castle Gro., Leigh	59	R13
Castle Hill, Newt.	64	H18
Castle Hill Pk., Hind.	30	M8
Castle Hill Rd., Hind.	30	M9
Castle La., Orm.	11	SS5
Castle Ri., Hind.	30	M9
Castle St., Hind.	30	M9
Castle St., Tyld.	45	S11
Castlehey, Skel.	24	ZZ9
Castleton Way, Wgn.	39	E11
Castleway, Hind.	30	M9
Brookdale Rd.		
Catherine St., Leigh	58	P13
Catherine St., Wgn.	29	J8
Catherine Ter., Wgn.	29	J8
Catherines La., Orm.	21	QQ7
Caunce Av., Gol.	65	K16
Caunce Rd., Wgn.	29	J8
Causeway, The, Leigh	57	O14
Cavendish Dr., Wgn.	39	E11
Cavendish St., Leigh	44	P12
Cawdor Av., Farn.	35	W7
Cawdor St., Farn.	35	W7
Cawdor St., Hind.	30	M9
Cawdor St., Wgn.	27	F9
Caxton Clo., Wgn.	39	F11
Cecil Av., Wgn.	28	G7
Cecil St., Ince	41	J10
Cecil St., Leigh	58	Q14
Cecil St., Wgn.	29	J8
Cedar Av., Ath.	44	Q10
Cedar Av., Hind.	42	M10
Cedar Av., Low.	66	M16
Cedar Av., Stand.	16	F4
Cedar Cres., Orm.	10	PP6
Cedar Dr., Wgn.	28	H7
Cedar Gro., Asht.	53	E13
Cedar Gro., Farn.	35	W8
Cedar Gro., Hay.	63	F16
Cedar Gro., Orr.	26	C9
Cedar Gro., Skel.	23	WW7
Cedar Gro., Westho.	32	P8
Cedar Rd., Leigh	44	P12
Celandine Wk., Wgn.	38	D10
Cemetery Rd., Ince	29	J9
Cemetery St., Westho.	32	P7
Central Av., Ath.	45	S10
Central Av., Farn.	35	W8
Central Av., Leigh	59	R14
Central Dr., Hay.	62	D17
Central Dr., Shev.	15	D5
Central Dr., Westho.	32	P7
Central Pk. Way, Wgn.	28	H7
Centre, The, Leigh	59	S13
Richmond Dr.		
Chaddock La., Tyld.	60	U13
Chadwick St., Hind.	30	M9
Chadwick St., Leigh	58	P13
Chadwick St., Wgn.	28	G9
Chalbury Clo., Hind.	42	L10
Cashmore Dr.		
Chalfont Dr., Tyld.	46	T12
Chancery Clo., Tyld.	46	T12
Chandos St., Newt.	63	G18
Chanters Av., Ath.	45	S11
Chantry Clo., Westho.	32	P9
Chantry Wk., Asht.	53	F13
Chapel Flds. La., Hind.	30	M9
Chapel Grn. Rd., Hind.	30	M9
Chapel La., Parb.	5	YY3
Chapel La., Wgn.	28	H8
Chapel Meadow, Booth.	47	W12
Ellenbrook Rd.		
Chapel Ms., Orm.	10	QQ6
Chapel Pl., Asht.	54	G14
Chapel St.		
Chapel St., Asht.	54	G14
Chapel St., Asp.	18	K6
Chapel St., Ath.	45	R10
Bolton Old Rd.		
Chapel St., Bick.	42	M11
Chapel St., Hay.	63	F17
Chapel St., Hind.	30	L9
Chapel St., Ince	28	H9
Chapel St., Leigh	58	P14
Chapel St., Newt.	63	G18
Chapel St., Orm.	10	QQ6
Chapel St., Pemb.	26	D9
Chapel St., Platt Br.	41	K11
Chapel St., Tyld.	61	V13
Chapel St., Wgn.	28	H8
Chapel Ter., Low.	67	N16
Gregory Row		
Chapel Wk., Gol.	57	N15
Chapelfield Dr., Litt.H.	47	W10
Chapelstead, Westho.	32	P9
Charles St., Gol.	55	K15
Charles St., Hind.	30	M8
Charles St., Ince	29	J8
Pickup St.		
Charles St. (Orchard La.), Leigh	44	P12
Charles St. (The Av.), Leigh	58	Q13
Charles St., Orr.	26	D8
Charles St., Tyld.	45	S11
Charles St., Wgn.	28	H7
Charlesbye Av., Orm.	11	RR5
Charlesbye Clo., Orm.	11	RR5
Charleston Ct., Tyld.	45	S11
Charles St.		
Charlesworth Av., Farn.	35	W7
Charlock Av., Westho.	32	P9
Charnock, Skel.	24	ZZ9
Charnock Av., Newt.	63	F18
Charnock St., Abram	41	K11
Bickershaw La.		
Charnocks Yd., Wgn.	26	D9
Moss Ter.		
Charnwood Clo., Tyld.	46	T12
Merlewood Dr.		
Charterhouse St., Ince	28	H9
Chatburn Av., Gol.	56	L15
Chatham St., Ince	29	K8
Chatham St., Wgn.	29	J8
Chatsworth Av., Ince	41	J10
Chatsworth Clo., Asht.	53	F14
Chatsworth Dr., Leigh	45	S12
Chatsworth St., Wgn.	27	E9
Chatteris Clo., Hind.	42	M10
Chaucer Gro., Ath.	33	R9
Milton Clo.		
Chaucer Gro., Leigh	43	O12
Chaucer Pl., Platt Br.	41	K11
Chaucer Pl., Wgn.	17	H6
Chedworth Cres., Litt.H.	35	W9
Cheetham Fold, Gol.	67	N16
Cheetham Gro., Wgn.	27	F9
Cheethams, The, Black.	19	M4
Chelburn Clo., Bick.	42	M11
Chelford Av., Gol.	66	L16
Chelford Clo., Wgn.	39	F11
Chelford Dr., Tyld.	60	U13
Chelmarsh Av., Asht.	54	H14
Chelmer Clo., Westho.	32	Q7
Chelmsford Dr., Wgn.	40	G10
Cheltenham Av., Ince	28	H9
Cheltenham Dr., Bill.	37	B11
Cheltenham Dr., Newt.	64	H18
Cheltenham St., Wgn.	29	J7
Whelley		
Cheltmorton Gro., Win.	39	E11
Chemical St., Newt.	63	G18
Queen St.		
Chepstow Gro., Leigh	45	S12
Chequer La., Skel.	24	ZZ9
Chequers St., Wgn.	28	G8
Cherington Dr., Tyld.	46	U11
Cherry Clo., Newt.	63	F18
Cherry Cft., Wgn.	28	H7
Cherry Grn., Orm.	20	OO7
Cherry Gro., Leigh	44	P12
Cherry Gro., Wgn.	16	F6
Cherry Tree Av., Farn.	35	V8
Cherry Tree Cotts., St.H.	49	A15
Cherry Tree Ct., Stand.	8	E3
Moores La.		
Cherry Tree Gro., Ath.	45	R10
Cherry Tree Gro., Leigh	57	O13
Cherry Tree La., Orm.	20	OO7
Cherry Tree La., St.H.	49	A15
Cherry Tree Rd., Gol.	66	M16
Cherrycroft, Skel.	24	ZZ9
Cherrytree Gro., Hay.	62	D17
Cherrywood Av., Westho.	34	T8
Cherrywood Clo., Wors.	47	W12
Chervil Wk., Wgn.	39	E10
Cherwell Clo., Asp.	19	L5
Cherwell Rd., Westho.	32	P7
Chesham St., Farn.	34	T7
Cheshire Clo., Newt.	64	H18
Chester Av., Gol.	66	L16
Chester Dr., Asht.	54	H15
Chester Rd., Tyld.	46	U12
Chester St., Ath.	45	S11
Chester St., Leigh	58	P13
Chesterton Clo., Wgn.	28	G9
Chestnut Av., Ath.	45	R10
Chestnut Av., Hay.	62	D17
Chestnut Av., Leigh	58	P14
Chestnut Dr., Leigh	58	P15
Chestnut Dr., Westho.	32	P8
Chestnut Gro., Asht.	54	H14
Chestnut Gro., Gol.	66	M16
Chestnut Gro., Hind.	43	N10
Chestnut La., Leigh	58	P15
Chestnut Rd., Wgn.	28	H7
Chetwode Av., Asht.	54	G15
Cheviot Clo., Wgn.	39	E11
Cheviot Wk., Platt Br.	41	K11
Chew Moor La., Westho.	32	Q7
Chichester Av., Ath.	44	Q11
Chilham St., Farn.	34	T7
Chilham St., Orr.	26	D9
Chapel St.		
Chillingham Dr., Leigh	58	Q14
Chiltern Av., Ath.	45	S10
Chiltern Clo., Asht.	54	H15
Chiltern Dr., Wgn.	39	E10
Chiltern Rd., St.H.	62	D18
Chiltern Way, Tyld.	46	T12
Chilton Clo., Leigh	44	P12
Chimes Rd., Asht.	53	F13
Chinnor Clo., Leigh	44	P12
Chisacre Dr., App.Br.	14	B4
Chisholm Clo., Stand.	7	D2
Chisnall Av., Wri.	7	C1
Chisnall La., Wri.	7	D1
Chiswell St., Wgn.	27	E9
Chisworth Clo., Leigh	44	P12
Chorley La., Stand.	9	G3
Chorley Rd., Stand.	17	G5
Chorley Rd., Wri.	5	YY2
Chorley St., Ince	29	J9
Chowbent Clo., Ath.	45	S10
Christleton, Shev.	15	D5
Christopher St., Ince	29	J9
Church Av., Bick.	42	M12
Church Ct., Wgn.	29	J8
Church Dr., Orr.	25	B9
Church Gro., Wgn.	29	J8
Church La., Aug.	20	OO8
Church La., Gol.	66	L16
Church La., Shev.	15	D5

Church Rd., Hay.	63	F16
Church Rd., Platt Br.	41	K10
Church Rd., Rainf.	48	XX13
Church Rd., Skel.	23	WW7
Church Rd., Tyld.	60	U13
Church St., Ath.	45	R10
Church St., Gol.	55	K15
Church St., Haigh	18	K5
Church St., Hind.	30	L9
Church St., Ince	29	J9
Church St., Leigh	58	P13
Church St., Newt.	64	H18
Church St., Orm.	10	QQ5
Church St., Orr.	25	B9
Church St., Pemb.	26	D9
Church St., Stand.	8	F3
Church St., Up Holl.	25	B8
Church St., Westho.	32	P7
Church St., Wgn.	28	H8
Church Ter., Asht.	54	G15
Church Vw., Aug.	20	OO8
Church Vw. Ct., Orm.	10	QQ5
Derby St. W.		
Church Wk., Westho.	32	P7
School St.		
Churchfield, Shev.	15	D5
Churchfields, Orm.	10	QQ5
Churnet Clo., Westho.	32	P7
Churton Gro., Stand.	7	D3
Cinnamon Av., Hind.	43	N10
Cinnamon Brow, Ince	30	L8
Cirencester Clo., Litt.H.	35	W9
City Rd., Orr.	26	D8
Clanwood Clo., Wgn.	39	F11
Clap Gate La., Wgn.	39	F10
Clarance Yd., Wgn.	28	H8
Hallgate		
Clare St., Wgn.	28	G8
Claremont Av., Bill.	50	C13
Claremont Av., Hind.	30	M9
Claremont Dr., Litt.H.	35	W9
Claremont Dr., Orm.	10	PP6
Claremont Rd., Bill.	50	C13
Claremont Rd., Cul.	67	O18
Clarence St., Asht.	53	F13
Clarence St., Ath.	45	S11
Clarence St., Gol.	55	K15
Clarence St., Ince	29	K8
Clarence St., Leigh	58	Q14
Clarence St., Newt.	63	F18
Clarence St., Wgn.	28	H8
Clarendon St., Ince	29	J9
Clarington Gro., Wgn.	29	J8
Clark Cres., Litt.H.	35	V9
Clarke St., Leigh	58	P14
Claude St., Wgn.	27	E9
Clay Brow Rd., Skel.	24	ZZ9
Clay Ho., Hind.	43	O11
Claydon Dr., Ince	41	J10
Clayton Av., Low.	66	M16
Clayton Ms., Skel.	22	VV7
Clayton St., Skel.	22	VV7
Clayton St., Wgn.	28	G8
Cleeve Av., Leigh	43	O12
Clegg St., Astley	60	T13
Clegg St., Ince	29	J8
Clegg St., Skel.	22	VV7
Cleggs La., Litt.H.	35	W9
Clement Av., Ath.	44	Q11
Clevedon Dr., Wgn.	39	E10
Cleveland Av., Wgn.	39	E11
Cleveland Dr., Asht.	54	H14
Cleveland Dr., Gol.	66	L16
Cleworth Clo., Tyld.	60	U14
Cleworth Hall Rd., Tyld.	46	U11
Clieves Hills La., Orm.	20	NN7
Clifford St., Leigh	58	Q14
Clifton Av., Cul.	67	O18
Clifton Av., Tyld.	60	U13
Clifton Cres., Wgn.	28	H7
Clifton Ho., Wgn.	28	G9
Clifton Rd., Asht.	53	F13
Clifton Rd., Bill.	50	B14
Clifton Rd., Leigh	58	P15
Clifton St., Farn.	35	W7
Clifton St., Leigh	57	O13
Clifton St., Wgn.	28	H7
Clifton St., Wors.M.	40	G10
Clipsley Cres., Hay.	62	D16
Clipsley La., Hay.	62	D17

Clive Rd., Westho.	32	P9
Clock Twr. Clo., Litt.H.	47	V10
Quarry Pond Rd.		
Cloister Av., Leigh	43	O11
Cloisters, The, Westho.	32	P9
Close, The, Bolt.	33	S9
Close La., Bick.	43	N11
Close La., Hind.	42	M10
Close St., Hind.	30	M9
Closebrook Rd., Wgn.	27	E9
Cloudstock Gro., Litt.H.	35	V9
Clough Av., Westho.	32	P8
Clough Fold, Westho.	32	P8
Clough Gro., Asht.	53	F13
Clough Ho. Dr., Leigh	58	Q13
Cloughwood Cres., App.Br.	14	B5
Clovelly Av., Leigh	44	P12
Clovelly Dr., Parb.	4	XX3
Clover St., Wgn.	28	G7
Club St., St.H.	49	A15
Clucas Gdn., Orm.	10	QQ5
Clyde Rd., Tyld.	46	U12
Clyde St., Leigh	58	Q14
Co-operative St., Leigh	57	O13
Coach Ho. Dr., Shev.	15	D5
Coach Rd., Tyld.	60	U13
Coach St., Ath.	45	R10
Coal Pit La., Ath.	44	Q10
Coal Pit La., Bick.	43	N11
Coal Pit La., Leigh	44	P12
Cob Moor Av., Bill.	37	B11
Cob Moor Rd., Bill.	37	B11
Cobbs Brow La., Parb.	4	XX3
Cobbs Clough Rd., Skel.	12	WW6
Cobden St., Newt.	64	H18
Cobden St., Tyld.	46	T11
Common La.		
Cocker St., Litt.H.	47	W10
Coffin La., Bam.	41	J12
Colburn Clo., Wors.M.	40	G11
Colby Rd., Wgn.	40	G10
Colchester Dr., Farn.	35	V7
Coldalhurst La., Tyld.	60	T13
Coldstone Dr., Asht.	53	E14
Cole Av., Newt.	64	H18
Cole Cres., Orm.	21	PP8
Coleridge Av., Orr.	26	D9
Coleridge Pl., Wgn.	39	F10
Warrington Rd.		
Coleridge Rd., Bill.	37	B11
Colerne Way, Wgn.	39	E11
Colesbourne Clo., Litt.H.	35	W9
Coleshill Rd., Wgn.	39	E11
Colin St., Wgn.	28	H7
Colinmander Gdns., Orm.	10	PP6
Colinton, Skel.	24	ZZ8
Collard St., Ath.	44	Q10
College Av., Wgn.	28	H8
College Rd., Up Holl.	25	A7
College St., Leigh	58	Q13
Colliery La., Ath.	44	Q10
Colling Rd., Newt.	63	G18
Collinge St., Platt Br.	41	K11
Collingwood St., Stand.	8	F3
Collingwood Way, Westho.	32	P7
Collins La., Westho.	32	P9
Collisdene Rd., Orr.	25	B9
Coln Brook, Stand.	7	D3
Shevington Moor		
Colonels La., Gol.	64	H17
Columbus St., Asht.	53	F13
Colwyn Dr., Hind.	43	O11
Colwyn Gro., Ath.	33	R9
Comet Rd., Wgn.	27	E8
Commodore Pl., Wgn.	27	F7
Common, The, Parb.	5	YY2
Common La., Leigh	57	N14
Common La., Tyld.	46	T11
Common Rd., Newt.	63	F18
Common St., Newt.	63	F18
Common St., Westho.	31	N8
Byng St.		
Commonside Rd., Tyld.	47	V12
Concorde Av., Wgn.	40	G10
Concourse, The, Skel.	23	XX7
Conder Pl., Platt Br.	41	J11
Congresbury Rd., Leigh	43	O12
Conifer Wk., Leigh	57	N13

Coniston Av., Asht.	54	G14
Coniston Av., Ath.	33	R9
Coniston Av., Farn.	35	V8
Coniston Av., Ince	29	K8
Coniston Av., Litt.H.	35	W9
Coniston Av., Orr.	26	C8
Coniston Av., Wgn.	17	G6
Coniston Dr., Abram	41	K12
Coniston Gro., Litt.H.	47	W10
Coniston Pk. Dr., Stand.	17	G5
Coniston Rd., Hind.	42	M10
Coniston Rd., Tyld.	46	T12
Coniston St., Leigh	58	P13
Conrad Clo., Wgn.	28	G9
Constantia St., Ince	41	J10
Convent Clo., Orm.	21	PP7
Conway Clo., Leigh	59	S13
Conway Cres., Bill.	50	C13
Conway Dr., Asp.	19	L5
Conway Dr., Bill.	50	C13
Conway Dr., Newt.	64	H18
Conway Rd., Asht.	55	J13
Conway Rd., Hind.	42	M10
Conway St., Wgn.	27	E9
Cook Av., Hay.	63	F16
Cook St., Abram	41	K11
Cook St., Leigh	58	P13
Cooling La., Tyld.	45	S12
Coombe Clo., Tyld.	46	T12
Coop St., Wgn.	28	H7
Cooper Av., Newt.	63	F18
Coopers Glen, Ince	29	K8
Nelson Dr.		
Coopers La., Hay.	62	E17
Coopers Row, Wgn.	28	H8
Market Pl.		
Copperas Clo., Shev.	15	D4
Copperas La., Haigh	18	K5
Copperfield, Wgn.	28	H7
Coppice Dr., Bill.	37	B11
Coppice Dr., Wgn.	39	F10
Coppull La., Wgn.	28	H7
Coppull Moor La., Cop.	8	E1
Copse, The, Newt.	63	G18
Coral Gro., Leigh	58	P14
Coral St., Wgn.	17	G6
Corfe Clo., Asp.	19	L5
Corhampton Cres., Ath.	33	S9
Alldford Dr.		
Corless Fold, Astley	60	U13
Corn St., Leigh	57	O13
Cornbrook, Skel.	24	ZZ8
Cornelian Gro., Asht.	39	F12
Corner Gate, Westho.	32	P9
Corner La., Hind.	43	O10
Cornwall Av., Tyld.	46	T10
Cornwall Av., Westho.	33	S8
Cornwall Cres., Stand.	9	G3
Cornwall Dr., Hind.	30	M9
Cornwall Pl., Wgn.	27	E9
Cornwall Rd., Tyld.	45	S10
Cornwallis Rd., Wgn.	27	F9
Coronation Av., Ath.	33	R9
Coronation Dr., Hay.	63	G16
Coronation Dr., Leigh	59	R13
Coronation Rd., Stand.L.G.	16	E6
Coronation St., Asht.	53	E13
Coronation St., Ince	41	J10
Coronation St., Wgn.	28	G9
Coronation Wk., Bill.	50	B14
Corporation St., Wgn.	28	G9
Corrie St., Litt.H.	47	W10
Corsey Rd., Hind.	42	M10
Corsock Dr., Wgn.	29	J7
Costessy Way, Win.	39	E10
Cosworth Clo., Leigh	58	Q14
Cotswold Av., Gol.	66	L17
Cotswold Av., Wgn.	26	D9
Cotswold Gro., St.H.	62	D18
Cottage Clo., Orm.	10	PP6
Cottage Gdns., Orm.	10	PP5
Cottage La., Orm.	10	PP5
Cottesmore Way, Gol.	55	K15
Cotton Dr., Orm.	10	PP5
Cotton St., Leigh	57	O13
Coultshead Av., Bill.	50	C13
Council Av., Asht.	54	G14
County Police St., Ince	29	J8
Careless La.		

County Rd., Litt.H. 47 V10
County Rd., Orm. 10 PP5
Coupes Grn., Westho. 32 P9
Coupland Rd., Hind. 43 N10
Courage Low La., Wri. 6 B2
Courier Pl., Wgn. 27 F7
Course La., Parb. 4 WW3
Court Grn., Orm. 10 PP4
Court La., Asht. 54 G15
Courtfield Rd., Orm. 10 QQ4
Coverdale Rd., Westho. 31 O8
Coverts, The, Wgn. 27 F7
Cow La., Farn. 34 T7
Cow Lees, Westho. 32 Q7
Cowburn St., Hind. 30 M8
Cowburn St., Leigh 57 O13
Cowling St., Wgn. 28 G9
Cowper Av., Ath. 33 R9
Cowper St., Leigh 57 O13
Coxfield, App.Br. 14 B4
Crab Brow, Ath. 44 Q10
Crab Tree La., Ath. 45 R10
Crabtree Rd., Wgn. 27 E8
Crag Gro., St.H. 49 A15
Cranberry Av., Wgn. 16 F6
Cranborne Clo., Stand. 8 E3
Cranbrook Av., Asht. 54 G14
Cranbrook Way, Wgn. 17 G6
Cranby St., Hind. 30 L9
Cranfield Rd., Wgn. 40 G10
Cranham Av., Gol. 66 M16
Cranham Clo., Litt.H. 35 W9
Crank Hill, Rainf. 49 ZZ14
Crank Rd., K.Moss 49 ZZ13
Crank Rd., St.H. 49 ZZ15
Crankwood Rd., Abram 56 L13
Cranleigh, Stand. 17 G4
Cranleigh Dr., Tyld. 46 T12
Cranstal Dr., Hind. 31 N9
Cranworth Av., Tyld. 60 T13
Craven Av., Gol. 66 M16
Crawford Av., Asp. 19 L5
Crawford Av., Tyld. 45 S10
Crawford Clo., Asp. 19 L5
Crawford Rd., Bill. 36 YY11
Crawford St., Asp. 19 L6
Crawford St., Wgn. 28 H8
Crawley Clo., Tyld. 46 U11
Crediton Dr., Platt Br. 41 K11
Crescent, The, Ince 29 K8
Petticoat La.
Crescent, The, Westho. 32 P8
Crescent, The, Wgn. 27 E9
Crescent Av., Asht. 54 G14
Crescent Av., Westho. 34 T8
Crescent Dr., Litt.H. 35 W9
Crescent Grn., Orm. 20 OO7
Crescent Rd., Farn. 35 W7
Cressell Pk., Stand. 7 D3
Crestfold, Litt.H. 47 W10
Crestwood Av., Wgn. 39 F10
Cricketers Way, Westho. 32 P8
Crippen St., Ath. 44 Q11
Croal Av., Platt Br. 41 K11
Croasdale Dr., Parb. 5 YY2
Croft, The, Bill. 37 B10
Croft Av., Ath. 45 R11
Croft Av., Gol. 55 J15
Croft Av., Orr. 25 B9
Croft Gro., Litt.H. 35 V8
Croft St.
Croft Heys, Orm. 20 OO7
Croft Pl., Tyld. 45 S12
Croft St., Litt.H. 35 V9
Crofters Arms Yd., Wgn. 28 H8
Market St.
Crofton St., Ath. 45 S10
Croftson Av., Orm. 10 QQ4
Croftwood Sq., Wgn. 27 E7
Crombouke Dr., Leigh 44 P11
Crombouke Fold, Booth. 47 W12
Cromedale Cres., Stand. 17 G4
Cromer Dr., Ath. 44 P11
Cromer Rd., Wgn. 39 F10
Cromfield, Orm. 21 PP7
Cromford Dr., Wgn. 26 D9
Crompton St., Ince 41 J10
Warrington Rd.
Crompton St., Platt Br. 41 K10
Crompton St., Wgn. 28 H8
Cromwell Clo., Orm. 21 PP7
Crook St., Hind. 42 L10
Lord St.
Crook St., Wgn. 28 G8
Fitzadam St.
Crooke Rd., Stand.L.G. 16 E6
Crookhurst Av., Bill. 50 B13
Croppers La., Orm. 21 QQ7
Crosby Gro., Ath. 45 S10
Crosby St., Ath. 45 S10
Cross Hall Brow, Orm. 11 RR5
Cross La., Bill. 37 B10
Cross La., Newt. 63 G18
Cross Pit La., Rainf. 48 XX13
Cross St., Ath. 44 Q10
Cross St., Gol. 65 K16
Cross St., Haigh 18 K5
Cross St., Hind. 30 L9
Cross St., Ince 41 J10
Cross St., Leigh 58 Q14
Cross St., Orr. 26 D9
Cross St., Stand. 8 F3
Cross St., Tyld. 45 S12
James St.
Cross St., Wgn. 28 H8
Crossdale Rd., Hind. 43 N10
Crossdale Way, St.H. 49 A15
Crossgill, Tyld. 60 T13
Crosslands Rd., Tyld. 61 V13
Crossway Clo., Asht. 55 J13
Crow La., Skel. 13 ZZ6
Crow La. E., Newt. 64 H18
Crow La. W., Newt. 63 F18
Crow Orchard Rd., Stand. 7 D3
Crow Orchard Rd., Wri. 7 C3
Crow Orchard Ter., Ince 29 J9
Crow Wd. Rd., Gol. 56 L15
Crowhurst Dr., Wgn. 17 G6
Crown Flds. Clo., Newt. 63 G17
Crown Gdns., Newt. 63 G18
Crown Gro., Leigh 59 R13
Crown Pk. Dr., Newt. 63 G17
Crown St., Ath. 45 R10
Crown St., Hind. 30 L9
Crown St., Newt. 63 G18
Crown St., Wgn. 28 G9
Crown Ter., Newt. 64 H18
Croydon Av., Leigh 44 P12
Crummock Dr., Wgn. 39 F10
Crummock Gro., Farn. 35 V8
Culcheth Av., Abram 41 K11
Culcross Av., Win. 39 E10
Cullen Clo., Ince 29 K8
Culvert La., Parb. 4 XX3
Culvert St., Wgn. 17 G6
Culzean Clo., Leigh 59 R14
Cumberbatch Pl., Ince 41 J10
Cumberland Av., Tyld. 45 S11
Cumberland Cres., Hay. 62 D17
Cumberland Rd., Ath. 45 S10
Cumberland St., Wgn. 29 J7
Cumbermere La., Tyld. 46 T11
Cumbrian Clo., Platt Br. 41 K11
Cunliffe Av., Newt. 63 G17
Cunliffe Ct., Gol. 57 N14
Cunningham, Westho. 31 O8
Curtis St., Farn. 34 U7
Curtis St., Wgn. 27 E9
Cuthbert St., Farn. 34 T7
Cuthbert St., Wgn. 27 E9
Cygnet Clo., Aug. 21 PP7
Cygnet St., Wgn. 28 G9
Cypress Rd., Wgn. 27 F9

D

Daffodil Rd., Farn. 35 W7
Dailton Rd., Up Holl. 25 A8
Daisy Av., Farn. 35 W7
Daisy Hall Dr., Westho. 32 P9
Daisy Rd., Wgn. 27 F9
Dakins Lea, Leigh 58 Q14
Dakins Rd., Leigh 58 Q15
Dalbeatie Ri., Wgn. 29 J7
Dalby Rd., Hind. 31 N9
Dale Clo., Parb. 4 XX3
Dale Gro., Leigh 57 O14
Dale Lee, Westho. 32 Q8
Dale Rd., Gol. 65 K16
Dale St., Ince 41 J10
Dale St., Leigh 57 O13
Dale St., Westho. 32 P9
Dale Vw., Newt. 64 H18
Dalebank, Ath. 33 R9
Dalecrest, Bill. 37 B11
Dalehead Pl., St.H. 49 A15
Dalesford Clo., Leigh 67 O16
Daleside Av., Asht. 40 G12
Dalkeith Rd., Hind. 31 N9
Dalston Dr., St.H. 49 A15
Dalston Gro., Wgn. 39 E10
Dalton Clo., Orr. 26 D8
Dalton Dr., Wgn. 39 F10
Dalton Fold, Westho. 32 P8
Dalton Gro., Asht. 54 G14
Dam Head Fold, Westho. 32 P7
Dam La., Gol. 55 J14
Damian Dr., Newt. 63 G17
Danbers, Skel. 24 ZZ9
Danes Av., Hind. 30 M9
Danesbury Clo., Bill. 50 C14
Danesway, Wgn. 17 G6
Daniels La., Skel. 24 YY8
Darby La., Hind. 30 L9
Darent Rd., Hay. 62 D17
Darfield, Skel. 24 ZZ8
Daric Clo., Leigh 57 O15
Dark La., Orm. 11 SS5
Darley Rd., Wgn. 40 G11
Darlington St., Ince 29 K8
Darlington St., Tyld. 46 T11
Darlington St., Wgn. 28 H8
Darlington St. E., Tyld. 46 T11
Darnhall St., Ince 41 J10
Darnley Av., Booth. 47 W11
Darran Av., Wgn. 39 F10
Darvel Av., Asht. 53 E14
David Brow, Farn. 34 T7
Davidson Wk., Wgn. 27 F8
Davies Av., Newt. 64 H17
Davies St., Platt Br. 41 K11
Dawber St., Asht. 54 H14
Dawber St., Wgn. 28 G8
Dawley Clo., Asht. 54 G14
Dawnwood Sq., Wgn. 27 E7
Dawson Av., Wgn. 17 G6
Dawson Rd., Orm. 10 QQ4
Dawson St., Ath. 45 R10
Daybrook, Skel. 24 ZZ8
Dayfield Ct., Up Holl. 25 A8
Dayton Wk., Asp. 29 K7
Ashbourne Av.
De Trafford Dr., Ince 29 K8
Deakin St., Ince 29 J9
Dean Clo., Bill. 50 B14
Dean Clo., Farn. 35 V8
Dean Clo., Up Holl. 25 B8
Dean Ct., Gol. 65 K16
Dean Cres., Orr. 26 D8
Dean Meadow, Newt. 64 H18
Dean Rd., Gol. 65 K16
Deans La., Parb. 4 WW2
Deansgate, Hind. 30 L9
Deanwood Av., Orr. 26 C7
Dearden Av., Litt.H. 35 W9
Dearden Ct., Up Holl. 25 A8
Debdale La., Tyld. 59 S14
Deben Clo., Stand. 8 E3
Dee Rd., Tyld. 46 U12
Deepdale, Leigh 59 R14
Defiance St., Ath. 45 R10
Delamere Av., Low. 66 M17
Delamere Rd., Skel. 23 WW7
Delamere Way, Up Holl. 25 A8
Delegarte St., Ince 29 J9
Dell, The, Up Holl. 25 A8
Dell Av., Wgn. 16 F6
Dell Side Clo., Asht. 53 E13
Delph, The, Parb. 5 YY2
Delph Clo., Aug. 21 PP7
Delph Common Rd., Orm. 21 PP7
Delph Gro., Leigh 43 O11
Delph La., Orm. 21 PP7
Delph Pk. Av., Orm. 20 OO7
Delph St., Wgn. 28 G7
Delph Top, Orm. 11 RR5
Delphside Clo., Orr. 25 B9
Delphside Rd., Orr. 25 B9
Denbigh Gro., Ath. 33 R9

Dene Av., Newt. 63 G18
Dene Gro., Leigh 57 N14
Dene St., Leigh 57 N14
Denford Clo., Wgn. 39 F10
Denham Dr., Wgn. 40 G10
Denholme, Skel. 24 ZZ8
Denshaw, Skel. 24 ZZ8
Denton Gro., Orr. 26 D8
Derby Clo., Newt. 63 G18
Derby Dr., Rainf. 48 XX13
Derby Hill Cres., Orm. 11 RR5
Derby Hill Rd., Orm. 11 RR5
Derby Rd., Gol. 56 L15
Derby Rd., Skel. 22 VV8
Derby St., Ath. 45 R10
Derby St., Ince 41 J10
Derby St., Newt. 63 G18
Derby St., Orm. 10 QQ5
Derby St., Tyld. 46 T11
Derby St., Westho. 32 P7
Derby St., Wgn. 29 J7
Derby St. E., Leigh 58 Q14
Derby St. W., Leigh 58 P14
Derby St. W., Orm. 10 QQ5
Derby Ter., Wgn. 28 H8
Derbyshire Hill Rd., St.H. 62 D18
Dereham Way, Wgn. 39 E10
Derngate Dr., Stand. 17 G4
Derwent Av., Gol. 56 L15
Derwent Av., Ince 29 K8
Derwent Clo., Litt.H. 47 W11
Derwent Pl., Wgn. 27 E8
Derwent Rd., Asht. 55 J13
Derwent Rd., Farn. 35 V8
Derwent Rd., Hind. 30 M9
Derwent Rd., Orr. 26 C8
Derwent St., Leigh 58 P14
Derwent St., Tyld. 46 T12
Desmond St., Ath. 44 Q11
Devoke Av., St.H. 49 A15
Devoke Gro., Farn. 35 V8
Devon Clo., Asp. 19 L5
Devon Clo., Wgn. 27 E9
Devon Dr., Stand. 17 G4
Devon Rd., Tyld. 46 T11
Devon St., Hind. 30 M9
Devon St., Leigh 59 S14
Devonshire Dr., Tyld. 61 V13
Devonshire Ho. Yd., Ince 29 K8
Devonshire Rd., Ath. 33 R9
Diamond St., Leigh 58 P14
Diamond St., Wgn. 17 G6
Diane Rd., Asht. 54 H13
Dicconson Cres., Wgn. 28 H7
Dicconson St., Wgn. 28 H7
Dicconson Ter., Wgn. 28 H7
Dicconson Way, Orm. 11 RR6
Dickens Dr., Abram 41 K12
Dickens Pl., Wgn. 39 F10
Dickenson Clo., Hay. 62 D17
Dickenson St., Hind. 42 M10
Dicketts La., Skel. 22 UU7
Didsbury Gro., Hind. 30 L9
Diggle St., Wgn. 28 G7
Digmoor Dr., Skel. 24 YY8
Daniels La.
Digmoor Rd., Skel. 24 ZZ8
Dingle Av., App.Br. 15 C4
Dingle Av., Up Holl. 25 B8
Dingle Clo., Orm. 21 PP7
Dingle Rd., Up Holl. 25 A8
Dingle Wk., Stand.L.G. 16 E6
Dixon Av., Newt. 64 H17
Dixon Av., Shev. 15 D5
Dixon Clo., Hay. 63 G16
Dixon Dr., Shev. 15 D5
Dixon Pl., Abram 41 K11
Dixon St., Platt Br. 41 K10
Moss La.
Dobb Brow Rd., Westho. 31 O8
Doctors Nook, Leigh 58 P13
Dodhurst Rd., Hind. 30 M9
Doe Hey Gro., Farn. 35 W7
Doe Hey Rd., Farn. 35 W7
Doe Meadow, Parb. 4 XX3
Doeford Clo., Cul. 67 O17
Donnington Clo., Leigh 57 O15
Dootson St., Abram 41 K11
Dootson St., Hind. 31 N9
Dorchester Rd., Up Holl. 25 A8
Doric Grn., Bill. 37 B10
Dorning St., Black. 19 M4
Dorning St., Leigh 58 P13
Dorning St., Tyld. 45 S11
Dorning St., Wgn. 28 G8
Dorothy Gro., Leigh 58 P14
Dorothy Wk., Bam. 41 J12
Dorset Av., Tyld. 45 S10
Dorset Clo., Wgn. 27 E9
Dorset Rd., Ath. 45 R10
Dorset Rd., Stand. 9 G3
Dorset St., Hind. 30 M9
Dorset St., Leigh 59 R14
Dorset St., Wgn. 29 J7
Dorstone Clo., Hind. 31 N9
Douglas Av., Bill. 50 B14
Douglas Av., Up Holl. 25 A8
Douglas Bk. Dr., Wgn. 27 F7
Douglas Dr., Orm. 10 QQ4
Douglas Dr., Orr. 26 C8
Douglas Dr., Shev. 15 C5
Douglas Pk., Ath. 45 S10
Douglas Rd., Ath. 45 S11
Douglas Rd., Leigh 43 O12
Douglas Rd., Stand. 7 D3
Douglas Rd., Wgn. 28 H7
Douglas St., Ath. 45 S10
Douglas St., Hind. 42 L10
Douglas St., Wgn. 28 G8
Douglas Ter., Wgn. 28 G8
Douglas Way, Platt Br. 41 K11
Lune Rd.
Dove St., Gol. 55 K15
Dove Wk., Litt.H. 35 V8
Dovecote La., Litt.H. 47 V10
Dovedale Cres., Asht. 40 G12
Dovedale Dr., Stand. 8 F3
Dovedale Rd., Asht. 40 G12
Dovey Clo., Tyld. 46 U12
Dower St., Platt Br. 41 K10
Dowling Clo., Stand.L.G. 16 E6
Downall Grn. Rd., Asht. 53 F13
Downham Wk., Bill. 37 B11
Downing Clo., Platt Br. 41 K11
Downing St., Leigh 58 P13
King St.
Downs, The, Wgn. 39 E10
Downton Av., Hind. 42 L10
Doyle Rd., Westho. 33 S6
Drake Clo., Aug. 21 PP7
Drake Hall, Westho. 32 P9
Drayton St., St.H. 62 D18
Druid St., Asht. 54 H15
Drummers La., Asht. 39 F12
Drummond Sq., Wgn. 27 F8
Dryden Av., Asht. 39 F12
Dryden Clo., Wgn. 28 G9
Dryden Ho., Wgn. 28 G9
Dryton Wk., Wgn. 29 K7
Ashbourne Av.
Dudley Rd., Leigh 58 P15
Dudley St., Asht. 54 G13
Duke St., Asht. 54 H14
Duke St., Gol. 55 K15
Duke St., G.Grn. 39 F10
Duke St., Leigh 58 Q14
Duke St., Newt. 63 G18
Duke St., Platt Br. 41 K10
Duke St., Swin. 28 H7
Duke St., Tyld. 60 U13
Dukes Ward La., Bill. 36 YY10
Dumbarton Grn., Wgn. 27 F7
Dunblane Clo., Asht. 53 E14
Duncan Av., Newt. 64 H17
Duncan Pl., Wgn. 27 F8
Dungeon La., Skel. 13 YY4
Dunham Av., Gol. 55 J15
Dunham Clo., Westho. 31 O9
Dunham Gro., Leigh 59 R15
Dunlin Av., Newt. 64 H18
Dunmail Av., St.H. 50 B15
Dunoon Rd., Asp. 19 L5
Dunscore Rd., Win. 39 F10
Dunsdale Dr., Asht. 54 H14
Walford Rd.
Dunster Clo., Platt Br. 41 K11
Dunster Dr., Wgn. 39 F10
Dunster Pl., Tyld. 47 V12
Dunster Rd., Tyld. 47 V12
Dunvegan Rd., Asht. 54 H15
Durban St., Abram 56 M14
Durban St., Ath. 44 Q11
Durham Clo., Tyld. 46 T10
Durham Rd., Hind. 30 M9
Durham St., Skel. 22 VV7
Durham St., Wgn. 29 J7
Dursley Dr., Asht. 54 H14
Dutton Gro., Leigh 59 R15
Dyer St., Gol. 55 J15
Dyers Ct., Orm. 10 QQ6
Dyers La., Orm. 10 QQ6

E

Eagle Cres., Rainf. 48 XX13
Earl St., Ath. 44 Q11
Earl St., Ince 29 K8
Earl St., Leigh 58 Q13
Earl St., Wgn. 27 F7
Earl St. (Ince), Wgn. 28 H7
Earle Clo., Newt. 63 F18
Earle St., Newt. 63 F18
Earlsdon Cres., Litt.H. 35 W9
Earlswood, Skel. 24 ZZ7
East Av., Gol. 56 L15
East Av., Leigh 59 R14
East Bond St., Leigh 58 Q13
East Bridgewater St., Leigh 58 Q14
East Dene, Parb. 4 XX3
East Lancashire Rd., Gol. 64 H16
East Lancashire Rd., Hay. 62 D16
East Lancashire Rd., Low. 67 N17
East Lancashire Rd., Tyld. 60 T14
East Mead, Orm. 20 OO7
East Meade, Farn. 35 V7
East Moor, Tyld. 47 W12
East Mt., Orr. 26 C9
East St., Asht. 54 H14
East St., Ath. 45 S11
East St., Hind. 43 N10
East St., Ince 28 H9
East Vw., Ince 29 K8
Eastgarth, Platt Br. 41 K11
Eastham Way, Litt.H. 35 W9
Eastleigh, Skel. 24 YY7
Eastleigh Cres., Leigh 58 Q14
Eastmoor Gro., Farn. 34 T7
Easton Clo., Wors.M. 40 G11
Eastwell Rd., Asht. 54 G14
Eastwell Rd., Wgn. 16 F6
Eastwood Av., Litt.H. 47 W11
Eastwood Av., Newt. 64 H18
Eastwood Gro., Leigh 57 O13
Eatock St., Platt Br. 41 K10
Eatock Way, Westho. 31 O9
Eaton St., Hind. 30 M9
Eavesdale, Skel. 24 ZZ8
Eccles La., Bisp. 4 XX1
Eccles Rd., Orr. 26 D7
Eccleston St., Wgn. 28 H7
Eckersley Av., Hind. 42 L10
Eckersley Fold La., Ath. 44 Q11
Eckersley St., Wgn. 29 J7
Edale Clo., Ath. 45 R10
Edale Dr., Stand. 8 F3
Edale Rd., Leigh 59 R14
Eddisford Dr., Cul. 67 O17
Eddleston St., Asht. 53 F13
Eden Gro., Leigh 57 O13
Edenbank, Leigh 58 Q13
Edenvale, Tyld. 47 W12
Edge Grn. La., Gol. 55 J15
Edge Grn. Rd., Gol. 55 J14
Edge Grn. St., Asht. 54 H14
Edge Hall Rd., Orr. 26 C9
Edge St., Tyld. 45 S11
Lime St.
Edgerley Pl., Asht. 54 G14
Edgerton Rd., Low. 66 M16
Edgeware Gro., Wgn. 39 E10
Edgeway Rd., Wors.M. 40 G11
Edgewood, Shev. 15 D5
Edgeworth Rd., Hind. 43 N10
Edgley Dr., Orm. 11 RR5
Edinburgh Clo., Ince 29 K8
Edinburgh Dr., Hind. 43 N10
Edinburgh Dr., Wgn. 27 E9

Edinburgh Wk., Asp. 19 L5
Edith St., Wgn. 28 G8
Edmund Dr., Leigh 57 O13
Edna Rd., Leigh 43 O12
Edward Dr., Asht. 54 G14
Edward St., Farn. 35 W7
Edward St., Hay. 62 D17
Edward St., Ince 29 J8
Edward St., Leigh 58 Q14
Edward St., Wgn. 28 H7
Edwin St., Wgn. 29 J8
Egerton, Skel. 24 YY8
Egerton St., Abram 41 K12
Egeworth Rd., Gol. 55 J15
Elaine Clo., Asht. 54 H13
Elcombe Av., Gol. 66 M16
Elderberry Clo., Wgn. 17 G6
Eldon Gdns., Asht. 54 G13
Eldon St., Leigh 57 O13
Eleanor Dr., Tyld. 46 U12
Eleanor St., Wgn. 28 G8
Elgin Av., Asht. 53 E14
Elgin Clo., Ince 29 K8
Eliot Dr., Wgn. 28 G9
Elizabeth Av., Bick. 42 M11
Elizabeth Rd., Hay. 63 F16
Elizabeth St., Ath. 45 R10
Elizabeth St., Ince 29 K8
Elizabeth St., Leigh 58 Q14
Elizabeth St., Wgn. 29 J8
Elizabethan Ct., Tyld. 45 S11
Ash St.
Elizabethan Dr., Ince 41 J10
Elizabethan Wk., Platt Br. 41 K11
Webster St.
Elkstone Clo., Litt.H. 35 W9
Earlsdon Cres.
Elkstone Clo., Wgn. 39 E11
Elkwood Clo., Wgn. 17 G6
Ellen St., Ince 29 J8
Ellen St., Wgn. 28 H8
Ellenbrook Rd., Booth. 61 W13
Ellendale Gra., Booth. 47 W12
Ellerbrook Way, Orm. 10 QQ5
Ellesmere Clo., Litt.H. 47 W10
Ellesmere Dr., Asht. 53 F13
Ellesmere Rd., Asht. 53 F14
Ellesmere Rd., Wgn. 27 E9
Ellesmere St., Astley 60 U13
Ellesmere St., Litt.H. 47 W10
Ellesmere St., Tyld. 45 S11
Elliot Av., Gol. 55 K15
Elliot Dr., Hind. 30 M8
Elliott St., Tyld. 45 S11
Ellis Cres., Litt.H. 47 W10
Ellis Rd., Bill. 50 B14
Ellis St., Wgn. 29 J7
Elm Av., Asht. 53 E13
Elm Av., Gol. 55 K15
Elm Av., Pemb. 27 F9
Elm Av., Stand. 16 F4
Elm Cft., Wgn. 17 G6
Elm Dr., Bill. 50 B13
Elm Gro., Farn. 35 W8
Elm Gro., Skel. 23 WW7
Elm Pl., Orm. 10 QQ6
Elm Rd., Abram 42 L12
Elm Rd., Hay. 63 F16
Wycliffe Rd.
Elm Rd., Westho. 32 P8
Elm St., Leigh 58 P14
Elm St., Platt Br. 41 K11
Elm St., Tyld. 46 T11
Elm Tree Rd., Gol. 66 M16
Elmers Grn., Skel. 24 YY7
Elmers Grn. La., Skel. 13 YY6
Elmers Wd. Rd., Skel. 24 YY7
Elmfield, Shev. 15 D5
Elmfield Av., Ath. 44 Q10
Elmfield Rd., Wgn. 17 G5
Elmhow Gro., Wgn. 40 G11
Elmridge, Leigh 58 Q13
Elmridge, Skel. 24 YY7
Elmsbury St., Asht. 53 F13
Elmsfield Pk., Aug. 20 NN9
Elmstead, Skel. 24 YY8
Elmwood, Skel. 13 YY6
Forest Dr.
Elmwood Av., Asht. 54 G15
Elmwood Clo., Westho. 34 T9
Elnup Av., Shev. 15 D5
Elsham Rd., Litt.H. 47 W10
Elstead Gro., Asht. 53 E14
Elston Av., Newt. 63 G17
Elswick, Skel. 24 YY8
Elton Av., Farn. 35 V8
Elton Clo., Gol. 66 M16
Elway Rd., Asht. 54 H14
Elworthy Gro., Wgn. 29 J7
Ely Dr., Tyld. 46 U12
Emerald Av., Leigh 58 P14
Emerald St., Wgn. 17 G6
Emlyn St., Hind. 30 L9
Empress Dr., Leigh 59 S13
Ena Cres., Leigh 43 O12
Endsleigh Gdns., Leigh 58 P13
Endsley Av., Booth. 47 W11
Enfield Gro., Leigh 58 Q13
Enfield St., Wgn. 27 E9
Engine Fold Rd., Litt.H. 47 W10
Engine La., Tyld. 46 T10
Engineer St., Ince 29 K8
English St., Leigh 58 Q14
Enid Pl., Bam. 41 J12
Ennerdale, Skel. 24 YY8
Ennerdale Av., Asht. 54 G14
Ennerdale Av., St.H. 49 A15
Ennerdale Dr., Orm. 21 PP7
Ennerdale Gro., Farn. 35 V8
Ennerdale Pl., Ince 29 K8
Ennerdale Rd., Hind. 30 M9
Ennerdale Rd., Leigh 58 Q13
Ennerdale Rd., Tyld. 46 T12
Enstone, Skel. 24 YY7
Enstone Way, Tyld. 46 U11
Entwistle Gro., Leigh 59 R14
Envoy Clo., Wgn. 27 F7
Ephraims Fold, Asp. 19 L5
Epsom Dr., Bam. 41 J12
Erica Wk., Leigh 57 N13
Erradale Cres., Wgn. 39 E11
Erskine Pl., Abram 41 K11
Esham Dr., Farn. 35 W7
Eskbank, Skel. 24 YY8
Eskbrook, Skel. 24 YY7
Eskdale, Skel. 23 XX8
Eskdale Av., Black. 19 M4
Eskdale Av., Orm. 21 PP7
Eskdale Av., Wgn. 17 G6
Eskdale Dr., Orm. 21 PP7
Eskdale Gro., Farn. 35 V8
Eskdale Rd., Asht. 54 G13
Eskdale Rd., Hind. 30 M9
Essex Pl., Tyld. 45 S10
Essex Rd., Stand. 17 G4
Essex St., Wgn. 29 J7
Esthwaite Dr., Tyld. 46 T12
Etherstone St., Leigh 58 P14
Eton St., Leigh 58 P14
Eton Ter., Ince 29 J9
Eton Way, Orr. 26 C8
Eva St., Leigh 43 O12
Evans Clo., Hay. 63 F16
Evans St., Leigh 58 P13
Even Clo., Stand.L.G. 16 E6
Evenwood, Skel. 24 YY7
Everard Clo., Wors. 47 W12
Everbrom Rd., Farn. 34 T7
Everest Pl., Wgn. 28 H7
Everest Rd., Ath. 33 R9
Eversley, Skel. 24 YY7
Everton St., Asht. 53 E13
Evesham Clo., Leigh 57 O15
Evington, Skel. 24 YY7
Exeter Av., Farn. 35 V7
Exeter Dr., Asp. 19 L5
Exeter Rd., Hind. 30 M9
Exford Av., Wgn. 40 G10
Exhall Clo., Litt.H. 35 W9
Earlsdon Cres.
Eyes La., Parb. 4 XX2
Eyet St., Leigh 58 P13

F

Factory Fold, Ince 29 K8
Factory St., Tyld. 45 S11
Factory St. W., Ath. 45 R10
Fair St., Farn. 34 U7
Fairacres, Stand. 7 D3
Fairbourne Av., Wgn. 40 G10
Fairburn, Skel. 12 XX6
Fairclough Cres., Hay. 62 D17
Fairclough St., Hind. 30 L9
Fairclough St., Newt. 63 G18
Fairclough St., Wgn. 28 H8
Darlington St.
Fairfield Av., Platt Br. 41 K11
Fairfield Av., Wgn. 27 E9
Fairfield Gdns., St.H. 49 ZZ15
Fairfield Rd., Farn. 35 W8
Fairfield St., Wgn. 27 E9
Fairhaven, Skel. 13 YY6
Fairhaven Av., Westho. 32 Q8
Fairholme Av., Asht. 54 G14
Fairhurst Av., Stand. 8 E2
Fairhurst Dr., Litt.H. 47 V11
Fairhurst Dr., Parb. 4 XX3
Fairhurst La., Stand. 17 G4
Fairhurst St., Leigh 58 P13
Fairlie, Skel. 13 YY6
Fairlyn Clo., Westho. 34 T8
Fairlyn Dr., Westho. 34 T8
Fairstead, Skel. 13 YY6
Fairview, Bill. 50 B13
Fairview Av., Bill. 50 B13
Fairview
Fairview Clo., Asht. 54 G14
Faith St., Leigh 57 O13
Falcon Dr., Litt.H. 35 W9
Falconers Grn., Wors.M. 28 G9
Falconwood Chase, Booth. 61 W13
Falconwood Clo., Wgn. 28 G7
Falkirk Dr., Ince 29 K8
Falkirk Gro., Wgn. 27 E8
Falkland, Skel. 13 YY6
Falkland Dr., Asht. 53 E14
Fallow Clo., Westho. 32 P7
Peel Ter.
Falstone Clo., Win. 39 E11
Fardon Clo., Wgn. 39 F10
Farefield Av., Gol. 55 J15
Farley La., R.Mill 14 A6
Farm La., Ince 29 K7
Farm Meadow Rd., Orr. 26 C9
Farndale Gro., Asht. 54 H15
Farnham Clo., Leigh 58 P13
Farnsfield, Wgn. 29 J7
Farnworth St., Leigh 58 Q14
Farr Clo., Wgn. 27 F9
Farrell St., Wgn. 27 E9
Farriers Cft., Wgn. 27 F7
Farrimonds Row, Wgn. 28 H8
Wallgate
Farrington Dr., Orm. 10 QQ5
Fawcett, Skel. 12 XX6
Fearnham Dr., Leigh 58 P15
Fell St., Leigh 57 N14
Fellbridge Clo., Westho. 32 Q7
Fellside, Wgn. 28 H7
Felsted, Skel. 24 YY7
Feltons, Skel. 23 XX7
Feltons Ms., Skel. 24 ZZ7
Fenney Ct., Skel. 24 YY7
Ferguson Ri., Wgn. 27 F8
Fern Clo., Ath. 45 R11
Fern Clo., Shev. 15 D5
Fern Clo., Skel. 23 WW7
Fern Lea Gro., Litt.H. 47 V10
Fernbray Rd., Hind. 30 M9
Ferndale, Skel. 24 YY7
Ferndale Wk., Leigh 57 N13
Fernhurst Clo., Ince 29 J9
Fernhurst Gate, Orm. 20 OO7
Fernlea Gro., Asht. 53 E13
Fernside Gro., Win. 39 E11
Festival Rd., Rainf. 48 XX13
Field St., Asht. 53 F13
Field St., Hind. 42 M10
Field St., Ince 41 J10
Field St., Skel. 22 VV7
School La.
Field St., Wgn. 28 G8
Field Wk., Orm. 11 RR5
Fieldbrook Wk., Westho. 32 Q7
Fieldhead Av., Tyld. 60 T13
Fields, The, Asp. 19 L6
Fieldsend Dr., Leigh 67 O16
Fieldway, Platt Br. 41 K11

Finch Av., Farn. 35 V8
Finch Av., Rainf. 48 XX13
Finch La., Wri. 6 A3
Finch Mill Av., App.Br. 14 B4
Finchdale Gdns., Leigh 67 N16
Finchley Cres., Wgn. 29 J7
Findlay St., Leigh 58 P13
Findon, Skel. 23 XX7
Finney Gro., Hay. 63 F17
Fir Gro., Wgn. 17 G6
Fir Rd., Farn. 35 W8
Fir Tree Av., Gol. 66 M16
Fir Tree Clo., K.Moss 36 ZZ12
Fir Tree Clo., Skel. 24 YY8
Fir Tree Cres., Ince 41 J10
Fir Tree Dr., Ince 41 J10
Fir Tree La., Orm. 20 NN7
Fir Tree St., Ince 41 J10
Fir Tree Wk., Low. 66 M16
Firbank Rd., Wgn. 40 G10
Firbeck, Skel. 23 XX7
Fircroft, Stand. 7 D3
Firecrest Clo., Booth. 47 W12
Firethorn Clo., Westho. 32 P7
Firs La., Leigh 57 O13
Firs La., Orm. 20 NN7
Firs Pk. Cres., Asp. 30 M7
Firs Rd., Westho. 33 S9
First Av., Astley 60 U14
First Av., Ath. 45 R10
First Av., Hind. 30 L9
First Av., Wgn. 28 G7
First St., Bam. 41 J12
Firsway, Leigh 57 N13
Firswood Rd., Skel. 22 UU7
Firtree Av., Booth. 61 W13
Firvale Clo., Leigh 57 O13
Firwood, Skel. 13 YY6
Firwood Gro., Asht. 54 G15
Fisher Av., Abram 42 L12
Fisher Clo., Wgn. 27 F9
Fisher Dr., Orr. 26 C9
Fishers Yd., Wgn. 28 H8
Fitzadam St., Wgn. 28 G8
Five Acres Sq., Low. 66 M16
Flamstead, Skel. 24 YY7
Flapper Fold La., Ath. 45 R10
Flaxton, Skel. 24 YY7
Fleet St., Wgn. 26 D9
Fletcher Av., Ath. 33 R9
Fletcher St., Ath. 45 R10
Fletcher St., Westho. 33 S8
Flimby, Skel. 24 YY7
Flockton Av., Stand.L.G. 16 E6
Flora St., Asht. 54 G15
Flordon, Skel. 24 YY7
Florence St., Wgn. 29 J8
Foggs St., Platt Br. 41 K11
Fold St., Gol. 55 K15
Foley St., Hind. 30 L9
Fordice Way, Ince 29 K8
Fordland Clo., Gol. 56 M15
Forest Av., Wgn. 16 F6
Forest Dr., Skel. 13 YY6
Forest Dr., Stand. 7 D3
Forest Dr., Westho. 32 Q8
Foresters Clo., Bick. 42 M12
Forge St., Ince 29 J8
Formby Av., Ath. 45 R10
Formby La., Orm. 20 NN7
Forres Gro., Asht. 53 E14
Forster St., Gol. 55 K15
Forth St., Leigh 59 R14
Forton Rd., Wgn. 39 F11
Foster Av., Ince 29 J9
Foster St., Wgn. 28 G7
Fosters Bldgs., Wgn. 28 G8
Fosters Grn. Rd., Skel. 24 YY7
Fotherby Pl., Wgn. 40 G10
Foundry La., Wgn. 39 E10
Foundry St., Leigh 58 Q14
Foundry St., Newt. 63 G18
Fountains Av., Hay. 63 F16
Fountains Clo., Tyld. 46 U12
Fountains Wk., Leigh 67 N16
Fourteen Meadows Rd., Wgn. 28 G9
Fourth St., Bam. 41 J12
Foxdene Gro., Wgn. 39 F11
Foxfold, Skel. 13 YY6
Foxglove Clo., Stand. 8 E3
Foy St., Asht. 54 G14
France St., Hind. 30 L9
France St., Westho. 32 P9
France St., Wgn. 27 F8
Frances Pl., Ath. 44 Q11
Francis St., Hind. 30 L9
Francis St., Leigh 44 P12
Francis St., Tyld. 46 U12
Sale La.
Frank St., Wgn. 28 H8
Fraser Rd., Wgn. 27 F8
Frawley Av., Newt. 64 H17
Freckleton St., Wgn. 28 H7
Frederica Gdns., Platt Br. 41 K10
Frederica St., Platt Br. 41 K10
Moss La.
Frederick St., Asht. 54 G13
Frederick St., Hind. 30 L9
Frederick St., Ince 28 H9
Frederick St., Wgn. 29 J8
Freelands, Tyld. 46 U11
Freesia Av., Litt.H. 47 V10
Freshfield Av., Ath. 45 R10
Freshfield Av., Farn. 34 U7
Freshfield Gro., Farn. 35 V7
Freshfield Rd., Hind. 30 M9
Freshfield Rd., Wgn. 39 F10
Friars Clo., Tyld. 46 U11
Frith St., Wgn. 28 G8
Frodsham Clo., Stand.L.G. 16 E6
Frog La., Parb. 4 WW2
Frog La., Wgn. 28 G7
Frome Clo., Tyld. 60 U13
Fulbeck Av., Wgn. 39 F11
Fullbrook Way, Tyld. 46 U11
Fulmar Clo., Westho. 31 O9
Fulwell Av., Tyld. 45 S12
Fulwood Rd., Gol. 66 M17
Furlong Clo., Bam. 41 J12
Furness Av., Orm. 10 QQ6
Furness Cres., Leigh 43 O11
Furnival St., Leigh 44 P12
Furze Av., Westho. 32 P8

G

Gable St., Newt. 63 G18
Gadbury Av., Ath. 44 Q10
Gainsborough Clo., Wgn. 39 E10
Galway Gro., Wgn. 17 H6
Gamble St., Leigh 58 Q13
Gambleside Clo., Booth. 47 W12
Gantley Av., Bill. 37 B10
Gantley Cres., Bill. 37 B10
Gantley Rd., Bill. 37 B10
Garden St., Tyld. 46 T12
Gardiners Pl., Skel. 23 WW8
Garnett Grn., Orm. 10 PP6
Garnett Lees, Skel. 24 ZZ8
Garnett Pl., Skel. 23 XX8
Garrett Hall Rd., Tyld. 47 V12
Garrett La., Tyld. 46 U12
Garside Av., Gol. 66 L16
Garside Gro., Wgn. 39 F11
Garston Av., Ath. 32 Q9
Garston Clo., Leigh 44 P11
Garswood Cres., Bill. 50 C14
Garswood Old Rd., St.H. 50 B16
Garswood Rd., Asht. 51 D13
Garswood Rd., Bill. 50 C13
Garswood Rd., Farn. 35 V7
Garswood St., Asht. 54 G14
Garth-mere Rd., Westho. 33 S9
Garton Dr., Gol. 56 M15
Gas St., Leigh 58 P13
Gas St., Platt Br. 41 K11
Gaskell St., Hind. 30 M8
Gaskell St., Wgn. 29 J8
Gaskells Brow, Asht. 53 F13
Gategill Gro., Bill. 37 B10
Gatehouse Rd., Litt.H. 47 W10
Gatemere Clo., Booth. 47 W12
Gathurst La., Shev. 15 D6
Gathurst Rd., Orr. 26 C8
Gaw Hill La., Orm. 10 PP6
Gawsworth Rd., Gol. 55 J15
Gaynor Av., Hay. 63 F16
Kenyons La.
Gayton Clo., Wgn. 39 E10
Gazebo Clo., Litt.H. 47 V10
Gellert Pl., Westho. 32 P9
Gellert Rd., Westho. 32 P9
George St., Asht. 54 H14
George St., Ath. 45 R10
George St., Farn. 35 W8
George St., Hind. 30 M9
George St., Ince 29 J8
George St., Newt. 63 G18
George St., Westho. 32 P8
George Ter., Orr. 25 B9
Georgian Ct., Leigh 58 Q14
Georgian Ct., Tyld. 45 S11
Ash St.
Georgian Sq., Platt Br. 41 K11
Georgiana St., Farn. 35 W7
Georgina Ct., Farn. 34 T7
Aldred St.
Georgina St., Farn. 34 T7
Gerard St., Asht. 54 G14
Gerrard Clo., Asp. 30 L7
Gerrard Pl., Skel. 23 WW8
Gerrard Rd., Bill. 50 C13
Gerrard St., Westho. 32 P7
Ghyll Gro., St.H. 49 A15
Giants Hall Rd., Stand.L.G. 16 F6
Gib Fold, Ath. 45 R10
Gibbons Rd., Asht. 53 E15
Gibson Gro., Litt.H. 47 W10
Gibson La., Litt.H. 47 W10
Gibson St., Bick. 42 L11
Gidlow Av., Wgn. 28 G7
Gidlow Cottage, Wgn. 28 G7
Gidlow La., Wgn. 17 G6
Gidlow New Hos., Wgn. 17 G6
Gidlow St., Hind. 30 L9
Gidlow St., Ince 29 K8
Gilbert St., Hind. 30 L9
Gilda Rd., Tyld. 47 V12
Gill Av., Shev. 15 D5
Gillan Rd., Wgn. 17 G6
Gillbrow Cres., Wgn. 29 J7
Gillibrands Rd., Skel. 23 XX8
Gilliburns Wk., Westho. 32 P9
Gilpin Pl., Platt Br. 41 J11
Gilroy St., Wgn. 28 H8
Girton Av., Asht. 53 F14
Girvan Cres., Asht. 53 E14
Gisburn Av., Gol. 55 J15
Gladden Pl., Skel. 23 WW8
Glade, The, Shev. 15 D5
Gladstone St., Westho. 32 P7
Glaisdale Clo., Asht. 54 H14
Glamis Clo., Leigh 59 R13
Glassbrook St., Wgn. 28 G7
Glastonbury Av., Leigh 67 N16
Glastonbury Rd., Tyld. 46 T12
Gleadlands Av., Win. 39 E11
Glebe Av., Asht. 54 H15
Glebe Clo., Stand. 8 F3
Glebe End St., Wgn. 28 G8
Glebe Rd., Skel. 23 XX8
Glebe Rd., Stand. 16 F4
Glebe St., Hind. 43 O11
Glebe St., Leigh 58 P13
Glebe St., Westho. 32 P7
Gleed La., Skel. 12 WW5
Glemsford Clo., Wgn. 40 H10
Glen Dr., App.Br. 15 C4
Glen Pk., Leigh 58 Q13
Glenburn Rd., Skel. 23 WW7
Glencar, Westho. 31 O8
Glendale Av., Asht. 54 H14
Glendale Clo., Tyld. 47 V12
Glendale Rd.
Glendale Rd., Tyld. 47 V12
Gleneagles Dr., Hay. 62 D17
Glenmaye Gro., Hind. 31 N9
Cranstal Dr.
Glenmore Av., Farn. 35 W7
Glenside, Wri. 6 A3
Glenside Dr., Farn. 35 V7
Gloucester Av., Gol. 65 K16
Gloucester Cres., Hind. 30 M9
Gloucester Pl., Ath. 45 R10
Gloucester Rd., Wgn. 27 E9

Gloucester St., Ath. 45 R10
Glover St., Leigh 43 O12
Glover St., Newt. 64 H18
Glovers Pl., Orr. 26 D8
Glynne St., Farn. 35 W8
Golborne Dale Rd., Gol. 65 K17
Golborne Pl., Wgn. 29 J8
Golborne Rd., Asht. 54 H14
Golborne Rd., Gol. 66 L16
Golborne St., Newt. 64 H18
Golborne St., Wgn. 29 J8
Goldcrest Clo., Booth. 47 W12
Goldenways, Wgn. 28 H7
Goldsmith Pl., Wors.M. 40 G10
Gordon Av., Asht. 53 F14
Gordon Av., Hay. 63 F16
Kenyons La.
Gordon Clo., Wgn. 27 F8
Gordon St., Leigh 58 P13
Gordon St., Wgn. 29 J8
Gordonstoun Cres., Orr. 26 C8
Gore Dr., Orm. 10 QQ6
Gore St., Wgn. 26 D9
Gores La., Rainf. 49 ZZ13
Gorman St., Wgn. 28 G7
Gorman Wk., Wgn. 27 F9
Gorse Dr., Litt.H. 35 V9
Gorse Wk., Leigh 57 N13
Gorses Dr., Asp. 19 L5
Gorsey Brow, Bill. 50 B13
Gorsey Brow Clo., Bill. 50 B13
Gorsey Hey, Westho. 32 P8
Gorsey Pl., Skel. 23 XX8
Gorton St., Farn. 35 W8
Gower St., Leigh 58 P14
Poets Nook
Gower St., Wgn. 27 F9
Goyt Hey Av., Bill. 50 C13
Grafton St., Ath. 44 Q11
Grafton St., Newt. 63 G18
Graham Av., Wri. 6 A3
Graham St., Abram 41 K11
Grampian Way, Gol. 56 L15
Grampian Way, Platt Br. 41 K11
Granchester Pl., Farn. 35 V7
Grange Av., Orr. 26 D8
Grange Av., Wgn. 28 G9
Grange Clo., Gol. 66 L17
Grange Rd., Asht. 53 F13
Grange Rd., Bick. 42 M11
Grange Rd., Farn. 35 W7
Grange Rd., Hay. 62 E17
Grange Rd., Tyld. 47 V12
Grange St., Leigh 58 P14
Grange Valley, Hay. 62 E17
Grangeway, Hind. 31 N9
Grant Rd., Wgn. 40 G10
Grant St., Farn. 35 W7
Grant St., Ince 29 J8
Grantham Gro., Wgn. 29 J7
Grantley St., Asht. 54 G13
Grantwood, Asht. 54 G13
Granville Clo., Orm. 20 OO7
Granville Pk. W., Orm. 20 OO8
Granville St., Hind. 30 M9
Granville St., Leigh 44 P12
Byron St.
Grasmere Av., Farn. 35 V8
Grasmere Av., Hind. 42 M10
Grasmere Av., Ince 29 K8
Grasmere Av., Orr. 26 C8
Grasmere Av., Up Holl. 25 A8
Grasmere Dr., Asht. 54 G13
Grasmere Rd., Wgn. 27 E8
Grasmere St., Leigh 58 P13
Grasmere Ter., Abram 41 K12
Grasscroft Rd., Hind. 43 N10
Gratton Pl., Skel. 23 XX8
Grave Oak La., Leigh 58 Q15
Gray Av., Hay. 62 E17
Graymar Rd., Litt.H. 47 W10
Grayson Rd., Litt.H. 47 W10
Graysons Clo., Wgn. 28 H7
Upper Dicconson St.
Great Fold, Leigh 59 S14
Great George St., Wgn. 28 G8
Greaves Clo., App.Br. 15 C4
Grebe Clo., Wgn. 38 D10
Green, The, Wgn. 26 D8
Green Acres Clo., Leigh 67 N16
Green Av., Litt.H. 35 V9
Green Av., Tyld. 59 S14
Green Bk. St., Tyld. 46 T12
Green Clo., Tyld. 45 S11
Green Common La., Westho. 32 Q8
Green Fold La., Westho. 32 P8
Green Hayes Av., Wgn. 17 H6
Green Heys Rd., Litt.H. 35 V9
Green La., Bill. 37 B10
Green La., Gol. 57 N15
Green La., Hind. 43 N10
Green La., Leigh 59 R13
Green La., Orm. 10 QQ5
Green La., Rainf. 48 XX13
Green La., Stand. 16 F4
Green La. Av., Orm. 10 QQ5
Green Meadows, Westho. 31 O8
Green Slate Ct., Bill. 38 C10
Green Slate Rd., Bill. 38 C10
Green St., Asp. 18 J6
Green St., Ath. 45 S11
Green St., Platt Br. 41 K11
Green St., Tyld. 46 T11
Green St., Wgn. 28 H9
Green Ways, Stand. 17 G5
Greenacre, Orm. 11 SS6
Greenacre, Westho. 32 P8
Greenacre, Wgn. 28 H7
Greenbank, Abram 41 K12
Greenbank Av., Bill. 37 B10
Greenburn Av., St.H. 50 B15
Greencourt Dr., Litt.H. 47 V10
Greendale, Ath. 45 S10
Greendale Cres., Leigh 59 R14
Greenfield Av., Ince 29 J8
Greenfield Av., Parb. 4 XX3
Greenfield Clo., Newt. 64 H18
Greenfield Clo., Westho. 32 Q7
Greenfield Rd., Ath. 33 S9
Greenfield Rd., Litt.H. 47 W10
Greenfield Vw., Bill. 50 B14
Greenfields, Wgn. 17 G6
Greenfields Clo., Hind. 30 M9
Greenfields Cres., Asht. 54 H14
Greenfold Av., Farn. 35 W8
Greenford Clo., Orr. 25 B9
Greenhall Clo., Ath. 45 S10
Greenhaven, Up Holl. 25 A8
Greenhey, Orr. 26 D8
Greenhey Pl., Skel. 23 WW8
Greenhill Cres., Bill. 50 C13
Greenhill Rd., Bill. 50 C13
Greenland Av., Stand. 8 F3
Greenland Clo., Tyld. 46 T12
Greenland Rd., Farn. 35 V7
Greenland Rd., Tyld. 60 T13
Greenlea Clo., Orr. 25 B9
Greenleaf Clo., Booth. 61 V13
Greenough St., Wgn. 28 H8
Greenshank Clo., Newt. 64 H18
Greenslaye Av., App.Br. 15 C4
Greensmith Way, Westho. 32 P7
Greensward Clo., Stand. 7 D3
Crow Orchard Rd.
Greenvale, Shev. 15 C6
Greenway, Asht. 54 G14
Greenway Av., Skel. 23 XX8
Greenway Clo., Skel. 23 WW7
School La.
Greenways, Bill. 37 B10
Greenways, Leigh 58 Q13
Greenwell Rd., Hay. 62 E17
Greenwood Av., Wgn. 27 F8
Greenwood Clo., Orm. 21 PP7
Greenwood Clo., Tyld. 47 V12
Greenwood Rd., Stand. 8 F3
Greetby Hill, Orm. 11 RR5
Greetby Pl., Skel. 23 XX8
Gregory Av., Ath. 33 R9
Gregory Row, Low. 67 N16
Gregory St., Hind. 29 K9
Gregory St., Leigh 58 P14
Gregory St., Westho. 31 N8
Gregsons Row, Leigh 43 O12
Grenaby Av., Hind. 31 N9
Grenfell Clo., Wgn. 28 G9
Greta Wk., Platt Br. 41 K11
Ribble Rd.
Grey Rd., Asht. 54 G14
Greyfriars, Asht. 53 F14
Greystokes, Orm. 21 PP7
Greystone Av., Asp. 19 L5
Grimrod Pl., Skel. 23 XX8
Grimshaw Rd., Orm. 10 QQ4
Grimshaw Rd., Skel. 23 XX8
Grimshaw St., Gol. 55 K15
Grindlow Wk., Wgn. 39 E11
Grosvenor Av., Gol. 66 L16
Grosvenor Rd., Hay. 62 D16
Grosvenor Rd., Leigh 57 O13
Grosvenor St., Hind. 30 L9
Grosvenor St., Wgn. 27 F9
Grove, The, Gol. 56 L15
Grove, The, Ince 29 J8
Grove, The, Orm. 21 PP8
Grove, The, Westho. 32 P8
Grove, The, Wri. 6 A3
Grove La., Stand. 16 F4
Grove Pk., Orm. 10 QQ4
Grove Pl., Stand. 16 F4
Grove Rd., Up Holl. 25 B8
Grove St., Asht. 54 G14
Grovehill, Booth. 61 V13
Grovewood Dr., App.Br. 15 C4
Grundy St., Gol. 65 K16
Grundy St., Leigh 58 Q14
Grundy St., Westho. 32 P7
Grundys Clo., Tyld. 60 U13
Guest St., Leigh 58 Q13
Guildford Cres., Wgn. 16 F6
Gun Site La., Rainf. 49 ZZ14
Gunters Av., Westho. 32 P9

H

Habel St., Westho. 32 P8
Hadbutt La., Tyld. 59 S13
Haddon Rd., Gol. 56 L15
Haddon Rd., Wgn. 39 F10
Haddon St., Asht. 53 F13
Haguebush Clo., Gol. 56 M15
Haigh Rd., Asp. 18 K5
Haigh St., Wgn. 28 G8
Haigh Vw., Ince 29 J9
Haigh Vw., Wgn. 28 H7
Haile Dr., Booth. 61 V13
Hale Clo., Leigh 59 R15
Hale Gro., Asht. 53 F13
Halesfield, Hind. 43 N11
Halewood Av., Gol. 55 J15
Hall Brow Clo., Orm. 11 RR6
Hall Clo., Shev. 15 D5
Hall Gate, Westho. 32 P9
Hall Grn., Up Holl. 25 A8
Hall Grn. Clo., Up Holl. 25 A8
Hall La., Asp. 30 L7
Hall La., Bill. 38 C10
Hall La., Parb. 4 XX1
Hall La., Wgn. 17 H6
Hall La., Wri. 6 A3
Hall La. Gro., Hind. 30 L8
Hall Lee Dr., Westho. 32 Q7
Hall Rd., Hay. 63 F16
Hall St., Ath. 44 Q11
Leigh Rd.
Hall St., Bam. 41 J12
Hall St., Ince 28 H8
Hallbridge Gdns., Up Holl. 25 A8
Hallcrop, Skel. 24 YY7
Hallgate, Wgn. 28 H8
Hallhouse La., Leigh 59 R14
Hallmoor Clo., Orm. 21 QQ7
Hallstead Av., Litt.H. 47 V10
Hallstead Gro., Litt.H. 47 V10
Hallworthy Clo., Gol. 57 N15
Halsall Ct., Orm. 10 PP5
Halsall Dr., Farn. 35 V7
Halsall La., Orm. 10 PP5
Halton Chase, Orm. 11 SS6
Halton St., Hay. 63 F17
Hamblett St., Leigh 57 N13
Hamilton Dr., Hind. 42 M10
Hamilton Rd., Asht. 53 E14
Hamilton Sq., Wgn. 27 F8
Hamilton St., Ath. 45 R11

Hamilton St., Leigh 57 O13
Hamilton St., Wgn. 27 F8
Hampden Pl., Wgn. 27 E7
Hampson Clo., Asht. 54 G15
Hampson St., Ath. 45 R10
Hampson St., Bick. 42 L11
Hampstead Rd., Stand. 8 E3
Hampton Gro., Leigh 45 S12
Hanborough Ct., Tyld. 45 S11
Blenheim St.
Hand La., Leigh 58 P15
Hanmer St., Hind. 30 L9
Hanover Rd., Hind. 30 L9
Hanover St., Leigh 58 Q13
Hants La., Orm. 10 QQ5
Harbern Dr., Leigh 43 O11
Harbury Clo., Wgn. 27 F7
Harbury Wk., Wgn. 27 F7
Hardacre St., Ince 28 H9
Hardacre St., Orm. 10 QQ5
Hardie Av., Farn. 35 W8
Hardman St., Wgn. 28 G9
Hardrow Clo., Wgn. 40 G11
Hardwick Rd., Asht. 54 G13
Hardy Clo., Westho. 32 P7
Hardy St., Wgn. 28 G7
Hardybutts, Wgn. 28 H8
Harebell Av., Litt.H. 47 V10
Harewood Rd., Hind. 30 L9
Harlea Av., Hind. 43 N10
Harlech Av., Hind. 43 N10
Harlech St., Asht. 53 F13
Harmuir Clo., Stand.L.G. 16 E6
Harold Av., Asht. 53 F13
Harold Rd., Hay. 63 F16
Harold St., Asp. 19 L5
Harp St., Hind. 42 L10
Harper Grn. Rd., Farn. 35 W7
Harper St., Farn. 35 W7
Harper St., Wgn. 29 J8
Harris Rd., Stand. 7 D2
Harrison Dr., Hay. 62 D17
Harrison St., Hind. 43 N10
Harrison St., Wgn. 27 F9
Harrison Way, Newt. 64 H18
Harrock La., Wri. 6 A1
Harrogate St., Wgn. 28 H8
Harrop St., Litt.H. 47 W10
Harrow Clo., Orr. 26 C8
Harrow Cres., Leigh 58 P14
Harrow Pl., Ince 41 J10
Harrow Rd., Wgn. 27 E7
Harrowby St., Farn. 35 W8
Harrowby St., Wgn. 27 F9
Harsnips, Skel. 24 YY7
Hart St., Tyld. 46 U12
Hart St., Westho. 31 N8
Hewlett St.
Hartland, Skel. 24 YY7
Hartland Clo., Tyld. 46 T12
Hartland Dr., Asht. 54 H14
Hartley Av., Wgn. 29 J8
Hartley Gro., Orr. 26 D8
Hartley St., Wgn. 26 D9
Hartley Ter., Wgn. 28 H8
Harts Fm. Ms., Leigh 44 P12
Leigh Rd.
Hartshead, Skel. 24 YY7
Harty Rd., Hay. 62 D17
Harvey Av., Newt. 63 F18
Harvey La., Gol. 55 J15
Harvey St., Ince 29 J9
Haseldine St., Asht. 53 F13
Haslam Dr., Orm. 10 PP4
Hassness Clo., Wors.M. 40 G11
Hatfield Clo., Ince 41 J10
Hatford Clo., Tyld. 46 U11
Hathaway Ct., Leigh 58 Q13
Hathaway Wk., Ince 41 J10
Hatton Av., Ath. 33 R9
Havannah La., St.H. 62 D18
Haven Brow, Orm. 21 PP8
Havenwood Rd., Wgn. 17 G6
Havercroft Clo., Win. 39 F10
Hawes Av., Farn. 35 V8
Hawes Cres., Asht. 54 G13
Haweswater Av., Hay. 62 D17
Haweswater Av., Ince 29 K8
Haweswater Av., Tyld. 46 T12
Hawkhurst St., Leigh 58 Q14
Hawkley Av., Wgn. 39 F11
Hawksclough, Skel. 24 YY7
Hawkshaw Clo., Asp. 18 K6
Hawkworth, Tyld. 60 T13
Haworth St., Hind. 30 L9
Hawthorn Av., Asht. 53 E13
Hawthorn Av., Farn. 35 W8
Hawthorn Av., Hind. 43 N10
Hawthorn Av., Newt. 64 H18
Hawthorn Av., Orr. 26 C9
Hawthorn Av., Stand. 17 G5
Hawthorn Av., Wgn. 27 E9
Hawthorn Clo., Bill. 50 B13
Hawthorn Clo., Hay. 62 D17
Hawthorn Cres., Skel. 23 WW7
Hawthorn Rd., Westho. 32 P8
Hawthornes, The, Parb. 4 XX3
Haydock Dr., Booth. 61 W13
Haydock La., Hay. 62 E16
Haydock Pk. Gdns., Asht. 54 G15
Haydock Pl., Newt. 63 G18
Wellington St.
Haydock St., Asht. 54 G15
Haydock St., Newt. 63 G18
Hayes Row, Low. 57 N15
Hayes St., Leigh 44 P12
Hayes St. 57 N14
(Firs La.), Leigh
Hayfell Rd., Wors.M. 40 G11
Hayfield Av., Astley 60 U13
Manchester Rd.
Hayfield Rd., Orm. 10 QQ4
Hayman Av., Leigh 57 O15
Haymill Av., Litt.H. 35 W9
Haysbrook Av., Litt.H. 47 V10
Haywood Clo., Low. 56 M15
Hazel Av., Litt.H. 35 V9
Hazel Av., Westho. 32 P8
Hazel Av., Wgn. 17 G6
Hazel Gro., Farn. 35 W8
Hazel Gro., Gol. 65 K16
Hazel Gro., Leigh 44 P12
Hazel La., Skel. 12 XX6
Hazel Rd., Ath. 45 R10
Hazelhurst Gro., Asht. 54 H14
Hazelmere Gdns., Hind. 42 M10
Borsdane Av.
Hazelwood Rd., Wgn. 17 G6
Hazleton Clo., Leigh 58 P15
Headen Av., Wgn. 26 D9
Headland Clo., Gol. 66 M17
Heald St., Newt. 63 F18
Heardman Av., Wgn. 28 G7
Heath Clo., Farn. 34 T7
Heath Gdns., Hind. 43 O10
Heath La., Gol. 66 L17
Heath La., Leigh 57 N13
Heath Rd., Asht. 54 G15
Heath St., Gol. 65 K16
Heather Brae, Newt. 63 G18
Heather Gro., Asht. 55 J14
Heather Gro., Leigh 44 P12
Heather Gro., Wgn. 27 F8
Heatherlea Clo., Up Holl. 25 B8
Wellcross Rd.
Heathfield Dr., Farn. 34 T7
Heathfield Dr., Tyld. 46 U11
Heathgate, Skel. 24 YY7
Heathmoor Av., Gol. 66 L17
Heaton Clo., Up Holl. 25 A8
Heaton St., Asp. 19 L5
Heaton St., Ince 29 J9
Heaton St., Stand. 8 F3
Heaton St., Wgn. 28 H7
Heatons Gro., Westho. 32 Q7
Hebdon Clo., Asht. 54 G13
Heber St., Ince 29 J8
Hector Rd., Wgn. 27 E7
Hedge Clo., Ath. 45 S10
Heeley St., Wgn. 28 G7
Helen St., Asht. 54 G14
Helen St., Gol. 55 J15
Helias Clo., Litt.H. 47 V10
Quarry Pond Rd.
Hell Nook, Gol. 55 J15
Helmsdale, Skel. 24 YY7
Helmsman Way, 28 G9
Wors.M.
Helsby Way, Wgn. 39 E11
Helston Way, Tyld. 46 U12
Helvellyn Rd., Wgn. 26 D9
Hemclough Way, Booth. 47 W12
Hemfield Rd., Ince 29 K8
Hen Fold Rd., Tyld. 46 U12
Hen St., Wgn. 29 J8
Hendon Gro., Leigh 44 P12
Hendon St.
Hendon Rd., Wgn. 27 E8
Hendon St., Leigh 44 P12
Henley St., Haigh 18 K5
Henniker Rd., Farn. 34 T7
Henrietta St., Leigh 58 P13
Henry Pk. St., Wgn. 29 J8
Henry St., Ince 41 J10
Henry St., Leigh 58 Q14
Henry St., Tyld. 46 T11
Henry St., Westho. 32 P7
Winward St.
Herbert St., Westho. 32 P7
Herbert St., Wgn. 28 G8
Hereford Av., Gol. 65 K16
Hereford Clo., Asht. 54 H15
Lincoln Dr.
Hereford Rd., Hind. 30 M9
Herevale Gra., Booth. 47 W12
Hermitage Clo., App.Br. 15 C4
Heron Av., Litt.H. 35 V8
Heron Dr., Wgn. 39 F11
Heron Gro., Rainf. 48 XX13
Heron Pl., Wgn. 27 E8
Hertford Dr., Tyld. 46 T10
Hesketh Dr., Stand. 7 D3
Hesketh Meadow La., 66 M16
Low.
Hesketh St., Ath. 45 R10
Hesketh St., Leigh 57 O13
Hesketh St., Wgn. 27 F8
Heskin La., Orm. 10 PP4
Heversham, Skel. 24 YY7
Hewlett St., Westho. 31 N8
Hewlett St., Wgn. 28 H8
Hexham Av., Wgn. 39 F10
Hey St., Ince 41 J10
Hey St., Wgn. 28 G8
Heyes Av., Hay. 62 E17
Heyes Av., Rainf. 48 XX13
Heyes Gro., Rainf. 48 XX13
Heyes Rd., Orr. 26 C9
Heyford Rd., Wgn. 27 E8
Heys St., Hind. 30 L9
Wigan Rd.
Heysham Rd., Orr. 26 D8
Heysome Clo., Rainf. 49 ZZ14
Heywood Av., Gol. 55 K15
Heywood Gdns., Gol. 55 K15
Heywood Av.
Hic-Bibi La., Cop. 8 F1
Hieland Rd., Wgn. 29 J7
Higginson St., Leigh 58 Q13
High Bk., Westho. 34 T9
High Beeches Cres., Asht. 54 G13
High La., Orm. 11 RR4
High Moor La., Wri. 5 ZZ2
High Moss, Orm. 10 PP6
High Pk., Shev. 16 E5
High Peak, Gol. 66 M16
High St., Asp. 18 K6
High St., Astley 60 T13
High St., Ath. 45 R10
High St., Gol. 65 K16
High St., Hind. 30 M8
High St., Ince 29 J9
High St., Leigh 58 Q13
High St., Newt. 64 H18
High St., Skel. 22 VV8
High St., Stand. 8 F3
High St., Swin. 28 H7
High St., Tyld. 45 S11
Higham Ct., Wgn. 29 J8
Higham St., Leigh 43 O12
Wigan Rd.
Highcliffe Ct., Stand. 16 F4
Higher Drake Meadow, 32 P9
Westho.
Higher Grn. La., Tyld. 60 U13
Higher La., Asp. 18 K6
Higher La., Parb. 4 XX3
Higher La., Rainf. 48 XX13
Higher La., Skel. 12 XX4
Higher La., Up Holl. 25 B8

Higher Southfield, Westho. 32 P8
Highfield, Wgn. 39 E10
Billinge Rd.
Highfield Av., Ath. 33 S9
Highfield Av., Gol. 64 H16
Highfield Av., Leigh 59 R14
Highfield Av., Shev. 15 D5
Highfield Av., Tyld. 47 V12
Highfield Av., Wgn. 29 J7
Highfield Dr., Rainf. 49 ZZ14
Highfield Dr., Stand. 16 F4
Highfield Gra. Av., Wgn. 39 E11
Highfield Gro., Asp. 19 L5
Highfield La., Gol. 66 L17
Highfield Rd., Farn. 35 V8
Highfield Rd., Hind. 30 L8
Highfield Rd., Litt.H. 35 V9
Highfield Rd., Orm. 10 QQ4
Highgate, Bolt. 33 R7
Highgate Cres., App.Br. 15 C4
Highgate Dr., Litt.H. 35 V9
Highgate La., Litt.H. 35 V9
Highgate Rd., Up Holl. 25 A8
Highwoods Clo., Asht. 54 G13
Hilary Av., Ath. 33 R9
Hilary Av., Gol. 56 L15
Hilda St., Leigh 57 O13
Hilden St., Leigh 58 P13
Hilgay Clo., Wgn. 39 E10
Hill Clo., App.Br. 15 C4
Hill Cres., Leigh 43 O12
Hill Crest, Bolt. 33 S9
Hill Crest Av., Leigh 43 O12
Hill Fld., Farn. 35 W8
Hill Ho. Fold La., Wri. 6 B1
Hill Ho. La., Wri. 6 A1
Hill St., Hind. 30 L9
Hill St., Ince 29 K7
Hill St., Leigh 58 P13
Twist La.
Hill St., Wgn. 28 G7
Hill Top, Bolt. 33 S9
Hill Top Fold, Hind. 30 M9
Hill Top Rd., St.H. 48 XX15
Hillary Av., Wgn. 27 E9
Hillbank, Stand. 17 G4
Hillbeck Cres., Asht. 53 E14
Hillbrae Av., St.H. 49 A15
Hillcrest, Platt Br. 41 K11
Hillcrest, Skel. 24 YY8
Hillcrest Rd., Orm. 10 QQ5
Hillcrest Rd., Tyld. 46 U12
Chester Rd.
Hilldean, Up Holl. 25 B8
Hillfield Dr., Booth. 47 W12
Birchfield Dr.
Hillock, The, Tyld. 60 T13
Hillock La., Skel. 13 YY5
Hillreed, Wgn. 27 F7
Knightshill Cres.
Hillside Av., Asht. 39 F12
Hillside Av., Ath. 45 S10
Hillside Av., Farn. 35 W8
Hillside Av., Orm. 10 PP6
Hillside Av., Wri. 5 YY1
Hillside Clo., Bill. 50 B13
Hillside Clo., Wgn. 39 E10
Hilltop Wk., Orm. 10 PP6
Hilton Bk., Litt.H. 47 W10
Hilton Clo., Leigh 58 Q13
Hilton Cres., Booth. 61 W13
Hilton La., Litt.H. 47 W11
Hilton Pl., Asp. 19 L5
Hilton St., Asht. 54 G14
Hilton St., Ath. 45 S10
Laburnum St.
Hilton St., Ince 29 J9
Hilton St., Litt.H. 47 W10
Hilton St., Wgn. 28 H7
Hindburn Dr., Tyld. 47 W12
Hindles Clo., Ath. 44 Q11
Hindley Mill La., Hind. 30 M8
Hindley Rd., Westho. 31 O9
Hindsford St., Tyld. 45 S11
Hoade St., Hind. 30 M8
Hob Hey La., Cul. 67 O18
Hodder Av., Platt Br. 41 J11
Hodder Clo., Wgn. 27 E8
Hodges St., Wgn. 17 G6
Hodnet Dr., Asht. 54 H14
Hodson St., Wgn. 28 H8
Holbeach Clo., Hind. 42 M10
Holbeck, Tyld. 60 T13
Holborn Av., Leigh 44 P12
Hendon St.
Holborn Av., Wgn. 28 G9
Holborn Dr., Orm. 10 PP6
Holborn Hill, Orm. 10 PP6
Holbrook Av., Litt.H. 35 W9
Holcombe Av., Gol. 66 L16
Holden Brook Clo., Leigh 58 Q13
Holden Rd., Leigh 58 P13
Holding St., Hind. 30 L9
Holford Way, Newt. 64 H18
Holgate Dr., Orr. 26 C9
Holland St., Wgn. 29 J8
Hollies, The, Wgn. 17 H6
Hollin Acre, Westho. 32 P8
Hollin Hey Clo., Bill. 50 B14
Hollinbrook, Wgn. 27 F7
Sandway
Hollington Way, Wgn. 39 E11
Castleton Way
Hollingwood Clo., Asht. 54 G14
Hollingwood Dr., Asht. 54 G14
Alderton Dr.
Hollins Clo., Asht. 53 E14
Hollins Clo., Tyld. 46 T12
Hollins Rd., Hind. 31 N9
Hollinswood Rd., Booth. 61 W13
Hollowford La., Parb. 4 WW3
Holly Av., Newt. 64 H18
Holly Clo., Orm. 11 SS6
Holly Clo., Skel. 23 WW7
Holly Cres., Rainf. 48 XX13
Holly Gro., Farn. 35 W8
Holly Gro., Leigh 44 P12
Holly Heath Dr., Wgn. 17 G6
Holly Rd., Asp. 18 K5
Holly Rd., Gol. 66 L16
Holly Rd., Hay. 62 D17
Holly Rd., Wgn. 27 F8
Holly St., Wgn. 29 J7
Hollybush Sq., Gol. 56 M15
Holme Av., Wgn. 28 H7
Holme Ter., Wgn. 17 G6
Holmes Ho. Av., Wgn. 39 E10
Holmeswood Rd., Farn. 34 U7
Holmrook, Tyld. 46 U11
Holmsfield Clo., Asp. 29 K7
Holmwood Clo., Asht. 54 G13
Holt Av., Bill. 50 B14
Holt Coppice, Aug. 20 OO8
Holt Cres., Bill. 50 B14
Holt St., Hind. 30 L9
Holt St., Ince 29 J8
Holt St., Leigh 44 P12
Holt St., Orr. 25 B9
Holt St., Swin. 27 F7
Holt St., Tyld. 46 T11
Holt St., Wors.M. 40 G10
Holtswell Clo., Gol. 56 M15
Holyrood Clo., Leigh 45 S12
Coronation Dr.
Homestead Av., Hay. 63 F17
Honeybourne Clo., Tyld. 46 U11
Honeysuckle Av., Wgn. 16 F6
Honister Rd., Wgn. 26 D9
Honister St., Leigh 58 P13
Honiton Clo., Leigh 43 O11
Hood Clo., Tyld. 46 U11
Heathfield Dr.
Hood Gro., Leigh 58 Q14
Hook St., Ince 29 J8
Hooten La., Leigh 59 R14
Hope Av., Litt.H. 47 W10
Hope Carr La., Leigh 58 Q15
Hope Carr Rd., Leigh 58 Q14
Hope Carr Ter., Leigh 58 Q15
Hope Cres., Shev. 15 D5
Hope Fold Av., Ath. 44 Q11
Hope Hey La., Litt.H. 35 V9
Hope La., Tyld. 59 S14
Hope St., Asp. 19 M6
Hope St., Hind. 30 M9
Hope St., Ince 41 J10
Hope St., Leigh 58 P13
Hope St., Newt. 63 G18
Hope St., Tyld. 60 T13
Hopwood Cres., Rainf. 48 XX13
Hordon, Skel. 24 YY7
Hornby Dr., Westho. 33 R7
Hornby Gro., Leigh 45 R12
Hornby St., Wgn. 28 H7
Horne Gro., Wgn. 27 F9
Hornsey Gro., Wgn. 39 E10
Horridge Av., Newt. 64 H17
Horridge Fold Av., Bolt. 33 S7
Horrocks St., Leigh 58 P13
Horrocks St., Tyld. 45 S11
Horsham Gro., Wgn. 29 J7
Horton St., Gol. 57 N14
Horton St., Wgn. 16 F6
Hoscar Moss Rd., Lath. 4 WW2
Hoskers, The, Westho. 31 O9
Hoskers Nook, Westho. 31 O8
Hotel St., Newt. 63 G18
Hough La., Tyld. 46 U12
Houghton Av., Wgn. 27 F7
Houghton Clo., Newt. 63 G18
Houghton St., Leigh 58 P13
Leigh Rd.
Houghtons La., Skel. 24 YY7
Houghtons Rd., Skel. 12 WW6
Houghwood Gra., Asht. 53 F14
Housley Clo., Wgn. 28 G9
Howard St., Wgn. 27 E9
Howards La., Orr. 26 C8
Howarth St., Leigh 58 Q14
Howarth St., Westho. 32 P8
Howbridge Clo., Booth. 47 W12
Howden Dr., Wgn. 40 G10
Hoylake Clo., Leigh 57 O15
Hugo St., Farn. 35 W7
Hullet Clo., App.Br. 15 C4
Hulme Av., Leigh 57 O13
Hulme Rd., Leigh 57 O13
Hulton Av., Litt.H. 47 W10
Hulton Rd., Farn. 34 U7
Humber Pl., Wgn. 27 E8
Humber Rd., Tyld. 46 U12
Humphrey St., Ince 29 K8
Hungerhill Av., Westho. 33 S7
Hunt Rd., Hay. 63 F17
Hunt St., Ath. 45 R10
Hunt St., Wgn. 29 J8
Hunter Rd., Wgn. 27 E7
Hunts Bk., Westho. 32 P9
Hurlston Dr., Orm. 10 QQ5
Hurst Clo., Bolt. 33 S8
Hurst Gro., Leigh 58 Q15
Hurst St., Hind. 30 L9
Hurst St., Leigh 58 Q14
Hurstfield Rd., Wors. 47 W12
Hutton Av., Tyld. 61 V13
Hutton Clo., Cul. 67 O17
Hutton Rd., Skel. 22 VV7
Hutton St., Stand. 9 G2
Hutton Way, Orm. 10 QQ5
Huxley Clo., Wgn. 28 G9
Hyacinth Clo., Hay. 63 F17
Hyatt Cres., Stand. 8 E2
Hyde Clo., Wors.M. 28 G9

I

Ice Ho. Clo., Litt.H. 47 V10
Quarry Pond Rd.
Ilkeston Dr., Asp. 19 M6
Imperial Dr., Leigh 45 R12
Ince Bar, Ince 29 J8
Ince Grn. La., Ince 29 J9
Ince Hall Av., Ince 29 J8
Inchfield, Skel. 23 XX7
Industrial St., Westho. 32 P8
Ingham St., Leigh 44 P12
Ingleby Clo., Stand. 8 E3
Inglemoss Dr., St.H. 48 XX15
Ingles Fold, Booth. 47 W12
Inglesham Clo., Leigh 57 O15
Ingleton Clo., Newt. 64 H18
Inglewhite, Skel. 23 XX7
Inglewhite Av., Wgn. 28 H7
Inglewhite Cres., Wgn. 28 H7
Inglewhite Pl., Wgn. 28 H7
Inglewood Ct., Pemb. 27 E9
Billinge Rd.
Inglewood Rd., St.H. 48 XX15
Ingram, Skel. 23 XX7

Ingram St., Platt Br. 41 K10
Ingram St., Wgn. 27 F7
Inskip, Skel. 23 XX7
Inverness Clo., Asp. 19 L5
Inward Dr., Shev. 15 D5
Ireland Rd., Hay. 62 E17
Iris Av., Farn. 35 W7
Ironmonger La., Wgn. 28 H8
Irvine Av., Booth. 61 W13
Irvine St., Leigh 58 P13
Irwell, Skel. 12 XX6
Irwell Av., Litt.H. 47 W10
Irwell Pl., Platt Br. 41 J11
Irwell Pl., Wgn. 27 E9
Irwell Rd., Orr. 26 C8
Isabella Sq., Wgn. 29 J8
Isherwood St., Leigh 44 P12
Ivanhoe Av., Gol. 56 L15
Ivy Clo., Litt.H. 47 V10
Ivy Gro., Farn. 35 W8
Ivy Ho. Rd., Gol. 56 L15
Ivy Rd., Gol. 65 K16
Ivy Rd., Westho. 32 P8
Ivy St., Asht. 54 G14
Ivy St., Wgn. 28 G8
Ivybridge, Skel. 23 XX7
Ivydale, Skel. 23 XX7
Ivydale Dr., Leigh 59 R13

J

Jacks La., Westho. 31 N8
Jackson St., Hay. 62 D16
Juddfield St.
Jackson St., Ince 29 K8
Jackson St., Leigh 58 Q14
Jacob St., Hind. 30 L9
Jaffrey St., Leigh 58 P13
James Pl., Stand. 8 E3
James Rd., Hay. 63 F16
James Sq., Stand. 8 E3
James St., Ath. 45 S11
James St., Bam. 41 J12
James St., Ince 28 H9
James St., Westho. 32 P7
Jasmine Rd., Wgn. 27 E8
Jean Av., Leigh 58 P15
Jeffrey St., Ince 29 K8
Jenkinson St., Hind. 30 L9
Jennet Hey, Asht. 53 F13
Jennets La., Leigh 59 R15
John St., Ath. 58 P13
John St., Gol. 65 K16
John St., Hind. 43 N10
Atherton Rd.
John St., Tyld. 46 T11
John St., Wgn. 27 E9
Johns Av., Hay. 63 F16
Johnson Av., Bick. 42 M11
Johnson Av., Newt. 63 G17
Johnson Clo., Leigh 57 N14
Johnson St., Leigh 44 Q11
Johnson St., Pemb. 26 D9
Johnson St., Tyld. 46 T11
Johnson St., Wgn. 28 H8
Johnson St. S., Tyld. 46 T12
Johnsons Ter., Wgn. 28 H8
Bradford St.
Jonquil Dr., Tyld. 47 V11
Jubilee Av., Bill. 37 B10
Jubilee Av., Orm. 10 QQ5
Jubilee Cres., Hay. 63 F16
Jubilee Dr., Skel. 23 WW8
Juddfield St., Hay. 62 D17
Junction La., Newt. 63 G18
Junction Ter., Ince 29 J9
June Av., Leigh 57 O13
Jupiter Gro., Wgn. 39 F11
Jury St., Leigh 44 P12
Jutland Gro., Westho. 32 P7

K

Karen Rd., Ince 29 J8
Kay Clo., Wgn. 28 H8
Kay St., Ath. 45 R11
Kearsley St., Leigh 57 O13
Kearsley St., Wgn. 28 G7
Keats Av., Ath. 33 R9
Spa Rd.
Keats Av., Bill. 37 B11
Keats Av., Stand.L.G. 16 F6
Keats Av., Wgn. 28 G9
Keats Clo., Ath. 33 R9
Keats St., Leigh 43 O12
Keats Way, Platt Br. 41 K11
Keble Gro., Leigh 43 O12
Keble St., Ince 29 J8
Kellbank Rd., Win. 39 F10
Kelvin Clo., Asht. 53 E13
Stirling Dr.
Kelvin Gro., Wgn. 39 F11
Kelway Ter., Wgn. 28 H7
Kempton Clo., Newt. 64 H17
Ken Way, Rainf. 48 XX13
Kendal Gro., Asht. 54 G14
Kendal Gro., Leigh 57 O13
Kendal Rd., Hind. 30 M9
Kendal Rd., Ince 29 K8
Kendal Rd., Tyld. 47 V12
Kendal St., Wgn. 28 G7
Kendrick Pl., Wgn. 29 J8
Kenhall Rd., Leigh 59 R14
Kenilworth Dr., Hind. 42 M10
Kenilworth Dr., Leigh 45 S12
Kenilworth Rd., Gol. 66 M16
Kenmore Gro., Asht. 53 E14
Kennedy Clo., Stand. 16 F4
Kennet Clo., Westho. 32 P7
Kennet Rd., Hay. 62 E17
Kennet Way, Leigh 44 P12
Kenneth Av., Leigh 57 O13
Kenneth Gro., Leigh 57 O13
Kensington Dr., Leigh 45 S12
Kensington Rd., Wgn. 27 E9
Kent Av., Platt Br. 41 K11
Kent Clo., Litt.H. 47 W11
Kent Rd., Ath. 45 R10
Kent Rd., Tyld. 46 T11
Kent St., Leigh 59 S14
Kent St., Wgn. 28 H8
Kentmere Av., St.H. 50 B15
Kentmere Dr., Tyld. 46 T12
Kentmere Gro., Farn. 35 V8
Kenton Gro., Litt.H. 47 V10
Kenwood Av., Leigh 59 R14
Kenyon Rd., Stand. 8 E3
Kenyon Rd., Wgn. 28 H7
Kenyon St., Leigh 44 P12
Kenyon Ter., Tyld. 47 V10
Kenyon Way, Litt.H. 47 V10
Kenyons La., Hay. 63 F16
Kerans Dr., Westho. 32 P7
Kerfoot St., Leigh 59 R14
Kerfoots La., Skel. 22 VV8
Kermishaw Nook, Astley 60 T13
Kersal Av., Litt.H. 47 W10
Kershaw St., Orr. 26 D9
Kershaw St., Tyld. 46 T11
Kershaw Way, Newt. 64 H17
Kestrel Av., Asht. 54 H13
Kestrel Av., Farn. 35 V8
Kestrel Av., Litt.H. 35 W9
Kestrel Ms., Skel. 13 YY6
Kestrel Pk., Skel. 13 YY6
Keswick Pl., Ince 29 K8
Kilbuck La., Hay. 63 F16
Kilburn Av., Asht. 54 H14
Kilburn Clo., Leigh 43 O11
Kilburn Dr., Shev. 15 D4
Kilburn Gro., Wgn. 39 E10
Kilburn Rd., Orr. 25 B9
Kildare Gra., Hind. 30 L9
Sutherland St.
Kildare St., Hind. 30 L9
Kildare St., Wgn. 27 F9
Killington Clo., Wors.M. 40 G11
Kiln La., Skel. 23 WW7
Kilshaw St., Wgn. 27 E9
Kimberley Pl., Asht. 54 H14
Princess Rd.
Kimberley St., Wgn. 28 G7
Kinder Gro., Asht. 53 F13
King George Rd., Hay. 63 G16
King St., Ath. 45 S10
King St., Hind. 30 L9
King St., Ince 29 K8
King St., Leigh 58 P14
King St., Newt. 63 G18
King St., Westho. 32 P7
King St., Wgn. 28 H8
King St. W., Wgn. 28 H8
King William St., Tyld. 45 S12
Kingfisher Ct., Asht. 54 G13
Kingfisher Dr., Farn. 35 V8
Kingfisher Pk., Skel. 13 YY6
Kings Av., Gol. 66 M16
Kings Ct., Tyld. 45 S11
Factory St.
Kings Cres., Tyld. 45 S12
Kings Gdns., Leigh 59 R13
King's Moss La., K.Moss 36 ZZ12
Kings Rd., Gol. 65 K16
Kings St., Hay. 62 E17
Kingsbury Ct., Skel. 13 YY6
Kingsdown Rd., Abram 41 K12
Kingsdowne Cres., Wgn. 17 H6
Kingsfield Way, Tyld. 46 T12
Kingshill Ct., Stand. 16 F4
Kingsland Rd., Farn. 35 V7
Kingsley Av., Wgn. 39 F10
Kingsley Rd., Hind. 30 M9
Kingsley St., Leigh 43 O12
Kingsmede, Wgn. 17 H6
Kingsoak Clo., Wgn. 28 H8
Kingston Clo., Wgn. 40 G10
Kingsway, Ince 29 J8
Kingsway, Wgn. 28 H7
Kingwood Cres., Wgn. 27 E9
Kinlet Rd., Wgn. 39 E10
Kinloch Way, Orm. 10 PP5
Kinnerley Gro., Mos.Com. 47 W11
Kinniside Gro., Wgn. 40 G11
Kinross Av., Asht. 53 E14
Kintbury St., Abram 41 J12
Kipling Av., Wgn. 39 F10
Kipling Gro., Leigh 43 O12
Kirby Av., Ath. 33 R9
Kirkbeck, Leigh 59 R14
Kirkhall La., Leigh 44 P12
Kirkham Av., Gol. 66 M17
Kirkham Rd., Leigh 57 O15
Kirkham St., Abram 41 K12
Kirkham St., Leigh 57 O15
Kirkham St., Litt.H. 35 W9
Kirkless La., Ince 29 K7
Kirkless St., Asp. 18 K6
Kirkless St., Wgn. 29 J8
Kirkless Vill., Asp. 29 K7
Kirkpatrick St., Hind. 43 N10
Atherton Rd.
Kirkstile Cres., Wgn. 39 E11
Kirkstone, Wgn. 27 E8
Kitt Grn. Rd., Wgn. 27 E8
Kiveton Dr., Asht. 54 H15
Knaresborough Rd., Hind. 42 M10
Knightscliff Cres., App.Br. 14 B5
Knightshill Cres., Wgn. 27 F7
Knowles Av., Wgn. 39 F10
Knowles Pl., Wgn. 29 J8
Knowles St., Ince 28 H9
Winchester Gro.
Knowsley Av., Ath. 45 R10
Knowsley Av., Gol. 65 K16
Knowsley Dr., Leigh 57 O15
Knowsley Ms., Orm. 10 QQ5
Knowsley Rd., Orm. 10 QQ6
Knowsley Rd., Wgn. 17 G6
Knowsley St., Leigh 57 O13
Knutshaw Cres., Westho. 33 R7

L

Laburnum Av., Ath. 45 S10
Laburnum Av., Ince 29 J9
Laburnum Av., Leigh 44 P12
Laburnum Dr., Skel. 22 VV7
Laburnum Gro., Tyld. 46 U11
Laburnum Gro., Wgn. 17 G6
Laburnum Rd., Farn. 35 W8
Laburnum Rd., Gol. 66 M16
Laburnum St., Asht. 54 G15
Laburnum St., Ath. 45 S10
Ladies La., Hind. 30 L9
Ladies Wk., Ath. 45 R11
Lady La., Wgn. 39 F10
Ladymere Dr., Booth. 47 W12

Ladys Wk., Orm. 11 RR5
Ladysmith Av., Asht. 54 G14
Ladywell Av., Litt.H. 47 W10
Ladywell Gro., Litt.H. 35 W9
Lafford La., R.Mill 25 B7
Lafford La., Up Holl. 25 B8
Laithwaite Rd., Wgn. 27 E8
Lake Side, Leigh 57 O13
Lake St., Leigh 58 Q13
Lake Wk., Wgn. 26 D8
Lakeland Av., Asht. 54 G14
Lakes Dr., Orr. 26 C9
Lakeside Av., Bill. 38 C10
Lakeside Av., Farn. 35 W7
Lakeside Gdns., Rainh. 48 XX13
Lamb St., Wgn. 29 J7
Lamberhead Rd., Wgn. 26 D9
Lambeth St., Ath. 44 Q10
Lambley Clo., Leigh 43 O12
Lambourne, Skel. 12 XX6
Lambourne Gro., St.H. 62 D18
Lambton St., Farn. 34 U7
Lambton St., Wgn. 27 E9
Lancaster Av., Ath. 45 S10
Lancaster Av., Farn. 35 V7
Lancaster Av., Gol. 66 L16
Lancaster Av., Tyld. 46 T10
Lancaster Clo., Newt. 63 F18
Lancaster Ct., Leigh 58 Q14
Lancaster Cres., Skel. 23 WW7
Lancaster La., Parb. 5 YY2
Lancaster Rd., Hind. 30 M9
Lancaster Rd., Wgn. 27 E7
Lancaster St., Ince 28 H9
Lancaster Wk., Wgn. 27 E7
Wessex Rd.
Lancewood Pl., Wgn. 27 E9
Land Gate La., Asht. 40 G12
Land St., Wgn. 28 G8
Landedmans, Westho. 32 P8
Landrace Dr., Booth. 61 W13
Landside, Leigh 58 P15
Lane Head Av., Gol. 66 M16
Langdale Av., Gol. 56 L15
Langdale Av., Ince 29 K8
Langdale Av., Wgn. 17 G6
Langdale Cres., Abram 41 K12
Langdale Cres., Orr. 26 D8
Langdale Gro., Platt Br. 41 K10
Langdale Rd., Hind. 30 M9
Langdale Rd., Orr. 26 D8
Langdale St., Leigh 58 P13
Langfield, Gol. 66 M16
Langham Rd., Stand. 8 E3
Langholm Clo., Win. 39 E10
Langholm Rd., Asht. 53 E14
Langley Clo., Gol. 56 L15
Langley Clo., Stand. 8 F3
Langley Dr., Tyld. 61 V13
Langley Platt La., Leigh 45 R12
Langley St., Wgn. 27 E9
Langton Av., Stand. 8 F3
Langton Pl., Stand. 8 F3
Langtree, Skel. 12 XX6
Langtree Clo., Booth. 47 W12
Langtree La., Stand. 8 E2
Langwood La., Bill. 36 YY11
Langworthy Av., Litt.H. 47 W10
Lansbury St., Orr. 26 D9
Lansdowne Rd., Bolt. 33 S9
Larch Av., Wgn. 27 E9
Larch Clo., Bill. 50 B13
Larch Clo., Gol. 66 M17
Larch Clo., Skel. 23 WW7
Larch Gro., Ath. 45 R10
Larch Rd., Hay. 63 F16
Wycliffe Rd.
Larch Rd., Leigh 44 P12
Larchwood Dr., Wgn. 17 G6
Larkfield Av., Litt.H. 35 V9
Larkfield Av., Wgn. 17 G6
Larkfield Gro., Litt.H. 35 V9
Larkhill, Skel. 12 XX6
Larkhill Av., Stand. 16 F4
Latham Av., Newt. 64 H18
Latham Av., Orm. 11 RR5
Latham La., Orr. 26 D8
Lathom Av., Parb. 4 XX2
Lathom La., Orm. 11 SS4
Latimer Clo., Orr. 26 C8
Launceston Rd., Hind. 43 O10
Laurel Av., Newt. 64 H18
Laurel Cres., Hind. 43 N10
Laurel Dr., Litt.H. 47 W10
Laurel Dr., Skel. 23 WW7
Laurel Gro., Asht. 54 G14
Laurel Gro., Gol. 66 L16
Laurel Gro., Leigh 44 P12
Lavender Rd., Farn. 35 W7
Lavender Rd., Wgn. 16 F6
Lawns Av., Orr. 25 B9
Lawnswood Dr., Tyld. 46 U11
Lawrence St., Newt. 63 G18
Wellington St.
Lawson Av., Leigh 44 P11
Laxey Av., Ath. 45 S11
Laxey Cres., Leigh 43 O12
Lazonby Av., Asp. 19 M6
Lazonby Cres., Asht. 53 F14
Lea Cres., Orm. 10 QQ4
Lea St., Wgn. 28 G8
Lea Vw., Wgn. 29 J7
Leacroft, Asht. 53 F13
Leadale Clo., Stand. 8 E3
Leader St., Pemb. 27 E9
Leader St., Wgn. 29 J8
Leafield, Tyld. 46 U11
Leagate Clo., Win. 39 F10
Leaholme Av., Asp. 18 K6
Leckenby Clo., Booth. 61 W13
Ledburn, Skel. 13 YY6
Ledbury St., Leigh 58 P13
Ledger Rd., Hay. 62 D17
Ledmore Gro., Asht. 53 E14
Ledson Gro., Aug. 20 OO8
Lee Bk., Westho. 32 Q8
Lee Gro., Farn. 35 V8
Lee La., Abram 41 K12
Lee St., Ath. 45 R11
Leeds St., Ince 29 K7
Leeds St., Wgn. 28 G8
Lees La., R.Mill 14 A4
Lees La., Skel. 13 YY4
Leeswood, Skel. 12 XX6
Legh Rd., Hay. 62 D17
Legh St., Asht. 54 G15
Legh St., Gol. 65 K16
Legh St., Newt. 63 G18
Leicester Av., Hind. 30 M9
Leicester Rd., Litt.H. 35 V9
Leicester Rd., Tyld. 46 T11
Leigh Rd., Booth. 61 W13
Leigh Rd., Hind. 43 N11
Leigh Rd., Leigh 58 P13
Leigh Rd., Westho. 32 P9
Leigh St., Asp. 19 M6
Leigh St., Ath. 44 Q10
Leigh St., Hind. 43 N11
Leigh St., Leigh 57 O13
Leigh St., Westho. 32 P7
Leigh St., Wgn. 28 H8
Leighton Av., Ath. 44 Q10
Leighton Dr., Gol. 57 N15
Leighton St., Ath. 44 Q10
Lemon St., Tyld. 45 S12
Lenfield Dr., Hay. 62 D17
Leominster Pl., Ince 29 J8
Leonard Ct., Leigh 57 N14
Leonard Pl., Leigh 57 N14
Leopold St., Wgn. 27 E9
Lessingham Av., Wgn. 17 G6
Lesters Row, Tyld. 60 U14
Letcombe Clo., Leigh 44 P12
Levens Pl., Ince 29 K8
Levens Wk., Wgn. 27 E8
Lever Clo. Sq., Tyld. 45 S11
Lever St.
Lever Edge La., Farn. 34 U7
Lever St., Tyld. 45 S11
Lever St., Westho. 32 P6
Lever St., Wgn. 28 H8
Lewis Clo., Wgn. 28 G9
Ley Cres., Tyld. 60 T13
Ley Rd., Astley 46 T12
Leyland Av., Hind. 42 L10
Leyland Av., Rainf. 48 WW13
Leyland Grn. La., Asht. 53 E13
Leyland Gro., Hay. 62 D17
Leyland Mill La., Wgn. 17 H6
Leyland St., Abram 41 K11
Leyland St., Hind. 42 L10
Leyland St., Platt Br. 41 K11
Leyland Way, Orm. 10 QQ5
Leyton Clo., Farn. 35 V7
Leyton Clo., Pemb. 27 E9
Library St., Westho. 32 P8
Library St., Wgn. 28 H8
Lichfield Av., Gol. 66 L16
Lichfield Av., Tyld. 46 U12
Lichfield Clo., Farn. 35 W7
Lichfield St., Wgn. 27 E9
Lidgate Clo., Wgn. 39 E10
Lightburne Av., Leigh 58 P14
Lightshaw La., Gol. 55 K14
Lightwood, Tyld. 47 W12
Lilac Av., Asht. 53 E13
Lilac Av., Leigh 44 P12
Lilac Av., Wgn. 17 G6
Lilac Gdns., Ince 41 J10
Lilac Gro., Bill. 50 B14
Lilac Gro., Skel. 23 WW7
Lilac Rd., Gol. 55 K15
Lilford St., Ath. 44 Q11
Lilford St., Leigh 58 P14
Lilian Dr., Wgn. 17 G6
Lily Av., Farn. 35 W7
Lily La., Abram 41 J12
Lily Pl., Asht. 54 H15
Lily St., Asht. 54 H13
Lime Av., Leigh 44 P12
Lime Clo., Abram 42 L12
Lime Ct., Skel. 23 WW7
Lime Gro., Gol. 66 M17
Lime Gro., Hind. 42 M10
Lime Gro., Skel. 23 WW7
Lime St., Ath. 44 P10
Lime St., Tyld. 45 S11
Lime St., Wgn. 28 H8
Lime Vale, Ince 41 J10
Lime Vale Rd., Bill. 50 B14
Limefield, Wgn. 28 H8
School St.
Limefield Dr., Skel. 24 ZZ8
Ormskirk Rd.
Limes, The, Stand. 17 G4
Limes Av., Stand. 17 G5
Linacre Av., Farn. 35 V7
Linbeck Gro., Gol. 56 M15
Linburne St., Bick. 42 L11
Lincoln Av., Gol. 56 L15
Lincoln Clo., Leigh 67 O16
Lincoln Clo., Tyld. 46 T10
Lincoln Dr., Asht. 54 H15
Lincoln Dr., Asp. 19 L5
Lincoln Gro., Ath. 44 Q10
Lincoln Pl., Wgn. 27 E7
Lincoln Rd., Hind. 30 M9
Lincroft Rd., Hind. 43 N10
Lindale Clo., Booth. 47 V12
Lindale Rd., Tyld. 47 V12
Linden Av., Asht. 53 F13
Linden Av., Ath. 44 Q10
Linden Av., Orr. 26 C9
Linden Ct., Orr. 26 C9
Linden Gro., Bill. 50 B14
Linden Gro., Leigh 44 P12
Linden Gro., Orr. 26 C9
Linden Ms., Booth. 61 V13
Linden Rd.
Linden Rd., Booth. 61 V13
Linden Rd., Hind. 30 M8
Linden St., Wgn. 27 E9
Linden Wk., Orr. 26 C9
Lindens, Skel. 12 XX6
Lindholme, Skel. 13 YY6
Lindisfarne Av., Low. 67 O16
Lindley Av., Orr. 25 B9
Lindley Clo., Stand.L.G. 16 E6
Lindley Dr., Parb. 5 YY2
Lindley St., Leigh 58 Q13
Lindow St., Leigh 57 O13
Lindsay Ter., Asp. 19 L5
Ling Dr., Ath. 45 R11
Lingard St., Leigh 58 Q14
Lingards Dr., Astley 60 T14
Lingards La., Astley 60 T14
Lingfield Cres., Wgn. 16 F6
Lingfield Dr., Tyld. 61 V13
Lingmell Av., St.H. 49 A15
Lingmoor Clo., Wors.M. 40 G11

Lingmoor Dr., Tyld. 46 T12
Linkway Av., Asht. 55 J14
Linley Rd., Wgn. 27 E9
Linnet Clo., Newt. 64 H18
Linnet Dr., Leigh 58 Q13
Linney Sq., Wgn. 29 J8
Linstock Way, Ath. 44 Q10
Linton Av., Gol. 55 J15
Linwood Clo., Hind. 42 L10
Liptrot St., Wgn. 27 F8
Liscard St., Ath. 44 Q10
Litchfield Gro., Asht. 54 H15
Litherland Rd., Farn. 35 V7
Little Ch. St., Wgn. 26 D9
Little Factory St., Tyld. 45 S11
Little Gate, Westho. 32 P9
Little La., Wgn. 27 F9
Little London, Wgn. 28 H7
Little Pasture, Leigh 43 O12
Littler Rd., Hay. 62 D17
Littleton Gro., Stand. 8 F3
Liverpool Rd., Asht. 53 F15
Liverpool Rd., Aug. 20 NN9
Liverpool Rd., Hay. 62 D16
Liverpool Rd., Orm. 20 OO7
Liverpool Rd., Platt Br. 41 K11
Liverpool Rd., Skel. 22 VV8
Liverpool St., Ince 29 K7
Livingstone St., Asht. 54 G13
Liza St., Leigh 44 P12
Lloyd Cres., Newt. 63 F18
Lobelia Av., Farn. 35 W7
Local Board St., Wgn. 29 J8
Loch St., Orr. 26 D9
Lock La., Westho. 33 R6
Locker La., Gol. 55 J14
Lockerbie Pl., Wgn. 39 F11
Lockett Rd., Asht. 54 G13
Lodge Dr., Tyld. 60 T13
Lodge Gro., Ath. 45 S11
Lodge La., Ath. 45 R11
Lodge La., Hay. 54 G15
Lodge La., Leigh 59 S13
Lodge Rd., Ath. 45 S11
Lodge Rd., Orr. 38 C10
Lodge St., Hind. 30 L9
Logwood Av., Wgn. 27 E8
Logwood Pl., Wgn. 27 F8
Lomax St., Platt Br. 41 K11
Lombard St., Ath. 44 Q10
London Clo., Wgn. 27 E8
London Flds., Bill. 50 C13
Long Causeway, The, Leigh 44 Q12
Long Hey, Skel. 13 YY6
Long Heys La., Skel. 13 ZZ6
Long La., Bill. 36 ZZ10
Long La., Hind. 43 N10
Long La., Orm. 10 PP6
Long La., Westho. 31 O7
Longbrook, Shev. 15 D4
Longcroft, Leigh 59 S14
Longden Rd., Asht. 54 G14
Longdowns Dr., Tyld. 46 T12
Longendale Rd., Stand. 16 E4
Longfellow Clo., Wgn. 28 G9
Longfield Rd., Farn. 34 T7
Longhurst Rd., Hind. 42 M10
Longmead Av., Asht. 54 H14
Longridge Av., Stand. 16 F4
Longridge Way, Stand. 16 F4
Longshaw Av., Bill. 38 C11
Longshaw Clo., Bill. 38 C11
Longshaw Common, Bill. 38 C12
Longshaw Dr., Litt.H. 47 W10
Longshaw Old Rd., Bill. 38 C11
Longton Av., Gol. 66 L16
Longton St., Hind. 42 L10
Longwall Av., Booth. 47 W12
Longwood Clo., St.H. 48 YY15
Lonsdale Av., Leigh 58 P15
Lonsdale Av., Orm. 10 QQ4
Lonsdale Wk., Orr. 26 D8
Silverdale Rd.
Lord St., Ince 29 J8
Lord St., Leigh 58 P13
Lord St., Newt. 63 G18
Lord St., Tyld. 59 S13
Lord St., Westho. 32 P7
Lord St., Wgn. 28 H7
Lorne St., Wgn. 29 J8
Lorton Av., St.H. 49 A15
Lorton Clo., Booth. 61 V13
Lostock Clo., Bill. 50 C13
Lostock Wk., Leigh 57 O13
Loughrigg Av., St.H. 49 A15
Louise Gdns., Westho. 32 P9
Lovers La., Ath. 44 P11
Loves Cotts., Orm. 10 PP5
Low Bk. Rd., Asht. 53 F14
Low Grn., Bolt. 33 S9
Low Hall Gdns., Platt Br. 41 K10
Eatock St.
Low Mill La., Hind. 30 L9
Lowcroft, Skel. 13 YY6
Lowe St., Gol. 65 K16
Lower Bri. St., Hind. 30 M9
Lower Drake Fold, Westho. 32 P9
Lower Grn. La., Tyld. 60 U14
Lower Landedmans, Westho. 32 P8
Lower Leigh Rd., Westho. 32 P9
Lower Longshoot, Wgn. 28 H8
Lower New Row, Tyld. 47 W11
Lower St. Stephen St., Wgn. 28 G8
Lower Southfield, Westho. 32 P8
Lower St., Farn. 35 W8
St. James St.
Lowes La., Skel. 12 WW4
Lowes Sq., Wgn. 28 H8
Hardybutts
Loweswater Av., Tyld. 46 T12
Loweswater Cres., Hay. 62 D17
Lowood St., Leigh 57 O13
Lowther Dr., Leigh 45 S12
Lowther St., Farn. 35 W7
Lowther Ter., App.Br. 14 B4
Lowton Gdns., Gol. 65 K17
Lowton Rd., Gol. 55 K15
Loxton Clo., Wgn. 40 G10
Lucas Rd., Farn. 35 W8
Luciol Clo., Tyld. 46 U11
Ludlow, Skel. 13 YY6
Ludlow Av., Hind. 43 N10
Ludlow Dr., Leigh 45 S12
Ludlow Dr., Orm. 10 PP4
Ludlow St., Stand. 8 E2
Ludovic Ter., Wgn. 17 H6
Lulworth, Skel. 12 XX6
Lulworth Dr., Hind. 43 N10
Lune Gro., Leigh 57 O13
Lune Rd., Platt Br. 41 J11
Lune St., Tyld. 45 S12
Lunehurst, Gol. 66 M16
Tarnway
Lupin Av., Farn. 35 W7
Lupin Dr., Hay. 63 F17
Lurdin La., Stand. 17 G4
Luther Gro., St.H. 62 D18
Luton Gro., Ath. 44 Q10
Lychgate, Wgn. 27 F9
Lydford Grn., Stand. 17 G4
Lyefield Av., Wgn. 29 J7
Lyelake La., Skel. 22 UU8
Lyme St., Hay. 63 F17
Lyme St., Newt. 63 F18
Lymefield Dr., Wors. 47 W12
Lymm St., Platt Br. 41 K10
Lymm St., Wgn. 28 H8
Lymn Clo., Litt.H. 47 W10
Lyndale, Skel. 12 XX6
Lyndhurst, Skel. 12 XX6
Lyndon Av., Shev. 15 D5
Lynmouth Clo., Wgn. 28 G7
Lynton Av., Wgn. 17 G6
Lynton Rd., Farn. 34 U7
Lynton Rd., Hind. 30 M9
Lynton Rd., Tyld. 46 U12
Lynton St., Leigh 57 O13
Lynwood Av., Farn. 35 W7
Lynwood Av., Gol. 66 M17
Lynwood Av., Orm. 10 PP6
Lynwood Clo., Skel. 24 YY8
Lynwood End, Orm. 10 PP6
Lynwood Gro., Ath. 44 Q10
Lyon St., Asht. 39 F12
Lyon St., Wgn. 28 G8
Lytham Rd., Asht. 53 F13

M

Mabel St., Wgn. 27 F9
Maberry Clo., App.Br. 14 B4
Macaulay Pl., Wgn. 39 F10
Macclesfield St., Hind. 30 L9
MacDonald Av., Farn. 35 W8
MacDonald Av., Wgn. 40 G10
MacDonald St., Orr. 26 D9
MacKenzie Av., Wgn. 40 G10
Madams Wd. Rd., Litt.H. 47 W10
Madeley Clo., Wgn. 39 F10
Maden St., Tyld. 59 S13
Mafeking Pl., Asht. 54 H14
Magdalen Dr., Asht. 53 F14
Main Clo., Hay. 62 D17
Main La., Gol. 66 M18
Main St., Bill. 50 C13
Mains Av., Abram 41 J12
Mains La., Lath. 4 WW1
Major St., Wgn. 27 E9
Makants Clo., Bolt. 33 S9
Makerfield Way, Ince 29 K8
Makinson Arc., Wgn. 28 H8
Makinson Av., Hind. 30 L8
Maldon Av., Stand. 16 F6
Maldon Clo., Wgn. 29 J7
Maldwyn St., Farn. 34 T7
Malham Av., Wgn. 40 G11
Malham Clo., Leigh 57 O13
Malika Pl., Asht. 53 F13
Mallard Clo., Aug. 21 PP7
Mallory Dr., Leigh 58 Q13
Mallowdale, Tyld. 47 W12
Malpas Av., Wgn. 29 J7
Maltkiln La., Bisp. 5 YY1
Maltkiln La., Orm. 21 QQ8
Malton Av., Gol. 66 M16
Malton Gro., Leigh 57 O13
Malton Rd., Tyld. 47 V12
Malvern Av., Ath. 33 S9
Malvern Av., Hind. 43 N10
Malvern Clo., Asht. 54 G14
Malvern Clo., Farn. 35 V7
Malvern Clo., Wgn. 39 E10
Malvern Cres., Ince 41 J10
Malvern Rd., St.H. 62 D18
Malvern St., Stand. 8 E2
Malvern Ter., Leigh 58 P14
Manchester Rd., Astley 60 T14
Manchester Rd., Black. 19 M4
Manchester Rd., Ince 29 J8
Manchester Rd., Leigh 59 R14
Manchester Rd., Tyld. 46 T11
Manchester Rd. (Blackmoor), Tyld. 60 T13
Manchester Rd., Westho. 32 P7
Manchester Rd. E., Litt.H. 47 W10
Manchester Rd. W., Litt.H. 34 U9
Manderville Clo., Wgn. 39 E11
Westbury Av.
Manfield, Skel. 12 XX6
Manley Av., Gol. 55 J15
Manley Clo., Leigh 43 O12
Manley Cres., Westho. 32 Q7
Manley St., Ince 29 J9
Manning Av., Wgn. 28 G7
Manor Av., Gol. 66 L16
Manor Av., Newt. 63 F18
Manor Clo., Asht. 53 E14
Manor Ct., Gol. 66 L16
Manor Grn., Orr. 26 D8
Manor Gro., Asp. 18 K5
Manor Gro., Leigh 59 R14
Manor Gro., Skel. 23 WW7
Manor Ho. Clo., St.H. 49 A15
Manor Ho. Dr., Skel. 36 ZZ10
Manor Pl., Ince 29 J9
Manor Rd., Hay. 63 F16
Manor Rd., Hind. 30 M9
Manor Rd., Shev. 15 C5
Manor Rd., Tyld. 60 U13
Manor St., Gol. 55 K15
Manor St., New. 27 F9
Manor St., Wgn. 28 H8
Manorial Dr., Litt.H. 35 V9

Manse Gdns., Newt. 64 H18
Mansleys Pas., Leigh 58 P13
King St.
Maple Av., Ath. 44 Q10
Maple Av., Gol. 66 M16
Maple Av., Hay. 62 D16
Maple Av., Hind. 42 M10
Maple Av., Ince 29 J9
Maple Clo., Bill. 50 B13
Maple Cres., Leigh 44 P12
Maple Dr., Abram 41 K12
Maple Gro., Wgn. 17 G6
Maple Rd., Farn. 35 W8
Maplefield Dr., Booth. 47 W12
Maplewood, Skel. 12 XX6
Marbury Gro., Stand. 16 F4
Marchbank, Asp. 29 K7
Ashbourne Av.
Marchbank Rd., Skel. 22 VV7
Mardale Av., St.H. 49 A15
Mardale Clo., Ath. 33 R9
Margaret Av., Stand.L.G. 16 E6
Margaret St., Hind. 30 L9
Margaret St., Wgn. 28 G7
Marian Av., Newt. 63 F18
Marian Rd., Hay. 63 F16
Marians Dr., Orm. 10 QQ4
Marigold St., Wgn. 27 E8
Marina Dr., Wgn. 27 E9
Marion Pl., Bam. 41 J12
Maritime Clo., Newt. 64 H17
Mark St., Tyld. 47 V12
Market Pl., Stand. 8 F3
Market Pl., Wgn. 28 H8
Market Sq., Wgn. 28 H8
Market St., Ath. 45 R10
Market St., Hind. 30 L9
Market St., Leigh 58 P13
Market St., Newt. 63 G18
Market St., Stand. 8 F3
Market St., Tyld. 45 S11
Market St., Westho. 32 P8
Market St., Wgn. 28 H8
Markland St., Ince 29 J8
Marklands Rd., Astley 60 T14
Marklands Sq., Tyld. 45 S11
Lime St.
Marl Gro., Bill. 37 B10
Marland, Skel. 12 XX6
Marlborough, Skel. 12 XX6
Marlborough Av., Ince 41 J10
Marlborough Gdns., Farn. 35 V8
Marlborough Rd., Ath. 45 S10
Marlbrook Dr., Westho. 32 P9
Marlbrook Ms., Westho. 32 P9
Marlowe Clo., Wgn. 28 G9
Marmion Clo., Gol. 56 M15
Marple Clo., Stand. 7 D3
Marrick Clo., Wgn. 40 G11
Marsden St., Booth. 61 V13
Marsden St., Ince 41 J10
Marsden St., New. 27 F8
Marsden St., Westho. 32 P8
Marsden St., Wgn. 28 H8
Mesnes St.
Marsh Brook Fold, Westho. 31 N8
Marsh Grn., Wgn. 27 E8
Marsh La., Farn. 35 W8
Marsh La., Orm. 10 PP4
Marsh La., Wgn. 28 H8
Marsh Rd., Litt.H. 47 W10
Marsh Row, Hind. 43 N10
Long La.
Marsh St., Westho. 32 P7
Marsh St., Wgn. 40 G10
Marshall St., Leigh 58 P14
Marshbrook Clo., Hind. 31 N9
Marsland Grn. La., Tyld. 59 S14
Martin Av., Farn. 35 V8
Martin Av., Newt. 64 H17
Martin St., Ath. 45 R10
Bradshaw St.
Martindale Cres., Wgn. 27 F9
Martindale Rd., St.H. 49 A15
Martins Ct., Hind. 31 N9
Martins La., Skel. 24 YY8
Martland Av., Gol. 66 L16
Martland Av., Shev. 15 C5
Martland Cres., Wgn. 16 F6
Martland Mill La., Wgn. 27 E7
Martlew Dr., Ath. 45 S10
Marton Dr., Ath. 45 S10
Marton St., Wgn. 28 H7
Marus Av., Wgn. 39 F10
Marwick Clo., Stand. 8 E3
Marylebone Ct., Wgn. 17 H6
Marylebone Pl.
Marylebone Pl., Wgn. 17 H6
Masefield Av., Leigh 43 O12
Masefield Av., Orr. 26 D9
Masefield Dr., Farn. 35 W8
Masefield Dr., Wgn. 27 F9
Masefield Ho., Wgn. 27 F9
Mason Clo., Asht. 54 H14
Mason St., Abram 41 K12
Mason St., Wgn. 28 G8
Massam Clo., Rainf. 48 XX13
Mather Av., Gol. 66 M17
Mather Fold Rd., Wors. 47 W11
Mather La., Leigh 58 Q14
Mather St., Ath. 45 R10
Matheson Dr., Wgn. 27 E8
Matlock Clo., Ath. 45 R11
Matthew St., Farn. 35 W7
Mawdsley St., Hind. 42 L10
Mawdsley Ter., Orm. 10 QQ4
May Av., Abram 41 K12
May Av., Leigh 57 O13
May St., Gol. 55 K15
May St., Leigh 57 O13
May Tree Dr., Wgn. 17 G6
Mayfair Dr., Asp. 30 L7
Mayfair Dr., Ath. 45 S10
Mayfair Dr., Wgn. 39 F11
Mayfield Dr., Leigh 67 O16
Mayfield Rd., Orr. 26 D8
Mayfield Rd., Up Holl. 25 A8
Mayfield St., Ath. 45 R10
Mayflower Cotts., Stand. 17 H4
Maytree Wk., Skel. 12 XX6
McCormack Dr., Wgn. 28 H8
McMinnis Av., St.H. 62 D18
Meade, The, Farn. 35 V7
Meadow Bk., Orm. 10 QQ5
School Ho. Grn.
Meadow Clo., Leigh 58 P15
Meadow Clo., Newt. 63 F18
Meadow Clo., Skel. 24 ZZ8
Meadow Cft., Westho. 32 P8
Meadow Dr., Orm. 21 PP7
Meadow Pit La., Haigh 18 J4
Meadow St., Tyld. 46 T11
Shuttle St.
Meadow Wk., Tyld. 60 T13
Meadowbank Av., Ath. 33 S9
Meadowbank Rd., Farn. 34 T7
Meadowcroft, Asht. 53 F13
Meadowcroft, Skel. 12 XX6
Meadowfield Dr., Booth. 61 W13
Meadows St., Wgn. 28 G7
Meadowside Av., Asht. 40 G12
Meadowside Rd., Hind. 42 M10
Meadowvale Dr., Pemb. 27 E9
Meads Gro., Farn. 34 U8
Meads Gro., Tyld. 60 U13
Meadway, Ince 29 J8
Meadway, Tyld. 46 U11
Meadway Clo., Gol. 66 L16
Mealhouse La., Ath. 45 R10
Meanley Rd., Tyld. 45 S12
Meanley St., Tyld. 45 S11
Elliott St.
Medlock Way, Platt Br. 41 K11
Medway Clo., Asht. 53 F13
Medway Clo., Leigh 67 O16
Medway Pl., Pemb. 27 E8
Medway Rd., Wors. 47 W12
Medway Wk., Pemb. 27 E8
Megfield, Westho. 32 P9
Melbreck, Skel. 12 XX6
Melford Dr., Asht. 54 G14
Melford Dr., Bill. 37 B10
Melling Clo., Leigh 58 P15
Melling St., Wgn. 27 F9
Melling Way, Win. 39 E11
Mellings Av., Bill. 38 C11
Melmerby Clo., Asht. 53 F14
Melrose Av., Leigh 43 O11
Melrose Cres., Asht. 53 E14
Melrose Dr., Wgn. 39 E10
Melton Clo., Tyld. 46 T12
Melverley Dr., Leigh 59 R13
Melverley St., Wgn. 28 G8
Mendip Av., Wgn. 39 E10
Mendip Ct., Platt Br. 41 K10
Mercer Rd., Hay. 62 E17
Mercer St., Newt. 64 H18
Merchants Cres., Gol. 56 M15
Mere Av., Leigh 57 O13
Mere Clo., Skel. 23 WW7
Mere Gro., St.H. 50 B15
Mere Rd., Asht. 54 H14
Mere Rd., Newt. 64 H18
Mere St., Leigh 57 O13
Merefold, Litt.H. 47 W10
Merewood, Skel. 12 XX6
Merlewood Dr., Tyld. 46 T12
Mersey Clo., Hind. 43 O10
Mersey Rd., Orr. 26 C8
Mersey Rd., Platt Br. 41 J11
Mersey St., Leigh 57 O13
Mersey St., St.H. 62 D18
Merton Gro., Tyld. 60 U13
Merton Rd., Wgn. 38 D10
Mervyn Pl., Wgn. 40 G10
Mesnes Av., Wgn. 28 G9
Mesnes Dr., Wgn. 28 G9
Mesnes Pk. Ter., Wgn. 28 H7
Mesnes Rd., Wgn. 28 H7
Mesnes St., Wgn. 28 H7
Mews, The, Hind. 30 L9
Meynell Dr., Leigh 58 P15
Mickering La., Aug. 21 PP9
Middlewood, Gol. 66 M16
Tarnway
Middlewood, Skel. 12 XX6
Middlewood Clo., Orm. 21 PP8
Middlewood Dr., Orm. 21 PP8
Middlewood Rd., Orm. 21 PP8
Midge Nook, Skel. 23 WW9
Midland Clo., Leigh 57 O13
Miles La., App.Br. 14 B4
Miles La., Shev. 15 C5
Milford Rd., Wgn. 29 J7
Milford St., Ince 29 J9
Milk St., Tyld. 46 T11
Milk St., Wgn. 28 H8
Milking La., Farn. 34 U7
Mill Bk., App.Br. 14 B4
Mill Gdns., Orm. 10 QQ6
Mill Hill, Litt.H. 35 V9
Mill Ho. Vw., Up Holl. 25 B8
Mill La., App.Br. 14 B4
Mill La., Asp. 19 M6
Mill La., Gol. 65 K16
Mill La., Leigh 58 Q14
Mill La., Newt. 64 H18
Mill La., Orm. 20 NN7
Mill La., Parb. 5 YY3
Mill La., Rainf. 48 XX15
Mill La., Skel. 23 WW7
Mill La., Up Holl. 25 A8
Mill La., Westho. 32 P9
Mill La., Wgn. 39 F10
Mill Leat, Parb. 5 YY3
Mill Leat Clo., Parb. 5 YY3
Mill Leat Ms., Parb. 5 YY3
Mill Rd., Orr. 25 B9
Mill Sq., Westho. 32 P8
Mill St., Asht. 54 H15
Mill St., Booth. 61 W13
Mill St., Gol. 65 K16
Mill St., Hind. 30 L9
Mill St., Leigh 58 Q14
Mill St., Orm. 10 QQ6
Mill St., Westho. 32 P8
Mill St., Wgn. 28 G8
Millbeck Cres., Pemb. 27 E9
Millbeck Gro., St.H. 49 A15
Millbrook Av., Ath. 33 S9
Millbrook Clo., Skel. 23 WW7
Millcroft Av., Orr. 25 B9
Milldale Clo., Ath. 45 R10
Milldale Rd., Gol. 57 N15
Millers La., Ath. 45 R12
Millers La., Platt Br. 41 J11
Millfield, Parb. 5 YY3
Millfield Dr., Booth. 61 W13

Millfield La., Hay. 53 F15
Millgate, Wgn. 28 H8
Millingford Av., Gol. 55 J15
Millingford Gro., Asht. 54 G14
Millrose Clo., Skel. 23 WW7
Millwood Clo., Asht. 54 G13
Milman Clo., Orm. 10 PP6
Milne Clo., Hay. 63 F16
Milton Av., Newt. 63 G18
Milton Clo., Ath. 33 R9
Milton Cres., Farn. 35 W9
Milton Dr., Orm. 11 RR6
Milton Gro., Bill. 37 B11
Milton Gro., Orr. 26 D9
Milton Gro., Wgn. 17 H6
Milton Rd., Gol. 66 L16
Milton St., Leigh 58 P13
Minehead Av., Leigh 43 O11
Minerva Rd., Farn. 35 V7
Minster Gro., Tyld. 46 T12
Mirfield Clo., Gol. 66 L16
Miry La., Parb. 5 YY3
Miry La., Westho. 32 P9
Miry La., Wgn. 28 G8
Mitchell Rd., Bill. 50 C13
Mitchell St., Gol. 65 K16
Mitchell St., Ince 29 K8
Mitchell St., Leigh 57 N13
Mitchell St., Wgn. 27 F9
Moat Ho. St., Ince 29 K8
Molyneux Rd., Orm. 21 PP8
Molyneux Rd., Westho. 32 Q7
Mona St., Wgn. 28 G8
Monica Ter., Asht. 54 G15
Monkleigh Clo., Tyld. 46 T12
Monmouth Cres., Asht. 54 H15
Monroe Clo., Wgn. 40 G10
Montford Ri., Asp. 29 K7
Ashbourne Av.
Montreal St., Abram 56 M14
Montrey Cres., Asht. 53 E14
Montrose Av., Wgn. 26 D8
Monument Rd., Wgn. 28 H7
Moor Av., App.Br. 15 C4
Moor Dr., Skel. 24 ZZ8
Moor Gate, Orm. 10 QQ6
Moor La., Leigh 44 P12
Moor Rd., Orr. 26 C9
Moor St., Orm. 10 QQ5
Moore Av., St.H. 62 D18
Moore Dr., Hay. 63 F17
Moore St., Wgn. 28 H7
Moore St. E., Wgn. 29 J7
Moores La., Stand. 8 E3
Moorfield, Tyld. 47 V12
Moorfield Cres., Gol. 67 N16
Moorfield St., Platt Br. 41 K10
Moorgate Dr., Tyld. 60 T13
Moorhey Rd., Litt.H. 35 V9
Moorings Clo., Ince 29 J8
Moorland Dr., Litt.H. 35 W9
Moorland Rd., Asht. 55 J14
Moorland Rd., Hind. 30 L9
Moorland Vill., Asp. 19 L6
Moorlands Av., Leigh 58 P14
Moorlands Vw., Farn. 34 T7
Moorside, Asp. 19 L5
Scot La.
Moorside Av., Farn. 35 W8
Moorside Wk., Orr. 26 D8
Silverdale Rd.
Morden Av., Asht. 54 G14
Moreton Clo., Gol. 55 J15
Moreton Clo., Wgn. 39 E11
Wirral Dr.
Moreton Dr., Leigh 57 O15
Morley St., Ath. 45 R10
Morleys La., Tyld. 59 S14
Mornington Rd., Bolt. 33 S9
Mornington Rd., Hind. 30 M9
Morris Clo., Hay. 62 D17
Morris Grn., Farn. 34 U7
Morris Grn. La., Farn. 34 U7
Morris Grn. St., Farn. 34 U7
Morris Rd., Up Holl. 25 A8
Morris St., Wgn. 28 H8
Mort Fold, Litt.H. 35 W9
Mort La., Tyld. 47 V11
Mort St., Hind. 31 N9
Mort St., Leigh 57 N13
Mort St., Tyld. 45 S11
Mort St., Wgn. 28 G7
Mortlake Clo., Tyld. 47 V11
Morton Av., Wgn. 28 G9
Mortons, The, Westho. 32 P7
Morville Dr., Wors.M. 40 G10
Mosedale Av., St.H. 49 A15
Mosley Common Rd., Tyld. 47 V12
Moss Av., Bill. 37 B10
Moss Av., Leigh 58 Q13
Moss Bk., Orm. 21 PP7
Moss Bk. Rd., St.H. 49 A15
Moss Delph La., Orm. 21 PP7
Moss Gro., Stand. 16 F4
Moss Ho. La., Booth. 61 W13
Moss La., Aug. 20 NN9
Moss La., Gol. 65 K17
Moss La., Platt Br. 41 K10
Moss La., Rainf. 48 YY13
Moss La., Skel. 23 WW9
Moss La., Tyld. 60 T15
Moss La., Wri. 7 C2
Moss La. Vw., Skel. 23 WW9
Moss Meadow, Westho. 32 P7
Peel St.
Moss Pit Row, Asp. 18 K6
Moss Rd., Bill. 37 B10
Moss Side, Bill. 36 ZZ10
Moss St., Ince 41 J10
Moss St., Platt Br. 41 K10
Sydney St.
Moss St., Skel. 22 VV8
Moss St., Wgn. 28 G7
Moss Ter., Wgn. 26 D9
Moss Vw., Tyld. 46 T12
Mossborough Rd., Rainf. 48 WW13
Mossbrook Dr., Litt.H. 35 V9
Mossdale Rd., Asht. 40 G12
Mossfield Rd., Farn. 35 W8
Mossland Gro., Bolt. 33 R7
Mossy Lea Fold, Wri. 7 C2
Mossy Lea Rd., Stand. 7 D3
Mossy Lea Rd., Wri. 7 C1
Mottram Dr., Wors.M. 28 G9
Mount, The, Skel. 23 XX8
Spencers La.
Mount Cres., Orr. 26 C9
Mount Pleasant Av., St.H. 62 D18
Mount Pleasant Rd., Farn. 35 V8
Mount Skip La., Litt.H. 47 W10
Mount St., Leigh 57 O14
Mount Vw., Wgn. 28 H9
Mountmorres Clo., Westho. 33 S8
Mountwood, Skel. 12 XX6
Muirfield Dr., Tyld. 46 U12
Mulberry Av., Gol. 66 M16
Mulberry Clo., Wgn. 27 E9
Mullins Av., Newt. 64 H17
Munro Av., Orr. 26 C9
Murphy Clo., Wgn. 28 G9
Murray St., Ath. 44 Q11
Mycroft Clo., Leigh 44 P12
Myrtle Av., Asht. 53 F13
Myrtle Av., Hay. 62 D16
Myrtle Av., Leigh 44 P12
Myrtle Gro., Bill. 50 B14
Myrtle St., Wgn. 28 G8

N

Nairn Clo., Stand. 8 E3
Nangreaves St., Leigh 57 O13
Narcissus Wk., Litt.H. 47 V10
Narrow Cft. Rd., Orm. 20 OO7
Narrow La., Orm. 20 OO7
Narrow Moss La., Orm. 10 QQ4
Naunton Av., Leigh 57 O13
Navenby Rd., Wgn. 40 G11
Navigation Clo., Leigh 58 P14
Naylor Av., Gol. 65 K16
Naylor Fm. Av., Shev. 15 C5
Naylor St., Ath. 45 R10
Neild Gdns., Leigh 58 P14
Neild St., Leigh 58 P14
Nel Pan La., Leigh 43 O12
Nells La., Aug. 20 NN9
Nelson Dr., Ince 29 K8
Nelson St., Ath. 44 Q10
Nelson St., Hind. 30 L9
Nelson St., Newt. 63 G18
Nelson St., Tyld. 46 T12
Netherby Rd., Wgn. 17 G6
Nethercott Ct., Tyld. 45 S11
Blenheim St.
Netherfield Rd., Farn. 34 U7
Netherfields, Leigh 43 O12
Netherton Gro., Farn. 35 W7
Neverstitch Clo., Skel. 23 WW7
Neverstitch Rd., Skel. 22 VV7
Neville St., Newt. 63 G18
Neville St., Platt Br. 41 K10
Nevison St., Leigh 57 N13
New Acres, Parb. 4 XX3
New Boston, Hay. 63 F16
New Brook Rd., Westho. 33 S8
New City Rd., Tyld. 47 W12
New Ct. Way, Orm. 10 QQ5
New Drake Grn., Westho. 32 P9
New Fold, Wgn. 26 D9
New Hall Dr., Tyld. 46 T12
Wycombe Dr.
New La., Orm. 21 QQ7
New Mkt. St., Wgn. 28 H8
New Miles La., Stand. 15 C5
New Rd., Haigh 18 K5
New Sq., Wgn. 28 G8
New St., Asht. 54 H14
New St., Pemb. 26 D9
New St., Platt Br. 41 K11
New St., Wgn. 27 F7
Newall Gro., Leigh 44 P12
Newark Rd., Hind. 42 L10
Newark St., Wgn. 27 F7
Newbarn Av., Asht. 54 H14
Newbridge Clo., Asht. 53 E14
Newburn Clo., Wgn. 39 F10
Newby Sq., Pemb. 26 D9
Newcombe Dr., Litt.H. 35 V9
Newearth Rd., Wors. 47 W12
Newenden Rd., Wgn. 17 G6
Newgate Av., App.Br. 15 C4
Newgate Dr., Litt.H. 35 V9
Newgate Rd., Skel. 24 ZZ8
Newhaven Av., Leigh 44 P12
Newland Av., Wgn. 27 E9
Newland Dr., Westho. 33 S8
Newlands Av., Tyld. 60 T13
Newlands Dr., Black. 19 M4
Newlands Dr., Gol. 66 L16
Newlands Rd., Leigh 58 P14
Newlodge, Wgn. 28 H7
Newlyn Dr., Asht. 54 G15
Newlyn Dr., Skel. 24 YY8
Newman Av., Wgn. 28 G7
Newman St., Wgn. 29 J7
Newsham Wk., Wgn. 27 F7
Ingram St.
Newstead Rd., Wgn. 39 F10
Newton Clo., Wgn. 28 H7
Newton La., Gol. 64 H17
Newton Pk. Dr., Newt. 64 H18
Newton Rd., Bill. 50 C13
Newton Rd., Gol. 66 L17
Newton Rd., St.H. 62 D18
Newton St., Leigh 58 P13
Newtons Fold, Gol. 57 N14
Nicol Mere Dr., Asht. 54 G13
Nicol Rd., Asht. 54 G13
Nightingale Ct., Wgn. 28 G7
Nipe La., Skel. 23 XX9
Nixons La., Skel. 24 YY8
Noble St., Leigh 58 Q13
Noble St., Wgn. 27 F7
Noel Gate, Orm. 20 OO7
Nook, The, App.Br. 15 C4
Nook, The, Orm. 21 PP8
Nook La., Gol. 65 K16
Nook La., Tyld. 60 U15
Norbreck Cres., Wgn. 28 G7
Norbury Av., Bill. 50 B13
Norbury St., Leigh 57 O13
Norfield, Orm. 11 RR5
Norfolk Clo., Hind. 31 N9
Norfolk Rd., Ath. 33 R9
Norfolk Rd., Bill. 38 C11

Norfolk St., New. 27 F9
Norfolk St., Swin. 28 G7
Norley Cottage, Wgn. 27 E8
Norley Hall Av., Wgn. 27 E8
Norley Rd., Leigh 57 N14
Norley Rd., Wgn. 26 D8
Norma Av., Hay. 63 G16
Norman Av., Newt. 64 H18
Norman St., Ince 41 J10
Normanby St., Farn. 34 T7
Normanby St., Wgn. 26 D9
Normanhurst, Orm. 11 RR6
Normanton Clo., Stand.L.G. 16 F6
Norris St., Tyld. 46 T12
Norrishouse Dr., Orm. 21 PP8
North Av., Abram 56 M14
North Av., Farn. 35 W8
North Av., Leigh 59 R14
North Av. W., Farn. 35 W8
North Dene, Parb. 4 XX3
North Dr., Wri. 6 A3
North Florida Rd., Hay. 62 E16
North La., Tyld. 60 T13
North Rd., Ath. 32 Q9
North St., Asht. 54 H14
North St., Hay. 63 F17
North St., Leigh 58 Q14
North St., Newt. 63 F18
North Way, Aug. 20 NN9
North Ways, Stand. 8 E3
Northam Clo., Stand. 8 E3
Northcroft, Wgn. 29 J7
Northfield, Skel. 12 XX6
Northfield Ct., Gol. 56 L15
Northledge, Leigh 58 Q13
Northolt Av., Leigh 44 P12
Northumberland St., Wgn. 29 J7
Northway, Skel. 12 XX6
Northway, Wgn. 28 H7
Northwell St., Leigh 44 P12
Northwold Clo., Wgn. 39 E10
Northwood Av., Newt. 64 H18
Norton Rd., Tyld. 47 V12
Norweb Way, Leigh 58 Q14
Norwich Av., Asht. 54 H14
Norwich Av., Gol. 66 L16
Norwood Av., Asht. 53 F13
Norwood Av., Gol. 66 M16
Norwood Av., Tyld. 60 T13
Norwood Av., Wgn. 17 G6
Norwood Gro., Rainf. 48 XX13
Nostell Rd., Asht. 54 G13
Nottingham Pl., Wgn. 29 J7
Nursery Av., Orm. 11 RR5
Nutt St., Wgn. 29 J7
Nuttall St., Ath. 45 S10

O

Oak Av., Abram 42 L12
Oak Av., Gol. 65 K16
Oak Av., Hay. 63 F16
Oak Av., Hind. 43 N10
Oak Av., Newt. 64 H18
Oak Av., Orm. 10 PP6
Oak Av., Stand. 16 F4
Oak Cres., Skel. 22 VV7
Oak Grn., Orm. 10 QQ5
School Ho. Grn.
Oak Hill Clo., Wgn. 17 G6
Oak St., Asht. 54 G13
Oak St., Ath. 44 Q11
Oak St., Leigh 58 P14
Oak St., Tyld. 46 T11
Oak St., Wgn. 29 J8
Oak Tree Clo., Ath. 44 Q11
Oakbank, Platt Br. 41 K10
Oakdale Dr., Tyld. 60 U13
Oakenden Clo., Asht. 54 G13
Oakengates, Stand. 8 F3
Oakfield Av., Ath. 45 R10
Oakfield Av., Gol. 55 J15
Oakfield Cres., Asp. 19 L5
Oakfield Dr., Litt.H. 35 V9
Oakhead, Leigh 59 R14
Oakhurst Gro., Westho. 31 O8
Oaklands Rd., Gol. 66 M16
Oaklea, Shev. 7 D3
Oakleigh, Skel. 36 YY11
Oakleigh Av., Farn. 35 W7
Oakley Av., Bill. 50 C13
Oaktree Ct., Skel. 13 YY6
Oakwood, Skel. 13 YY6
Oakwood Av., Asht. 54 G15
Oakwood Av., Shev. 15 C5
Oakwood Dr., Leigh 58 P15
Oban Dr., Asht. 53 E14
Oban Way, Asp. 19 L5
Dunoon Rd.
O'Connell Clo., Hay. 62 E17
Okell Gro., Leigh 57 O13
Old Boundary Way, Orm. 10 QQ5
Old Bri. Dr., Hind. 30 L9
Old Collier Yd., Asht. 53 E14
Old Engine La., Skel. 22 VV7
Old Fold, Wgn. 26 D9
Old Fold Rd., Asp. 19 L5
Old Fold Rd., Westho. 31 N8
Old Garswood Rd., Asht. 51 D15
Old Hall Dr., Asht. 54 G15
Old Hall La., Westho. 32 P9
Old Hall Mill La., Leigh 44 Q12
Old Hall St., Ince 29 J9
Old Ho. La., Leigh 58 P14
Old La., Aug. 20 NN9
Old La., Litt.H. 35 V9
Old La., Shev. 15 D5
Old La., Up Holl. 25 A9
Old La., Westho. 31 O8
Old La., Wgn. 17 G6
Old Mill Hill, Orm. 10 PP6
Old Mill La., Wri. 5 ZZ1
Old Penny La., Hay. 63 G16
Old Pepper La., Stand. 7 D2
Old Rectory Grn., Aug. 20 OO8
Old Rd., Asht. 54 G14
Old Sch. Pl., Asht. 54 G13
Old Vicarage, Westho. 32 P9
Old Vicarage Ms., Westho. 32 P9
Old Wargrave Rd., Newt. 64 H18
Old Wash La., Wri. 6 B1
Old Whint Rd., Hay. 62 D17
Oldcott Clo., Booth. 61 V13
Oldfield Clo., Westho. 32 P8
Oldham St., Tyld. 46 T12
Oldwells Clo., Litt.H. 35 V9
Olivant St., Leigh 58 Q13
Olive Gro., Skel. 23 WW7
Olive Gro., Wgn. 16 F6
Oliver St., Ath. 45 R10
Ollerton Clo., Asp. 29 K7
Opal Gro., Leigh 58 P14
Openshaw Pl., Farn. 35 W8
Orchard, The, Orm. 10 PP5
Orchard Av., Booth. 47 W12
Orchard Clo., Leigh 44 P12
Orchard Clo., Shev. 15 D5
Orchard La., Leigh 44 P12
Orchard St., Asht. 54 H14
Orchard St., Wgn. 28 H8
Orchard Vw., Orm. 21 PP7
Orchid Av., Farn. 35 W7
Ordsall Av., Litt.H. 47 W10
Organ St., Hind. 43 N10
Organ St., Leigh 58 P13
Oriel Rd., Asht. 53 F14
Oriole Dr., Booth. 47 W12
Ormond Av., Orm. 11 SS6
Ormsby Clo., Stand. 8 F3
Ormside Clo., Hind. 43 N10
Ormskirk Rd. (Blaguegate), Skel. 22 VV7
Ormskirk Rd. (Digmoor), Skel. 23 XX8
Ormskirk Rd., Up Holl. 25 A8
Ormskirk Rd., Wgn. 26 D9
Ormston Gro., Wgn. 44 P12
Orpington St., Wgn. 27 E9
Orrell Gdns., Orr. 26 C9
Orrell Hall Clo., Orr. 26 D8
Orrell Rd., Orr. 25 B8
Orrell St., Hind. 42 L10
Orrell St., Wgn. 28 H8
Orton Way, Asht. 53 F14
Osborne Gro., Leigh 59 R13
Osborne Rd., Asht. 54 G14
Osborne Rd., Gol. 66 M16
Oscott Av., Litt.H. 35 W9
Osprey Av., Westho. 31 O9
Ospreys, The, Wgn. 39 E10
Otterwood Sq., Wgn. 27 E7
Oval, The, Shev. 15 C5
Overhill Way, Wgn. 39 E10
Overton St., Leigh 58 P14
Owen Av., Orm. 10 QQ5
Owen St., Leigh 57 O13
Firs La.
Owenington Gro., Litt.H. 35 W9
Owlwood Dr., Litt.H. 47 V10
Oxburgh Rd., Ince 41 J10
Oxford Clo., Farn. 35 V8
Oxford Ct., Wgn. 28 H7
Oxford Rd., Ath. 32 Q9
Oxford Rd., Orr. 26 C8
Oxford Rd., Skel. 23 WW7
Oxford St., Hind. 30 M8
Oxford St., Leigh 58 P13
Oxhouse Rd., Bill. 37 B10
Oxlea Gro., Westho. 32 P8

P

Paddock, The, Asht. 53 F13
Paddock, The, Orm. 10 PP6
Paddock Clo., Ath. 33 S9
Paddock Ri., Wgn. 16 F6
Paddock Rd., Skel. 24 YY9
Pagefield Clo., Wgn. 28 G7
Pagefield St., Wgn. 28 G7
Paignton Clo., Bill. 38 C11
Palace Gro., Leigh 59 R13
Palatine Clo., Wgn. 39 F10
Palatine Sq., Leigh 57 O13
Palin St., Hind. 43 N10
Palm Av., Asht. 53 E13
Palm Ct., Skel. 23 WW7
Palm Gro., Wgn. 27 E9
Palmer Gro., Leigh 44 P11
Pansy Rd., Farn. 35 W8
Parbold Hill, Parb. 5 YY3
Parchments, The, Newt. 64 H18
Park Av., Bill. 38 C11
Park Av., Gol. 55 J15
Park Av., Hay. 62 D17
Park Av., Orm. 10 QQ5
Park Av., Shev. 15 D4
Park Bk., Bolt. 33 S9
Park Clo., Parb. 5 YY2
Park Cres., Wgn. 28 G7
Park Cres. W., Wgn. 28 G7
Park Edge, Westho. 32 Q8
Park Fld. Av., Farn. 35 W8
Park Gro., Litt.H. 47 V10
Park Hey Dr., App.Br. 15 C4
Park La., Abram 41 K12
Park La., Leigh 59 R14
Park Link, Orm. 20 OO7
Park Meadow, Westho. 32 Q8
Park Rd., Bill. 38 C11
Park Rd., Gol. 64 H16
Park Rd., Hind. 42 M10
Park Rd., Orm. 10 QQ5
Park Rd., Orr. 26 D9
Park Rd., Stand. 16 F4
Park Rd., Westho. 32 Q8
Park Rd., Wgn. 28 G7
Park Rd. N., Newt. 64 H18
Park St., Ath. 45 S10
Park St., Hay. 62 D17
Park St., Tyld. 46 T11
Park St., Wgn. 28 G9
Park Ter., Stand. 8 E2
Park Vw., Abram 41 K11
Park Vw., Asht. 54 G15
Park Vw., Ince 29 K8
Park Vw., Newt. 64 H18
Park Way, Litt.H. 47 V10
Parkbrook La., Shev. 15 D4
Parkdale, Tyld. 60 T13
Parkend Dr., Leigh 57 O15
Parker Cres., Orm. 10 QQ4
Parkfield, Shev. 15 D4
Parkfield Av., Tyld. 60 T13
Parkfield Clo., Leigh 44 Q12
Parkfield Clo., Tyld. 60 T13
Parkfield Dr., Tyld. 46 U11
Parklands, Skel. 24 YY7

Parklands Dr., Asp. 19 L5
Parks, The, Asht. 54 G15
Parkside, Hind. 30 M9
Parkside Av., Asht. 39 F12
Parkside Cres., Orr. 26 C9
Parkside Rd., Newt. 65 K18
Parkway, Shev. 7 D3
Parkway, Westho. 31 O9
Parkwood Clo., Ince 29 J9
Parkwood Dr., Westho. 33 S8
Parliament St., Ince 28 H9
Pitt St.
Parliament St., Up Holl. 25 B8
Parr Clo., Farn. 35 W8
Plodder La.
Parr Gro., Hay. 62 D17
Parr St., Tyld. 45 S12
Elliott St.
Parrs La., Orm. 21 PP8
Parsonage Rd., Hind. 30 L8
Ladies La.
Parsonage Rd., Up Holl. 25 A8
Parsons Wk., Wgn. 28 G7
Part St., Westho. 32 P7
Partington St., Farn. 34 U7
Partington St., Wgn. 27 F8
Pasture Clo., Asht. 53 F13
Pasture La., Rainf. 48 XX14
Patchett St., Tyld. 46 T12
Elliott Sq.
Pateley Sq., Wgn. 28 G7
Patricroft Rd., Ince 29 J9
Patt St., Westho. 31 N8
Patterdale Pl., Ince 29 K8
Patterdale Rd., Asht. 40 G12
Patterdale Rd., Leigh 59 R14
Patterson St., Newt. 63 G18
Pauline St., Hind. 43 N11
Paxton Pl., Bill. 36 YY10
Peace Haven, Skel. 23 WW7
Peace St., Ath. 45 S10
Peace St., Tyld. 59 S13
Peach Av., Hay. 63 F16
Peacock Fold, Leigh 57 O13
Peak Av., Ath. 33 R9
Pear Tree Gro., Tyld. 47 V11
Pearl St., Wgn. 17 G6
Peebles Clo., Asht. 53 E14
Peel Clo., Ath. 45 S10
Peel Dr., Litt.H. 47 V10
Peel La., Litt.H. 47 V10
Peel La., Tyld. 60 T14
Peel Pk. Cres., Litt.H. 47 V10
Peel Rd., Skel. 24 ZZ9
Peel St., Leigh 58 P13
Peel St., Platt Br. 41 K11
Peel St., Westho. 32 P7
Peel Ter., Westho. 32 P7
Peelwood Av., Litt.H. 35 W9
Peet Av., Orm. 10 PP6
Pemberlei Rd., Asp. 30 L7
Pemberton Rd., Win. 38 D11
Pemberton St., Litt.H. 47 W10
Pembroke Rd., Hind. 43 O10
Pembroke Rd., Wgn. 27 E7
Penbury Rd., Wgn. 17 G6
Pendeen Clo., Tyld. 46 T12
Pendennis Cres., Hind. 43 N10
Pendle Clo., Wgn. 27 E9
Pendle Dr., Orm. 11 RR5
Pendle Pl., Bill. 36 YY10
Pendle Rd., Gol. 56 L15
Pendlebury Fold, Bolt. 33 R7
Pendlebury La., Haigh 17 H5
Penketh Av., Astley 60 T13
Penketh Pl., Skel. 24 YY9
Penketh St., Wgn. 28 G7
Penkford St., Newt. 63 F18
Penleach Av., Leigh 58 Q13
Penn Gdns., Leigh 58 P14
Pennine Av., Wgn. 39 E10
Pennine La., Gol. 56 L15
Pennine Pl., Skel. 24 YY9
Pennine Wk., Platt Br. 41 K11
Pennington Av., Leigh 58 P14
Pennington Av., Orm. 10 QQ5
Pennington Grn., Asp. 30 M7
Pennington La., Ince 29 K8
Pennington La., St.H. 62 E18
Pennington La., Stand. 18 J4
Pennington Pl., Litt.H. 47 V10
Pennington Rd., Leigh 58 P14
Pennington St., Hind. 30 L9
Penny La., Hay. 63 F16
Pennygate Clo., Hind. 30 L9
Pennyhurst St., Wgn. 28 G8
Penrhyn Gro., Ath. 33 R9
Penrice Fold, Booth. 47 W12
Penrith Cres., Asht. 54 G14
Penrose Pl., Bill. 36 ZZ10
Penshaw Av., Wgn. 40 G10
Penson St., Wgn. 28 H7
Pepper La., Stand. 7 D2
Pepper Mill La., Wgn. 28 H8
Pepys Pl., Wgn. 40 G10
Perch St., Wgn. 29 J7
Perryn Pl., Wgn. 8 F3
Perth Av., Ince 29 K8
Peter St., Asht. 54 H14
Peter St., Gol. 65 K16
Peter St., Hind. 30 L9
Peter St., Ince 29 J8
Peter St., Leigh 58 Q14
Peter St., Orr. 26 D8
Peter St., Westho. 31 N8
Peterhouse Wk., Asht. 53 F14
Petticoat La., Ince 29 K8
Petunia Wk., Litt.H. 47 V10
Petworth Av., Wgn. 39 E11
Pewfist, The, Westho. 32 P8
Pewfist Grn., Westho. 32 P9
Philip Clo., Wgn. 27 E9
Phillips St., Leigh 44 P12
Piccadilly, Bill. 50 C13
Pickley Grn., Leigh 44 P11
Picksley St., Leigh 58 Q14
Pickthorn Clo., Platt Br. 41 K10
Pickup St., Ince 29 J8
Piele Rd., Hay. 63 F16
Pierpoint St., Gol. 65 K16
Piggotts Clo., Hind. 30 L8
Pike Av., Ath. 44 Q11
Pikelaw Pl., Skel. 24 YY9
Pilkington St., Hind. 30 L9
Pilkington St., Rainf. 48 XX13
Pilling Pl., Skel. 24 YY9
Pilling St., Leigh 57 O13
Pilsley Clo., Orr. 26 D7
Pimblett Rd., Hay. 63 F16
Pimblett St., Gol. 65 K16
Pimbo La., K.Moss 36 ZZ11
Pimbo Rd., K.Moss 36 ZZ12
Pimbo Rd., Skel. 24 YY9
Pine Av., Orm. 11 RR4
Pine Clo., Hay. 62 E17
Pine Clo., Parb. 4 XX3
Woodrow Dr.
Pine Clo., Skel. 23 WW7
Pine Crest, Aug. 20 OO7
Pine Crest, Orm. 10 PP6
Pine Dr., Orm. 11 RR5
Pine Gro., Farn. 35 W8
Pine Gro., Gol. 66 L16
Pine Gro., Orm. 11 RR4
Pine Gro., Westho. 32 P8
Pine Rd., Wgn. 27 F9
Pine St., Tyld. 46 T11
Pine Vw., Win. 38 D11
Pines, The, Leigh 58 P14
Pinewood, Asht. 54 G15
Pinewood, Skel. 13 YY6
Pinewood Clo., Abram 42 L12
Pinewood Cres., Ince 29 J9
Pinewood Cres., Orr. 26 C9
Pinfold Pl., Bill. 36 YY10
Pinfold St., Ince 29 K8
Pingot, The, Leigh 57 O13
Pingot Rd., Bill. 50 C13
Pipers, The, Gol. 66 M16
Pipit Av., Newt. 64 H18
Pit Hey Pl., Skel. 24 YY9
Pitt St., Ince 28 H9
Pitt St., Wgn. 28 G8
Plane Av., Wgn. 27 F8
Plane Tree Rd., Hay. 63 G16
Plank La., Leigh 57 N14
Platt Cft., Leigh 59 R14
Platt Fold Rd., Leigh 58 Q13
Platt Fold St., Leigh 58 Q13
Platt La., Hind. 30 L9
Platt La., Stand. 9 G2
Platt La., Westho. 32 Q8
Platt La., Wgn. 29 J8
Platt St., Leigh 58 P13
Platt St., Platt Br. 41 K11
Pleasance Way, Newt. 64 H18
Plodder La., Farn. 34 T8
Plover Clo., Newt. 64 H18
Plymouth Dr., Farn. 35 V8
Pocket Nook La., Gol. 67 N16
Poets Nook, Leigh 58 P14
Poke St., Wgn. 26 D9
Polding St., Ince 41 J10
Pole St., Stand. 8 F3
Polegate Dr., Hind. 43 O11
Pond St., Gol. 67 N16
Pool St., Hind. 42 L10
Pool St., Wgn. 28 G9
Poolstock, Wgn. 28 G9
Poolstock La., Wgn. 39 F10
Poplar Av., Asht. 53 E13
Poplar Av., Newt. 64 H18
Poplar Av., Wgn. 27 E9
Poplar Dr., Skel. 23 WW7
Poplar Gro., Hay. 62 E17
Poplar Gro., Hind. 43 N11
Poplar Gro., Westho. 32 P8
Poplar Rd., Hay. 62 E17
Poplar St., Gol. 55 K15
Poplar St., Leigh 58 P14
Poplar St., Tyld. 46 T11
Poplars, The, Gol. 55 K15
Poplar St.
Poplars, The, Leigh 67 O16
Porlock Clo., Platt Br. 41 K11
Porter Av., Newt. 64 H17
Porters Wd. Clo., Orr. 26 D8
Silverdale Rd.
Porthleven Cres., Tyld. 46 U12
Portland Clo., Platt Br. 41 K11
Portland St., Newt. 63 F18
Portland St., Wgn. 27 F9
Portside Clo., Booth. 61 W13
Potter Pl., Skel. 24 YY9
Pottery Rd., Wgn. 28 G8
Pottery Ter., Wgn. 28 G8
Poulton Dr., Asht. 53 F13
Powell Dr., Bill. 50 B14
Powell St., Abram 41 K11
Powell St., Wgn. 28 H7
Pownall St., Leigh 58 Q13
Powys St., Ath. 45 S11
Poynt Chase, Booth. 61 W13
Prefect Pl., Wgn. 27 E8
Presbyterian Fold, Hind. 30 L9
Market St.
Prescot Av., Gol. 55 J15
Prescot Av., Tyld. 46 U11
Prescot Grn., Orm. 10 PP6
Prescot Rd., Aug. 21 PP9
Prescott Av., Ath. 45 S10
Prescott La., Orr. 26 D7
Prescott Rd., Bill. 36 ZZ10
Prescott St., Gol. 55 K15
Prescott St., Hind. 30 L9
Prescott St., Leigh 58 P13
Prescott St., Litt.H. 47 W10
Prescott St., Wgn. 28 G8
Prestbury Av., Wgn. 39 F10
Preston Rd., Stand. 8 E2
Preston St., Ince 28 H9
Prestt Gro., Wgn. 27 F9
Prestwich Av., Leigh 58 Q13
Prestwich St., Ath. 44 Q10
Prestwood Pl., Bill. 36 ZZ10
Prestwood Rd., Farn. 35 W7
Pretoria Rd., Asht. 54 G14
Primrose Av., Farn. 35 W7
Primrose Av., Litt.H. 47 W11
Primrose Gro., Hay. 63 F16
Primrose Gro., Wgn. 27 F8
Primrose La., Stand. 8 E3
Primrose Pl., Asht. 54 G15
Primrose St., Leigh 57 O13
Primrose St., Tyld. 46 T11
Primrose St. N., Tyld. 46 T11
Primrose St. S., Tyld. 46 T12
Primrose Vw., Asht. 54 G15
York Rd.
Prince St., Asht. 54 G13

Princes Av., Hay. 63 G16
Princes Av., Tyld. 60 T13
Princes Gdns., Leigh 59 R13
Princes Pk., Shev. 15 C6
Princes St., Newt. 63 G18
Princess Av., Asht. 54 H14
Princess Av., Ath. 33 R9
Princess Rd., Asht. 54 G14
Princess Rd., Stand.L.G. 16 E6
Princess St., Hind. 30 L9
Princess St., Leigh 58 Q13
Princess St., Wgn. 28 H8
Printshop La., Tyld. 45 S11
Priorswood Pl., Bill. 36 ZZ10
Priory Av., Leigh 43 O11
Priory Gro., Orm. 10 PP6
Priory Nook, Up Holl. 25 B8
Priory Rd., Asht. 53 F13
Priory Rd., Up Holl. 25 B8
Proctor Clo., Wgn. 27 F7
Prodesse Ct., Hind. 30 L9
Progress St., Hind. 30 L9
Prospect Cotts., Haigh 18 K5
Prospect Pl., Skel. 24 ZZ9
Prospect Rd., Stand. 16 F4
Prospect St., Hind. 30 L9
Platt La.
Prospect St., Tyld. 45 S11
Prosperity, Tyld. 46 U12
Prosser Av., Ath. 44 Q11
Provident St., St.H. 62 D18
Pump St., Hind. 30 L9
Punch La., Westho. 33 R7
Purbeck Way, Tyld. 46 T12
Pye Clo., Hay. 63 G16
Pyke St., Wgn. 28 H7

Q

Quakerfields, Westho. 31 O8
Quakers Pl., Stand. 8 F3
Quakers Ter., Stand. 8 E2
Quantock Clo., Wgn. 39 E11
Quarry Dr., Orm. 21 PP7
Quarry Pl., Wgn. 29 J8
Quarry Pond Rd., Litt.H. 47 V10
Quayside Clo., Booth. 61 W13
Quebec St., Abram 56 M13
Queen Anne Dr., Booth. 47 W12
Queen St., Gol. 65 K16
Queen St., Hind. 30 L9
Queen St., Leigh 58 Q13
Queen St., Litt.H. 47 W10
Manchester Rd.
Queen St., Orm. 10 QQ6
Queen St., Orr. 26 D9
Queen St., Pemb. 27 E9
Queen St., Platt Br. 41 K11
Queen St., Westho. 32 P7
Queen St., Wgn. 28 H8
Queens Av., Asht. 54 G14
Queens Av., Ath. 33 R9
Queens Clo., Tyld. 47 V12
Queens Dr., Gol. 66 L16
Queens Dr., Newt. 63 G17
Queens Gdns., Leigh 59 R13
Queens Rd., Asht. 54 G14
Queens Rd., Hay. 63 G16
Queens Rd., Orr. 25 B9
Queens Rd., Platt Br. 41 K10
Queens St., Newt. 63 G18
Queens Way, Ince 29 K8
Queensway, Leigh 59 R13
Queensway, Rainf. 48 XX13
Queensway, Shev. 15 C6
Queensway, Wgn. 28 G7
Queensway, Wors. 47 W12

R

Radcliffe Gro., Leigh 44 P12
Radnor Clo., Hind. 43 N10
Radnor Dr., Leigh 57 O14
Radway, Tyld. 46 U11
Radwell Clo., Low. 67 N16
Railway App., Orm. 10 QQ5
Railway Rd., Gol. 65 K16
Railway Rd., Leigh 58 P13
Railway Rd., Orm. 10 QQ5
Railway Rd., Skel. 22 VV7
Railway St., Ath. 32 Q9
Railway St., Hind. 30 L8
Railway St., Ince 28 H9
Railway St., Wgn. 28 G7
Railway Ter., Asht. 54 G13
Railway Vw., Tyld. 46 T12
Rainford By-Pass, Rainf. 48 XX14
Rainford Rd., Bill. 49 A13
Rainford Rd., Skel. 22 UU9
Raithby Dr., Wgn. 40 G11
Ram St., Litt.H. 47 V10
Rampit Clo., Hay. 63 F16
Ramsay Av., Farn. 35 W8
Ramsden Clo., Wgn. 28 G9
Ramsey Clo., Asht. 54 G15
Ramsey Clo., Ath. 45 S11
Randall Av., Shev. 15 D5
Randle St., Hind. 30 L9
Randsclough Dr., Booth. 61 W13
Ranleigh Dr., Parb. 4 XX3
Ranmore Av., Asht. 53 E14
Rannicar St., Hind. 43 O10
Ransey Rd., Leigh 58 Q14
Mather La.
Ransthorne St., Tyld. 46 U12
Rassey Clo., Stand. 17 G4
Ratcliffe Rd., Asp. 19 L5
Ratcliffe St., Leigh 44 P12
Ratcliffe St., Tyld. 46 T11
Ratcliffe St., Wgn. 28 G7
Rathbone St., Newt. 63 G18
Rathen Av., Ince 29 K7
Ravenhead Dr., Up Holl. 25 A8
Ravenscraig Rd., Litt.H. 35 W9
Ravenscroft Av., Orm. 10 QQ6
Ravenswood Av., Wgn. 39 E10
Ravenswood Dr., Hind. 30 M9
Rawthey Pl., Platt Br. 41 J11
Raydale Clo., Gol. 56 M15
Rayden Cres., Westho. 32 P9
Rayner Av., Hind. 42 L11
Recreation Av., Asht. 54 H14
Recreation Dr., Bill. 50 C13
Rectory Av., Gol. 66 L16
Rectory Gdns., Westho. 32 P9
Rectory La., Stand. 8 F3
Rectory Rd., Asht. 53 E13
Red Barn Rd., Bill. 50 B13
Red Cat La., Rainf. 49 ZZ14
Red Rock La., Stand. 17 G4
Red Rose Gdns., Litt.H. 47 W10
Red St., Ath. 45 S10
Redburn Clo., Wgn. 28 G9
Redcliffe Gdns., Orm. 10 QQ6
Redford Clo., Leigh 58 Q13
Gamble St.
Redgate, Orm. 10 PP5
Redgate Rd., Asht. 54 G13
Redgrave Ri., Wgn. 39 E10
Redhill Way, Hind. 30 L9
Redland Ct., Bam. 41 J12
Redmain Gro., Gol. 66 M16
Redmayne Clo., Newt. 63 G18
Rednal Wk., Wgn. 28 G9
Redpoll Clo., Booth. 47 W12
Redsands, Orm. 10 PP6
Redshank Clo., Newt. 64 H18
Redstock Clo., Westho. 32 Q7
Molyneux Rd.
Redwaters, Leigh 58 Q13
Redwood, Shev. 15 D5
Redwood, Westho. 31 O9
Redwood Av., Orr. 26 D9
Redwood Av., Wgn. 16 F6
Redwood Dr., Orm. 10 PP6
Reed Cres., Wgn. 40 G10
Reed La., Wors.M. 40 H11
Reeds, The, Orm. 10 PP5
Reeds Brow, Bill. 36 XX12
Reeds La., St.H. 48 XX14
Reedsmere Clo., Wgn. 27 F9
Reepham Clo., Wgn. 39 E10
Reeves St., Gol. 67 N16
Reeves St., Leigh 58 P13
Regaby Gro., Hind. 31 N9
Alder La.
Regency Ct., Wgn. 28 H8
Orchard St.
Regent Av., Asht. 53 F13
Regent Av., Litt.H. 47 W10
Regent Dr., Leigh 45 R12
Regent Rd., Platt Br. 41 K10
Regent St., Ath. 45 S11
Regent St., Hind. 30 L9
Regent St., Newt. 63 G18
Regent St., Wgn. 39 F10
Regents Av., Hay. 62 D16
Regina Cres., Leigh 59 S13
Reginald St., Farn. 34 T7
Renfrew Clo., Wgn. 40 G10
Renfrew Rd., Asp. 19 L5
Renfrey Clo., Orm. 10 QQ4
Renwick Sq., Asht. 53 F14
Repton Av., Ince 41 J10
Reservoir St., Asht. 54 H14
Reservoir St., Asp. 19 M6
Reservoir St., Ince 29 K8
Restormel Av., Asp. 19 L5
Reynolds Clo., Bolt. 33 S9
Reynolds Dr., Westho. 33 S8
Ribbesford Rd., Wgn. 39 E10
Ribble Cres., Bill. 50 B14
Ribble Dr., Tyld. 61 V13
Ribble Dr., Wgn. 27 E8
Ribble Gro., Leigh 57 O13
Ribble Rd., Platt Br. 41 K11
Ribble Rd., Stand. 7 D3
Richard St., Ince 28 H9
Richards Rd., Stand. 7 D2
Richmond Av., Hay. 62 D16
Richmond Clo., Cul. 67 O18
Richmond Clo., Stand. 17 G4
Richmond Dr., Leigh 45 R12
Richmond Gdns., Farn. 35 W7
Richmond Gro., Farn. 35 W7
Richmond Gro., Leigh 59 S13
Richmond Hill, Wgn. 27 E9
Richmond Rd., Asht. 53 F13
Richmond Rd., Hind. 43 N10
Richmond Rd., Tyld. 47 V12
Richmond St., Ath. 45 R11
Stanley St.
Richmond St., Wgn. 28 G8
Richmond St., Wors.M. 28 G9
Rickford Av., Leigh 43 O12
Ridge Av., Stand. 17 G4
Ridgemount Dr., Tyld. 61 V13
Ridgeway, Gol. 66 M16
Ridgewell Av., Gol. 66 L16
Riding Clo., Tyld. 46 U12
Riding La., Asht. 55 J13
Ridyard St., Litt.H. 47 W10
Ridyard St., Platt Br. 41 K10
Ridyard St., Wgn. 27 E8
Rigby Gro., Litt.H. 47 V10
Rigby St., Asht. 54 G14
Rigby St., Gol. 65 K16
Rigby St., Hind. 30 M9
Rigbys La., Asht. 54 H14
Riley La., Haigh 18 K4
Riley Sq., Wgn. 28 H8
Riley St., Ath. 44 Q11
Rilston Av., Cul. 67 O18
Rimmington Av., Gol. 56 L15
Rindle Rd., Tyld. 60 U15
Ringley Av., Gol. 55 J15
Ringway Av., Leigh 44 P12
Ripley Dr., Leigh 58 P13
Ripley Dr., Wgn. 39 E10
Ripon Av., Gol. 66 L16
Ripon Av., Wgn. 17 G6
Ripon Clo., Newt. 64 H18
Ripon Dr., Asht. 54 H14
Rise, The, Stand.L.G. 16 E6
Rishton Av., Farn. 35 V7
Rishton La., Farn. 35 V6
River St., Leigh 58 Q14
River Way, Wgn. 28 H8
Riverdale, Stand.L.G. 16 E6
Rivers St., Orr. 26 C9
Riverside Av., Wgn. 28 H7
Riversmead, Leigh 58 Q13
Rivington Av., Gol. 56 L15
Rivington Av., Platt Br. 41 K10
Rivington Av., Wgn. 28 G7
Rivington Dr., Bick. 42 M12
Rivington Dr., Up Holl. 25 B8
Rivington St., Ath. 44 Q11
Rivington Way, Stand. 16 F4
Rixton Dr., Tyld. 46 T12

Roach Grn., Wgn. 29 J7
Roadside Ct., Gol. 66 L16
Rob La., Newt. 64 H18
Robert St., Ath. 45 S11
Robert St., Platt Br. 41 K10
Roberts Av., Hay. 62 D17
Robertshaw St., Leigh 44 P12
Robin Clo., Litt.H. 35 V8
Robin Hill Dr., Stand. 7 D3
Robin Hill La., Stand. 8 E2
Robin Hood La., Wri. 6 A2
Robin La., Wri. 5 YY1
Robin Pk. Rd., Wgn. 27 F8
Robinson St., Leigh 58 Q14
Brewery La.
Robinson St., Tyld. 46 T11
Robson Pl., Abram 41 K12
Roby Well Way, Bill. 50 B13
Roch Pl., Platt Br. 41 J11
Rochester Clo., Gol. 65 K16
Rock Rd., Booth. 61 W15
Rock St., Gol. 55 K15
Rockbourne Clo., Hind. 42 L10
Rodgers Clo., Westho. 32 P9
Rodgers Way, Westho. 32 P9
Rodney St., Ath. 45 R11
Rodney St., Wgn. 28 H8
Roebuck St., Hind. 43 O10
Roeburn Wk., Platt Br. 41 J11
Roecliffe Clo., Wgn. 28 G9
Tipping St.
Rogerton Clo., Leigh 58 Q14
Rokeby Av., Gol. 56 L15
Rokeden, Newt. 64 H18
Roman Rd., Asht. 54 G13
Romford Av., Leigh 58 P13
Romford Pl., Hind. 30 M9
Romford St., Hind. 30 L9
Romiley Dr., Skel. 23 WW7
Romley Sq., Stand. 16 F4
Romney Way, Wgn. 17 G6
Romsey Gro., Win. 39 E11
Rookery, The, Newt. 64 H18
Rookery Av., App.Br. 15 C4
Rookery Av., Asht. 54 G15
Rookery Dr., Rainf. 48 XX13
Rookery La., Rainf. 48 XX13
Roscoe Av., Newt. 64 H18
Roscoe St., Wgn. 29 J8
Roscoes Ct., Westho. 32 P8
Rose Av., Abram 41 K12
Rose Av., Hay. 63 F17
Rose Av., Wgn. 16 F6
Rose Bk. Clo., Wgn. 17 G6
Rose Bri. Ter., Ince 29 J8
Rose Cres., Skel. 23 WW7
Rose Dr., Rainf. 48 XX13
Rose Hill Av., Wgn. 27 E9
Rose Hill Vw., Asht. 39 F12
Rose Pl., Orm. 21 PP7
Rose Pl., Rainf. 48 XX13
Rose St., Hind. 30 L9
Platt La.
Rose St., Ince 29 J8
Roseacre, Tyld. 47 W12
Roseberry, Westho. 32 P8
Roseberry Rd., Asht. 54 G13
Rosebury Av., Leigh 58 Q13
Rosecroft Clo., Orm. 10 QQ5
Rosedale Av., Ath. 45 R10
Rosedale Av., Gol. 66 L16
Rosedale Dr., Leigh 59 R13
Rosehill Dr., Orm. 21 PP7
Rosemary Cres., Wgn. 28 H7
Rosemary La., Farn. 34 T8
Roseneath Gro., Farn. 34 U7
Rosewood, Westho. 31 O9
Rosewood Clo., Abram 41 K12
Rosina Clo., Asht. 53 F13
Rosley Rd., Wgn. 40 G10
Ross Clo., Bill. 50 B13
Ross Clo., Wgn. 29 J7
Rossall Cres., Leigh 58 Q14
Rossdale Gro., Stand. 17 G4
Rostherne Av., Gol. 66 L16
Rosthwaite Clo., Wgn. 40 G11
Navenby Rd.
Rosthwaite Gro., St.H. 49 A15
Rothay St., Leigh 58 Q14
Rothwell Clo., Orm. 10 PP5
Rothwell Cres., Litt.H. 35 V9
Rothwell Dr., Orm. 20 OO7
Rothwell La., Litt.H. 35 V9
Rothwell Rd., Gol. 55 K15
Roughlea Av., Cul. 67 O18
Roundhouse Av., Wgn. 29 J7
Roundmoor Rd., Stand. 17 G4
Roundthorne La., Westho. 32 P8
Rowan Av., Gol. 66 M16
Rowan Av., Wgn. 16 F6
Rowan Hill, Wgn. 28 H7
Rowan La., Skel. 12 XX6
Rowans, The, Aug. 20 OO8
Rowbottom Sq., Wgn. 28 H8
Wallgate
Rowe St., Tyld. 46 T12
Rowland St., Ath. 45 R10
Rowton Ri., Stand. 17 G4
Roxby Clo., Litt.H. 47 W10
Royal Arc., Wgn. 28 H8
Standishgate
Royal Dr., Leigh 59 R13
Royden Av., Wgn. 40 G11
Royden Cres., Bill. 50 C13
Royden Rd., Bill. 50 C13
Ruabon Cres., Hind. 43 N10
Ruby Gro., Leigh 58 P14
Rudyard Av., Stand. 8 F3
Ruff La., Orm. 10 QQ6
Rufford Dr., Farn. 34 U7
Rufford Gro., Farn. 34 U7
Rufford Pl., Tyld. 59 S14
Rufford St., Asht. 53 F13
Rugby Dr., Orr. 26 C8
Rugby Rd., Leigh 58 P14
Runnymead Dr., Hay. 62 D17
West Side Av.
Runshaw Av., App.Br. 15 C4
Rupert St., Wgn. 28 H8
Rushdene, Wors.M. 40 G10
Rushmoor Av., Asht. 55 J14
Rushton Av., Leigh 43 O12
Rushton Av., Newt. 63 G18
Ruskin Av., Newt. 64 H18
Ruskin Av., Wgn. 39 F10
Ruskin Cres., Abram 41 K11
Russeldene Rd., Wgn. 39 F10
Russell Ct., Litt.H. 47 W10
Russell St., Ath. 45 R10
Russell St., Hind. 43 O11
Russell St., Litt.H. 47 W10
Rutherford Dr., Westho. 33 S8
Rutland Av., Bolt. 33 S9
Rutland Av., Gol. 66 L16
Rutland Cres., Orm. 10 PP4
Rutland Dr., Asht. 54 H14
Rutland Rd., Hind. 30 M9
Rutland Rd., Tyld. 45 S11
Rutland St., Leigh 59 S14
Ryburn Rd., Orm. 10 QQ6
Rydal Av., Hind. 30 M9
Rydal Av., Orr. 26 C8
Rydal Clo., Asht. 54 H14
Rydal Clo., Tyld. 46 T12
Rydal Gro., Farn. 35 V8
Rydal Pl., Abram 41 K12
Rydal Pl., Ince 29 K8
Rydal St., Leigh 58 P13
Rydal St., Newt. 64 H18
Ryde St., Wgn. 27 F9
Ryder Clo., Orm. 21 PP7
Ryder Cres., Orm. 21 PP7
Ryder Gro., Leigh 59 R15
Ryecroft Av., Gol. 56 M15
Ryeford Clo., Ince 29 J9
Ryehill, Westho. 32 P8
Ryelands, Westho. 32 P8
Rylands St., Wgn. 28 G7
Ryton Clo., Wgn. 28 G9

S

Saddle Tree Fold, Gol. 56 M15
Saddleback Clo., Booth. 61 W13
Saddleback Cres., Wgn. 26 D9
Saddleback Rd., Wgn. 26 D8
Sagar Fold, Aug. 21 PP8
St. Aidans Clo., Bill. 50 C13
St. Albans Clo., Hay. 63 F16
St. Ambrose Rd., Tyld. 60 T13
St. Andrews Cres., Hind. 30 L9
St. Andrews Dr., Leigh 59 R13
St. Andrews Dr., Wgn. 27 F7
St. Annes Av., Ath. 45 S11
St. Annes Ct., Shev. 15 C5
St. Annes Dr., Shev. 15 D5
St. Annes Rd., Orm. 10 PP6
St. Aubyns Rd., Wgn. 17 H6
St. Austell Av., Tyld. 46 U12
St. Bedes Av., Farn. 34 T7
St. Bedes Clo., Orm. 10 PP6
St. Clements Ct., Wgn. 28 G9
Mesnes Dr.
St. Clements Rd., Wgn. 17 H6
St. Clements St., Ince 41 J10
Warrington Rd.
St. Davids Cres., Asp. 18 K5
St. Elizabeths Rd., Asp. 18 K5
St. Gabriels Clo., R.Mill 14 A6
St. Georges Av., Westho. 32 P9
St. Georges St., Tyld. 45 S12
St. Helens Rd., Gol. 67 O16
St. Helens Rd., Leigh 58 P14
St. Helens Rd., Orm. 10 QQ6
St. Helens Rd., St.H. 48 XX15
St. Helens Rd., Westho. 33 S7
St. James Clo., Orm. 11 SS6
St. James Cres., Bick. 42 M12
St. James Gro., Wgn. 28 G9
St. James Rd., Orr. 25 B9
St. James St., Farn. 35 W8
St. James St., Westho. 32 P9
St. John St., Ath. 45 R10
St. John St., Newt. 63 G18
St. John St., Wgn. 26 D9
St. Johns Rd., Asp. 18 K5
St. Johns Rd., Tyld. 47 V12
St. Johns St., Abram 41 K12
St. Lukes Av., Gol. 66 L16
St. Lukes Dr., Bill. 37 B10
St. Malo Rd., Wgn. 17 H6
St. Marks Av., Wgn. 27 F8
St. Marks St., Hay. 62 D17
Park St.
St. Marys Av., Bill. 50 B14
St. Marys Clo., Ath. 45 S10
St. Marys Rd., Asp. 18 K5
St. Marys Way, Leigh 58 P13
St. Matthews Clo., Wgn. 39 E10
St. Michael Rd., Aug. 20 OO8
St. Michaels Av., Ath. 44 Q11
St. Michaels Av., Farn. 35 W7
St. Michaels Pk., Aug. 20 OO8
St. Nicholas Rd., Low. 57 N15
St. Oswalds Rd., Asht. 54 G15
St. Patricks Way, Wgn. 28 H8
St. Pauls Av., Wgn. 39 F10
St. Stephens Av., Wgn. 29 J7
St. Stephens Clo., Astley 60 T13
St. Stephens Rd., Stand. 8 E3
St. Thomas St., Wgn. 28 H8
St. Thomas's Ct., Up Holl. 25 B8
Church St.
St. Wilfreds Pl., Stand. 8 F3
St. Wilfreds Rd., Stand. 8 F3
St. Wilfreds Way, Stand. 8 F3
Rectory La.
Salcombe Clo., Wgn. 29 J7
Sale La., Tyld. 46 U11
Salesbury Way, Wgn. 40 G10
Salford Rd., Farn. 34 T8
Salisbury Av., Hind. 30 M9
Salisbury Rd., Hay. 63 F16
Salisbury St., Gol. 65 K16
Salisbury Way, Tyld. 46 T12
Salkeld Av., Asht. 53 F14
Salmon St., Wgn. 29 J7
Saltram Rd., Wgn. 39 E10
Samuel St., Ath. 45 S11
Sandalwood Dr., Wgn. 16 F6
Sandbrook Gdns., Orr. 25 B9
Sandbrook Rd., Orr. 25 B9
Sanderling Clo., Westho. 31 O9
Sanderling Rd., Newt. 64 H18
Sanderson St., Leigh 57 O13
Sandersons Cft., Leigh 59 R14
Sandfield Clo., Gol. 66 M16
Sandford Rd., Orr. 25 B9
Sandgate Clo., Leigh 58 P13

Sandiacre, Stand. 16 F4
Sandon Gro., Rainf. 48 XX13
Sandown Rd., Wgn. 16 F6
Sandpiper Clo., Newt. 64 H18
Sandpiper Rd., Wgn. 38 D10
Sandra Dr., Newt. 64 H18
Sandringham Clo., Wgn. 27 F9
Sandringham Dr., Leigh 45 S12
Sandringham Rd., Booth. 61 W13
Sandringham Rd., Hind. 42 M10
Sandstone Rd., Win. 39 E11
Sandwash Clo., Rainf. 48 XX14
Sandway, Wgn. 27 F7
Sandwith Clo., Wors.M. 40 G11
Sandy La., Aug. 20 OO9
Sandy La., Bill. 37 B10
Sandy La., Gol. 55 J15
Sandy La., Hind. 30 M9
Sandy La., Low. 57 N15
Sandy La., Orm. 11 SS4
Sandy La., Parb. 4 WW3
Sandy La., St.H. 49 ZZ15
Sandy La., Skel. 22 VV7
Sandy La. (Astley), Tyld. 60 T15
Sandy La. (Town La.), Tyld. 60 T14
Sandy Pk., Hind. 31 N9
Sandy Way, Hind. 30 M9
Sandyacre Clo., Westho. 34 T9
Sandycroft Av., Wgn. 28 H7
Sankey St., Gol. 65 K16
Sankey St., Newt. 63 G18
Santon Dr., Gol. 66 M16
Sapling Rd., Farn. 34 T7
Sarah Clo., Hind. 43 N11
Sarah St.
Sarah St., Hind. 43 N11
Sarsfield Av., Gol. 66 L16
Sawley Av., Gol. 56 L15
Sawley Av., Wgn. 27 F7
Saxthorpe Clo., Wgn. 39 E10
Scafell Dr., Wgn. 26 D9
Scafell Gro., Platt Br. 41 K11
Scarisbrick Av., Parb. 5 YY3
Scarisbrick St., Orm. 10 QQ5
Scarisbrick St., Wgn. 28 H7
Scarth Hill La., Orm. 21 QQ7
Sceptre Clo., Newt. 63 G18
Schofield Gdns., Leigh 58 P14
Schofield La., Ath. 44 P10
Schofield St., Leigh 58 P14
Schofield St., Tyld. 46 T12
Scholefield La., Wgn. 28 H8
Scholes, Wgn. 29 J8
School Av., Wgn. 29 J7
School Brow, Bill. 50 C13
School Clo., Asp. 19 L6
School Clo., Orm. 21 PP7
School Dr., Bill. 50 C13
School Ho. Grn., Orm. 10 QQ5
School La., Asht. 53 E14
School La., Haigh 18 J4
School La., Orm. 11 SS6
School La., R.Mill 14 A6
School La., Skel. 22 VV7
School La., Stand. 8 E3
School La., Up Holl. 25 B8
School La., Wgn. 28 H8
School St., Abram 41 K11
School St., Asht. 54 H13
School St., Asp. 18 J6
School St., Astley 45 S12
School St., Ath. 44 Q11
School St., Gol. 65 K16
School St., Ince 29 J8
School St., Leigh 44 P12
School St., Newt. 63 G18
School St., Tyld. 45 S12
School St., Westho. 32 P8
School St., Wgn. 28 H8
School Way, Wgn. 27 E9
Scot La., Asp. 19 L5
Scot La., Wgn. 27 F7
Scot St., Tyld. 60 U14
Scotia Wk., Low. 66 M16
Scott Av., Hind. 30 M9
Scott Dr., Orm. 10 QQ4
Scott Rd., Gol. 56 L15
Scott St., Leigh 57 O13
Scott St., Westho. 32 P7
Scott St., Wgn. 28 G7
Seaforth Av., Ath. 45 R10
Seaman Way, Ince 29 K9
Seascale Cres., Wgn. 28 H7
Seathwaite Clo., Tyld. 46 T12
Seatoller Pl., Wgn. 26 D8
Seaton Pl., Skel. 12 WW6
Second Av., Ath. 45 R10
Second Av., Tyld. 60 T14
Second Av., Wgn. 28 G7
Seddon Clo., Ath. 45 R10
Seddon Ho. Dr., Wgn. 16 F6
Seddon Pl., Skel. 12 WW6
Seddon St., Litt.H. 35 V9
Seddon St., Westho. 32 P6
Sedgefield Dr., Wgn. 16 F6
Sedgeley, Stand. 17 G4
Sedgley Dr., Westho. 32 P9
Sedwyn St., Wgn. 28 H7
Seedley Av., Litt.H. 47 W10
Sefton Av., Ath. 33 R9
Sefton Av., Orr. 25 B9
Sefton Clo., Orr. 25 B9
Sefton Fold Dr., Bill. 50 B13
Sefton Fold Gdns., Bill. 50 B13
Sefton Fold Dr.
Sefton Gdns., Orm. 21 PP8
Sefton Rd., Asht. 53 F13
Sefton Rd., Orr. 25 B9
Sefton Rd., Wgn. 39 F10
Sefton St., Leigh 58 P13
Sefton St., Newt. 63 F18
Sefton Vw., Orr. 25 B9
Selbourne Clo., Westho. 32 Q7
Selbourne St., Leigh 44 P12
Selby Dr., Wgn. 39 E10
Selby Pl., Skel. 12 WW6
Selkirk Av., Asht. 53 E14
Selkirk Gro., Wgn. 26 D8
Sellside, Wgn. 40 G11
Selwyn St., Leigh 58 P13
Senecar Clo., Asp. 29 K7
Sennicar La., Haigh 17 H5
Sephton Dr., Orm. 10 QQ4
Sephton St., Ince 29 J9
Serin Clo., Newt. 64 H18
Serpentine, The, Orm. 21 PP8
Seven Stars Rd., Wgn. 28 G8
Sevenoaks, Leigh 58 Q13
Severn Clo., Bill. 50 B14
Severn Dr., Hind. 43 N10
Severn Dr., Wgn. 27 E9
Severn Rd., Asht. 55 J13
Severn St., Leigh 58 Q14
Seymour Gro., Farn. 35 W7
Shadwell Gro., Leigh 43 O12
Shaftesbury Rd., Orr. 26 D8
Shaftway Clo., Hay. 63 F16
Shakerley La., Tyld. 45 S10
Shakerley Rd., Tyld. 45 S11
Shakespeare Gro., Wors.M. 40 G10
Shap Gate, Wgn. 26 D8
Shared St., Wgn. 28 H8
Sharon Sq., Bam. 41 J12
Sharp St., Ince 29 J9
Delegarte St.
Sharp St., Wgn. 28 G8
Shaw St., Asht. 54 G13
Shaw St., Hay. 63 F17
Shaw St., Wgn. 28 H7
Shawbrook Av., Wors. 47 W12
Shearwater Dr., Westho. 31 O9
Shed St., Ince 41 J10
Shefford Cres., Win. 39 E11
Sheilings, The, Gol. 66 M16
Sheldon Av., Stand. 8 F3
Sheldon Clo., Farn. 35 W7
Shelley Dr., Abram 41 K11
Shelley Dr., Orm. 10 PP5
Shelley Dr., Orr. 26 D9
Shelley Rd., Litt.H. 35 W9
Shelley St., Leigh 43 O12
Shelley Wk., Ath. 33 R9
Spa Rd.
Shellingford Gro., App.Br. 14 B4
Shelmorton Gro., Win. 39 E11
Shepton Av., Platt Br. 41 K11
Sheraton Clo., Pemb. 26 D7
Sherborne Rd., Orr. 26 D8
Sherburne Av., Hind. 31 N9
Sheridan Av., Gol. 66 L16
Sheriffs Dr., Tyld. 46 U11
Sherlock Av., Hay. 63 F16
Sherrat St., Skel. 22 VV7
Sherwood Av., Asht. 54 H14
Sherwood Av., Orm. 21 PP7
Sherwood Av., Tyld. 60 T13
Sherwood Cres., Platt Br. 41 K11
Sherwood Cres., Wgn. 27 E8
Sherwood Dr., Skel. 13 YY6
Sherwood Dr., Wgn. 27 E9
Sherwood Gro., Leigh 58 Q15
Sherwood Gro., Wgn. 27 E8
Shevington La., Shev. 15 D5
Shevington La., Stand. 7 D3
Shevington Moor, Stand. 7 D3
Shevington Rd., Stand. 7 D3
Shildon Clo., Wgn. 29 J7
Shillingten Clo., Litt.H. 47 V10
Quarry Pond Rd.
Shipham Clo., Leigh 43 O10
Congresbury Rd.
Short St., Ath. 45 S11
Short St., Gol. 55 K15
Short St., Hay. 63 F17
Short St., Newt. 63 F18
Short St., Wgn. 26 D9
Shrewsbury Clo., Hind. 30 M9
Shrub St., Farn. 34 U7
Shudehill Rd., Tyld. 47 W11
Shurdington Rd., Bolt. 33 S9
Shuttle Hillock Rd., Bick. 42 M12
Shuttle St., Hind. 30 M9
Shuttle St., Tyld. 45 S11
Sibley Av., Asht. 54 H14
Sidbrook St., Hind. 30 L9
Siddeley Dr., Newt. 63 F18
Siddeley St., Leigh 57 O13
Siddow Common, Leigh 58 Q14
Sidmouth Gro., Wgn. 39 F10
Sidney St., Leigh 58 Q13
Silcock St., Gol. 65 K16
Silk St., Leigh 58 P13
Silk St., Westho. 32 P7
Sillitoe Dr., Wgn. 28 G7
Silsbury Gro., Stand. 17 G4
Silsden Av., Gol. 67 N16
Silver Av., Hay. 62 D17
Silver Birch Gro., Asht. 54 G13
Silverdale, Wgn. 28 H7
Silverdale Av., Ince 29 K8
Silverdale Av., Litt.H. 35 W9
Silverdale Rd., Farn. 35 W7
Silverdale Rd., Hind. 30 M9
Silverdale Rd., Newt. 63 G18
Silverdale Rd., Orr. 26 D8
Silvington Way, Wgn. 29 K7
Ashbourne Av.
Simms Sq., Asp. 19 L6
Simms Yd., Asp. 19 M6
Simpkin St., Bick. 41 K11
Simpson Gro., Booth. 61 W13
Simpson Rd., Tyld. 61 W13
Sinclair Pl., Wgn. 27 F8
Singleton Gro., Westho. 32 Q8
Sisken Clo., Newt. 64 H18
Sittingbourne Rd., Wgn. 17 H6
Size Ho. Pl., Leigh 58 Q14
Skelmersdale Rd., Skel. 22 UU8
Skelton St., Asht. 53 F13
Skelwith Av., Farn. 35 V7
Skiddaw Pl., Wgn. 27 E9
Skipton Av., Hind. 43 N10
Skull Ho. La., App.Br. 6 B3
Slack Fold La., Farn. 34 U7
Slack La., Westho. 32 P6
Slackey Fold, Hind. 43 N11
Slag La., Gol. 66 L16
Slag La., Hay. 62 D16
Slaidburn Clo., Wgn. 40 G11
Raithby Dr.
Slaidburn Cres., Gol. 55 J15
Slate La., Skel. 22 VV7
Slater St., Leigh 57 O13
Sledbrook St., Wgn. 27 E9
Sloane St., Farn. 34 T7
Small La., Orm. 10 QQ6
Smallbrook La., Leigh 44 P10

Smalley St., Stand.	8	F3
Smallshaw Clo., Asht.	54	G13
Smethurst Hall Pk., Bill.	37	B11
Smethurst La., Farn.	34	T7
Smethurst La., Wgn.	27	E9
Smethurst Rd., Bill.	37	B11
Smethurst St., Wgn.	27	E9
Smith Av., Orr.	26	D8
Smith St., Asp.	19	L5
Smith St., Ath.	45	R10
Smith St., Leigh	58	Q13
Smith St., Skel.	22	VV7
Smithfold La., Litt.H.	47	W10
Smiths La., Bick.	42	M12
Smiths Pl., Ath.	45	R10
Smithwood Av., Hind.	30	M9
Smithy Brow, Parb.	4	XX3
Smithy Grn., Ince	29	J8
Smithy La., Aug.	20	NN9
Smithy St., Leigh	58	P14
Smock La., Asht.	53	E14
Snape St., Wgn.	28	G8
Snowden Av., Wgn.	39	F10
Snowshill Dr., Wgn.	39	E10
Snydale Clo., Westho.	32	Q7
Snydale Way, Bolt.	33	R7
Soham Clo., Hind.	42	M10
Soho St., Wgn.	27	F8
Sole St., Wgn.	29	J7
Solway Clo., Asht.	54	G14
Somerset Av., Tyld.	45	S10
Somerset Rd., Ath.	32	Q9
Somerset Rd., Wgn.	27	E8
Somerton Clo., Stand.	8	E3
Somerville Rd., Wgn.	17	H6
Soughers La., Asht.	53	F13
South Av., Abram	56	M14
South Av., Leigh	59	R14
South Ct., Leigh	58	Q13
South Dene, Parb.	4	XX3
South Dr., Wri.	6	B3
South Hey, Leigh	57	O14
South La., Tyld.	60	T13
South Milnes Av., Leigh	58	P15
South St., Tyld.	45	S11
Tyldesley Rd.		
South Ter., Orm.	10	QQ6
South Vw., Ath.	45	R10
Southdown Dr., Tyld.	61	V13
Southern St., Wgn.	27	E9
Southerns Fold, Asp.	18	K6
Southerns La., Rainf.	48	XX13
Southery Av., Wgn.	39	E10
Southfield, Platt Br.	41	K11
Southfield Dr., Westho.	32	P8
Southlands Av., Stand.	16	F4
Southover, Westho.	32	P9
Southport Rd., Orm.	10	PP4
Southport St., St.H.	62	D18
Southward Rd., Hay.	63	G16
Southway, Skel.	23	XX7
Southwell Clo., Gol.	66	L16
Southworth Rd., Newt.	64	H18
Sovereign Fold Rd., Leigh	44	P11
Sovereign Rd., Wgn.	28	H8
Spa Cres., Litt.H.	35	V9
Spa Gro., Litt.H.	35	W9
Spa La., Litt.H.	35	W9
Spa La., Skel.	12	WW6
Spa Rd., Ath.	33	R9
Spawell Clo., Gol.	66	M16
Speakman Av., Leigh	58	Q13
Speakman Av., Newt.	64	H17
Spelding Dr., Stand.L.G.	16	E6
Spencer Rd., Wgn.	17	G6
Spencer Rd. W., Wgn.	17	G6
Spencers La., Orr.	25	B8
Spencers La., Skel.	23	XX8
Spenlow, Leigh	59	R14
Spey Clo., Stand.	8	E3
Spilsby Sq., Wgn.	40	G11
Spindle Hillock, Asht.	53	F14
Spindle Wk., Westho.	32	P7
Spindlewood Rd., Ince	29	J9
Spinney Clo., Orm.	10	PP6
Spion Kop, Asht.	54	G14
Sportsman St., Leigh	58	P13
Spring Bk., App.Br.	14	B4
Spring Bk., Astley	60	T13
Spring Gdns., Ath.	45	R10
Matthew St.		
Spring Gdns., Litt.H.	35	V9
Spring Gdns., Wgn.	28	G8
Spring Gro., Wgn.	28	H8
Spring St.		
Spring Pool, Win.	38	D11
Spring Rd., Orr.	26	C8
Spring St., Ince	41	J10
Spring St., Wgn.	28	H8
Springborne, Wgn.	27	F7
Springburn Clo., Booth.	61	W13
Border Brook La.		
Springfield Av., Gol.	55	J15
Springfield Pk., Hay.	62	E16
Springfield Rd., Ath.	45	S10
Springfield Rd., Aug.	20	NN9
Springfield Rd., Farn.	35	W7
Springfield Rd., Hind.	30	L9
Springfield Rd., Wgn.	16	F6
Springfields, Wgn.	28	H7
Springmount, Gol.	66	M16
Springmount Dr., Wri.	5	YY1
Sprodley Dr., Wri.	6	A3
Spruce Clo., Gol.	66	M16
Spruce Rd., Wgn.	16	F6
Squires La., Tyld.	45	S12
Stafford St., Hind.	30	L9
Stafford St., Ince	41	J10
Stafford St., Leigh	59	R14
Stafford St., Skel.	22	VV7
Stainburn Clo., App.Br.	15	C5
Stamford Rd., Skel.	22	VV7
Stamford St., Ath.	45	S10
Stancliffe Gro., Asp.	19	L5
Standfield Dr., Booth.	47	W12
Standhouse La., Orm.	21	PP7
Standish Cres., Bill.	50	C13
Standish St., Tyld.	46	T12
Standish Wd. La., Stand.	16	F5
Standishgate, Wgn.	28	H8
Stanedge Gro., Wgn.	40	G11
Stanley Bk. Rd., Hay.	62	D16
Stanley Clo., Westho.	32	P8
Stanley Dr., Leigh	43	O12
Stanley La., Haigh	19	L4
Stanley Nook, Asp.	19	L5
Stanley Pl., Wgn.	29	J8
Stanley Rd., Asp.	19	L5
Stanley Rd., Farn.	35	V8
Stanley Rd., Platt Br.	41	K10
Stanley Rd., Up Holl.	25	A8
Stanley St., Ath.	45	R11
Stanley St., Ince	29	K8
Stanley St., Newt.	63	G18
Stanley St., Orm.	10	QQ5
Stanley St., Tyld.	46	T11
Stanley St., Wgn.	27	F9
Stanley Way, Skel.	12	WW6
Stanmoor Dr., Asp.	19	L5
Stannanought Rd., Skel.	13	YY6
Stansfield Clo., Leigh	59	R15
Stanstead Clo., Wgn.	29	J7
Stanton Clo., Hay.	62	E17
Stanton Clo., Wgn.	40	G10
Stapleford Clo., Westho.	34	T9
Stapleton St., Platt Br.	41	K11
Starling Dr., Farn.	35	V8
Stars Brow, Stand.	8	E1
Start Av., Bill.	50	B14
Statham Rd., Skel.	12	WW6
Statham Way, Orm.	10	QQ6
Station App., Orm.	10	QQ5
Station Av., Bick.	42	L11
Station Av., Orr.	25	B9
Station Rd., Asht.	53	E14
Station Rd., Hay.	62	E17
Station Rd., Orm.	10	QQ5
Station Rd., Parb.	5	YY3
Station Rd., Wgn.	28	H8
Staveley Rd., Skel.	12	WW6
Stepfield, Westho.	32	P9
Stephen St., Platt Br.	41	K11
Stephens Way, Wgn.	27	F9
Stephenson St., Abram	41	K12
Sterndale Av., Stand.	8	F3
Sterndale Rd., Tyld.	61	V13
Stetchworth Dr., Booth.	47	W12
Stevenson Clo., Wgn.	28	G9
Stevenson Sq., Farn.	35	W8
Stevenson St., Litt.H.	47	W10
Stewart Av., Farn.	35	W8
Stewart Rd., Wgn.	40	G10
Stiles, The, Orm.	10	QQ5
Stirling Av., Ince	29	J8
Stirling Clo., Leigh	59	R13
Stirling Dr., Asht.	53	E14
Stirling Rd., Hind.	42	M10
Stirling St., Wgn.	28	G7
Stirrup Brook Gro., Booth.	61	V13
Stockley Dr., App.Br.	15	C4
Stocksfield Dr., Litt.H.	35	V9
Stockwell Clo., Wgn.	39	E10
Holmes Ho. Av.		
Stone Cross La., Gol.	66	L17
Stone Hall La., R.Mill	14	A5
Stone Pit Clo., Gol.	56	M15
Stone Row, Asp.	18	K6
Stonechat Clo., Booth.	47	W12
Stonecroft Ter., Asht.	54	G14
Stonefield, Tyld.	46	U11
Stonehaven, Win.	39	E11
Erradale Cres.		
Stonethwaite Clo., Wgn.	40	G11
Stoney Brow, Up Holl.	25	A7
Stoneygate La., Wri.	6	A3
Stony La., Wri.	5	YY2
Stonyhurst Av., Ince	28	H9
Stonyhurst Pl., Ince	29	J9
Stopford St., Ince	29	J8
Stopforth St., Wgn.	28	G7
Stour Rd., Tyld.	46	T12
Stourbridge Av., Litt.H.	35	W9
Stout St., Leigh	57	O13
Straits, The, Astley	60	T13
Strand, The, Asht.	54	G14
Strand Av., Asht.	54	G14
Strange Rd., Asht.	53	E14
Strange St., Leigh	57	N14
Stranraer Pl., Wgn.	27	E7
Stratford Clo., Farn.	35	V7
Stratford St., Wgn.	28	G7
Strathmore Av., Asht.	54	G13
Stratton Dr., Platt Br.	41	K11
Stretton Av., Bill.	50	C13
Stretton Av., Gol.	66	L16
Stretton Clo., Stand.	16	E4
Stringer St., Leigh	58	P13
Stroud Clo., Wgn.	29	J7
Stuart Av., Hind.	43	N10
Stuart Cres., Bill.	50	B13
Studley Ct., Tyld.	45	S11
Sturgess Clo., Orm.	10	QQ4
Sturgess St., Newt.	63	F18
Sturton Av., Wgn.	39	F10
Sudbury Clo., Wgn.	40	G11
Sudell La., Aug.	20	NN8
Suez St., Newt.	63	G18
Suffolk Clo., Stand.	17	G4
Suffolk Gro., Leigh	57	O14
Sullivan Way, Wgn.	28	H7
Summer Ct., Tyld.	46	T12
Summer St., Skel.	12	WW6
Summerfield Dr., Tyld.	46	T12
Sumner St., Asp.	19	L5
Sumner St., Ath.	45	R10
Sumner St., Farn.	34	T7
Sumner St., Hay.	62	D16
Sunbeam St., Newt.	64	H18
Sunderland Pl., Wgn.	27	E7
Sunleigh Rd., Hind.	30	M9
Sunningdale Gro., Leigh	45	R12
Sunny Dr., Orr.	26	C9
Sunny Garth, Westho.	32	P8
Sunnybank Clo., Newt.	64	H18
Sunnybank Rd., Tyld.	46	T12
Sunnyfields, Orm.	11	RR5
Sunnyfields, Wgn.	39	E11
Sunnyside, Orm.	21	PP8
Sunnyside Rd., Asht.	53	F13
Surrey Av., Leigh	59	S14
Sussex Clo., Hind.	31	N9
Sussex Clo., Stand.	17	G4
Sussex Pl., Tyld.	46	T10
Sussex St., Leigh	59	S14
Sutherland Rd., Wgn.	40	G10
Sutherland St., Hind.	30	L9

Sutherland St., Wgn. 27 F9
Ormskirk Rd.
Swain Delph, Aug. 21 PP7
Swallowfield, Leigh 58 Q13
Swan La., Aug. 20 NN9
Swan La., Hind. 43 N10
Swan Meadow Rd., Wgn. 28 G8
Swan Rd., Newt. 62 E18
Swann St., Wgn. 28 G8
Swanpool La., Orm. 21 PP7
Swift St., Wgn. 27 F8
Swifts Fold, Skel. 22 VV8
Swinburn Clo., Bill. 37 B11
Swinley La., Wgn. 28 H7
Swinley Rd., Wgn. 28 H7
Swinley St., Wgn. 28 H7
Swinside, Wgn. 29 J7
Sycamore Av., Gol. 55 K15
Sycamore Av., Hay. 62 D17
Sycamore Av., Hind. 42 M10
Sycamore Av., Newt. 64 H18
Sycamore Av., Tyld. 46 U11
Sycamore Av., Wgn. 16 F6
Sycamore Dr., Skel. 23 WW7
School La.
Sycamore Dr., Win. 38 D11
Sycamore Rd., Ath. 45 S10
Sydney Av., Leigh 57 O15
Sydney St., Platt Br. 41 K10
Sydney St., Wgn. 39 F10
Syresham St., Platt Br. 41 K11

T

Tabbys Nook, Parb. 4 XX3
Taberner Clo., Stand. 8 F3
Taberner St., Platt Br. 41 K11
Tadmor Clo., Litt.H. 47 V10
Talbot Rd., Gol. 57 N14
Talbot St., Gol. 65 K16
Tamar Rd., Hay. 62 E17
Tamer Gro., Leigh 43 O12
Tamneys, The, Skel. 23 WW7
Tamworth Dr., Wgn. 29 J7
Tamworth St., Newt. 63 G18
Tan Ho. Av., Tyld. 46 U12
Tan Ho. Clo., Parb. 5 YY2
Tan Ho. Dr., Wgn. 39 E11
Tan Ho. La., Wgn. 39 E11
Tancaster, Skel. 23 WW7
Tanfield Nook, Parb. 5 YY3
Tanfields, Skel. 23 WW7
Tanhouse La., Parb. 5 YY3
Tanhouse Rd., Skel. 24 YY7
Tank St., Asp. 29 K7
Tanners La., Gol. 65 K16
Tansley Sq., Wgn. 27 E9
Tarleton Av., Ath. 32 Q9
Tarlswood, Skel. 23 WW7
Tarn Brow, Orm. 10 PP6
Tarn Clo., Asht. 54 G13
Tarnrigg Clo., Win. 39 F10
Tarnside Rd., Orr. 25 B9
Tarnway, Gol. 66 M16
Tarrant Clo., Wgn. 39 E11
Andover Cres.
Tarvin Clo., Gol. 66 M16
Tatlock Clo., Bill. 50 C13
Tatton Dr., Asht. 53 F13
Taunton Av., Leigh 43 O11
Taunton Dr., Farn. 35 V7
Tavistock Rd., Hind. 43 N10
Tavistock St., Ath. 44 Q10
Tawd La., Lath. 4 WW2
Tawd Rd., Skel. 24 YY8
Tawdor Ct., Farn. 35 W7
Taylor Av., Orm. 11 RR5
Taylor Rd., Hay. 63 F17
Taylor Rd., Hind. 43 O10
Taylor St., Gol. 56 L15
Taylor St., Leigh 43 O12
Taylor St., Skel. 22 VV7
Taylor St., Tyld. 47 V12
Taylor St., Wgn. 28 G8
Taylors La., Ince 41 J10
Taylors Yd., Wgn. 28 H8
Hallgate
Tayton Clo., Tyld. 46 U11
Taywood Rd., Westho. 33 R7
Teal Clo., Aug. 21 PP7
Teal Clo., Wgn. 38 D10
Tears La., Parb. 12 WW4
Teesdale Av., Litt.H. 47 V10
Teesdale Dr., Leigh 59 R13
Teesdale Rd., Hay. 62 E16
Telford Cres., Leigh 43 O12
Telford St., Ath. 44 Q11
Templemartin, Skel. 23 WW7
School La.
Templeton Rd., Platt Br. 41 K11
Tenbury Dr., Asht. 53 F14
Tenby, Skel. 23 WW7
School La.
Tenement St., Abram 41 K11
Tennyson Av., Leigh 43 O12
Tennyson Dr., Bill. 37 B11
Tennyson Dr., Orm. 10 PP5
Tennyson Dr., Wgn. 17 H6
Tennyson Rd., Farn. 35 W9
Tensing Av., Ath. 33 R9
Tenter Dr., Stand. 17 G4
Tern Av., Farn. 35 V8
Tetley St., Bam. 41 J12
Teversham, Skel. 23 WW7
Thornton
Teviot, Skel. 23 WW7
School La.
Tewkesbury, Skel. 23 WW7
School La.
Tewkesbury Rd., Gol. 65 K16
Thackeray Ho., Wgn. 28 G9
Thackeray Pl., Wgn. 28 G9
Thames Av., Leigh 58 P15
Thames Dr., Orr. 26 C8
Thames St., Haigh 18 K5
Thanet, Skel. 23 WW7
Thanet Gro., Leigh 58 Q13
Thealby Clo., Skel. 23 WW7
Thelwall Clo., Leigh 57 N14
Thetford Clo., Hind. 42 M10
Thicknesse Av., Wgn. 16 F6
Thickwood Moss La., Rainf. 48 XX13
Third Av., Tyld. 60 T14
Third Av., Wgn. 28 G7
Third St., Bam. 41 J12
Thirlmere Av., Abram 41 K12
Thirlmere Av., Asht. 54 H14
Thirlmere Av., Ince 29 K8
Thirlmere Av., Orr. 26 C8
Coniston Av.
Thirlmere Av., Stand. 17 G4
Thirlmere Av., Tyld. 46 T12
Thirlmere Av., Up Holl. 25 A8
Beacon Vw. Dr.
Thirlmere Dr., Litt.H. 35 W9
Thirlmere Gro., Farn. 35 V8
Thirlmere Rd., Bolt. 33 S8
Thirlmere Rd., Gol. 56 L15
Thirlmere Rd., Hind. 30 M9
Thirlmere Rd., Wgn. 26 D8
Thirlmere St., Leigh 58 P13
Thirsk, Skel. 23 WW7
School La.
Thistledown Clo., Wgn. 28 G7
Thomas St., Ath. 45 R10
Thomas St., Hind. 43 N10
Thomas St., Leigh 58 Q14
Severn St.
Thompson Av., Orm. 11 RR5
Thompson St., Leigh 57 N13
Thompson St., Wgn. 29 J7
Thompson St., Wors.M. 40 G10
Thomson St., Asht. 54 H14
Thorburn Rd., Wgn. 27 E9
Thoresby Clo., Wgn. 39 F10
Thorn Clo., Farn. 35 W8
Thorn Well, Westho. 32 P8
Thornbury, Skel. 23 WW7
Thornbury Av., Gol. 66 M16
Thornbush Clo., Gol. 56 M15
Thornby, Skel. 23 WW7
School La.
Thorndale, Skel. 23 WW7
Thornton
Thorneycroft, Leigh 59 R13
Thornfield Clo., Gol. 66 L16
Thornfield Cres., Litt.H. 35 V9
Thornfield Gro., Litt.H. 35 V9
Thornhill, Orm. 20 OO8
Thornhill Rd., Asht. 53 E14
Thornton, Skel. 23 WW7
Thornton Clo., Asht. 53 F14
Thornton Clo., Booth. 47 V12
Thornton Clo., Leigh 58 P15
Thornton Clo., Low. 57 N15
Hayes Row
Thornton Rd., Tyld. 47 V12
Thornvale, Abram 42 L12
Thornway, Tyld. 47 W12
Thornwood, Skel. 23 WW7
Thorpe, Skel. 23 WW7
Three Sisters Rd., Asht. 54 G13
Throstle Nest Av., Wgn. 28 G7
Thrush Av., Farn. 35 V8
Thurcroft Dr., Skel. 23 WW7
Thurlby Clo., Asht. 54 H14
Thurston, Skel. 23 WW7
Thurston Av., Wgn. 40 G10
Tickle St., Leigh 44 P12
Tickle St., Wgn. 28 G8
Tideswell Av., Orr. 26 D7
Tig Fold Rd., Farn. 35 V8
Tilbury Gro., App.Br. 14 B4
Tilcroft, Skel. 23 WW7
Timperley La., Leigh 58 Q14
Tinkersfield, Leigh 43 O12
Tintagel, Skel. 23 WW7
Tintagel Rd., Hind. 43 N10
Tintern Av., Asht. 54 H14
Tinwald Pl., Wgn. 29 J7
Tipping St., Wgn. 28 G9
Tithe Barn Rd., Asht. 53 E15
Tithe Barn St., Westho. 32 P7
Tithebarn St., Up Holl. 25 A8
Rivington Dr.
Tiverton Av., Leigh 43 O11
Tiverton Av., Skel. 23 WW7
Tiverton Clo., Tyld. 46 U12
Tobermory Clo., Hay. 62 D17
Toddington La., Haigh 18 K4
Tolketh St., Ince 29 K8
Toll St., Platt Br. 41 K11
Tollgreen Clo., Hind. 30 L8
Tolver Rd., Asht. 54 G13
Tongbarn, Skel. 23 WW7
Tontine Rd., Up Holl. 25 B9
Toogood La., Wri. 6 B1
Toothill St., Asht. 54 G13
Topcliffe St., Hind. 30 M9
Torquay Dr., Bill. 38 C12
Torridon Clo., Stand. 17 G4
Torver Clo., Wors.M. 40 G11
Tower Gro., Leigh 59 R13
Tower Hill Rd., Up Holl. 24 ZZ9
Tower Nook, Up Holl. 25 A9
Towerhill, Orm. 11 RR5
Town Grn. La., Orm. 21 PP8
Townfield Av., Asht. 54 G15
Townfields, Asht. 54 G14
Townsfield Rd., Westho. 32 P8
Townshends Yd., Orr. 37 B10
Townson Dr., Leigh 58 P15
Tracey Dr., Newt. 64 H18
Tracks La., Bill. 37 B10
Trafalgar Rd., Hind. 30 L9
Trafalgar Rd., Wgn. 28 H7
Trafford Dr., Litt.H. 35 W9
Trafford Rd., Hind. 30 L9
Tram St., Platt Br. 41 K11
Trecastell Clo., Wgn. 29 J7
Treen Rd., Tyld. 46 U12
Tregaron Gro., Hind. 43 N10
Trent Dr., Hind. 43 O10
Trent Dr., Litt.H. 47 W11
Trent Gro., Leigh 57 O14
Trent Rd., Asht. 55 J13
Trent Rd., Bill. 50 B14
Trent Rd., Wgn. 27 E8
Trentham St., Wgn. 28 G8
Trescott Ms., Stand. 16 F4
Trevelyan Dr., Bill. 37 B11
Trevor Av., Farn. 34 U6
Troon Clo., Hay. 62 D17
Troutbeck Av., Newt. 63 F18
Troutbeck Dr., Tyld. 46 T12
Troutbeck Gro., St.H. 49 A15
Troutbeck Ri., Wgn. 26 D9
Troutbeck Rd., Asht. 54 G13
Truro Rd., Tyld. 46 U12

Tuckers Hill, Haigh 18 K4
Tudor Av., Farn. 35 W8
Tudor Ct., Orm. 10 QQ5
Tudor Gro., Wgn. 39 F11
Tulip Av., Farn. 35 W7
Tulip Dr., Wgn. 16 F6
Tulip Rd., Hay. 63 F17
Tully Av., Newt. 63 F18
Tunley La., Wri. 7 C1
Tunnicliffes New Row, Leigh 57 O13
Tunnicliffes Old Row, Leigh 57 O13
Tunstall La., Wgn. 27 E9
Turnberry, Skel. 22 VV7
Turnberry Way, Tyld. 46 U12
Carnoustie Clo.
Turncroft Way, Tyld. 47 V12
Turner Av., Bick. 42 M11
Turner St., Hind. 30 L8
Turner St., Leigh 58 Q14
Turner St., Westho. 32 P9
Turner St., Wgn. 28 H8
Turnpike Rd., Orm. 20 OO7
Turnstone Av., Newt. 64 H18
Turret Hall Dr., Gol. 66 M16
Turriff Gro., Ince 29 K7
Turton St., Gol. 65 K16
Twiss Grn. La., Cul. 67 O18
Twist Av., Gol. 66 L16
Twist La., Leigh 57 O13
Tybyrne Clo., Tyld. 47 V12
Tyldesley Old Rd., Ath. 45 S11
Tyldesley Pas., Tyld. 45 S11
Tyldesley Rd., Ath. 45 R10
Tyrer Av., Wgn. 27 F9
Tyrer Rd., Orm. 10 QQ4
Tyrer Wk., Low. 66 M16

U

Uganda St., Farn. 34 U7
Ullswater Av., Asht. 54 G13
Ullswater Av., Orr. 26 C8
Ullswater Dr., Farn. 35 V8
Ullswater Dr., Ince 29 K8
Ullswater Rd., Gol. 56 L15
Ullswater Rd., Tyld. 46 T12
Ullswater St., Leigh 58 P13
Ulverston Clo., Hay. 62 D17
Ulverston Rd., Wgn. 39 F10
Umberton Rd., Westho. 33 S8
Underwood Ter., Tyld. 46 T11
Shuttle St.
Union St., Ince 29 K8
Union St., Leigh 58 P13
Union St., Tyld. 45 S11
Unsworth Av., Gol. 56 L15
Unsworth Av., Tyld. 46 T12
Unsworth St., Hind. 42 L10
Aughton St.
Unsworth St., Leigh 44 P12
Unsworth St., Tyld. 46 T12
Unsworth Ter., Hind. 30 L9
Wigan Rd.
Upholland Rd., Bill. 37 B11
Upland Dr., Asht. 54 H14
Upland Rd., Litt.H. 35 V9
Upper Dicconson St., Wgn. 28 H7
Upper George St., Tyld. 46 T12
Upper Lees Dr., Westho. 32 Q7
Upper St. Stephen St., Wgn. 28 G8
Upton Clo., Gol. 66 L16
Upton La., Tyld. 46 U12
Upton Rd., Ath. 45 S10
Upwood Rd., Gol. 66 L16
Urmston Av., Newt. 64 H17
Urmston St., Leigh 57 O13

V

Vale, The, App.Br. 14 B4
Vale Clo., App.Br. 15 C4
Vale La., Skel. 12 WW6
Valentine Rd., Newt. 63 F18
Valiant Rd., Wgn. 27 E8
Valley, The, Ath. 45 S10
Valley Rd., Wgn. 27 E9
Vanbrugh Gro., Pemb. 26 D7
Varlan Clo., Orm. 11 SS6
Vauxhall Rd., Wgn. 28 H8
Verbena Av., Farn. 35 W7
Verda St., Abram 41 K12
Vernon St., Leigh 58 P13
Viaduct Row, Ince 29 J9
Viaduct St., Newt. 63 G18
Vicarage Clo., Orm. 11 RR6
Vicarage Clo., Platt Br. 41 K11
Vicarage Dr., Hay. 62 D16
Vicarage La., Orm. 11 SS6
Vicarage La., Shev. 15 D5
Vicarage Rd., Abram 41 K11
Vicarage Rd., Asht. 54 G15
Vicarage Rd., Hay. 62 D16
Vicarage Rd., Orr. 37 B10
Vicarage Sq., Leigh 58 P13
Vicarage Wk., Orm. 10 QQ5
Vicars Hall Gdns., Booth. 61 V13
Vicars Hall La., Booth. 61 V13
Victor Clo., Wgn. 27 E8
Victoria Av., Bick. 42 M11
Victoria Av., Wgn. 28 G7
Victoria Clo., Booth. 61 W13
Victoria St.
Victoria Clo., Haigh 18 K5
Victoria Ct., Skel. 22 VV7
Victoria Cres., Stand. 16 F4
Victoria Pk., Skel. 22 VV7
Victoria Rd., Asht. 53 E14
Victoria Rd., Newt. 64 H18
Victoria Rd., Platt Br. 41 K11
Victoria St., Booth. 61 W13
Victoria St., Farn. 35 W7
Victoria St., Haigh 18 K5
Victoria St., Ince 29 J8
Victoria St., Leigh 44 P12
Victoria St., Platt Br. 41 K11
Victoria St., Westho. 32 P8
Victoria St., Wgn. 27 F9
Victoria Ter., Bick. 42 M12
Vigo St., Wgn. 29 J7
Villa Av., Wgn. 17 G6
Village Vw., Leigh 58 Q14
Vincent Way, Wgn. 27 E8
Vine Gro., Wgn. 28 H8
Chapel St.
Vine St., Hind. 30 L9
Viola Clo., Stand. 8 E3
Violet Av., Farn. 35 W7
Violet St., Asht. 54 G15
Violet St., Ince 29 J9
Virginia Way, Wgn. 27 E8
Viscount Rd., Wgn. 27 E8
Vista Av., Newt. 63 G18
Vista Rd., Hay. 63 G16
Vulcan Dr., Wgn. 28 H8
Vulcan Rd., Wgn. 27 E8

W

Waddington Clo., Low. 66 M16
Wade Bk., Westho. 32 P8
Wagon La., Hay. 62 D17
Wainfleet Clo., Win. 39 F10
Wakefield Cres., Stand. 17 G4
Wakefield St., Gol. 65 K16
Walcot Pl., Wgn. 40 G11
Waldorf Clo., Wgn. 39 E11
Waldron, Skel. 22 VV8
Walford Rd., Asht. 54 H14
Walk, The, Ath. 45 R10
Walkden Av., Wgn. 28 G7
Walkden Av. E., Wgn. 28 H7
Walkden Dr., Litt.H. 47 W10
Walkdens Av., Ath. 44 Q11
Walker St., Westho. 32 P8
Wall Cft. St., Skel. 23 WW8
Wall St., Wgn. 27 F7
Wallace La., Wgn. 29 J7
Wallbrook, Bill. 37 B11
Wallbrook Cres., Litt.H. 35 W9
Wallgarth Clo., Wgn. 39 E11
Wallgate, Wgn. 28 G8
Walls St., Hind. 43 O11
Wallwork Rd., Astley 60 U13
Walmer Rd., Hind. 31 N9
Belmont Rd.
Walmesley Av., Wgn. 28 H9
Walmesley Dr., Ince 29 K8
Walmesley Dr., Rainf. 48 XX13
Walmesley Rd., Leigh 58 P13
Walmesley St., Newt. 64 H18
Walmesley St., Wgn. 28 H8
Walney Rd., Win. 39 E11
Walnut Av., Wgn. 28 H7
Walnut Gro., Leigh 44 P12
Walpole Av., Wgn. 39 F10
Walsh Clo., Newt. 64 H17
Walter Scott Av., Wgn. 17 G6
Walter St., Asht. 54 H14
Walter St., Farn. 35 W7
Walter St., Leigh 57 N13
Walter St., Wgn. 27 E9
Waltham Av., Wgn. 16 F6
Waltham Gdns., Leigh 59 R14
Walthew Ho. La., Wgn. 26 D7
Walthew La., Platt Br. 41 K10
Walton St., Ath. 45 S10
Wanborough Clo., Leigh 44 P12
Wanes Blades Rd., Lath. 4 WW2
Warbeck Clo., Hind. 42 M10
Warburton Pl., Ath. 45 R10
Ward St., Hind. 30 L8
Wardend Clo., Litt.H. 35 W9
Wallbrook Cres.
Wardens Bk., Westho. 32 P9
Wardley Av., Litt.H. 47 W11
Wardley Rd., Tyld. 46 U12
Wardley Sq., Tyld. 46 U12
Wardley St., Wgn. 26 D9
Wardlow Av., Orr. 26 D7
Wardour St., Ath. 45 R11
Wareing St., Tyld. 45 S12
Waring Av., St.H. 62 D18
Warlow Dr., Leigh 43 O11
Warminster Gro., Wgn. 39 E11
Warnford St., Wgn. 28 H7
Warren Clo., Ath. 45 S10
Warren Dr., Newt. 64 H18
Warrington La., Wgn. 28 H8
Warrington Rd., Abram 41 K11
Warrington Rd., Asht. 54 G15
Warrington Rd., Gol. 65 K17
Warrington Rd., Ince 28 H9
Warrington Rd., Leigh 58 Q14
Warrington Rd., Wgn. 27 F9
Warwick Av., Asht. 54 H15
Warwick Dr., Hind. 30 M9
Warwick Gdns., Farn. 34 T7
Warwick Rd., Asp. 19 L5
Warwick Rd., Ath. 33 R9
Warwick Rd., Tyld. 46 T11
Warwick St., Leigh 59 S14
Wash Acre, Westho. 32 P8
Wash End, Gol. 67 N16
Wash La., Leigh 59 R13
Washacre Clo., Westho. 32 P8
Washbrook Av., Booth. 47 W11
Washbrook Way, Orm. 10 QQ6
Statham Way
Washburn Clo., Westho. 32 P7
Washwood Clo., Litt.H. 35 W9
Wallbrook Cres.
Wastdale Rd., Asht. 40 G12
Water Heyes, Wgn. 28 H8
Water St., Ath. 45 R10
Water St., Newt. 64 H18
Water St., Wgn. 28 H8
Waterbeck Clo., Wgn. 29 J7
Waterdale Clo., Booth. 61 W13
Watergate Dr., Westho. 34 U8
Watergate La., Westho. 34 U8
Waterloo St., Wgn. 28 G7
Watermede, Bill. 38 C10
Waters Edge, Farn. 35 W7
Waters Nook Rd., Westho. 32 Q8
Waterview Pk., Leigh 58 P14
Waterworks Dr., Newt. 64 H18
Waterworks Rd., Orm. 11 RR5
Watkin St., Wgn. 28 H8
Watkins Av., Newt. 63 F18
Watson Av., Asht. 54 H14
Watson Av., Gol. 55 J15
Watson Rd., Farn. 35 V8
Waverley, Skel. 22 VV8
Waverley Ct., Wgn. 39 E10
Waverley Gro., Leigh 59 R13

Waverley Rd., Gol. 56 L15
Waverley Rd., Hind. 30 L9
Waverley Rd., Wors. 47 W11
Wavertree Av., Ath. 33 R9
Wayfarers Dr., Newt. 64 H18
Wayfaring, Westho. 32 P7
Wearish La., Westho. 31 O9
Weaste Av., Litt.H. 47 W10
Weaver Av., Litt.H. 47 W11
Weaver Gro., Leigh 57 O14
Weaver Gro., St.H. 62 D18
Webster St., Platt Br. 41 K11
Wedge Av., Hay. 62 D17
Wedgewood Dr., Stand.L.G. 16 E6
Weedon Av., Newt. 63 G17
Welbeck Rd., Asht. 54 H14
Welbeck Rd., Wors.M. 39 F10
Welbourne, Skel. 22 VV8
Welch Hill St., Leigh 58 P14
Weldon Av., Farn. 34 T7
Weldon Dr., Orm. 10 QQ6
Weldon Gro., Wgn. 29 J7
Welford Av., Gol. 66 L16
Welham Rd., Wgn. 40 H10
Well Rd., Leigh 43 O11
Well St., Tyld. 46 T12
Well St., Wgn. 29 J8
Welland, The, Westho. 32 P8
Welland Rd., Asht. 55 J13
Wellcross Rd., Up Holl. 25 A9
Wellesley Clo., Wgn. 27 F8
Wellfield La., Orm. 11 SS6
Wellfield Rd., Hind. 43 N10
Wellfield Rd., Wgn. 16 F6
Wellington Gro., Ince 28 H9
Wellington Rd., Bolt. 33 S9
Wellington St., Newt. 63 G18
Wellington St., Westho. 32 P7
Wellington St., Wgn. 28 H8
Wells Av., Bill. 50 B13
Wells Clo., Tyld. 46 U12
Wells Dr., Wgn. 29 J7
Wells Pl., Wgn. 29 J8
Wellstock La., Litt.H. 35 V9
Welton Clo., Leigh 59 R13
Wendlebury Clo., Leigh 58 P15
Wenlock Gro., Hind. 42 L10
Wenlock Rd., Hind. 42 L10
Wenlock Rd., Leigh 58 P15
Wenlock St., Hind. 42 L10
Wenning Wk., Platt Br. 41 K11
Ribble Rd.
Wensley Rd., Gol. 66 M16
Wensleydale, Leigh 59 R13
Wentworth Rd., Asht. 53 F13
Wescoe Clo., Orr. 26 C9
Wesley Av., Hay. 63 F16
Elizabeth Rd.
Wesley Clo., Westho. 32 P7
Wesley St.
Wesley Ct., Westho. 32 P7
Wesley St.
Wesley St., Westho. 32 P7
Wesley St., Wgn. 27 E9
Wesse Clo., Stand. 9 G3
Wessex Rd., Wgn. 27 E7
West Av., Gol. 55 K15
West Av., Leigh 59 R14
West Bk. St., Ath. 45 S11
West Bridgewater St., Leigh 58 P14
West Clo., Tyld. 45 S11
West Dene, Parb. 4 XX3
West End Gro., Hay. 62 D17
West End Rd., Hay. 62 D17
West Gro., Westho. 32 P9
West Meade, Farn. 34 U7
West Mt., Orr. 26 C9
West Side Av., Hay. 62 D17
West St., Hind. 43 N10
West St., Ince 29 K8
West St., Wgn. 28 G7
West Way, Litt.H. 35 W9
Westbourne Av., Leigh 44 P12
Westbury Av., Wgn. 39 E11
Westbury Clo., Westho. 32 Q7
Molyneux Rd.
Westcott Dr., Wgn. 39 E10
Westcourt Rd., Farn. 34 U7
Westcroft, Platt Br. 41 K11
Westfield Av., Asht. 54 G14
Westfield Gro., Wgn. 17 G6
Westfield Rd., Ath. 45 S11
Westfield Rd., Farn. 34 T7
Westgate, Skel. 22 VV7
Westgate Dr., Orr. 25 B9
Westgate Dr., Tyld. 60 U13
Westhaven Cres., Orm. 21 PP7
Westhead Av., Gol. 66 M16
Turret Hall Dr.
Westlake Gro., Hind. 43 N10
Westleigh La., Leigh 43 O11
Westleigh Vw., Leigh 44 P12
Westlock, Wgn. 28 G9
Westmead, Stand. 16 F4
Westminster Dr., Hay. 63 F16
Westminster Dr., Leigh 45 S12
Westminster St., Wgn. 27 F9
Westmorland Rd., Tyld. 46 T11
Westmount, Wgn. 28 H7
Weston Pk., Stand.L.G. 16 E6
Weston St., Ath. 45 S10
Weston St., Tyld. 46 T11
Westrees, Leigh 44 Q12
Westview, Parb. 4 XX3
Westwell Gro., Leigh 44 P12
Westwell St.
Westwell St., Leigh 44 P12
Westwood Av., Litt.H. 47 W11
Westwood La., Ince 28 H9
Westwood Rd., Wgn. 28 H9
Wetheral Clo., Hind. 43 O10
Wetherby Clo., Newt. 64 H18
Cheltenham Dr.
Wexham Gdns., Platt Br. 41 K10
Moss La.
Weybourne Dr., Wgn. 39 F10
Weymouth Dr., Hind. 43 N10
Whalley Av., Rainf. 48 WW13
Whalley Clo., Wgn. 40 G11
Whalley Dr., Orm. 21 PP8
Whalley Gro., Leigh 43 O11
Abbey La.
Whalley St., Hind. 30 L9
Whalleys Rd., Skel. 12 XX5
Wharf Rd., Newt. 63 F18
Wharf St., Leigh 58 Q14
Wharfedale, Westho. 32 P7
Wharmby Rd., Hay. 63 F17
Wharncliff St., Hind. 30 L9
Wharton La., Litt.H. 46 U10
Wheatacre, Skel. 23 WW8
Wheatlea Rd., Wgn. 39 F11
Wheatley Av., Newt. 64 H17
Whelley, Wgn. 29 J7
Whimbrel Av., Newt. 64 H18
Whimbrell Rd., Tyld. 46 U12
Whinchat Av., Newt. 64 H18
Whins Av., Farn. 35 V8
Whistle La., Cop. 9 G1
Whistlecroft Ct., Ince 29 J9
Whistley St., Platt Br. 41 K10
Whitburn, Skel. 23 WW7
Whitburn Clo., Asht. 53 E14
White Horse Gro., Westho. 32 Q7
White Lady Clo., Litt.H. 47 V10
Quarry Pond Rd.
White Moss Rd., Skel. 22 VV8
White Moss Rd. S., Skel. 22 VV8
White Stocks, Skel. 23 WW8
White St., Leigh 59 R14
White St., Wgn. 26 D9
Whiteacre, Stand. 7 D3
Whitebeam Wk., Westho. 32 P7
Whitecroft Av., Gol. 66 M16
Whitecroft Rd., Wors.M. 40 G11
Whitefield Clo., Gol. 64 H16
Whitefield Gro., Hay. 62 D17
Harrison Dr.
Whitegate, Bolt. 33 R7
Whitehall Av., App.Br. 15 C4
Whitehall St., Ince 29 J9
Whitehey, Skel. 23 WW8
Whitehey Rd., Skel. 23 WW8
Whitehouse Clo., Hay. 62 D17
Whiteledge Rd., Skel. 24 YY9
Whiteleys La., Orm. 11 SS6
Whitelodge Dr., Asht. 55 J14
Whiterails Dr., Orm. 10 PP5
Whiterails Ms., Orm. 10 PP5
Whiteside Av., Hind. 30 L8
Whiteside Av., Wgn. 28 G7
Whiteside Rd., Hay. 62 D17
Whitewood Clo., Asht. 54 G13
Whitfield St., Leigh 59 R14
Whitledge Grn., Asht. 54 G13
Whitledge Rd., Asht. 54 G13
Whitley Cres., Abram 41 K12
Whitley Cres., Wgn. 17 G6
Whitley Rd., R.Mill 14 B6
Whitlow Av., Gol. 55 K15
Whitsbury Av., Hind. 42 L10
Whitstone Dr., Skel. 24 YY8
Whitsundale, Westho. 32 P7
Whittle Av., Hay. 62 D17
Whittle Dr., Orm. 10 QQ4
Whittle La., Wri. 5 ZZ1
Whittles Ter., Westho. 32 P7
Whitwell Clo., Stand. 8 E3
Wichbrook Rd., Litt.H. 47 V11
Wicheaves Cres., Litt.H. 47 W10
Wicheries, The, Litt.H. 47 V10
Widdows St., Leigh 58 Q14
Widdrington Rd., Wgn. 28 H7
Wide Cross La., R.Mill 25 A7
Wiend, Wgn. 28 H8
Wigan La., Cop. 9 H1
Wigan La., Wgn. 17 G5
Wigan Lwr. Rd., Stand.L.G. 16 E6
Wigan Rd., Asht. 54 G13
Wigan Rd., Asp. 18 K6
Wigan Rd., Ath. 44 Q11
Wigan Rd., Bill. 38 C12
Wigan Rd., Gol. 55 K15
Wigan Rd., Hind. 30 L9
Wigan Rd., Leigh 43 O12
Wigan Rd., Orm. 10 QQ5
Wigan Rd., Shev. 15 D5
Wigan Rd., Skel. 23 WW8
Wigan Rd., Stand. 16 F4
Wigan Rd., Westho. 31 N8
Wigan St., Platt Br. 41 K11
Wigshaw Clo., Leigh 58 P15
Wigshaw La., Cul. 67 O18
Wilbraham St., Leigh 57 O13
Wilbraham St., Westho. 32 P8
Wilcock St., Wgn. 28 G8
Wilcove, Skel. 23 WW7
Wilcox Rd., Hay. 63 G16
Wildbrook Gro., Litt.H. 47 V10
Wildbrook Rd., Litt.H. 47 V10
Wilding St., Ince 29 J9
Wildman La., Farn. 35 V8
Wilds Pas., Leigh 58 P14
King St.
Wilfred St., Wgn. 27 F8
Wilkesley Av., Stand. 16 E4
Wilkinson St., Leigh 58 P13
Willard Av., Bill. 37 B10
William Rd., Hay. 62 D17
William St., Hind. 30 M9
William St., Ince 28 H9
William St., Leigh 58 Q13
Williams Av., Newt. 64 H17
Willow Av., Newt. 64 H18
Willow Av., Tyld. 60 T13
Willow Bk., Newt. 64 H18
Willow Bk. Est., Newt. 64 H18
Willow Cres., Leigh 44 P12
Willow Dr., Hind. 42 M10
Willow Dr., Skel. 23 WW7
Willow Grn., Orm. 10 QQ5
School Ho. Grn.
Willow Gro., Asht. 55 J13
Willow Gro., Gol. 55 K15
Willow Hey, Skel. 23 WW7
Willow Lo., Abram 41 K11
Willow Rd., Hay. 63 F16
Willow Rd., Newt. 64 H18
Willow Rd., Wgn. 16 F6
Willow St., Abram 41 K11
Willow St., Ath. 45 R10
Willow St., Wgn. 39 F11
Willow Tree Clo., Wgn. 17 G6
Willow Wk., Skel. 12 XX6
Willowbrook Dr., Shev. 15 D4

Willowcroft Av., Asp. 19 M6
Willowdale, Newt. 64 H18
Willowfield Gro., Asht. 54 G15
Wilsford Clo., Gol. 55 K15
Wilson Av., Wgn. 28 G7
Wilson Rd., Platt Br. 41 K11
Wilton Av., Wgn. 29 J7
Wilton La., Gol. 67 N17
Wilton Rd., Shev. 15 D5
Wilton St., Wgn. 28 H8
Wiltshire Pl., Wgn. 27 E9
Wimborne Rd., Orr. 26 D8
Wimbreck Cres., Orm. 10 PP6
Winchcombe Dr., Leigh 58 P15
Winchester Av., Asht. 54 G14
Winchester Av., Tyld. 46 U12
Winchester Clo., Orr. 26 C8
Winchester Gro., Wgn. 28 H9
Winchester Rd., Bill. 37 B11
Winchester Rd., Hay. 53 F15
Windale, Litt.H. 47 W10
Windermere Av., Ath. 33 R9
Windermere Av., St.H. 49 A15
Windermere Rd., Abram 41 K12
Windermere Rd., Farn. 35 V8
Windermere Rd., Hay. 62 D17
Windermere Rd., Hind. 30 M9
Windermere Rd., Ince 29 K8
Windermere Rd., Leigh 58 P13
Windermere Rd., Orr. 26 C8
Windermere St., Wgn. 29 J7
Windlehurst Dr., Booth. 47 W12
Windlesham St., Ince 29 J9
Windmill Av., Orm. 10 QQ5
Windmill Clo., Wgn. 28 H8
Windmill La., Tyld. 59 S14
Windmill Rd., Skel. 24 ZZ8
Windover Clo., Westho. 34 T8
Windrows, Skel. 23 WW8
Windrush Dr., Westho. 32 P7
Windsor Av., Astley 60 T13
Windsor Av., Litt.H. 35 W9
Windsor Cres., Asp. 19 L5
Windsor Dr., Hay. 63 G16
Windsor Gro., Hind. 43 N10
Windsor Rd., Asht. 54 G15
Windsor Rd., Bill. 50 C13
Windsor Rd., Gol. 66 L16
Windsor Rd., Leigh 59 S13
Windsor Rd., Up Holl. 25 A8
Windsor St., Wgn. 28 H7
Windybank Av., Gol. 66 M16
Wingate Rd., Litt.H. 47 W10
Wingates Rd., Wgn. 17 H6
Winifred La., Orm. 20 OO7
Winifred Rd., Farn. 35 W7
Winifred St., Ince 29 J9
Winmarleigh Gdns., Leigh 58 P14
Winnard St., Gol. 55 K15
Winsford Clo., Hay. 63 F16
Kenyons La.
Winslow Rd., Westho. 33 R7
Winsor St., Ath. 45 S11
Winstanley Pl., Ince 29 J9
Winstanley Rd., Asht. 51 D13
Winstanley Rd., Bam. 41 J12
Winstanley Rd., Bill. 38 C10
Winstanley Rd., Skel. 23 WW8
Winstanley St., Wgn. 27 F9
Winster Dr., Platt Br. 41 J11
Winsters, The, Skel. 23 WW7
Winston Av., Newt. 64 H18
Winter Gro., St.H. 62 D18
Winterton Clo., Westho. 32 Q7
Winton Av., Wgn. 27 E9
Winton Rd., Gol. 66 M17
Winward St., Leigh 57 N13
Winward St., Westho. 32 P7
Winwick La., Low. 66 M18
Wirral Dr., Westho. 39 E11
Witham Clo., Stand. 8 E3
Witham Rd., Skel. 22 VV7
Withington Dr., Tyld. 46 U12
Withington Hill, Asp. 30 L7
Withington La., Asp. 18 K6
Withins Rd., Hay. 63 F16
Woburn Av., Leigh 43 O11
Woburn Clo., Hay. 63 F16
Wolford Dr., Tyld. 46 U11
Wolfson Sq., Asht. 53 F14
Wolmer St., Asht. 54 G14
Wolsey Clo., Asht. 54 G13
Wolver Clo., Litt.H. 35 W9
Wolverton, Skel. 23 WW8
Wood Dagger Clo., Hind. 30 M9
Wood Garth, Leigh 57 O14
Wood La., Lath. 4 WW1
Wood St., Ath. 44 Q10
Wood St., Gol. 65 K16
Wood St., Hind. 43 N10
Wood St., Newt. 63 G18
Wood St., New. 27 F8
Wood St., Tyld. 46 T12
Wood St., Westho. 32 P8
Wood St., Wgn. 28 H8
Wood Yd., Hind. 30 L9
Wigan Rd.
Woodbrook Dr., Wgn. 39 E10
Woodchurch, Wgn. 29 J7
Woodcock Dr., Platt Br. 41 K11
Woodcott Clo., Litt.H. 47 V10
Quarry Pond Rd.
Woodcourt, Wgn. 28 G9
Woodcroft, App.Br. 15 C5
Woodcroft, Skel. 23 WW8
Woodedge, Asht. 53 F14
Woodfield Cres., Asht. 54 G15
Woodfield Dr., Booth. 61 W13
Woodfield Rd., Orm. 10 PP6
Woodfield St., Asp. 18 K6
Woodfield St., Wgn. 26 D9
Woodford Av., Gol. 66 L16
Woodford St., Hind. 30 M9
Castle Hill Rd.
Woodhead Gro., Wgn. 40 G11
Woodhouse Dr., Wgn. 16 F6
Woodhouse La., Wgn. 16 F6
Woodhurst Dr., Stand. 8 E3
Woodland Av., Farn. 35 W7
Woodland Av., Ince 29 J9
Woodland Av., Newt. 64 H18
Woodland Dr., Asht. 54 G13
Woodland Dr., Stand. 8 F3
Woodlands, The, Wgn. 17 H6
Woodlands Av., Hind. 43 N10
Woodlands Av., Leigh 58 P14
Woodlands Clo., Orm. 11 RR6
Woodlands Dr., Bolt. 33 S9
Woodlands Dr., Shev. 15 C6
Woodlands Rd., Tyld. 46 T12
Woodley Gro., Leigh 57 O14
Woodley Pk. Rd., Skel. 12 XX6
Woodnook Rd., App.Br. 15 C4
Woodrow, Skel. 23 WW8
Woodrow Dr., Parb. 4 XX3
Woodrush Rd., Stand.L.G. 16 E6
Woods Clo., Hind. 43 N10
Atherton Rd.
Woods Ct., Hind. 43 N10
Atherton Rd.
Woods Gro., Wgn. 28 H8
Chapel St.
Woods La., Asht. 54 H13
Woods Rd., Asp. 19 L6
Woods St., Wgn. 28 H8
Woodshaw Gro., Booth. 47 W12
Woodside Av., Asht. 40 G12
Woodside Clo., Up Holl. 25 B8
Woodside Rd., Hay. 63 F16
Woodstock Clo., Leigh 58 P15
Woodvale Av., Asp. 19 M6
Woodvale Av., Ath. 32 Q9
Woodvale Av., Farn. 34 U7
Woodvale Dr., Farn. 34 U7
Woodvale Gdns., Farn. 34 U7
Woodvale Gro., Farn. 34 U7
Woodview, Shev. 15 D5
Woodville Rd., Ince 41 J10
Woodwards Rd., Westho. 32 P9
Woolden St., Wgn. 27 F9
Woolston Dr., Tyld. 46 U12
Woolton Clo., Asht. 53 F13
Worcester Av., Gol. 65 K16
Worcester Av., Hind. 30 M9
Wordsworth Av., Ath. 33 R9
Spa Rd.
Wordsworth Av., Bill. 37 B11
Wordsworth Av., Farn. 35 W8
Wordsworth Av., Leigh 43 O12
Wordsworth Av., Orr. 26 C9
Wordsworth Av., Wgn. 17 H6
Wordsworth Clo., Orm. 10 PP5
Wordsworth Rd., Litt.H. 35 W9
Worsley Av., Litt.H. 47 W11
Worsley Clo., Wgn. 26 D9
Worsley Grn., Wgn. 26 D9
Worsley Gro., Litt.H. 47 W11
Worsley Mesnes Dr., Wgn. 27 F9
Worsley St., Gol. 65 K16
Worsley Ter., Wgn. 28 H7
Worsley Vw., Astley 60 U13
Worth St., Wgn. 28 G8
Worthington Fold, Ath. 44 Q10
Worthington Gro., Ath. 44 Q10
Worthington St., Hind. 30 L9
Worthington Way, Wgn. 39 F11
Wraxhall Cres., Leigh 43 O12
Shelley St.
Wray St., Ince 29 J8
Wren Clo., Farn. 35 V8
Wrenbury Clo., Wgn. 26 D9
Wright St., Abram 41 K12
Wright St., Platt Br. 41 K10
Wright St., Wgn. 29 J7
Wrightington St., Wgn. 28 H7
Wrigley Rd., Hay. 63 F17
Wrington Clo., Leigh 43 O10
Shelley St.
Wycliffe Rd., Hay. 63 F16
Wycombe Dr., Tyld. 46 T12
Wyedale Rd., Hay. 62 E16
Wykeham Clo., Ince 29 J9
Wynard Av., Wgn. 28 H7
Wyndham Av., Farn. 34 T7
Wynne St., Litt.H. 47 W10
Wynne St., Tyld. 45 S11
Wynton Clo., Leigh 58 P15
Wyre Av., Platt Br. 41 K11
Wyre Dr., Booth. 47 W12

Y

Yarn Cft., Tyld. 46 T12
Yarrow St., Hind. 42 L10
Yarrow Wk., Platt Br. 41 J11
Yates Dr., Litt.H. 47 W10
Yates Gro., Wgn. 16 F6
Yates St., Leigh 44 P12
Yates St., Wgn. 28 G8
Yeadon, Skel. 23 XX7
Yealand Rd., Hind. 31 N9
Yellow Lo. Dr., Westho. 32 Q7
Yellowbrook Clo., Asp. 19 L5
Yew Gro., Wgn. 16 F6
Yew Tree Av., Newt. 63 G18
Yew Tree Rd., Orm. 10 QQ4
Yewdale, Shev. 15 D4
Yewdale, Skel. 23 XX7
Yewdale Av., St.H. 49 A15
Yewdale Cres., Wgn. 17 G6
Yewdale Rd., Asht. 40 G12
Yewtree Av., Ath. 45 R10
York Av., Tyld. 46 T11
York Rd., Asht. 54 G14
York Rd., Hind. 30 M9
York Rd. S., Hind. 54 H15
York St., Ath. 45 R10
York St., Gol. 55 K15
York St., Ince 29 K8
York St., Leigh 59 R14
York St., Wgn. 28 G8
Yorkshire Row, Orr. 26 C7
Youd St., Leigh 58 P13
Young St., Leigh 59 S14

Z

Zetland Av., Farn. 34 T7